mmonwealth states

Name Dependent territories of Commonwealth states (in brackets)

(as of 01/2021)

Blue Line 5

Ausgabe für Bayern (Mittelschulen) Klasse 9 R-Zug

Die Mediencodes (Beispiel: Find more online: nd4r3a) enthalten zusätzliche Unterrichtsmaterialien, die der Verlag in eigener Verantwortung zur Verfügung stellt.

Im Lernmittel wird in Form von Symbolen (/) auf Medien verwiesen. Diese umfassen – bis auf die Hörverstehensübungen – ausschließlich optionale Unterrichtsmaterialien und unterliegen nicht dem staatlichen Zulassungsverfahren.

Zusatzmaterial für Schülerinnen und Schüler u. a.:
Blue Line 5 Bayern R-Zug Workbook mit Audio-CD (ISBN 978-3-12-548355-2)

1. Auflage 1 5 4 3 2 | 25 24 23

Alle Drucke dieser Auflage sind unverändert und können im Unterricht nebeneinander verwendet werden.
Die letzte Zahl bezeichnet das Jahr des Druckes.
Das Werk und seine Teile sind urheberrechtlich geschützt. Jede Nutzung in anderen als den gesetzlich zugelassenen Fällen bedarf der vorherigen schriftlichen Einwilligung des Verlages. Hinweis § 60a UrhG: Weder das Werk noch seine Teile dürfen ohne eine solche Einwilligung eingescannt und in ein Netzwerk eingestellt werden. Dies gilt auch für Intranets von Schulen und sonstigen Bildungseinrichtungen. Fotomechanische, digitale oder andere Wiedergabeverfahren nur mit Genehmigung des Verlages.

© Ernst Klett Verlag GmbH, Stuttgart 2021. Alle Rechte vorbehalten. www.klett.de
Das vorliegende Material dient ausschließlich gemäß § 60b UrhG dem Einsatz im Unterricht an Schulen.

Herausgeber: Wolfgang Hamm, Marktredwitz
Autorinnen und Autoren: Daniel Shatwell, Hanau; Wolfgang Hamm, Marktredwitz sowie Sheila McBride, Leinfelden-Echterdingen; Chris Caridia, Frankfurt; Monika Münzenloher, Dorfen; Joanne Popp, editing etc., Korntal-Münchingen
Beratung: Michaela Cavallucci, München; Gaby Fruhmann, Parsberg; Michael Meisenzahl, Karlstadt; Lisa Schubert, Altdorf; Anna Weber, Taufkirchen
Externe Redaktion: Birgit Piefke-Wagner, Korntal-Münchingen; Anette Dralle, Stuttgart

Entstanden in Zusammenarbeit mit dem Projektteam des Verlages.

Umschlaggestaltung und Gestaltungskonzept: know idea, Freiburg; Koma Amok, Stuttgart
Umschlagfotos: Avenue Images GmbH (Dave and Les Jacobs), Hamburg; plainpicture GmbH & Co. KG (Angela Elbing), Hamburg
Satz: graphitecture book & edition; Fotosatz Kaufmann, Stuttgart
Reproduktion: Schwabenrepro GmbH, Stuttgart
Druck: Firmengruppe APPL, aprinta druck, Wemding

Printed in Germany
ISBN 978-3-12-548265-4

9 783125 482654

Blue Line 5

Ausgabe für Bayern (Mittelschulen) Klasse 9 R-Zug

Herausgeber: Wolfgang Hamm

Ernst Klett Verlag GmbH
Stuttgart • Leipzig • Dortmund

Inhalt

	Kompetenzen / Themen / I can …	Kommunikative Fertigkeiten	Seite
	So lernst du mit Blue Line		**6**
Zoom in – A world language			
	Informationen über Englisch als weltweite Verkehrssprache	R, S	**8**
Unit 1 Around Australia			
Intro	**… Informationen über Australien verstehen.** *Australia is one of the largest countries in the world. Most Australians live in cities near the coast, like Sydney.* Einblicke in Gesellschaft, Kultur, Natur, Umwelt und nachhaltiges Handeln	V, S, R, L	**10**
Topic 1	**… einen Blogeintrag über eine Reise schreiben.** *Hi everyone! I really enjoyed my visit to Uluru, the big, beautiful rock in the Australian outback.* Einblicke in Gesellschaft und Kultur – ein Reisebericht – Revision: simple past – Revision: will-future Sounds: Betonung von Silben	R, S	**12**
Topic 2	**… darüber sprechen, wenn ich krank bin.** *I have a bad headache and a cold. You'll have to stay in bed for a few days if you want to get better.* Gesundheit und Krankheit – Dienstleistungen: Arztpraxis – If-clauses I – If-clauses with can / with commands	R, S, L	**16**
Text	**… Texte über Umweltprobleme verstehen.**	R	**20**
Mediation	**… Informationen in einer Apotheke weitergeben.**	M, S	**22**
Film	**… einen Film über Tiere in Australien verstehen.**	V, S	**23**
Checkout	**Wissen und Strategien anwenden; den Lernstand überprüfen.**		**24**
Look at Australia	**Life in Australia**	S	**26**
Speaking skills	**Tipps und Strategien zu einem Gespräch über ein Bild (*picture-based interview*)**	S	**28**
Test practice 1	**Vorbereitung auf eine schriftliche Prüfung**		**30**

L = Listening M = Mediation R = Reading S = Speaking V = Viewing W = Writing

	Kompetenzen / Themen / I can …	Kommunikative Fertigkeiten	Seite
Unit 2 Exploring India			
Intro	**… Informationen über Indien verstehen.** *India is more than nine times the size of Germany. English is one of India's 22 official languages, and most Indians speak it.* Einblicke in Gesellschaft, Kultur, Natur, Umwelt und nachhaltiges Handeln – berühmte Persönlichkeiten – Feiertage und Feste	V, S, R, L	**36**
Topic 1	**… eine Firma vorstellen.** *We work in a team. We write computer programs for many different international customers.* Leben, Arbeiten, Kommunizieren in der globalisierten Welt – Revision: simple present	S, R, L	**38**
Topic 2	**… ein Poster über Nachhaltigkeit gestalten.** *We need to make farming more sustainable so that we can grow food in the future too. There is a lot of pollution.* Umwelt und nachhaltiges Handeln – Revision: word order	R	**42**
Text	**… einen Text über eine berühmte Person verstehen.**	S, R	**46**
Mediation	**… Informationen über verschiedene Jobs weitergeben.**	M, S	**48**
Film	**… einen Film über einen Lieferservice verstehen.**	S, V	**49**
Checkout	**Wissen und Strategien anwenden; den Lernstand überprüfen.**		**50**
Look at India	**Out and about in India**	S	**52**
Writing skills	**Tipps und Strategien zum Schreiben einer Geschichte (*picture-based story*)**	W	**54**
Test practice 2	**Vorbereitung auf eine schriftliche Prüfung**		**56**

L = Listening M = Mediation R = Reading S = Speaking V = Viewing W = Writing

Inhalt

	Kompetenzen / Themen / I can …	Kommunikative Fertigkeiten	Seite
Unit 3	**Discover South Africa**		
Intro	**… Informationen über Südafrika verstehen.** *South Africa has three capitals: Pretoria, Cape Town and Bloemfontein. Apartheid ended in 1994, and a black South African, Nelson Mandela, became president.* Einblicke in Gesellschaft, Kultur, Natur, Umwelt und nachhaltiges Handeln – berühmte Persönlichkeiten	V, S, R, L	62
Topic 1	**… über einen Unfall sprechen.** *The driver braked and the car skidded. A car hit our bus while we were travelling to the cricket match.* ein Unfallbericht – Dienstleistungen: Polizeistation – past progressive – while and when Sounds: /ɒ/, /əʊ/	S, R, L	64
Topic 2	**… einen Text über mein Vorbild schreiben.** *I admire Miriam Makeba because she fought against apartheid. The government took away her passport when she left South Africa.* Einfluss von Vorbildern – berühmte Persönlichkeiten – Revision: present perfect with for and since	R, L, S	68
Text	**… Texte über das Leben junger Menschen verstehen.**	R	72
Mediation	**… Informationen in einem Krankenhaus weitergeben.**	M, S	74
Film	**… einen Film über das Leben in Kapstadt verstehen.**	S, V	75
Checkout	**Wissen und Strategien anwenden; den Lernstand überprüfen.**		76
Look at South Africa	**South Africa – People and places**	S	78
Mediation skills	**Tipps und Strategien zur Sprachmittlung**	M	80
Test practice 3	**Vorbereitung auf eine schriftliche Prüfung**		82

L = Listening M = Mediation R = Reading S = Speaking V = Viewing W = Writing

	Kompetenzen / Themen / I can …	Kommunikative Fertigkeiten	Seite
Unit 4	**News from New Zealand**		
Intro	**… Informationen über Neuseeland verstehen.** *New Zealand is about 1,000 miles (1,600 km) from Australia, its nearest neighbour. New Zealand has amazing landscapes.* Einblicke in Gesellschaft, Kultur, Natur, Umwelt und nachhaltiges Handeln – Freizeit im Freundeskreis, Vereinsleben	V, S, R, L	88
Topic 1	**… über Jobmöglichkeiten und Fähigkeiten sprechen.** *I see you find it easy to talk to people that you don't know. We're going to have a careers day at the school at the beginning of July.* Berufsberatung – Revision: going to-future	S, R, L	90
Topic 2	**… einen Bericht über ein Praktikum schreiben.** *Supermarkets buy their products from other local companies. These companies are called suppliers.* Ausbildung und Stellenmarkt – eine Betriebsbesichtigung – Revision: simple past – Revision: passive voice Sounds: /ɜ:/, /eɪ/, /aɪ/	R, S	94
Text	**… eine Geschichte über verschiedene Generationen verstehen.**	R	98
Mediation	**… Informationen über einen Verein weitergeben.**	M	100
Film	**… einen Film über Vulkane und Erdbeben verstehen.**	S, V	101
Checkout	**Wissen und Strategien anwenden; den Lernstand überprüfen.**		102
Look at New Zealand	**More about New Zealand**	S	104
Writing skills	**Tipps und Strategien zum Schreiben einer Bewerbung**	W	106
Test practice 4	**Vorbereitung auf eine schriftliche Prüfung**		108
Diff corner – D	Parallelaufgaben zu den Units 1–4 auf leichterem Niveau		114
Grammar – G	Erklärungen und Übungen Lösungen zur Selbstkontrolle List of irregular verbs		126 137 138
Methods – M	Anleitung zu kooperativen Lernformen		140
Vocabulary – V	Vocabulary tips Word banks Vocabulary (unitbegleitendes Vokabular) Dictionary (English-German, German-English) Instructions (Arbeitsanweisungen mit Operatoren) Classroom phrases		144 146 154 172 221 223

L = Listening M = Mediation R = Reading S = Speaking V = Viewing W = Writing

So lernst du mit Blue Line

So lernst du mit deinem Buch.
Das Buch hat vier *Units* (Kapitel).
Jede *Unit* ist gleich aufgebaut.

Intro

Hier steigst du in das neue Thema ein.
Dazu gibt es auch einen kurzen Film.

Im gelben Kasten siehst du, was du in der *Unit* lernen wirst.

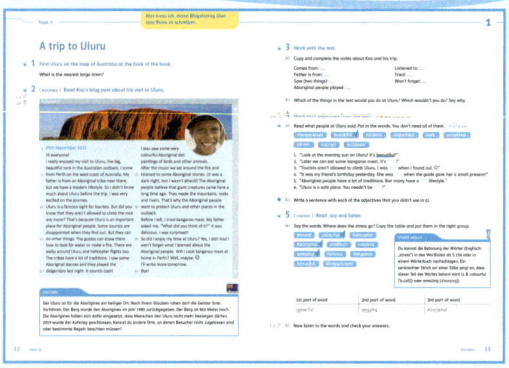

Topics

In jeder *Unit* gibt es zwei *Topics*.
Hier kannst du erkennen, wie schwer eine Übung ist:

● schwer ◒ mittel ○ leicht

In der *Task* kannst du zeigen, dass du alles verstanden hast, und deine eigenen Ideen einbringen.

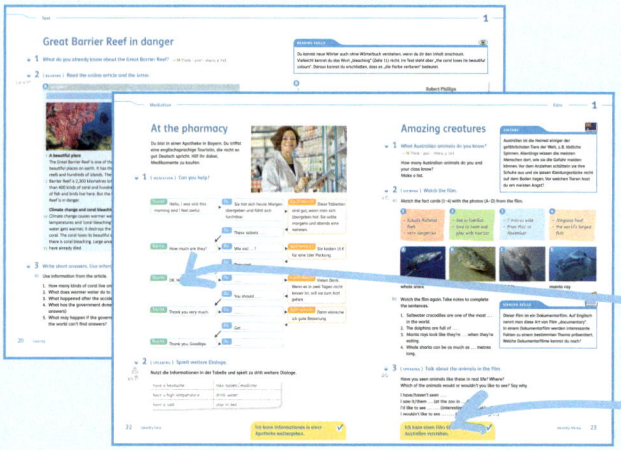

Text

Auf den *Text*-Seiten findest du spannende Geschichten, Sachtexte und Artikel.

Mediation/Film

Auf der linken Seite geht es darum, englische Informationen auf Deutsch wiederzugeben und zwischen englisch- und deutschsprechenden Personen zu vermitteln. Das nennt man *Mediation*.

Auf der *Film*-Seite geht es um einen Film in englischer Sprache.

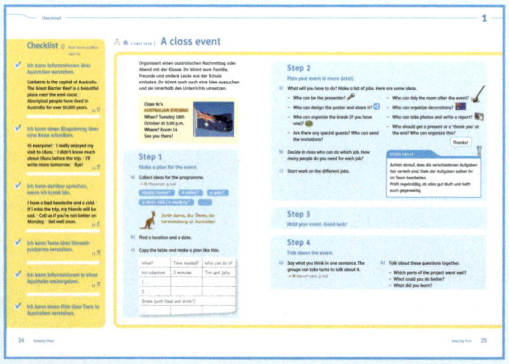

Checkout

Auf dieser Seite findest du eine Übersicht über die Kompetenzziele der *Unit*.

Die Abschlussaufgabe (*Unit task*) könnt ihr meist zu zweit oder in der Gruppe lösen.

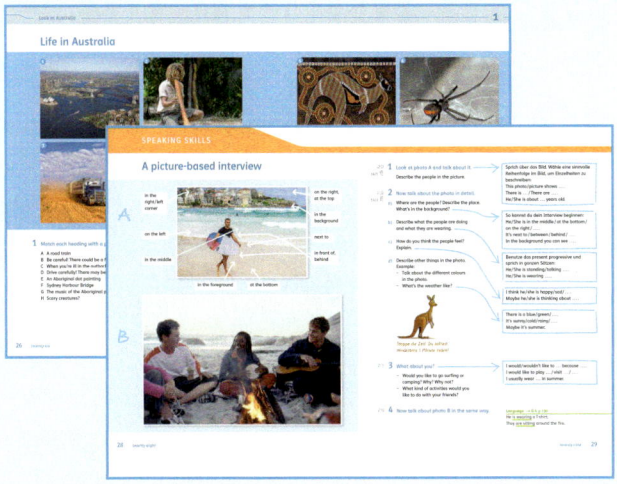

Look at ...

Hier kannst du Australien, Indien, Südafrika und Neuseeland weiter entdecken.
Schau genau hin. Vieles kannst du verstehen oder erraten.

Skills

Auf jede *Unit* folgt eine Doppelseite, auf der du eine bestimmte Fertigkeit (*Skill*) oder Lernstrategie besonders trainieren kannst.

Test practice

Hier kannst du für eine schriftliche Abschlussprüfung trainieren.

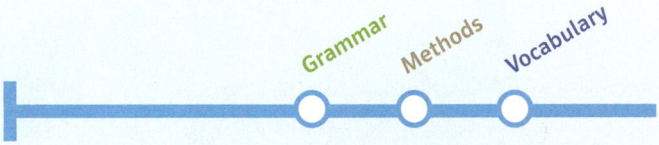

Im Anschluss an die vier *Units* gibt es noch weitere nützliche Seiten:

Grammar: Hier findest du alle Regeln und Erklärungen zur Grammatik, Übungen und eine Liste der unregelmäßigen Verben.

Methods: Manche Übungen könnt ihr auf eine bestimmte Art und Weise bearbeiten.
Das erkennst du an diesem Symbol: → M.
Wie es genau funktioniert, kannst du hier nachlesen.

Vocabulary: Im *Vocabulary* findest du alle neuen Wörter in der Reihenfolge, in der sie in der *Unit* auftauchen, sowie *Word banks*, die dir bei der Bearbeitung der *Task* helfen. Im *Dictionary* sind die Wörter noch einmal alphabetisch aufgelistet: zuerst Englisch–Deutsch und dann Deutsch–Englisch.

Symbol	Erklärung
○ ◒ ●	leicht/mittel/schwer (Niveaudifferenzierung)
❀	individualisierende Aufgabe (natürliche Differenzierung)
→ ○ p.120	Verweis auf leichtere Parallelübung auf der *Diff corner*-Seite
OR	Aufgabe zur Auswahl (Wahldifferenzierung)
	Entwicklung von Schlüsselkompetenzen für Ausbildung und Beruf
P	Hier entsteht ein Produkt für das Portfolio.
4/3	Verweis auf eine Übung im *Workbook*
→ G1, p.127	Verweis auf den Grammatikanhang (*Grammar*)
→ M	Verweis auf die Methodenseiten (*Methods*)
→ V	Verweis auf eine *Word bank* im Vokabular (*Vocabulary*)
	Partnerarbeit
	Gruppenarbeit
	Verweis auf die Lehrer-CD (Audio)
	Verweis auf die Lehrer-DVD (Film)
Find more online: 3h58uu	Code auf www.klett.de eingeben und Zusatzinformationen erhalten

1,1

Zoom in – A world language

1

Over a billion people all around the world speak English, and it is an official language in 67 countries. The majority of these speakers have learned English as a second language. So you can often talk to people in English when you don't know their language.

Top 5 languages by number of speakers (native and non-native)

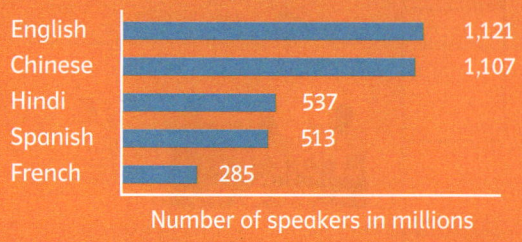

Source: SIL International, Dallas

2

English is the language of computers – most software programs use English. Over half of the websites on the internet are in English too. People who speak different languages can also chat on social media in English.

3

Many of the biggest pop songs are in English. A lot of artists sing in English, but it isn't their first language. That means that people in other countries can understand their songs. Artists in competitions often sing in English too.

1 (READING) Answer the questions with short answers.

1. How many countries have English as an official language?
2. How many people speak English?
3. Where can you find English in the world of computers?
4. Why do pop singers who speak other languages often sing in English?
5. Why do sports stars who move to different countries use English?
6. Which three tasks do people at work sometimes have to do in English?

4 Sports stars often move to play in other countries. When they need to communicate with fans or the people in their new team, it's easier for them to use English. Sports stars often use English like this when they aren't in an English-speaking country.

5 English is the language of international business. Many people write e-mails, give presentations and meet other employees in their job. If they work with companies and customers from other countries, they often have to do these tasks in English.

2 (SPEAKING) Find examples.

a) Talk in a group. Think about these questions.

1. Which programs, websites and social media sites do you use?
2. Which songs and artists do you like? Which series do you enjoy? Why?
3. Which international sports stars do you know and like? Why do you like them?
4. Which international companies do you know? What do they make or sell?

b) Collect new English words for each of these topics. Add to the lists during the year. (You can make lists for other topics too!)

computers | music | sport | work and business

1 1,2 Unit 1 Intro

Around Australia

Most Australians live in cities near the coast, like Sydney. Many people love sport, barbecues and the beach. The Great Barrier Reef is a beautiful place near the east coast. Thousands of creatures live there.

1 (SPEAKING) Choose a photo and tell your partner about it.

a) Describe the photo.

There is / There are ....
A person is ...ing .... / Some people are ...ing.

b) Would you like to travel to Australia? Why or why not?

cool beaches | beautiful animals | very hot | expensive | ...

2 (READING) Which three sentences are right? 2/1

1. The capital of Australia is Sydney.
2. In Australia spring starts in September.
3. Many animals live in the Great Barrier Reef near the east coast.
4. Fifty thousand years ago Australia was a part of Antarctica.
5. Many Aboriginal people were killed after the British settlers came.
6. There are a lot of schools in the centre of the country.

Am Ende dieser Unit kann ich ...
- Informationen über Australien verstehen.
- einen Blogeintrag über eine Reise schreiben.
- darüber sprechen, wenn ich krank bin.
- Texte über Umweltprobleme verstehen.
- Informationen in einer Apotheke weitergeben.
- einen Film über Tiere in Australien verstehen.

1

3

Australia is one of the largest countries in the world. It broke away from Antarctica millions of years ago. There are many animals that only live in Australia, like the koala and the kangaroo.

4

Aboriginal people have lived in Australia for over 50,000 years. In the 18th century the first British settlers arrived. Thousands of Aboriginal people were killed after that. They have struggled for their rights since then.

5

The flat, hot centre of Australia is called the 'outback'. Not many people live there, and they live a long way away from each other. That's why children have their school lessons online at the School of the Air.

3 (LISTENING) Listen to Peter's talk about the School of the Air.

1, 3
2/2

a) There is one mistake in each sentence. Listen and find the word which is wrong.

1. I'm a Year 10 student at the School of the Air.
2. I sit in front of the TV when the lesson begins.
3. There isn't any time for online shopping, computer games or videos.
4. I have the same homework as other students in Australia.
5. Three times a year the students spend a month together in town.
6. The music day is the best part of the school year.

b) Write the correct sentences in your exercise book.

Ich kann Informationen über Australien verstehen. ✓

Hier lerne ich, einen Blogeintrag über eine Reise zu schreiben.

A trip to Uluru

1 Find Uluru on the map of Australia at the back of the book.

What is the nearest large town?

2 (READING) Read Koa's blog post about his visit to Uluru.

1,4
3/1

INTERNET

25th September 2021

Hi everyone!
I really enjoyed my visit to Uluru, the big, beautiful rock in the Australian outback. I come from Perth on the west coast of Australia. My father is from an Aboriginal tribe near there, but we have a modern lifestyle. So I didn't know much about Uluru before the trip. I was very excited on the journey.

Uluru is a famous sight for tourists. But did you know that they aren't allowed to climb the rock any more? That's because Uluru is an important place for Aboriginal people. Some tourists are disappointed when they find out. But they can do other things. The guides can show them how to look for water or make a fire. There are walks around Uluru and helicopter flights too. The tribes have a lot of traditions. I saw some Aboriginal dances and they played the didgeridoo last night. It sounds cool!

I also saw some very colourful Aboriginal dot paintings of birds and other animals.
After the music we sat around the fire and listened to some Aboriginal stories. (It was a dark night, but I wasn't afraid!) The Aboriginal people believe that giant creatures came here a long time ago. They made the mountains, rocks and rivers. That's why the Aboriginal people want to protect Uluru and other places in the outback.
Before I left, I tried kangaroo meat. My father asked me, "What did you think of it?" It was delicious. I was surprised!
So did I enjoy my time at Uluru? Yes, I did! And I won't forget what I learned about the Aboriginal people. Will I cook kangaroo meat at home in Perth? Well, maybe. ☺
I'll write more tomorrow.
Bye!

CULTURE

Der Uluru ist für die Aborigines ein heiliger Ort. Nach ihrem Glauben ruhen dort die Geister ihrer Vorfahren. Der Berg wurde den Aborigines im Jahr 1985 zurückgegeben. Der Berg ist 863 Meter hoch. Die Aborigines haben sich dafür eingesetzt, dass Menschen den Uluru nicht mehr besteigen dürfen. 2019 wurde der Aufstieg geschlossen. Kennst du andere Orte, an denen Besucher nicht zugelassen sind oder bestimmte Regeln beachten müssen?

3 Work with the text.

a) Copy and complete the notes about Koa and his trip.

Comes from: ...
Father is from: ...
Saw (two things): ...
Aboriginal people played: ...
Listened to: ...
Tried: ...
Won't forget: ...

b) Which of the things in the text would you do at Uluru? Which wouldn't you do? Say why.

3/2 **4 Work with adjectives from the text.** → M Bus stop, p.140

a) Read what people at Uluru said. Put in the words. You don't need all of them. → p.114

disappointed | beautiful ✓ | modern | important | dark | surprised | afraid | excited | delicious

1. "Look at the evening sun on Uluru! It's beautiful!"
2. "Later we can eat some kangaroo meat. It's ___ !"
3. "Tourists aren't allowed to climb Uluru. I was ___ when I found out. ☹"
4. "It was my friend's birthday yesterday. She was ___ when the guide gave her a small present!"
5. "Aboriginal people have a lot of traditions. But many have a ___ lifestyle."
6. "Uluru is a safe place. You needn't be ___ !"

b) Write a sentence with each of the adjectives that you didn't use in a).

5 (SOUNDS) Read, say and listen.

a) Say the words. Where does the stress go? Copy the table and put them in the right group.

around | colourful ✓ | helicopter | Aboriginal ✓ | tradition | modern | amazing ✓ | famous | kangaroo | beautiful | disappointed

STUDY SKILLS

Du kannst die Betonung der Wörter (Englisch: „stress") in den Wortlisten ab S.154 oder in einem Wörterbuch nachschlagen. Ein senkrechter Strich vor einer Silbe zeigt an, dass dieser Teil des Wortes betont wird (z. B. colourful [ˈkʌləfl]) oder amazing [əˈmeɪzɪŋ]).

1st part of word	2nd part of word	3rd part of word
colourful	amazing	Aboriginal

1,5 b) Now listen to the words and check your answers.

Language detectives → G1, p.127

They played the didgeridoo last night.
Giant creatures came here a long time ago.
I didn't know much about Uluru.
"What did you think of it?"

In welcher Zeitform sind diese Sätze? Achte auf die Signalwörter!

4/3 **6 Complete the story about Omeo, a tour guide at Uluru.** → M Peer correction, p.141

a) Put in the right form of the words in brackets. → ○ p.114

Last week a group of tourists from Germany (1) visited (visit) Uluru. They (2) —— (arrive) at three o'clock on Monday afternoon and they (3) —— (go) on a helicopter flight around the rock. It (4) —— (be) very exciting! After that they (5) —— (ask) Omeo a lot of questions. They (6) —— (sing) songs with Omeo in the evening, but he (7) —— (not play) the didgeridoo for them. Later the tourists (8) —— (try) some delicious Aboriginal food.

b) Make more sentences about the tourists' visit to Uluru.

1. climb the rock (✗) They didn't climb ....
2. enjoy the helcopter flight (✓) They ....
3. listen to stories (✓) They ....
4. leave rubbish there (✗)
5. take photos of Uluru (✓)
6. see any koalas (✗)

4/4 **7 Make the questions and find the right answers.** → M Bus stop, p. 140

a) Make the questions that Koa's friend asked. Then find the right answers. → ○ p.114

Friend:
1. Uluru? • visit • did • when • you
   When did you visit Uluru?
2. did • there? • how long • stay • you
3. around Uluru? • go • you • on a walk • did
4. like • did • best? • you • what
5. you • to Uluru? • travel • did • how
6. go • did • on a helicopter tour? • you

Koa:
a. We went by plane.
b. Yes, we did. We walked for three hours!
c. No, we didn't. The flights are expensive.
d. We stayed for five days.
e. We went to the rock in September.
f. I liked the didgeridoo music best!

b) Write the questions for these answers. visit Uluru? play the didgeridoo? take photos?

1. No, we didn't. But we listened to an Aborginal man who played it!
2. Because I wanted to know more about Aboriginal culture and traditions.
3. Yes, I did. I took more than a hundred. I can show them to you now.

Language → G 2, p.128

I'll write more tomorrow.
I won't forget what I learned.
Will I cook kangaroo meat at home in Perth?

8 (SPEAKING) Talk about the future.

a) Think about these questions. Make notes. You can use a dictionary for help.

> What kind of job will you have in ten years?
> Where will you live?
> What will you do in your free time?

b) Ask your classmates the questions from a) and answer them. → M Milling around, p.141

I think I'll … Maybe I'll …
I won't …

work as a …. live in ….
play …/watch …/make ….

9 Choose the right words for Koa's blog post.

Yesterday I **talk** • **talked** (1) to my friend Daku about the future. Daku **wants** • **want** (2) to be a guide at Uluru. Then he **take** • **will take** (3) tourists on tours. He thinks that the job is interesting **before** • **because** (4) you work with people. **Next year** • **Last year** (5) I want to look for a job at a supermarket in Perth **so that** • **but** (6) I can travel to the USA. Maybe I **will** • **doesn't** (7) spend a year there and see **many** • **much** (8) great places!

10 (TASK) A blog post → V Talking about experiences, p.146

a) Think of a class trip or another interesting journey. Make notes in your exercise book for a blog post.

Trip to: …			
How did you travel? – …	Who went with you? – …	How long? – …	What did you see? – …

b) Add to your notes. How did you feel when you were there?

excited | surprised | disappointed | afraid | …

When did you arrive and leave?

c) Use your notes to write a blog post about the trip. Look at the checklist on page 145 to check your draft.

BLOG

Hi everyone!
This was my first trip to …. We stayed there for … days. I went with my class and our teachers, Mr … and Mrs …. We went by ….
I was very … when I saw ….
I won't forget …. It was great!
Maybe I'll go again one day.
Bye,
…

d) Share your blog post with a partner. Give feedback. → M Tip top, p.143

Ich kann einen Blogeintrag über eine Reise schreiben. ✔

Hier lerne ich darüber zu sprechen, wenn ich krank bin.

A few days in bed

1 Talk about the photo.

What do you think the woman's job is?

2 (READING) Read the dialogues.

1,6

1 Penny doesn't feel very well and is at the doctor's.

1.

Receptionist: Hello, how can I help you?
Penny: Hello. My name is Penny Watkins. I have an appointment at 11 o'clock to see Doctor Robson.
Receptionist: I can't find you in our list of patients. Are you new in Canberra?
Penny: Yes, my family moved here from Sydney two months ago.
Receptionist: If you're new, you have to register with us as a patient. If you register, we can get your medical records from your last doctor.
Penny: OK.

2.

Doctor: Hello Penny, take a seat. How are you today?
Penny: Hello Doctor Robson. I feel really ill.
Doctor: Oh dear. What's the matter?
Penny: I have a bad headache and a cold.
Doctor: Do you have a high temperature?
Penny: I don't know. I feel quite hot.
Doctor: Well, let's look at you. ... OK, Penny, I think you've caught the flu.
Penny: Oh no. I want to go surfing tomorrow. If I miss the trip, my friends will be sad.
Doctor: If you go surfing, the flu will get much worse.
Penny: What? You mean I can't go surfing?
Doctor: I'm afraid not. You'll have to stay in bed for a few days if you want to get better. You'll have to drink lots of water too.
Penny: Well, OK. Do I have to make another appointment?
Doctor: Call us if you're not better on Monday. Here's a prescription for some medicine. Take one tablet every morning before breakfast. There's a pharmacy on Darwin Road.
Penny: Thank you.
Doctor: You're welcome. Goodbye Penny, and get well soon.

3 Choose the right answers.

1. There is a problem because Penny **forgot her last appointment** • **is a new patient.**
2. She has a headache and a cold. She also feels **hot** • **tired.**
3. The doctor thinks that Penny has **the flu** • **a bad cold.**
4. Penny wants to go **rafting** • **surfing.**
5. The doctor gives Penny **some medicine** • **a prescription.**
6. She should take a tablet every **morning** • **evening.**

5/1 **4 Work with the words.** → M Think – pair – share, p.143

a) Make a mind map with the words and phrases. → ○ p.115

a headache | take tablets | being ill ✓ | a high temperature | drink tea | tired | stay in bed | the flu | a cold

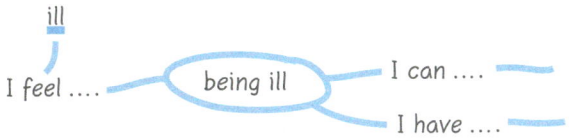

STUDY SKILLS

Du kannst neue Wörter besser behalten, wenn du sie mit Wörtern verbindest, die du schon kennst. Sammle sie in Wörternetzen und ergänze neue Wörter.

b) Add more words and phrases to the mind map.

5 (SPEAKING) Sort out the mixed-up dialogue.

a) Put the phrases in the right order. Act the dialogue. → ○ p.115 → M Read and look up, p.142

5/2

Receptionist:

1. Can you come today at 2:30 p.m.?
2. No problem. Goodbye.
3. Hello. How can I help you?
4. Good. What was the name again?
5. OK, Mr Hogan. See you at 2:30 p.m.

Patient:

6. Thank you. Goodbye.
7. Yes, I can.
8. Hogan. That's H-O-G-A-N.
9. Hello. My name is Mr Hogan. I would like to make an appointment. I have a high temperature.

b) Change the name, the time and the problem. Act the new dialogue.

6 (LISTENING) Listen to the dialogue between Penny and her father.

1,7

6/3–4

Complete the sentences. You don't need all the words.

a breakfast | swimming | last | sad | surfing | happy | first | a barbecue

1. Penny feels … about the trip to the beach.
2. It's the … time. All her friends are going.
3. She will miss … with her friends too.
4. Her father will go … with her one day.

LISTENING SKILLS

Achte beim Hören darauf, wie die Sprecherinnen und Sprecher klingen. Wann geht die Stimme nach oben oder nach unten? So kannst du erschließen, wie sich die Personen fühlen.

Language detectives → G3, p.129

If I miss the trip, my friends will be sad.
If you go surfing, the flu will get much worse.
You'll have to stay in bed for a few days if you want to get better.

In diesen Sätzen findest du eine Bedingung und die Folge davon. In welchem Teil des Satzes steht die Bedingung, in welchem Teil die Folge? Wo findest du immer das will-future?

7 Choose the right answers.

6/5

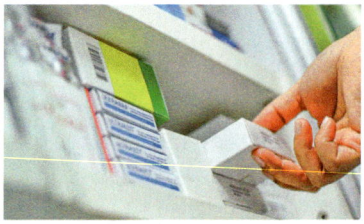

1. If Penny goes to the pharmacy, they **give** • **will give** her the tablets.
2. If she takes the tablets and stays in bed, she **will get** • **gets** better soon.
3. If she **stays** • **will stay** at home tomorrow, she will sleep a lot.
4. Dad: If you go surfing tomorrow, you **will be** • **are** very ill!
5. But if you **will call** • **call** Lara, she will tell you the news.
6. Penny: If I **don't feel** • **won't feel** better on Monday, I will go to the doctor's again.

6/6 8 Write sentences about Penny. → M Bus stop, p.140

a) Complete the sentences. → ○ p.115

1. If Penny goes to school on Monday, she ___ cricket (play)
   If Penny goes to school on Monday, she will play cricket.
2. If she wants to talk, she ___ her friends. (call)
3. They will have a barbecue too if they ___ longer. (stay)
4. Penny will work with her best friend if she ___ a project at school. (do)
5. If her dad isn't too busy, they ___ surfing in a few weeks. (go)
6. She will take photos if she ___ her cousin in Sydney next month. (visit)
7. Her cousin will come to Canberra in December if she ___ time. (have)

b) Write four sentences about yourself. Use these ideas.

… if my grades are good next week …
… if there is enough time on Saturday …
… will watch a film tomorrow if …
… will help my … at the weekend if …

Wie bildet man solche Sätze aus Bedingung und Folge im Deutschen? Wie bildet man sie in anderen Sprachen, die es in eurer Klasse gibt?

9 Put in the right words to complete the message. You don't need all of them.

come | hours | visited | if | was | where | you ✓ | barbecue | were | because

E-MAIL

Hi Penny,
Are you (1) feeling better now? I hope so!
The surfing trip ___ (2) fun yesterday. But we missed you! ☹ The waves ___ (3) very big and we spent two ___ (4) at the beach. I wore a hat ___ (5) the sun was very hot. If you ___ (6) next time, I'll show you the café ___ (7) we had a burger. I'll visit you ___ (8) you're better tomorrow.
See you,
Lara

10 Match the sentence halves.

7/7–8

1. If my leg doesn't hurt any more,
2. If I don't sleep much,
3. If you need some medicine,
4. If you work hard at school,
5. If the doctor doesn't speak so fast,
6. If we are late,

a. I get tired.
b. wait for us.
c. you can get a good grade.
d. Penny can understand her.
e. go to the pharmacy.
f. I can play basketball at the weekend.

Language → G 3, p.129

If you're new, you have to register with us.
If you register, we can get your medical records.
Call us if you're not better on Monday.

11 (TASK) A dialogue → V Talking about being ill, p.147

7/9

a) Use the phrases to make a dialogue. Partner B doesn't feel well. Partner A gives advice.

A: Hi. ...
B: Hi. ...
A: Oh dear. ...
B: I .... And my ....
A: Maybe you should ....
B: OK, I'll do that.
A: ... ((Give more advice.))
B: Thanks. That's good advice!
A: ... ((Look at page 16 to see how you can finish the dialogue.))

How are you today?
I feel really ill. | I don't feel very well.
What's the matter? | What's the problem?
I have a bad .... | My ... hurts. | ...
... go to the doctor's | ... take medicine
... go to the pharmacy | ...
If you drink ..., you'll .... | ...

b) Change roles.

Ich kann darüber sprechen, wenn ich krank bin. ✓

Great Barrier Reef in danger

1 What do you already know about the Great Barrier Reef? → M Think – pair – share, p.143

2 (READING) Read the online article and the letter.

1,8–9

A INTERNET

9 June 2019

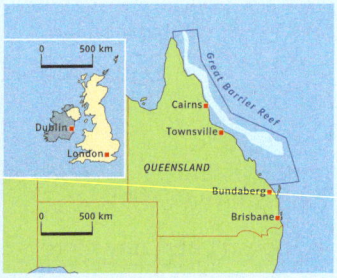

A beautiful place

The Great Barrier Reef is one of the most beautiful places on earth. It has thousands of reefs and hundreds of islands. The Great Barrier Reef is 2,300 kilometres long. More than 400 kinds of coral and hundreds of kinds of fish and birds live here. But the Great Barrier Reef is in danger.

Climate change and coral bleaching

Climate change causes warmer water temperatures and 'coral bleaching'. When the water gets warmer, it destroys the algae on the coral. The coral loses its beautiful colours and there is coral bleaching. Large areas of the reef have already died.

Ships and oil spills

A lot of ships go past the Great Barrier Reef. The worst accident happened in 2010, when a Chinese ship hit the reef. This caused damage to three kilometres of coral and there was a big oil spill. It will take years for the reef to recover.

Can we save the reef?

The Australian government has started programmes to protect the reef. It has also changed laws. However, Australia can't stop climate change alone. It has to work with other countries. The governments of the world have struggled to find answers. If they can't, the reef may die completely. Will we be able to protect this beautiful place?

3 Write short answers. Use information from the texts.

a) Use information from the article.

1. How many kinds of coral live on the reef?
2. What does warmer water do to the algae?
3. What happened after the accident in 2010?
4. What has the government done? (Two answers)
5. What may happen if the governments of the world can't find answers?

b) Use information from the letter.

1. Who sent the letter?
2. In which city does he or she live?
3. When did he or she write the letter?
4. When did the person visit the reef?
5. How does the person feel about the future of the reef?

READING SKILLS

Du kannst neue Wörter auch ohne Wörterbuch verstehen, wenn du dir den Inhalt anschaust. Vielleicht kennst du das Wort „bleaching" (Zeile 11) nicht. Im Text steht aber „the coral loses its beautiful colours". Daraus kannst du erschließen, dass es „die Farbe verlieren" bedeutet.

B

Robert Phillips
XX Martens Place
Brisbane
QLD X000

Australian Government
Department of the Environment and Energy
Barbara Thompson
GPO Box XXX
Canberra ACT XXXX

10th October 2019

Dear Mrs Thompson,

I am writing to protest about the destruction of the Great Barrier Reef. Last month I visited the reef. In the past there were beautiful colours. But some parts of the reef look awful now!

Coral bleaching is a very big problem. The coral and the animals that live on the reef are dying because the water is getting warmer. The government has changed some laws but it can do much more.

Oil spills from ships are a problem too. It takes years for the reef to recover from a bad oil spill. Why can't ships avoid the reef completely?

I am very worried about the future of the Great Barrier Reef. We must try to save the reef before it is too late. If we don't do anything now, we will lose this amazing place forever.

Yours sincerely,

Robert Phillips
Robert Phillips

4 Choose one of these tasks.

9/1–2 **a)** Give a short presentation about the Great Barrier Reef and its problems.

→ M 1-minute-presentation, p.140

Use information from the texts and find more photos. Say how you feel about the problems and where the photos are from.

OR

b) Write a short letter about the reef to Mrs Thompson. Say:

- why you are writing and how you feel
- how you heard about the problem
- what the government should do

There is more about letters on pages 106 and 107.

Ich kann Texte über Umweltprobleme verstehen. ✓

At the pharmacy

Du bist in einer Apotheke in Bayern. Du triffst eine englischsprachige Touristin, die nicht so gut Deutsch spricht. Hilf ihr dabei, Medikamente zu kaufen.

1 (MEDIATION) Can you help?

Tourist Hello, I was sick this morning and I feel awful.

Du Sie hat sich heute Morgen übergeben und fühlt sich furchtbar.

Apotheker/in Diese Tabletten sind gut, wenn man sich übergeben hat. Sie sollte morgens und abends eine nehmen.

Du These tablets ....

Tourist How much are they?

Du Wie viel ...?

Apotheker/in Sie kosten 15 € für eine 10er Packung.

Du They cost ....

Tourist OK. Here you are.

Du ....

Apotheker/in Vielen Dank. Wenn es in zwei Tagen nicht besser ist, soll sie zum Arzt gehen.

Du You should ....

Tourist Thank you very much.

Du ....

Apotheker/in Dann wünsche ich gute Besserung.

Du Get ....

Tourist Thank you. Goodbye.

Du ....

2 (SPEAKING) Spielt weitere Dialoge.

8/1

Nutzt die Informationen in der Tabelle und spielt zu dritt weitere Dialoge.

have a headache	*take tablets/medicine*
have a high temperature	*drink water*
have a cold	*stay in bed*

Ich kann Informationen in einer Apotheke weitergeben. ✓

Amazing creatures

1 What Australian animals do you know?

→ M Think – pair – share, p.143

How many Australian animals do you and your class know?
Make a list.

CULTURE

Australien ist die Heimat einiger der gefährlichsten Tiere der Welt, z. B. tödliche Spinnen. Allerdings wissen die meisten Menschen dort, wie sie die Gefahr meiden können. Vor dem Anziehen schütteln sie ihre Schuhe aus und sie lassen Kleidungsstücke nicht auf dem Boden liegen. Vor welchen Tieren hast du am meisten Angst?

2 (VIEWING) Watch the film.

2

a) Match the fact cards (1–4) with the photos (A–D) from the film.

1
- Kakadu National Park
- very dangerous

2
- live in families
- love to swim and play with tourists

3
- 7 metres wide
- from May to November

4
- Ningaloo Reef
- the world's largest fish

whale shark

saltwater crocodile

dolphin

manta ray

b) Watch the film again. Take notes to complete the sentences.

1. Saltwater crocodiles are one of the most … in the world.
2. The dolphins are full of ….
3. Manta rays look like they're … when they're eating.
4. Whale sharks can be as much as … metres long.

VIEWING SKILLS

Dieser Film ist ein Dokumentarfilm. Auf Englisch nennt man diese Art von Film „documentary". In einem Dokumentarfilm werden interessante Fakten zu einem bestimmten Thema präsentiert. Welche Dokumentarfilme kennst du noch?

3 (SPEAKING) Talk about the animals in the film.

Have you seen animals like these in real life? Where?
Which of the animals would or wouldn't you like to see? Say why.

I have/haven't seen ….
I saw it/them … (at the zoo in …/in …)
I'd like to see …… (interesting/beautiful/…)
I wouldn't like to see …… (dangerous/scary/…)

Ich kann einen Film über Tiere in Australien verstehen. ✔

Checklist

Find more online: nd4r3a

Ich kann Informationen über Australien verstehen.

Canberra is the capital of Australia. • The Great Barrier Reef is a beautiful place near the east coast. • Aboriginal people have lived in Australia for over 50,000 years. 10

Ich kann einen Blogeintrag über eine Reise schreiben.

Hi everyone! • I really enjoyed my visit to Uluru. • I didn't know much about Uluru before the trip. • I'll write more tomorrow. • Bye! 10

Ich kann darüber sprechen, wenn ich krank bin.

I have a bad headache and a cold. • If I miss the trip, my friends will be sad. • Call us if you're not better on Monday. • Get well soon. 10

Ich kann Texte über Umweltprobleme verstehen. 11

Ich kann Informationen in einer Apotheke weitergeben. 11

Ich kann einen Film über Tiere in Australien verstehen.

(UNIT TASK) A class event

Organisiert einen australischen Nachmittag oder Abend mit der Klasse. Ihr könnt eure Familie, Freunde und andere Leute aus der Schule einladen. Ihr könnt euch auch eine Idee aussuchen und sie innerhalb des Unterrichts umsetzen.

Class 9c's
AUSTRALIAN EVENING
When? Tuesday 18th October at 5:00 p.m.
Where? Room 14
See you there!

Step 1

Make a plan for the event.

a) Collect ideas for the programme.
→ M Placemat, p.142

music/dance? | a video? | a quiz? | a short talk / a reading? | ...

Denkt daran, das Thema der Veranstaltung ist Australien!

b) Find a location and a date.

c) Copy the table and make a plan like this:

What?	Time needed?	Who can do it?
Introduction	5 minutes	Tim and Julia
1. ...		
2. ...		
Break (with food and drink?)		
...		

Step 2

Plan your event in more detail.

a) What will you have to do? Make a list of jobs. Here are some ideas.

- Who can be the presenter?
- Who can design the poster and share it?
- Who can organize the break (if you have one)?
- Are there any special guests? Who can send the invitations?
- Who can tidy the room after the event?
- Who can organize decorations?
- Who can take photos and write a report?
- Who should get a present or a 'thank you' at the end? Who can organize this?

Thanks!

b) Decide in class who can do which job. How many people do you need for each job?

c) Start work on the different jobs.

STUDY SKILLS

Achtet darauf, dass die verschiedenen Aufgaben fair verteilt sind. Viele der Aufgaben solltet ihr im Team bearbeiten.
Prüft regelmäßig, ob alles gut läuft und helft euch gegenseitig.

Step 3

Hold your event. Good luck!

Step 4

Talk about the event.

a) Say what you think in one sentence. The groups can take turns to talk about it.
→ M Round robin, p.142

b) Talk about these questions together.

- Which parts of the project went well?
- What could you do better?
- What did you learn?

Life in Australia

1 Match each heading with a photo.

A A road train
B Be careful! There could be a fire!
C When you're ill in the outback
D Drive carefully! There may be kangaroos!
E An Aboriginal dot painting
F Sydney Harbour Bridge
G The music of the Aboriginal people
H Scary creatures?

INFO

Australien ist ein sehr großes Land. Von Perth an der Westküste bis Brisbane an der Ostküste sind es mehr als 4.300 Kilometer auf der Straße. Im Vergleich dazu beträgt die Entfernung auf der Straße von München nach Hamburg rund 800 Kilometer.

2 (SPEAKING) Talk about the photos.

Which of the things in Australia would or wouldn't you like to see or do? Say why.

I'd like to
I wouldn't like to

+ see .... look at .... go to ....
ride on .... listen to ....

+ I like ....
I'm interested in ....
I don't like ....
I'm not interested in ....

A picture-based interview

A

in the right/left corner

on the right, at the top

in the background

on the left

next to

in front of, behind

in the middle

in the foreground

at the bottom

B

14/1

1 Look at photo A and talk about it.

Describe the people in the picture.

Sprich über das Bild. Wähle eine sinnvolle Reihenfolge im Bild, um Einzelheiten zu beschreiben:
This photo/picture shows ....
There is .../There are ....
He/She is about ... years old.

14/2

2 Now talk about the photo in detail.

a) Where are the people? Describe the place. What's in the background?

So kannst du dein Interview beginnen:
He/She is in the middle/at the bottom/on the right/....
It's next to/between/behind/....
In the background you can see ....

b) Describe what the people are doing and what they are wearing.

Benutze das present progressive und sprich in ganzen Sätzen:
He/She is standing/talking ....
He/She is wearing ....

c) How do you think the people feel? Explain.

I think he/she is happy/sad/....
Maybe he/she is thinking about ....

d) Describe other things in the photo. Example:
- Talk about the different colours in the photo.
- What's the weather like?

There is a blue/green/....
It's sunny/cold/rainy/....
Maybe it's summer.

Stoppe die Zeit! Du solltest mindestens 1 Minute reden!

3 What about you?

- Would you like to go surfing or camping? Why? Why not?
- What kind of activities would you like to do with your friends?

I would/wouldn't like to ... because ....
I would like to play .../visit .../....
I usually wear ... in summer.

4 Now talk about photo B in the same way.

Language → G 4, p.130

He is wearing a T-shirt.
They are sitting around the fire.

Ein zweisprachiges Wörterbuch in Printform ist für die gesamte schriftliche Prüfung erlaubt.

A Listening Comprehension (Hörverstehen)

You will hear the recordings twice.

1,10 **1 Read the sentences. Then listen to the teenagers. Are the sentences true (T) or false (F)? There is an example (0.) at the beginning.**

Katie

Max

Lynn

Lucas

0. Katie liked working at her mum's school. (T)
1. Classroom assistants often teach a class of students alone.
2. Max is planning to have a holiday on a ship in Europe.
3. Max is looking forward to the summer on a ship.
4. Lynn wants to work as an assistant in a sports shop.
5. Shop assistants only have to work during the day.
6. Lucas is going to leave for Brisbane next year.
7. The most important thing for Lucas is that he can go surfing in Brisbane.

1,11 **2 Read the sentences. Listen to the four Australian teenagers again and fill in the information. There is an example (0.) at the beginning.**

0. Last year Katie did work experience at a school. Many of the children aren't good at reading or writing.
1. Katie will probably not work at a school ___.
2. Before Max starts his training, he wants to travel around ___ ___.
3. Life on a ship is hard. Maybe Max will be ___.
4. Lynn says that shop assistants have to listen carefully to the ___.
5. Yesterday Lynn ___ for the job online.
6. During his work placement Lucas will change departments every ___ ___.
7. Lucas will have a room in the hotel so he will ___ some money.

B Use of English (Sprachgebrauch)

1 Read the text about food in Australia. Find nine mistakes and write the correct word. There is an example (0.) at the beginning.

Eating in Australia

People who are on holiday in other countries think different about food and eating. Some are interested in trying new food. Others likes going to the fast food restaurants they know from there home country.
If you travelled to Australia, you will not be disappointed. Australian food is not at all boring. There are much immigrants in Australia and they brought their multicultural influences to the country. So you will find Chinese and Bavarian restaurant, for example. But of course, there are a lot of British traditions in Australia food too!
Australians are famously for their barbecues, and there are many free barbecue grills. If you eat a meal like this at Sydney or another city, you will understanding why barbecues are popular with Australians.

0 differently
1
2
3
4
5
6
7
8
9

2 Read the text about Australia's capital and complete it with words from the box. Use one word for each gap. There is an example (0.) at the beginning.

about • again • because • do • did • for • however • isn't • means • more • most ✓ • new • quiet • quite • since • too • when

Australia's capital

Which city is Australia's capital? Sydney or Melbourne is what (0) most people would probably say. But Canberra is the capital of Australia. How (1) —— that happen?
In 1908 the Australian people decided to have one capital for all the Australian states. At first they talked (2) —— Sydney and Melbourne, but finally they decided on a (3) —— capital, Canberra. The name (4) —— 'meeting point'. That's (5) —— a good name because they planned and built the city as the business and cultural centre of Australia. Canberra has been the official capital (6) —— 1927. (7) ——, Canberra (8) —— a spectacular city. People say that it hasn't got enough character and that it is (9) —— small with its population of only 322,000 people.

C Reading Comprehension (Leseverstehen)

Work and travel in Australia

An online guide

Would you like to visit Australia? Would you like to see the outback and visit the Great Barrier Reef? Worried that it could be too expensive?

The Australian Working Holiday visa can help you. It gives young people between 18 and 30 the chance to have an adventure for up to 24 months. More than 200,000 young people get one every year.

This is what you need: a Working Holiday visa and enough money to live until you find a job. The visa allows you to work in Australia, but you're only allowed to work at each job for six months.

What type of work can you do? A lot of jobs are on farms. Many farms in the outback are 100 kilometres away from the nearest neighbour or supermarket, so finding workers is a problem.

Also, a lot of the work, like fruit picking, is seasonal. Farm work can be fun, and you don't need to have experience. But don't forget, it's hard work and you will get dirty.

They also need teachers in the outback who live with families on large farms and teach small groups of children. You should like kids and be flexible. Children often help on the farm during busy times, so they have lessons in the evenings.

If you're not very interested in the outback, you can find factory jobs, office jobs or jobs in restaurants (like waiters, etc.) in towns.

There are many organizations in Australia which help people when they first arrive. They welcome you at the airport and find you a place to stay for the first few nights. They also give you information about the job market, places to stay, travel and safety.

But you won't just come to Australia to work. You'll do some exploring between your jobs, so it's often best to plan what you want to see. This will help you to find job locations that are best for your travel plans.

Linda (18): I took a job on a sheep farm with 6,000 sheep. I worked with an Italian girl and an English girl. I've never worked so hard in my life, and it really brought us together. I'm so thankful for those three months in the outback.

1 Answer the questions. Short answers are possible.

1. How many people get a holiday visa each year? more than 200,000
2. Why is it difficult for many farms in the outback to find workers?
3. What is working on a farm like? (3 aspects)
4. What can a child's day in the outback look like at busy times?
5. How can the organizations help people when they arrive?

2 In which line or lines of the text do you find the following information?

1. The Australian Working Holiday visa gives young people the chance to stay in Australia for up to two years. → lines 7–9
2. It's difficult to find workers for farms in the outback.
3. The children sometimes have to help on farms, so people who give lessons in the evenings are needed.
4. You can find jobs in towns as well as in the outback.
5. There are organizations which can help you from the beginning of your visit.
6. If you want to explore and work in Australia, you should plan it well.

D Text Production (Schreiben)

1 Du bewirbst dich auf einen Ferienjob in Australien.

Du hast vor, nach Australien zu reisen, aber du weißt noch nicht, wie du die Reise bezahlen sollst. In einer Zeitung hast du folgende Anzeige gelesen und du willst diese Gelegenheit nutzen. Schreibe einen Brief, in dem du

- eine passende Einleitung schreibst und dich vorstellst (Name, Alter, Hobbys)
- über deine Vorkenntnisse berichtest: Arbeit mit Kindern/Tieren, Aushilfsjobs, usw.
- über deine Erwartungen sprichst: dein Englisch verbessern, neue Leute treffen, usw.
- nach den Arbeitszeiten und deiner freien Zeit fragst
- weitere Fragen stellst: Dauer deines Aufenthalts, Entfernung vom Flughafen, usw.
- einen geeigneten Schlusssatz findest.

Sheep farming family is looking for help

Are you flexible and interested in helping on a farm and earning some money for free-time activities? If so, then we'd like to hear from you!

Who? *We are a nice sheep farming family and we are looking for someone to help us on the farm.*

Where? *About 100 km west of Brisbane*

What?
- *We need help with the sheep: counting, feeding, shearing*[1],
- *helping in the fruit and vegetable garden and at the market,*
- *babysitting and helping the children with their homework,*
- *cooking and helping in the house. You can live and eat with us for free.*

When?
- *We need help during the summer.*

Send your application to Tim Baker at ...

1 to shear – *scheren*

Schreibe einen Brief von ungefähr 100 Wörtern auf ein gesondertes Blatt. Achte auf eine ansprechende äußere Form und eine gut lesbare Handschrift.

E Mediation (Sprachmittlung)

1 Situierung und Text

Deine Schule veranstaltet eine Projektwoche zum Thema Umwelt. Deine Klasse hat sich für das Land Australien entschieden. Du findest Informationen dazu im Internet. Lies die Website aufmerksam durch.

INTERNET

Australia and the environment

Beautiful Australia

Australia is a huge country (and continent) with a unique environment. The climate is very hot and dry – especially in the outback – but there are also vast forests, blue oceans and some amazing food. It attracts a lot of tourists who like eating fish and go diving to see the coral. This experience should still be available to our children and grandchildren as well, so we need to take action now to save it for the future.

Climate change

Everyone is talking about climate change. One major cause concerns the fuel we burn. Using coal, for example, means that our atmosphere is being polluted by CO2. This leads to rising temperatures. It also makes people ill and kills the beautiful coral on the Great Barrier Reef. We should act now and find new energy sources so that we can close coal mines around the world.

Deforestation

Many of the world's forests have been destroyed and we should protect those which are left. Thousands of trees are cut down every year to make space for new houses as well as factories. But trees are important for producing fresh air. They are also home to many species of animals. For every tree that is cut down, new ones should be planted.

Blue oceans

There are a lot of blue oceans around Australia. Oceans are important for our health – they give us food and a space for free-time activities. A lot of people have jobs connected with the ocean. Governments set limits about how many fish can be taken from our oceans, both by individual fishermen and by industries. These limits need to be kept to and checked so that our oceans stay alive.

2 Aufgabe

Verwende die Informationen von der Website, um deine Klasse über die Situation in Australien zu informieren. Lies dafür die folgende Zusammenfassung auf Deutsch. Suche dann die fehlenden Informationen im englischen Text und ergänze die Lücken 1–10 mit Angaben in deutscher Sprache. Schreibe die Angaben in dein Heft.

Australien und seine Umweltprobleme

Wunderschönes Australien
Australien hat ein heißes, trockenes Klima, es gibt dort aber auch riesige Wälder, blaue Ozeane und unglaublich tolles Essen. Viele Touristen wollen ihren Urlaub in Australien verbringen. Diese (1) —— sollte auch für unsere Kinder und Enkelkinder noch (2) ——. Deshalb müssen wir jetzt beginnen, sie für die Zukunft zu bewahren.

Klimawandel
Leider wird häufig (3) —— als Brennstoff benutzt. Das macht Menschen krank und tötet die (4) —— am Great Barrier Reef. Es wird nach anderen Energiequellen gesucht, die die Umwelt nicht schädigen. Wenn das gelingt, können die Kohlebergwerke (5) —— werden.

Abholzung der Wälder
Viele Wälder (6) ——, um Platz zu machen für den Bau neuer Häuser und Industrieanlagen. Wir sollten also die verbleibenden (7) ——, da sie wichtig sind für unsere frische Luft. Auch geben sie vielen (8) —— ein zu Hause.

Blaue Ozeane
Es gibt viele schöne blaue Ozeane rund um Australien. (9) —— setzen Grenzen, wie viele Fische aus dem Meer gefischt werden dürfen. Diese Grenzen sollten (10) —— und kontrolliert werden, damit unsere Meere am Leben bleiben.

That's the end of Test practice 1!

3 1,12 Unit 2 Intro

Exploring India

India is more than nine times the size of Germany. It has a population of more than a billion people. New Delhi and Mumbai are the biggest cities. Tourists can see beautiful buildings like the Taj Mahal. But millions of poor people live in slums in big cities.

Most people in India work on farms, but jobs with computers are important too. India is less expensive than Europe. English is one of India's 22 official languages, and most Indians speak it. So India is an interesting place for international companies.

1 (SPEAKING) Talk about the photos.

Choose a photo and describe it to your partner.

There is a ....
He is .... She is .... It is ....
There are ....
They are ....
The photo shows a/some ....

2 (READING) Read and take notes.

22/1

What do you find out about these things?

1. India's population
2. the Taj Mahal
3. languages in India
4. India's independence
5. water in India
6. Holi
7. weddings in India

Am Ende dieser Unit kann ich ...
- Informationen über Indien verstehen.
- eine Firma vorstellen.
- ein Poster über Nachhaltigkeit gestalten.
- einen Text über eine berühmte Person verstehen.
- Informationen über verschiedene Jobs weitergeben.
- einen Film über einen Lieferservice verstehen.

2

India was a British colony for many years. But an Indian man, Mahatma Gandhi, led protests against the British. He helped India become an independent country in 1947. Gandhi died a few months after independence.

India has a lot of environmental problems. Many parts of the country are very dry, and sometimes people don't have enough water. There are also problems with pollution and waste in India. This is because so many people live together.

Family is very important in India, and young and old people often live together. There are many Indian traditions. One of them is Holi, the festival of colours. There are a lot of arranged marriages, and Indian weddings can last for several days.

3 (LISTENING) Listen to an Indian girl and her grandmother.

1,13

a) Find the missing information.

1. There will be a —— next week.
2. Grandma thinks there will be —— guests.
3. Amita and Krish first met at ——.
4. Young people in India are —— now.
5. When she was younger, Grandma didn't meet people from ——.

b) How does the girl feel about the event?

Ich kann Informationen über Indien verstehen. ✓

Hier lerne ich, eine Firma vorzustellen.

Working in India

1 (SPEAKING) Look at the photos. What are they doing?

I think he is working in a ....
Maybe she is working with ....

factory | computers | tourists | ...

2 (READING) Read the internet page about different jobs in India.

1,14
23/1

INTERNET

I'm Vibhu. I work as a computer programmer for a big IT company in Bangalore, here in the south of India. We work in a team. We write computer programs for different international customers. There are six people in my team. (I'm 22 and I'm the youngest!) I often try to solve problems in my job. I really enjoy doing that!

My name is Kashida and I'm 18 years old. I work as a tour guide at the Taj Mahal in Agra. That's in the north of India. I show tourists the building every day. They always want to know about the famous prince who lived here. I often meet people from other countries in my job. I like that! I sometimes need first-aid skills too.

Hi, I'm Manjit. I'm a factory worker. I work on the assembly line of a European company in Sanand, a city in the north of India. We make car parts. The company produces its goods in India and sells them all over the world. Sometimes people are late for work. My boss doesn't like that! He sometimes gets very angry. Today machines do a lot of things. I'm 24, so I'm fit. But it's true that the work is very hard.

My name is Prisha and I'm 24. I work as a 'virtual assistant' in New Delhi. I work from home and I'm always online. I help different companies with their office jobs. For example I write e-mails and organize trips for my customers. I like working from home, but I don't usually meet my customers. I never travel to work. That saves me a lot of time.

CULTURE

Arbeitsbedingungen in Indien unterscheiden sich sehr von denen in Europa. Rangordnungen sind sehr wichtig in der indischen Kultur und das zeigt sich in den Firmen. Für Europäer erscheinen indische Chefs manchmal sehr unhöflich und unfreundlich gegenüber ihren Angestellten. Was könnt ihr über Arbeitsbedingungen wie z. B. Arbeits- und Urlaubszeit in Firmen in eurer Nähe herausfinden?

3 Collect information about the people.

Copy the table and put in the information.

Name	How old	Job	One fact about job
Vibhu			
Kashida			
...			

4 (SPEAKING) Talk about the jobs with a partner.

Which of the jobs would or wouldn't you like to do? Say why. Use the information from Ex. 3.

I'd like to work as a ... because ....
I wouldn't like to work as a ... because ....

23/2

5 Work with words for jobs. → M Peer correction, p.141

a) Match the sentence parts to say what the people do. → ○ p.116

1. A computer programmer
2. A farmer
3. A tour guide
4. A virtual assistant
5. A chef
6. A factory worker
7. A nurse

a. makes meals in a restaurant.
b. makes car parts, for example.
c. produces food and keeps animals.
d. shows interesting sights to tourists.
e. does office work for different people.
f. looks after people who are ill.
g. writes computer programs.

b) Find the words in the text.

1. A group of people who work or play together
2. A visitor from another country, for example
3. The things that a company makes and sells
4. Another word for a journey

6 (LISTENING) Listen to Kashida at the Taj Mahal. Choose the right answers.

1,15
23/3

1. The prince met the girl at a **market** • **school**.
2. The wedding was five **months** • **years** later.
3. They **were happy** • **often had arguments**.
4. They designed **cities** • **buildings** together.
5. They had **four** • **fourteen** children.
6. The prince died in **1666** • **1696**.

Language detectives → G 5, p.131

I show tourists this in the building every day.
He gets very angry.
I often solve problems in my job.
I don't usually meet my customers.
My boss doesn't like that!

Schau dir die Sätze und die Signalwörter an.
Was drückst du mit dieser Zeitform aus?
Was musst du bei *he*, *she* und *it* beachten?
Wie bildest du die Verneinung?

7 Complete what Manjit says about his work.

a) Complete the sentences. Where do you need the -s? → ○ p.116

Manjit: I (1) work (work) between 40 and 65 hours every week. But I (2) —— (like) my job. I often (3) —— (listen) to music on the assembly line. Our boss (4) —— (visit) us most days. He (5) —— (work) in an office near the assembly line. He sometimes (6) —— (shout) at people when they (7) —— (arrive) late. Every Friday I (8) —— (finish) work at six o'clock. I (9) —— (go) home and the weekend (10) —— (start). No more work until Monday!

b) Use the notes to give more information.

1. more than 500 people – work – factory
2. boss – often – show – visitors – factory
3. we – not talk – to visitors (loud machines!)
4. best friend – work – another factory

8 Complete the sentences about the others.

a) Complete the sentences. → ○ p.116

24/4–5
25/6

1. Prisha: My father lives with me. (live)
2. My father —— any more. (not work)
3. Vibhu —— for an IT company. (work)
4. He —— programs with other workers. (write)
5. They —— computers. (not repair)
6. Kashida —— tourists the Taj Mahal. (show)
7. She —— souvenirs. (not sell)

Language → G 5, p.131
She likes … ☺
She doesn't like … ☹

b) Tell your partner three things about your daily routine. Two are true, one isn't true. Can your partner guess which thing isn't true? You can use these ideas:

A: I sometimes …. I don't …. I often ….
(I never …. My brother …. My sister ….)
B: I think that's true! / I don't think that's true!
A: You're right!

9 Match the questions and the answers.

1. What's your job?
2. How do you travel to work?
3. How many hours do you work every week?
4. What does your company make?
5. Where are your customers?
6. Do you work from home?
7. What time do you usually start work?
8. Do you work in a team?

a. We have customers all around the world.
b. Yes, I do. There are six people in my team.
c. No, I don't. I work in an office.
d. I work as a receptionist.
e. I travel by bus.
f. I usually start work at 9 a.m.
g. I work 40 hours every week.
h. My company makes computer parts.

10 (SPEAKING) Act an interview about work.

25/7

Your partner asks you five questions from Ex. 9. You can use the answers from the exercise or make up your own answers. Start and finish like this:

A: Excuse me, can I ask you about your job, please?
B: Yes, of course. What would you like to know?
...
A: Thank you for the interview!
B: You're welcome!

Language → G 5, p.131
How do you travel to work?
Do you work from home?

SPEAKING SKILLS

Falls du deine Partnerin oder deinen Partner nicht sofort verstehst, helfen dir Fragen wie „What do you mean?" oder „Sorry, can you say that again?"

11 (TASK) A presentation about a company → V Presenting a company, p.148

a) Choose a company. It can be a local, national or international company.

b) Find information about the company. Search online. Take notes about the company.

What does the company make or do?
Where does the company produce its goods?
Where does it sell its goods?
How many people work there?

STUDY SKILLS

Überlege dir zunächst, welche Quellen du verwenden kannst. Du solltest nicht nur auf der Website der Firma nachschauen, sondern z. B. auch Zeitungsartikel und Berichte lesen.

c) Organize your information and make a plan.
Find pictures of the things that the company makes.

d) Present the company. → M 1-minute-presentation, p.140

Today I'd like to tell you about ....
It's a company in .... It .....

1. *Say what my presentation is about*
2. *Give information about the company*
3. *Answer questions about my presentation*

Ich kann eine Firma vorstellen. ✔

Hier lerne ich, ein Poster über Nachhaltigkeit zu gestalten.

In the country

1 (READING) Read this article from a British youth magazine.

1,16
26/1

Deepali Chandra

What do Indian teenagers think?

By Deepali Chandra *20th August 2021*

1 The economy is growing fast in the big cities of India. But I wanted to find out about life in the country and on farms, where most people still live. What environmental problems do teenagers in Indian villages worry about? I spoke to Kyra, Tanvi and Moti, three teenagers from villages in different parts of India.

2 Kyra is a 16-year-old girl from a village in the north of India. She told me, "We need to make farming more sustainable so that we can grow food in the future too. There is a lot of pollution. We use fertilisers that help the crops to grow. But they are slowly damaging the soil. Another problem is that there are more people, so we need more food for them. We grow two or three different crops in the same field every year. This is not good for the soil. The crops don't grow well here."

3 I also spoke to Tanvi (15), from the east of the country. She said, "Villages in India don't have good sanitation. Many houses don't have bathrooms or toilets. People wash themselves and their clothes in rivers every day. Waste pollutes the soil and water."

4 Sixteen-year-old Moti is a boy from a village in Gujarat, in the west of India. "Our village doesn't have good drinking water," Moti said. "We have to walk to another village every day, so we use the water very carefully."

5 Indian villages have many problems. However, the situation is changing. Sustainable living is important for the young people there. Some villages have changed their crops, and this has helped the soil. Others have raised money for better sanitation and drinking water. What about where you live? What can you do to help the environment?

READING SKILLS

Wenn du dir die Struktur eines längeren Textes anschaust, kann sie dir helfen den Text leichter zu verstehen. Versuche als erstes zu erkennen, welche Aufgabe jeder Abschnitt hat. (Dieser Text hat fünf Abschnitte: eine Einleitung, drei Abschnitte, die zeigen, was die Teenager der Reporterin gesagt haben, und am Schluss eine Zusammenfassung.)

2 Match the headings with the parts 1–5 of the text. You don't need all of the headings.

A A walk to get water
B Things are getting better!
C Problems with farming
D Can machines help?
E Pollution in rivers
F What do they worry about?

3 Work with the text.

a) Answer the questions. You can use short answers. → p.117

1. What kind of problems did Deepali ask about?
2. What is the problem with fertilisers?
3. What can happen when there are two or three crops in the same year?
4. Why is bad sanitation a problem?
5. Why do they use water carefully in Moti's village?
6. What have some villages done to get better sanitation and drinking water?

b) Use information from the text to complete these sentences.

1. Most Indian people still ....
2. Crops grow better when ....
3. People wash themselves in rivers because ....
4. Young Indian people think ....

4 Work with words from the text.

a) What is it? Put in the right words. You don't need all of them. → p.118

drinking | teenagers | sustainable | field | fertilisers | environment | village

1. People who are between 13 and 19 are —.
2. A — is a group of houses and other buildings in the country.
3. Farmers use — to help plants to grow.
4. Water that is safe to drink is called — water.
5. If farming is —, we will have food in the future too.
6. The — is another word for the world around us.

b) Find the words in the text for these definitions.

1. plants which a farmer grows (Part 2)
2. where plants grow (Part 2)
3. the smallest room in the house (Part 3)
4. make something dirty (Part 3)

5 (SOUNDS) Listen, read and say.

1,17
26/2

1. There is a lot of pollution.
2. Many houses don't have bathrooms.
3. We have to walk to another village every day, so we use the water very carefully.
4. Some villages have changed their crops, and this has helped the soil.

SPEAKING SKILLS

Höre dir die Sätze genau an und versuche, sie nachzusprechen. Lange Sätze bestehen aus mehreren Abschnitten, die sinnvoll zusammenhängen (z. B. Verb und Objekt). Beim Zuhören kannst du diese Abschnitte erkennen.

Language detectives → G 6, p.132

The economy is growing fast in the big cities.
The crops don't grow well here.
We walk to another village every day.

Schau dir die Sätze an. Wo im Satz stehen die Adverbien der Art und Weise und wo stehen die Angaben des Ortes und der Zeit?

6 Copy the table. Put the words and phrases in the right groups. → M Peer correction, p.141

27/3

every day | fast | in the evening | at home ✓ | yesterday | well | here | every morning | carefully | in other countries | slowly | in India

Where?	When?	How?
at home	...	...
...		

7 Write sentences about village life in India.

27/4

a) Use the words to write a sentence for each photo. Put the parts of the sentences in the right order. → ○ p.118

1. The people have breakfast at home every day.

The people **every day** • **at home** • **have breakfast**

They **in the river** • **wash clothes** • **in the morning**

People **very hard** • **every day** • **work**

They **to get drinking water** • **a long way** • **walk**

Moti **on the farm** • **feeds the goats** • **every evening**

Crops **don't grow** • **in the soil** • **very well**

b) Write five sentences about your daily routine. Use two words or phrases from Exercise 6 in each sentence.

28/5 **8 Deepali's blog** → M Bus stop, p.140

a) Choose the right answers. → ○ p.119

BLOG

Hi everyone!
Village life in India **am** • **is** • **are** (1) very different from in Europe. Most houses have chickens, so the people can get eggs **easiest** • **easy** • **easily** (2). They know each other **good** • **well** • **best** (3) and chat with **their** • **them** • **they** (4) neighbours.
Most people in villages **work** • **works** • **working** (5) on farms. Many **don't have** • **doesn't have** • **didn't have** (6) drinking water so they have to **getting** • **get** • **gets** (7) it from another village.
Tomorrow **I talked** • **I talk** • **I'll talk** (8) to two other teenagers in Gujarat.
What do you like about where you live?
Bye,
Deepali

b) Write a short comment about Deepali's blog and answer her question.

9 Find the right words for the gaps. You don't need all the words.

28/6

are | is | lot ✓ | make | many | money | most | much | next

Kyra: Many farmers grow crops which need a lot (1) of water. Then the villages don't have enough water. That's why some farmers —— (2) now growing more crops which don't need so —— (3) water. Also, —— (4) villages don't have good sanitation. This causes water pollution, which can —— (5) people very ill. But things are changing. They have raised —— (6) to build new houses with bathrooms and toilets.

10 (TASK) A poster about sustainable living → V Sustainable living, p.149

28/7

a) Work in groups of four. What can you and your family do to help the environment? Collect topics and ideas. → M Placemat, p.142

Topics:
pollution waste farming holidays traffic shopping ...

Ideas:
use ... buy more/less ... travel by ... save ... ...

b) Find pictures for your ideas. Organize your information and make a poster about sustainable living.

c) Look at the other posters. Which posters have the best ideas? → M Gallery walk, p.141

d) Talk in the group about how you worked together. What would you do again, and what would you do differently another time?

Ich kann ein Poster über Nachhaltigkeit gestalten. ✓

Mahatma Gandhi and the Salt March

1 (SPEAKING) Talk about the photo of Gandhi.

What kind of person do you think he was? strong? friendly? ...?

2 (READING) Read the article about Gandhi and the Salt March.

1, 18

2nd October 1869

1 Mohandas Gandhi was born in Porbandar, a city in the west of India, in 1869.

1870s–1914

Gandhi was the youngest of four children. He wasn't always good at school and he didn't like sport. He was very small and didn't look strong. But when Gandhi wanted something, he certainly fought hard to get it. When he left school, he trained as a lawyer.
India was a British colony at this time. Many Indians were very poor and had to work very hard. Gandhi saw this and wanted to change the lives of the poorest people in India.

1914–1929

Gandhi decided to help India become an independent country. He believed in non-violent protest. He wasn't afraid to break the law and he was sent to prison several times. Gandhi was a vegetarian. He never wore expensive clothes and he wasn't interested in money. Indians started to call Gandhi 'Mahatma'. This means 'great soul'.

3 Work with the text.

30/1–2

a) Check your answers to Ex. 1. Were you right?

b) Complete the sentences about Gandhi and India.

1. Gandhi's parents had ... children.
2. Gandhi trained as ... after he left school.
3. Gandhi didn't eat ....
4. The first Salt March started because there was ....
5. Indians had to ... from British shops.
6. Thousands of Indians ... the march.
7. More than 60,000 were ... after the march.
8. India got its ... in August 1947.
9. Gandhi ... a Hindu extremist in 1948.

c) Find the parts of the text which show that Gandhi was popular with most people in India.

INFO

Indien war eine der wichtigsten Kolonien Großbritanniens. Von 1858–1947 gehörte es zum britischen Weltreich („British Empire"). Als Indien 1947 unabhängig wurde, forderten auch andere Kolonien ihre Unabhängigkeit. Es war der Anfang vom Ende des British Empire.

March 1930

In 1930 Gandhi started the first 'Salt March', a protest against the British. After a new law Indians weren't allowed to make their own salt. They had to buy expensive salt from British shops. So Gandhi and 78 followers decided to send a peaceful message to the British. They walked 400 kilometres together. More and more Indians joined the march.

When they arrived at the coast, thousands of people were with Gandhi. He showed them how to make salt. When he did this, he broke the law. The British put Gandhi and more than 60,000 other Indians in prison after the march. The British used violence at another march, but the Indians did not use violence.

August 1947

India became an independent country in 1947. Unfortunately there was violence between Hindus and Muslims in India when independence came.

30th January 1948

Gandhi was a Hindu, and he respected other religions and cultures. Some Hindus were angry when he was friendly to the Muslims in India. A few months after independence Gandhi was shot and killed by a Hindu extremist.

4 Choose one of these tasks.

P 31/3–5

a) Take notes from the text and write your own timeline about Gandhi.
Use the internet to find this information: Which other countries did Gandhi live in, and when? → M Writers' conference, p.143

OR

b) Think about what you have learned in this unit. Collect information about one of these aspects of India.

Gandhi | villages in India | jobs in India | the Taj Mahal

Use the information to give a topic-based talk. → M 1-minute-presentation, p.140

Ich kann einen Text über eine berühmte Person verstehen. ✓

Jobs around the world

Sanjay is a shop assistant in Mumbai in India. He works in a large supermarket. He often has to help customers. Sanjay works in the evening and at weekends. He works with many different products. He has to know all their prices, be quick and be good with numbers.

Sanjay

Hannah is a cook. She works in a restaurant in Toronto in Canada. She helps to plan menus and she cooks meals. Her food always has to taste and look good. She works every evening from 5:00 p.m. until 11:00 p.m. and she often has to work at weekends. She has to stand for long hours in her job.

Hannah

Jasmine is an assistant gardener who lives near Cambridge in England. She usually works outdoors in gardens and parks. But she often works in greenhouses in the winter. Jasmine helps to take care of plants. Jasmine has to be fit and she often uses machines in her job.

Jasmine

1 (MEDIATION) **Du informierst dich über verschiedene Berufsbilder.**

29/1

Auf einer Website für Jugendliche aus der ganzen Welt hast du diese drei Profile von jungen Menschen und ihren Berufen gefunden. Übertrage die Tabelle in dein Heft und ergänze die Informationen auf Deutsch.

	Beruf	Tätigkeiten	Besondere Anforderungen
Sanjay	Verkäufer		
Hannah			
Jasmine			

Ich kann Informationen über verschiedene Jobs weitergeben. ✓

Feeding Mumbai

1 (SPEAKING) Talk about delivery services for food. → M Think – pair – share, p.143

What delivery services for food do you know? Think about these questions.

What kind of food?
Who delivers it?
How do the people deliver the food?
Where and when do the people work?

2 (VIEWING) Watch the film about a delivery service in Mumbai.

4

a) Put the photos from the film in the right order.

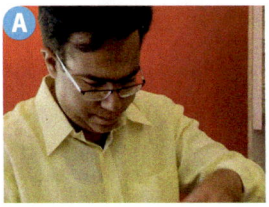

b) Watch again. Take notes to answer these questions.

1. Who makes the meal?
2. Where does he or she make it?
3. How do the people who deliver the food travel? (three ways)
4. How do they know who gets which meal?
5. How does the man feel when he gets his meal?

VIEWING SKILLS

In Dokumentarfilmen werden verschiedene Szenen häufig aneinandergereiht. Damit kann man längere Zeitabschnitte zusammenfassen. Am Anfang einer Szene wird oft im Untertitel angezeigt, wo und wann die Szene spielt.

CULTURE

In Indien sitzt man beim Essen oft auf dem Fußboden. Vieles wird ohne Besteck gegessen. Es wird aber nur die rechte Hand benutzt, die linke gilt als unrein. Welche Nahrungsmittel isst du mit der Hand?

3 (SPEAKING) Talk about the delivery service in the film.

How is the delivery service different from what you talked about in Ex. 1? What things are the same? Use your notes from Ex. 2b).

don't travel by ... | travel by ... | don't make ... | don't use ... | ...

Ich kann einen Film über einen Lieferservice verstehen. ✓

Checklist

Find more online: nd4r3a

Ich kann Informationen über Indien verstehen.

India has a population of more than a billion people. • English is one of India's 22 official languages.

32

Ich kann eine Firma vorstellen.

We work in a team and we write computer programs. • The company produces its goods in India. • I don't usually meet my customers.

32

Ich kann ein Poster über Nachhaltigkeit gestalten.

We need to make farming more sustainable. • The crops don't grow well here. • People wash themselves in rivers every day.

33

Ich kann einen Text über eine berühmte Person verstehen.

33

Ich kann Informationen über verschiedene Jobs weitergeben.

33

Ich kann einen Film über einen Lieferservice verstehen.

(UNIT TASK) An e-mail project

In diesem Projekt könnt ihr eine Partnerschule in Indien finden, der ihr E-Mails und Videos schicken könnt.

Step 1

Find out about schools in India.

Search online and find schools in India. Look for a school in India that matches your school or class.

STUDY SKILLS

Schaut euch die Websites der Schulen an, die ihr im Internet findet. Wählt diejenigen aus, die euch ansprechen. Speichert die Seiten als Favoriten, damit ihr sie jederzeit wieder finden könnt.

Step 2

Make a list of schools that you could write to.

Look at the school websites again and take notes about how to contact them.

Step 3

Plan your e-mail. Make a mind map.

Work in groups of three or four.
What can you say about your school?
What would you like to ask the school in India?

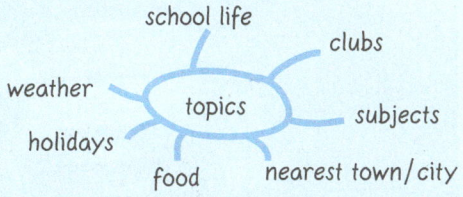

STUDY SKILLS

Eine Mindmap oder ein Wörternetz kann dir helfen, deine Ideen zu ordnen. Verwende zunächst einen Bleistift, damit du leichter etwas ändern kannst. Schreibe Stichpunkte auf Englisch. Es gibt auch Apps, mit denen du Mindmaps erstellen kannst.

Step 4

Write a draft.

Check your spelling, your grammar and the content.

WRITING SKILLS

Nutzt die Checkliste auf S.145, um euren Entwurf zu überprüfen. Schaut dann in einem Wörterbuch nach, wie man die Wörter richtig schreibt.

Dear friends, / Hi everyone,
We are ....
Our school is .... There are ... students.
Could you tell us something about ...?
Could you send us ...? / What about ...?
What is ... like?
Bye,
Your friends at ... School

Step 5

Read the e-mails from two other groups. → M Tip top, p.143

Give feedback. What is good about the e-mails? What could be better?

Step 6

Send your e-mails to the school or schools that you found in Step 1.

Be patient if you don't get an answer right away. There are also websites that help you find penfriends all over the world.

Out and about in India

1 (SPEAKING) **Talk about the photos with a partner.**

Think about these questions.

What is happening?
What people can you see?
Where are they?
What are they doing?
What can you see in the background?
Could you see things like this in Germany?

train, station | cricket, slum | cow | Holi | tea | wedding | dance

2 (SPEAKING) Talk about India.

What do or don't you like about India? Explain why you like or don't like it.

I like … because ….
I don't like … because ….

loud | pollution | exciting | food | clothes | colours | many people | …

INFO

Der Großteil der Menschen in Indien sind Hindus und alle Hindus sind Vegetarier, sie essen also auch kein Rindfleisch. Die Kuh hat allerdings auch eine besondere Bedeutung im Hinduismus – sie ist ein Symbol des Lebens und Kühe werden wertgeschätzt. Der Verkehr steht also still, wenn eine Kuh auf der Straße ist.

A picture-based story

Sieh dir die Bilder an und schreibe eine Geschichte auf Englisch. Beginne wie folgt:

Just in time
Mr and Mrs Singh and their daughter Layla live in England. They flew to India last month for the wedding of Layla's cousin Chandran. When the Singh family arrived at the airport in London …

Schreibe eine Geschichte von ungefähr 12 Sätzen bzw. etwa 100 Wörtern auf ein gesondertes Blatt.

1.

2. 10 hours later

3. 2 hours later

4. The next day

36/1 **1 Look, think and take notes.**

First look at the pictures and read the signs. Take notes.

People: Layla Singh, ...
Places: London, airport, ...
What happens: fly to India, plane is late, ...

Überlege dir zuerst, um was es in der Geschichte geht. Wer sind die Personen und an welchen Orten spielt die Geschichte? Die **Überschrift**, hier: Just in time („Gerade noch rechtzeitig") gibt einen guten Hinweis auf die Handlung.

36/2 37/3 **2 Start writing.**

Write a first draft. Do not worry if the story is not perfect. You can add details later.

Schreibe die Geschichte im **simple past** (saw, were, waited, landed, felt, phoned). Verwende auch die **Zeitangaben** in den Kästchen.

Use the speech bubbles.

Verwende auch die **Sprechblasen**. Oft ist es einfacher, die Personen in einer Geschichte miteinander sprechen zu lassen. (He/She said, "....")

37/4–5 **3 Read your text again and check it.**

- Did you use the simple past?
- Is your text interesting to read?
- Did you use the English word order?
- Is your text easy to read?
- Correct your text.

So machst du deine Geschichte spannend:
1. Benutze **Adjektive** um die Personen und die Sachen zu beschreiben: Layla was annoyed. The people were all happy.
2. Verwende auch **Adverbien** um zu beschreiben, wie jemand etwas tut: They ran quickly. He shouted loudly.

Denke an die **Satzstellungsregel**: Ort vor Zeit: They arrived in New Delhi ten hours later.

Verbinde die Sätze mit **Bindewörtern**. Sie machen den Text verständlicher und leichter lesbar: and/or/but/because/however/so/then ...

Überprüfe die richtige **Schreibweise** mit Hilfe eines Wörterbuchs.

4 Ask for feedback.

Show your text to your partner.
What tips can he or she give you?

Ein zweisprachiges Wörterbuch in Printform ist für die gesamte schriftliche Prüfung erlaubt.

A Listening Comprehension (Hörverstehen)

You will hear the recordings twice.

1,19 **1** **Listen to text 1. Choose the right answer. There is an example (0.) at the beginning.**

You will hear five short announcements from India.

0. At the pool this afternoon at 3:30 there will be ——.
   a) cakes and cookies
   b) activities only for children
   c) boring games
   d) drinks

1. You have to call Doctor Harris on ——.
   a) 504-374-23
   b) 54-274-23
   c) 94-374-33
   d) 54-274-83

2. Mumbai zoo will be closing in ——.
   a) 45 minutes
   b) 30 seconds
   c) half an hour
   d) one hour

3. You can save money on —— at the Kumar Shopping Mall.
   a) clothes
   b) vegetables
   c) fruit
   d) drinks

4. Trains from platforms 5–7 to Delhi will be leaving ——.
   a) earlier
   b) an hour later
   c) from different platforms
   d) tomorrow

1,20 **2** **Listen to text 2 and write the missing information. There is an example (0.) at the beginning.**

Maya is a girl from India who talks about her life in a radio interview.

0. Maya works at a clothes factory in Bangalore.
1. Most girls in her village marry when they are ....
2. Maya's dad said that he wanted her to see ....
3. The journey to Bangalore by train was exciting but ....
4. Now she lives with a lot of ....
5. Maya didn't like the factory because it was ....
6. Her boss spoke a different ....
7. She has to work for ....
8. In the evenings she is always ....

B Use of English (Sprachgebrauch)

1 Write the right form of the verb. There is an example (0.) at the beginning.

Trains in India

India (0 have) has an amazing railway system. We (1 visit) —— India last summer and (2 see) —— its busy railway stations but we still (3 think) —— that travelling by train would be a great experience. (4 see) —— you ever —— a photo of a crowded train like this one? Sometimes people (5 sit) —— on top. A year ago, we (6 choose) —— the fastest of the many types of trains. Our journey (7 take) —— four hours and cost as much as €10, but the same journey could take nine hours and be a lot cheaper. Don't forget that there (8 be) —— a special reservation for seats on certain trains. If you (9 not have to) —— travel quickly, it's best to (10 take) —— the night train from city centre to city centre. We (11 go) —— from New Delhi to Mumbai last year. That (12 not be) —— expensive, but we (13 not sleep) —— a lot. Next year we (14 do) —— it again.

2 Write the word that matches the definition. There is an example (0.) at the beginning.

0. Something that you think is really special is amazing.
1. When a lot of people and cars in the streets of a city are moving around, it is ——.
2. To remember their holidays, many people use their camera to take a lot of ——.
3. When there are no more seats and people have to stand the train is ——.
4. When you travel from A to B, you go on a ——.
5. You should make a —— if you want a seat on a train.
6. When you go from one place to another, for example by train, you ——.
7. The building where a train arrives and leaves is a railway ——.
8. This train doesn't go very fast. It is ——.
9. Many train journeys in India don't cost much. They are very ——.

C Reading Comprehension (Leseverstehen)

Tigers in trouble

India is home to most of the world's wild tigers today, but their numbers have gone down a lot. At the time of independence from Britain, in 1947, there were about 40,000 tigers in India. Today, there may be less than 2,000. Some people believe that in the future the only tigers left will be the tigers living in zoos.

India's economy is growing fast, which means that more space is needed for cities, factories, roads and railway systems. Unfortunately, the areas where tigers can live and move about are getting smaller every year. The growing economy is not only a big threat to tiger reserves, but also to the areas of woods between them. These areas are extremely important because they mean tigers can move to new areas and find different partners. This is important to keep the tiger population healthy.

As the areas where tigers can live are getting smaller, they are moving closer to people and towns and cities. They sometimes hunt farm animals or even kill people living in villages. Farmers often kill tigers to protect themselves, their animals and their family. Tigers are also hunted and killed so that people can earn money. The black market for tiger body parts is growing all over Asia. Some tiger body parts are sold as medicine.

There have been surveys recently with good news. Between 2011 and 2014 the population of tigers increased to about 2,220. It is too early to celebrate as there was a similar increase in the past but it unfortunately stopped.

India has tried very hard in the past to increase the tiger population by improving how and where tigers live. For a time this was very successful.

In the 1970s the number of tigers was not high. But between then and 1984 there was a huge increase in the population (to about 4,000). This was after important conservation work, which cost millions of dollars. However, between 1984 and 2008 cities grew and people hunted tigers. The number of tigers dropped again, this time to about 1,400.

It seems that the growing economy is good for companies but not for the environment. Governments must do something soon to protect these amazing animals. If they don't, it will be too late. There will be no tigers left in the wild.

Could zoos be the answer?

Wildlife groups and tiger experts are working hard to protect tigers, but it is very expensive. Some people believe that zoos are the answer:

- new generations can grow up safely,
- scientists can find out about animal food and health,
- animals which are born in zoos can be let into the wild.

But there are also people who see the problems of keeping animals in zoos:

- the cages and areas they live in are often too small for the animals,
- the animals are often bored or under a lot of stress.

Jeff Sparks (2016) in 'The Conservationist'

1 **Read the text about tigers in India and decide if the following statements are true, false or not in the text. There is an example (0.) at the beginning.**

0. There are more tigers today than in 1947. → fewer
1. People think that in the future you will only be able to see tigers in zoos.
2. More space is needed for parks and farms.
3. Tigers have less space to live than in the past.
4. Tigers sometimes kill cows, pigs, sheep and people.
5. Between 2011 and 2016 there was the first increase in the tiger population in India.
6. It is easy to protect tigers.
7. Everyone agrees about zoos.

2 **Copy the table into your exercise book. Use the information from the text to complete the table with the right number of tigers.**

Year	1947	1984	2008	2011–2014
Number of tigers (about ...)				

D Text Production (Schreiben)

1 **Du hast eine E-Mail von Tariq aus Indien erhalten. Schreibe ihm eine Antwort.**

Du hast dich auf einer Plattform angemeldet, die Kontakte zu Jugendlichen aus anderen Ländern vermittelt, und hast eine E-Mail von Tariq aus Indien erhalten.
Antworte ihm auf Englisch und gehe dabei auf seine E-Mail ein. Stelle ihm auch Fragen, z. B. zum Schulalltag und zum Essen in Indien. Schreibe eine E-Mail von ungefähr 100 Wörtern auf ein gesondertes Blatt. Achte auf eine ansprechende äußere Form und eine gut lesbare Handschrift.

E-MAIL

Hi there,
I'm Tariq. I'm 16 and I'm from Surat in the state of Gujarat in India. Surat is one of the largest cities in India and it is 289 miles north of Mumbai. Over 4.4 million people live in Surat. I play cricket and love watching the boats on the river in the city centre. I want to work on a boat when I leave school.
I'd like to hear more about you. Please tell me about where you live and go to school in Bavaria. What are your interests and your plans for the future? And why do you want a penfriend from India?
Hope to hear from you soon.
Bye for now,
Tariq

E Mediation (Sprachmittlung)

1 Situierung und Text

Deine Klasse vergleicht die beiden Länder Indien und Deutschland. Du interessierst dich für das Thema Umwelt und hast diesen Zeitungsartikel über Neu-Delhi gefunden. Lies ihn aufmerksam durch.

Zeitungsartikel

Air pollution in Delhi
Air pollution in the north of India reached new heights last month. The levels in many areas were so dangerous that they were causing people in the country's capital extreme breathing problems. Measurements of the air quality showed that the number of toxic particles in the air was nine times above the limit. The government have said that the air is so bad that there is a serious health emergency in the city at the moment.

Short-term action
Schools were closed for two days and people were advised not to go outside. Building sites were closed as they were too dangerous – the workers couldn't breathe, and they couldn't see what they were doing.
Rules were introduced to reduce the number of cars on the road. People nowadays do anything to make money and in 2019 a bar in Delhi started to sell fresh air to its customers – at a very high price, obviously. The government has been handing out millions of masks. They filter the air that people breathe.

Long-term action
There are plans to replace the polluting diesel buses with 500 electric buses. But this is only a start. Delhi's taxis are often toxic auto rickshaws. The government wants to replace them with 1.5 million electric rickshaws.
There are already solar-powered underground stations. These are the world's first stations that work with new energy sources only.
In a statement the Indian government say that by 2030 CO2 emissions will be reduced by 30 %, although more energy will be needed.
They argue that their pollution affects the whole world so everyone should help.

2 Aufgabe

Lies den Zeitungsartikel. Schreibe anschließend auf Deutsch in dein Heft, mit welchem Problem Delhi im Moment konfrontiert ist und was unternommen wird, um die Bewohner davor zu schützen. Nenne kurz- und langfristige Hilfen.

a) Problem:

b) Kurzfristige Hilfen (5)

(1) Kneipen verkaufen frische Luft.
(2) ...

c) Langfristige Hilfen (4)

(1) ...

That's the end of Test practice 2!

Discover South Africa

South Africa has three capitals: Pretoria, Cape Town and Bloemfontein. The parliament is in Cape Town. The city is also famous for Table Mountain, one of South Africa's most beautiful sights. The population of the country is 80 % African and 20 % European and others.

After independence from Britain in 1934, apartheid started in South Africa in the 1940s. This separated black and white people. Black people had to live in 'townships'. Apartheid ended in 1994, and a black man, Nelson Mandela, became president.

1 (SPEAKING) Talk about the photos.

a) Describe one of the photos to a partner.

There is .... There are ....
Photo ... shows ....

b) Talk about the photo. Would you like to spend a holiday in South Africa? Why? Why not?

You can use these words:

beautiful | hot | modern | poor

2 (READING) Correct the sentences.

38/1

1. Table Mountain is in Bloemfontein. That's wrong. Table Mountain is in ....
2. In 1934 Nelson Mandela became president of South Africa.
3. South Africa is often called the rainbow nation because it has interesting weather.
4. Many rich people still live in townships.
5. Tourists can see farm animals in South Africa's national parks.

Am Ende dieser Unit kann ich ...
- Informationen über Südafrika verstehen.
- über einen Unfall sprechen.
- einen Text über mein Vorbild schreiben.
- Texte über das Leben junger Menschen verstehen.
- Informationen in einem Krankenhaus weitergeben.
- einen Film über das Leben in Kapstadt verstehen.

3

There are eleven official languages and many traditions in South Africa. That's why it is often called the 'rainbow nation'. Many young people have moved to the cities to find work. However, many black South Africans don't finish high school.

Some people in South Africa are very rich. But many parts of the country are still poor, and many black people still live in townships in or near the cities. A lot of the houses there don't have sanitation or electricity.

Many tourists visit South Africa. They go on safari in the national parks and see wild animals like lions, elephants and buffaloes. Kruger National Park is the largest park. It has an area of 19,485 square kilometres.

3 (LISTENING) Listen to a South African radio news programme.

2,2

Choose the right answers.

1. There was a large **concert** • **protest** in Cape Town yesterday.
2. The woman is **worried** • **happy**.
3. Rangers in Kruger National Park found five dead **elephants** • **buffaloes** yesterday.
4. A new programme will help young people for **a year** • **six months**.
5. The man **is looking forward to** • **isn't sure about** the programme.
6. The weather in Cape Town will be **cold and wet** • **hot and sunny** today.
7. Steve has the news about **traffic** • **sport**.

Ich kann Informationen über Südafrika verstehen. ✓

Hier lerne ich, über einen Unfall zu sprechen.

After the accident

1 (SPEAKING) Why do road accidents often happen?

People drive too ... | They look at ... | There is too much ... | ...

2 (READING) Read the report and the text message.

2,3

A INTERNET

Daily News | News | Sports | Lifestyle

Accident in Durban

10 Jan – A car hit a school bus with students yesterday. The accident happened in Umlazi, Durban, at about 1 p.m.

The bus driver was seriously injured. A student, Piet Jansen (16), and the car driver, Lunga Sekibo (23), a man from Cape Town, also had to go to hospital.

Police officer Riah Nkosi told us, "We don't know what caused the accident yet. The car was going very fast. The driver didn't have a driving licence," she added.

Phil Davidson, a tourist from the USA, saw the accident. "The car was going fast when it happened," Phil said. "The driver braked and the car skidded. It crashed into the bus."

The police are looking for more information about the accident.

B

Nicole: Jade. It's Nicole here. There's just been an accident and Piet has gone to hospital! I really hope he's OK! A car hit our bus while we were travelling to the cricket match. We were really looking forward to it. Cebile was showing me her new wallet when we heard an awful noise and then, bang! I still can't believe it! I really want to see you, Jade, but we have to go to the police station now. The police want all the details. Call me later, OK?

INFO

In Südafrika herrscht Linksverkehr, wie in Großbritannien und Australien. Das stammt noch aus der Zeit Südafrikas als britische Kolonie und zeigt, wie die Kolonialzeit das Leben dort bis heute beeinflusst.

3 Work with the texts.

a) Match the parts of the sentences. → p.119

1. **Text A:** Piet and the two drivers
2. Phil Davidson
3. Riah Nkosi
4. **Text B:** Nicole
5. Nicole and Cebile
6. Jade

a. is looking for more information.
b. tells Jade about the accident.
c. saw the car hit the bus.
d. should phone Nicole later.
e. were injured in the accident.
f. were on the bus when it happened.

b) Find the parts of the text that give you the information. Write the lines.

1. Nicole is worried about Piet.
2. The students are interested in sport.
3. Nicole is surprised about what happened.
4. Jade is one of Nicole's best friends.

39/1 **4 Work with words from the text.** → M Bus stop, p.140

a) Complete the online comment about the report. → ○ p.120

Why are there so many car (1) accidents on South Africa's roads?

We often read about people who drive without a (2) d— l— .

Many drivers look at their (3) p— and go too (4) f— .

Every day cars (5) s— and drivers have to (6) b— hard.

b) Make word families for these words. Use your dictionary to find suitable words.

drive | ride | swim | visit | read | play

1. drive

driver — **drive** — driving licence

STUDY SKILLS

Wörternetze können dir helfen, deinen Wortschatz zu erweitern. Du kannst auch später immer wieder Wörter aus der gleichen Wortfamilie ergänzen.

2,4 39/2 **5 (LISTENING) Listen to the dialogue at the police station.**

Which two sentences are right?

1. Cathy has lost her passport.
2. She was swimming in the sea when it happened.
3. Cathy is staying at a hotel in Durban.
4. She will be there for one more week.
5. She should come back to the police station before she leaves.

LISTENING SKILLS

Manchmal sind Namen oder Adressen schwer zu verstehen. Wenn man nicht nachfragen kann, schreibt man sie am besten so auf, wie man sie hört. Das ist besser, als gar keinen Anhaltspunkt zu haben.

39/3 **6 (SOUNDS) Read, say and listen.** → M Peer correction, p.141

a) The words below are spelled with the letter 'o' but sound different. Make a chart. Say the words to a partner and put them in the right group.

/ɒ/	/əʊ/
on	know

told | gone | know ✓ | so | Nicole | won't | hospital | not | on ✓ | going | from

2,5 b) Listen to the words and check the chart.

40/4 **7 What did they do?**

a) What did they do on the morning of the accident? → p.120

1. Piet walked to school after breakfast. (walk)
2. Cebile and Nicole — at break. (talk)
3. They — Piet in the cafeteria at lunchtime. (meet)
4. Nicole's phone — at 12:22 p.m. (ring)
5. She — it. (not hear)
6. Phil — his hotel at about 11:30 a.m. (leave)
7. He — to his friend in the USA. (not talk)

Language → G1, p.127
The accident happened yesterday.
Phil saw the accident.
The driver didn't have a driving licence.

b) What did or didn't you do last weekend? Use the pairs to write five or more sentences.

play / not play ... | go to / not go to ... | eat / not eat ... | meet / not meet ...

Language detectives → G7, p.133

The car was going fast when the accident happened.
Cebile was showing me her new wallet when we heard an awful noise.
A car hit our bus while we were travelling to the cricket match.

Schau dir die Sätze an. Welche Handlung war noch nicht zu Ende und dauerte noch an, als etwas Neues passierte? Wie wird die Zeitform gebildet? Achte auf Einzahl (was) und Mehrzahl (were).

40/5 **8 Use the words and the pictures below to write what they were doing at 2 p.m. on Saturday.**

was | were | looking for | playing | talking to ✓ | swimming | working | visiting

Nicole ... her friend

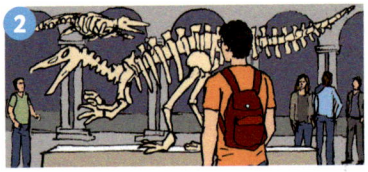
Phil Davidson ... a museum

Cebile ... a new wallet

Riah Nkosi ... at the police station

Jade and her mum ... in the sea

Piet and his friends ... on the beach

1. At 2 p.m. on Saturday Nicole was talking to her friend.

9 (SPEAKING) What were you doing?

41/6

a) Think about what you were doing at 8 p.m. yesterday. Make notes. Use these ideas:

I was + listening to … / making … / watching … / talking to … / playing … / … + with my brother/sister. / with my friend. ….

b) Ask other students what they were doing. → M Milling around, p.141

A: What were you doing at 8 p.m. yesterday?
B: I was listening to music with my brother. We were listening to ….

41/7–8

10 Nicole is telling a friend about the accident. Complete her sentences.

a) Put the verbs in the right form. → ○ p.120

1. We were going to the cricket match when a car crashed into the bus. (crash)
2. Cebile was showing me her new wallet when we — a loud bang. (hear)
3. The car driver was talking on his phone when the police —. (arrive)
4. While the police officer — to the car driver, the witness came to help. (talk)
5. While I — in the police car, I sent a message to Jade. (sit)
6. While I — at the police station, my parents arrived. (wait)

b) Complete the sentences.

1. Piet — (listen) to music when the car — (hit) us.
2. Jade — (get) the message while she — (talk to) her mum in the kitchen.
3. I — (go) home with my parents when I — (get) a message from Cebile.

11 (TASK) A role play at the police station → V Talking about an accident, p.150

a) Look at the texts about the accident on page 64. What happened? What did the different people see? What does the police officer want to know? Take notes.

b) Decide who is the police officer and who is the witness. Use your notes to make a dialogue. The phrases will help.

Police officer Riah Nkosi

Phil Davidson | Nicole | Piet Jansen

Police officer:
What is your name?
Please tell me what you saw.
Was the … travelling fast? …
What other information can you give us?
Thank you. You may leave now.

Witness:
My name is ….
I saw a ….
Yes, it was.
I think ….There was ….
You're welcome!

c) Present your dialogue to the class. → M Tip top, p.143

Ich kann über einen Unfall sprechen. ✓

Hier lerne ich, einen Text über mein Vorbild zu schreiben.

South African role models

1 (READING) Read the dialogue.

2,6

Miriam Makeba

Zackie Achmat

Kungawo: Hi everyone and welcome to our podcast about inspiring South Africans. With me now is Mia, who is going to tell us about her very special South African role model.

Mia: Yes, Kungawo. We've already talked about music on the show. My role model is the South African singer and songwriter Miriam Makeba.

Kungawo: Miriam Makeba? OK, tell us more.

Mia: Well, she became famous all around the world during apartheid. Life was hard for black people in South Africa at that time. They had to live in townships and many other places were for white people only. I admire Miriam Makeba because she fought against apartheid. The government took away her passport when she left South Africa. She couldn't go home.

Kungawo: That sounds awful!

Mia: Yes, it was. Her life has been an inspiration for a long time. She achieved a lot. What about you? Who do you admire?

Kungawo: My role model is Zackie Achmat.

Mia: Who's he?

Kungawo: Zackie Achmat is a South African film director. He fought against apartheid and has fought for gay and lesbian rights too. He has helped many South Africans with HIV and AIDS. He has made films about people who have the diseases.

Mia: HIV and AIDS have been serious problems in South Africa for many years.

Kungawo: That's right. There is medication for HIV, but at first it was very expensive. Zackie Achmat has been HIV-positive since 1990 but he didn't take medication right away. He fought for cheaper drugs. He only took medication in August 2003, when it was cheaper, and poorer people could pay for it too.

Mia: He was really brave. South Africans have achieved a lot since 1994 and before that.

Kungawo: Yes, there's a lot that this country can be proud of.

INFO

HIV ist ein Virus, der durch den Austausch von Körperflüssigkeiten übertragen wird. Aids ist die Krankheit, die nach einer längeren Zeit der Ansteckung mit HIV ausbrechen kann. In Südafrika waren 2018 mehr als 7 Millionen Menschen entweder HIV-positiv oder aidskrank. Heutzutage kann man mit HIV und Aids ein weitgehend normales Leben führen. Seit Längerem gibt es wirkungsvolle Medikamente, aber erst seit 2003 sind günstige Medikamente in Südafrika für alle zugänglich.

2 Complete the sentences. → p.121

42/1

1. Mia's role model is a South African singer and songwriter.
2. During apartheid Miriam Makeba became famous ___.
3. Miriam Makeba couldn't go back to her country when the government ___.
4. Zackie Achmat's films are about ___.
5. At first medication for HIV ___.
6. Zackie Achmat was brave because he only took medication when ___.

3 Work with words from the text. → M Bus stop, p.140

a) Put the words into the right groups (nouns, verbs or adjectives). → p.122

brave | achieve | inspiration | sing | admire | proud | role model | singer | inspiring

Du kannst manchmal eine Silbe an den Anfang oder an das Ende eines Wortes stellen, um neue Wörter zu bilden.

b) Use the endings to make new words. Use your dictionary if you are not sure.

admir(e) | pay | music | achieve | help | -ment | -ful | -ian | -ation

4 Choose the right answers to complete Mia's blog.

INTERNET

Today we talked about Miriam Makeba, the (1) **sing** • **singer** and songwriter. I really (2) **admire** • **achieve** her. She has been an (3) **inspiration** • **inspiring** to many South (4) **Africa** • **African** people. Miriam Makeba fought (5) **again** • **against** apartheid. She couldn't go home when the government took (6) **away** • **out** her passport. That was (7) **awesome** • **awful**!

5 (LISTENING) Listen to another podcast. Which three sentences are right?

2,7
42/2

1. Nelson Mandela trained as a doctor when he was young.
2. He was sent to prison near Cape Town.
3. He worked with the government to end apartheid.
4. He was president until 2002.
5. He helped to fight against AIDS and HIV.
6. He was 90 when he died. That was in 2013.

6 What has Zackie Achmat done in his life? Complete the sentences.

43/3

1. Zackie Achmat has worked with poor people in South Africa. (work)
2. He ___ to many people with AIDS and HIV. (talk)
3. He ___ for gay and lesbian rights. (fight)
4. He ___ several prizes for his work. (win)
5. He ___ concerts for people with AIDS and HIV. (not organize)
6. He ___ many young South Africans. (help)
7. He ___ a film about music. (not make)

Language → G 8, p.134

We've already talked about music on the show.
He has helped South Africans with HIV.
They haven't made a podcast about animals yet.

Language detectives → G 8, p.134

Miriam Makeba's life has been an inspiration for a long time.
HIV and AIDS have been serious problems in South Africa for many years.
South Africans have achieved a lot since 1994.

Schau dir die Sätze an. Wie würdest du die Sätze auf Deutsch sagen?
For und since sind wichtige Signalwörter für das present perfect. Welches Wort verwendest du für eine Zeitspanne, welches für einen Zeitpunkt?

43/4

7 How long have they done it? → M Peer correction, p.141

a) Make sentences with for or since. Put in the right form of the verb. → p.122

1. Mia – (be) in Cape Town – two days
   Mia has been in Cape Town for two days.
2. She – (live) in her flat – January
3. She – (work) at a hairdressing salon – two years
4. Her parents – (be) on holiday in Durban – last Friday
5. Kungawo – (share) a flat with his friend – six months
6. He – (work) at a large supermarket – November last year
7. Kungawo and Mia – (make) podcasts together – they met
8. Mia – (be) interested in music – a long time

Mia, 18

Kungawo, 19

b) How long? Make a sentence with each verb.

live in ... | be interested in ... | know ... | have ... | enjoy ...

I've lived in ... for ..../since ....
I've ....

8 (SPEAKING) Ask a partner. → M Milling around, p.141

43/4

a) Ask your partner questions. → ○ p.122

listen to South African music | meet a famous person | see a lion | organize a flea market | work with ... | ...

A: Have you ever listened to ...? B: Yes, I have. / No, I haven't. Have you ...?

Language → G 8, p.134
Have you ever seen this film?
Yes, I have. / No, I haven't.

b) Ask another partner about his or her interview.

A: Has Sophia ever listened to ...? B: Yes, she has. No, she hasn't.

9 Find the right words for the gaps. You don't need all the words.

for | from | has | have | hears | her | his | listens ✓ | many | much | of | since

Mia often listens (1) to different kinds of South African music. She's a big fan —— (2) the singer Karen Zoid, for example. Mia —— (3) heard all Karen Zoid's songs and has been to —— (4) of her concerts. Karen Zoid has been a big star —— (5) many years. She played with —— (6) band at the Nelson Mandela HIV / AIDS charity concert in 2005.

10 (TASK) An e-mail to a magazine → V Describing a role model, p.151

P

You have seen a competition in a magazine to win a 'meet and greet' with your favourite star.

a) Which star would you like to meet? Think of someone from music, film and TV or sport.

b) Think about why you are a fan. Make notes. Use these ideas:

have watched his/her films | read his/her updates on ... | want to go to his/her concerts | have liked him/her since/for ... | ...

c) Find out about other reasons why your star is great.

has helped with ... | has done a lot for ... | has worked with ... | ...

Karen Zoid

Meet & Greet

Send us an e-mail.
Say why you think
Karen Zoid is great!

d) Use your notes and the phrases on the right to write an e-mail to the magazine. Explain why you should win the 'meet and greet'. Use the checklist on page 145. → M Peer correction, p.141

Dear ...,
I want to meet and greet ... because .....
I look forward to hearing from you.
Yours sincerely,

Ich kann einen Text über mein Vorbild schreiben. ✓

Young people in South Africa

1 (READING) Read the texts from a magazine article about young South Africans.

2, 8–11

Shaka, 19

1 Hi, I'm Shaka and I live in Durban. Many young black South Africans are poor and unemployed. It's also not easy for me because I am in a wheelchair. But I was lucky because I got a job as an office worker with the organization *Working For Water*. Our workers cut down trees and control the plants in the area. We have a problem with plants and trees that aren't from here. These need much more water than local ones, so we cut some of the trees down. One day I'd like to be in charge of the office. In my free time I play the guitar a bit.

2 My name is Keeya and I work as a nurse at Tshepong Hospital in Klerksdorp. That's a town in the north of South Africa. My partner Bertha and I would like to share a flat together next year when we have saved some money. Fortunately my parents will help me with that. I speak English and Afrikaans. I enjoy working as a nurse – I like working with other people and it's great to help them. I don't think I could work at a desk all the time. I play hockey with the hospital team every week. We always have a lot of fun.

Keeya, 21

2 Copy the table and put in the information from the texts.

Name	Where they live	Job	Hobbies	Hopes for the future
Shaka	Durban	office ...	plays ...	be in charge of ...
Keeya				
Uuka				
Amahle				

3 Choose the right meaning in German for these words from the texts.

1. plant (... control the **plants** in our area) — a. Pflanze — b. pflanzen
2. save (... when we have **saved** some money) — a. retten — b. sparen
3. programme (a new preschool **programme**) — a. Programm — b. Sendung
4. use (... things that people don't **use** ...) — a. verwenden — b. Gebrauch
5. train (... to **train** as an engineer ...) — a. (Sport) trainieren — b. eine Ausbildung machen

Uuka, 19

3 I'm Uuka and I live in Soweto, a township in Johannesburg. I was born in Soweto too. I speak the Sesotho language at home but English at work. I work as a kindergarten teacher in a new preschool programme here in Soweto. A good preschool education is very important for poor children. Then they are ready for primary school and life outside the home. At the kindergarten I often do handicrafts with things that people don't use any more, like cans or boxes. I also enjoy painting pictures after work. One day I hope to sell my pictures at markets.

4 My name is Amahle and I live with my family in Makhanda, a town in the Eastern Cape. I'm still at school. I have two younger sisters and a younger brother. My father left us eight years ago, so I have to help my mother at home. I have school five days a week and lots of homework too, so it's quite hard. I often worry about my family because we don't have medical insurance. It's too expensive. My big hope for the future is this: I'd like to train as an engineer one day and build bridges. I like playing football too.

Amahle, 16

4 Choose one of the tasks.

45/1–2

a) Write a short text like the ones in the article about your own life. Write 10–12 sentences. You can use these ideas:

→ M Writers' conference, p.143

- I live in ....
- I was born in ....
- That's ....
- I live with ....
- I speak ....
- I ... in my free time.
- I also like ....
- I worry about ....
- My hope for the future is this: ....
- ... is great.
- ...

OR

b) Work in groups of three. Copy the table in Ex. 2 and do a survey with students in your class.

Ask them questions in English and make a chart with the most popular answers.

- Where do you live?
- What job do you want ...?
- What are your ...?
- What ...?
- ...

Ich kann Texte über das Leben junger Menschen verstehen. ✓

At the hospital

Du bist mit deiner Familie im Urlaub in Südafrika. Deine Mutter hat sich am Arm verletzt. Leider kann sie nicht so gut Englisch sprechen. Hilf ihr dabei, sich in der Notaufnahme im Krankenhaus zu verständigen.

1 (MEDIATION) Can you help?

Mutter Kannst du ihnen bitte sagen, was passiert ist?

Du Hello. My mother has hurt her arm.

Hospital employee Oh dear! OK. I need to know if you have medical insurance if you're not from South Africa.

Du Sie wollen wissen, ob ....

Mutter Ja, sag Ihnen, dass wir eine weltweite Reiseversicherung haben. Hier sind die Papiere.

Du Yes, we have ... for .... Here ....

Hospital employee OK. Is your mother taking any medicine?

Du ....

Mutter Eigentlich nicht. Aber ich habe heute Morgen Kopfschmerztabletten genommen.

Du No, ... But she ....

Hospital employee Right. That's not a problem. Does she have any allergies?

Du ....

Mutter Ja, ich habe eine Katzenhaarallergie.

Du ....

Hospital employee OK. She should sign this form here. If you just wait over there, the doctor will come and see you. It may take twenty minutes.

Du ....

Mutter Haben Sie vielen herzlichen Dank!

Du ....

Hospital employee You're welcome.

Du Sie sagt: ....

2 (MEDIATION) Erkläre auf Deutsch, welche Vorschriften es im Krankenhaus gibt.

44/1–2

Die Krankenhausangestellte erklärt dir, was im Krankenhaus erlaubt ist und was nicht. Gib die Informationen für deine Familie auf Deutsch wieder.

Hospital employee: There is no food and drink allowed in the hospital. Visitors can come and visit between 2–4 p.m. and 7–8 p.m.

Ich kann Informationen in einem Krankenhaus weitergeben. ✓

Different faces of Cape Town

1 (SPEAKING) Talk about where you live.

a) What do you think about the city, town or village where you live?

I like .... I don't like ....
The ... is cool/OK. ...

b) What would you show a visitor? Why?

I would show a visitor ... because ....

2 (VIEWING) Watch the film about Cape Town.

6

a) Which of these things is **not** in the film?

animals | a hospital | a mountain | people in a factory | colourful buildings | a football game on a beach

b) Watch the film from 01:25 to 02:10. Answer the questions (short answers).

1. What do the baboons in the film do?
2. Who can help with the problem?

CULTURE

Die Architektur kann viel über die Geschichte einer Stadt erzählen. Die farbenfrohen Häuser in Bo-Kaap, einem Stadtteil Kapstadts, wurden z. B. von Menschen errichtet, die aus Malaysia gekommen waren. Es gibt aber auch viele Gebäude aus der Kolonialzeit. Was kannst du über alte Gebäude oder Plätze in deinem Wohnort berichten?

VIEWING SKILLS

Am Anfang des Dokumentarfilms werden die Gesichter verschiedener Menschen gezeigt, die direkt in die Kamera sehen. Mehr erfährt man über sie jedoch nicht. Dennoch erhalten die Zuschauer einen ersten Eindruck von der Stadt und ihren Menschen. Achte darauf, welchen Eindruck die Bilder bei dir als Zuschauer oder Zuschauerin erwecken.

3 (SPEAKING) Talk about the film.

a) What do you think life in Cape Town is like? How do the people there feel?

b) Compare Cape Town to your city, town or village.

people | flowers and mountains | colourful buildings | animals in the roads | different kinds of people | ...

In Cape Town there is/are .... We have ... / We don't have ... where I live.

Ich kann einen Film über das Leben in Kapstadt verstehen. ✓

Checklist

Find more online: nd4r3a

Ich kann Informationen über Südafrika verstehen.

South Africa has three capitals. • Apartheid separated black and white people. • South Africa is often called the 'rainbow nation'. 46

Ich kann über einen Unfall sprechen.

The accident happened in Umlazi, Durban, at about 1 p.m. • The driver braked and the car skidded. • A car hit our bus while we were travelling to the cricket match. 46

Ich kann einen Text über mein Vorbild schreiben.

My role model is Miriam Makeba. • Her life has been an inspiration for a long time. • Zackie Achmat has helped many South Africans with HIV and AIDS. 47

Ich kann Texte über das Leben junger Menschen verstehen. 47

Ich kann Informationen in einem Krankenhaus weitergeben. 47

Ich kann einen Film über das Leben in Kapstadt verstehen.

(UNIT TASK) A feature story

Du bist Reporterin oder Reporter für deine englische Partnerschule. Du sollst einen Artikel über deine Stadt schreiben und Fotos machen. Stellt anschließend alle Artikel zu einer Wandzeitung zusammen und hängt sie in der Klasse auf.

Das ist eine „feature story". Das Thema ist „early birds" (Frühaufsteher). Die Autorin beschreibt darin eine Situation, die zum Thema passt: Leute warten vor einer Imbissbude auf ihr Frühstück. Mit einer feature story kannst du deine Leserinnen und Leser auf ein Thema aufmerksam machen, über das sie vorher noch nicht nachgedacht haben.

Early birds
(by Mika Hensing)
13th January 2020

headline, writer, date

It's seven o'clock in the morning. I'm in the city centre. I can only see a few people in the street. However, the small snack bar around the corner is already crowded with people. They are all waiting. Most of them want to buy something for breakfast. The snack bar opens at 7 a.m. every morning. Some people here are looking at their phones. Some are looking in their bags. Others are talking. Almost everyone looks tired, but the shop assistant .... I feel .... "I come here every day," a woman says ....

describe the scene

describe details

describe emotions

direct speech

Step 1

Choose a topic.

students on their journey to school | alone in the city | an afternoon in the park | ...

Step 2

Choose a place and a time.

Choose a place in your town or village and a time.
Go there, watch the people and take notes.
What can you see, hear, smell, feel?
How do you think the people feel? Why?
What do people there say?
Take photos.

STUDY SKILLS

Du kannst z. B. tagsüber die Leute an einer Bushaltestelle, auf dem Schulhof oder im Park beobachten. Finde andere Schülerinnen und Schüler, die den gleichen Ort ausgewählt haben. Geht gemeinsam dorthin. Wenn du Fotos von einer einzelnen Person oder einer kleinen Gruppe machst, musst du sie vorher um Erlaubnis fragen.

Step 3

Use your notes to write a draft. You can use these phrases:

It's ... in the morning/afternoon/evening.
I'm in ....
There is ..../There are .... I can also see ....
Some people are ....
One person is .... He/She looks/feels ....
Maybe he/she wants to ....
"...," says one ....

Step 4

Write your feature story.

Check your draft and write the feature story. Ask the other people in your group for help.
→ M Writers' conference, p.143

STUDY SKILLS

Nutze diese Liste, um deinen Entwurf zu prüfen:
- Hast du eine Überschrift, einen Einleitungssatz und ein Foto? ✓
- Hast du deinen Namen und das Datum angegeben? ✓
- Hast du alle Wörter richtig geschrieben? ✓
- Hast du die richtige Grammatik verwendet? ✓

Step 5

Make a wall newspaper in class. → M Gallery walk, p.141

South Africa – People and places

1 Work with photos 1–6.

a) Look at the photos. Match each photo with a caption on the right.

b) Describe one of the photos to a partner.

This is a photo of .... It's ....
There is / There are....
The people are ...
In the foreground / In the background ...

- The Cape Town Cycle Tour
- The Cape of Good Hope – where two oceans meet
- Rock art in a cave near Cape Town
- South Africa's rugby team after the 2019 World Cup
- A safari in Kruger National Park
- A football stadium in Durban

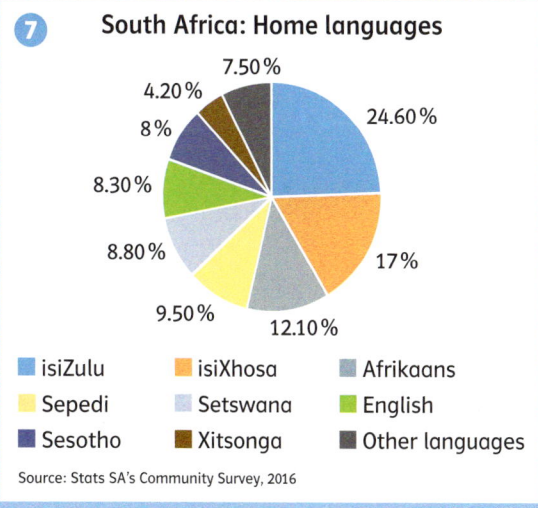

2 Look at the chart.

a) Which language is used at home by the largest group of South Africans?

b) What do you find most interesting about the chart? Why?

c) What languages are spoken at home by the students in your class? Use a dictionary if you need to.

INFO

Englisch ist die meist gesprochene Sprache im öffentlichen Leben (Wirtschaft, Politik und Medien) in Südafrika. Aber es ist nicht die meist gesprochene Sprache zu Hause. Die meisten Südafrikaner sind mehrsprachig und sprechen zwei oder mehr Sprachen.

Visiting a national park

Du machst gerade Urlaub in Südafrika mit deinem Onkel. Heute wollt ihr den „Kruger National Park" besuchen. Am Eingang gibt euch ein Park Ranger Auskunft. Dein Onkel, der nicht so gut Englisch spricht, hat ein paar Fragen. Er bittet dich, diese dem Ranger auf Englisch zu stellen und seine Antworten dann auf Deutsch wiederzugeben.

Onkel Hallo. Ich habe eine Frage. Wir wollen jetzt in den Park fahren. Kann man aus dem Auto aussteigen, wenn man Fotos von den Tieren machen will?

Du My uncle asks if we can ....

Park ranger No, sorry. You have to stay in your car all the time with the doors closed. But you'll find signs which show the distance to the nearest camp.

Du Der Ranger sagt, dass wir ....

Onkel OK. Können wir im Park mit dem Handy telefonieren?

Du He asks: "Can we ...?" / He wants to know if we ....

Park ranger No, you can only use your phones in camps, at gates or in emergencies.

Du Er betont, dass wir ....

Onkel Frage ihn doch mal, ob man die Tiere im Park füttern darf.

Du He asks: "...?" / He also wants to know if we ....

Park ranger Of course not. Never feed or disturb the animals.

Du Er weist darauf hin, dass wir ....

Onkel Das verstehe ich. Mir liegt die Natur ja sehr am Herzen. Frage ihn doch noch, ob es im Park gefährlich werden kann.

Du He says: "..." / He says that he ....

Park ranger You'll be safe as long as you follow all the rules. You must be at your camp before the gates close. They are closed to protect visitors against wild animals. But I've worked in the park for five years. There has never been a dangerous situation.

Du Er sagt, dass wir ....

Onkel Vielen Dank für die Informationen! Thank you.

50/1 **1 Read the dialogue on the left and the tips about how to pass on information.**

My uncle asks: "..."/ My ... wants to know if/when/what ....
He says: "..."

Der Ranger sagt/erklärt/betont, dass ....

Bei „Mediation" vermittelst du zwischen zwei Gesprächspartnern. Dabei kannst du – wie im Beispiel – die Fragen und Sätze mit verschiedenen Ausdrücken einleiten.

50/2 **2 Tips and tricks**

a) „Mir liegt die Natur ja sehr am Herzen."
(He says) he likes nature very much.

Versuche niemals, alles wortwörtlich zu „übersetzen". Vereinfache die Aussagen, ohne wichtige Infos auszulassen.

b) ... as long as you follow the rules.
... man muss die Regeln befolgen./
Man darf nur tun, was erlaubt ist.

Wenn dir einmal ein Wort (z. B. follow) unbekannt ist, solltest du versuchen, es im Zusammenhang mit bekannten Wörtern zu erraten oder ein Ähnliches im Deutschen denken: z. B. distance – Distanz, Entfernung

3 Be careful with verb forms.

a) My uncle asks ....
He wants to know if ....

b) I've worked ... for five years.
Er sagt, er arbeitet schon seit fünf Jahren.

Denke auch daran, die richtige Form des Verbs zu verwenden, besonders nach he/she/it.
Beachte: Verben im present perfect mit for/since werden auf Deutsch mit der Gegenwartsform wiedergegeben.

50/3 **4 Ask for help.**

Could you repeat that, please?
Could you speak more slowly, please?
I'm sorry, but could you explain that again, please?

Bitte deinen Gesprächspartner darum, langsam zu sprechen oder etwas zu wiederholen, wenn du etwas nicht verstanden hast.
Du kannst auch bitten, das Gesagte anders auszudrücken oder zu umschreiben.

5 Your turn

Gestaltet nun das Gespräch mit drei Personen.

→ M Peer correction, p.141

Ein zweisprachiges Wörterbuch in Printform ist für die gesamte schriftliche Prüfung erlaubt.

A Listening Comprehension (Hörverstehen)

You will hear the recordings twice.

2,12 **1** **Listen to text 1. There is one mistake in every sentence. Write the wrong words in your exercise book and then write the correct ones. There is an example (0.) at the beginning.**

0. It's quite difficult to get around in South Africa if you travel on your own.
   difficult → easy
1. There are almost 19 smaller airports.
2. Travel by train or taxi if you want to meet South Africans.
3. You need an international driving licence to buy a car in South Africa.
4. Watch your things, especially when you are alone.
5. It's very important to start learning English before you leave your country.

2,13 **2** **Listen to text 2 and complete the sentences with the information you hear. You don't need all the sentence parts on the right. There is an example (0.) at the beginning.**

0. The name of the airline is … → c
1. You need gate 41 for the flight to …
2. The L&G train is travelling to …
3. There has been an accident on the …
4. Don't forget to watch your bag at the …
5. Don't forget to wear a …

a) Pretoria.
b) hat.
c) SunAirlines.
d) train.
e) Johannesburg.
f) N12.
g) football stadium.
h) coat.

B Use of English (Sprachgebrauch)

1 Read the interview. Write the correct questions to complete the interview. There is an example (0.) at the beginning.

Charlie: With me in the studio today is Tony, a ranger at Kruger National Park.

0. Charlie: Why do you work as a ranger?
Tony: I work as a ranger because I love wild animals and being outdoors.

1. Charlie: ——?
Tony: It was in 1898 that President Paul Kruger started a nature reserve which later became Kruger National Park.

2. Charlie: ——?
Tony: Kruger National Park is in the northeast of South Africa, near the border with Zimbabwe.

3. Charlie: ——?
Tony: Today Kruger National Park is almost 20,000 square kilometres in size.

4. Charlie: ——?
Tony: For many years most tourists have wanted to see the 'Big Five' on their safaris.

5. Charlie: ——?
Tony: There are more than eleven thousand elephants at the moment in Kruger National Park.

6. Charlie: Thank you for answering my questions. I have just one more.
——?
Tony: That's difficult – I like all the animals, but I think my favourite is the lion.
Charlie: Thanks Tony.

2 Find a synonym (=) or an opposite (↔) for the underlined words. There is an example (0.) at the beginning.

0. From Table Mountain you get a bad view of the city. (↔) good
1. Tourists from all over the world hate the beaches. (↔)
2. Last year many people started their tour of South Africa at Robben Island. (=)
3. It is wrong that Cape Town is a beautiful city. (↔)
4. My mum and dad visited the Two Oceans Aquarium. (=)
5. We arrived a day ago. (=)
6. We think that South Africans drive really fast. (↔)
7. Our holiday in South Africa was worse than last year's at home. (↔)

C Reading Comprehension (Leseverstehen)

A surprise at the beach – a story

A It had been a hard time at school in Munich for Daniel, and he was glad that he had finished. Now he could start planning his future. **(x)** But first he needed a break.

B Then Daniel got a text message from his cousin Leo in Cape Town: *Just off to the beach. Great surf. A bit boring. Friends all away. Come visit!*
This was an exciting idea.
Cape Town. Some time in a foreign country would be the best medicine. And he could practise his English too.

C Daniel's parents protested at first. "South Africa is too expensive. And I don't think you really want to practise your English!" said his dad. "You only liked the word 'beach' in Leo's message."
"And it could be quite dangerous," his mum said. But Daniel told her, "Don't worry, Mum. I'm going to stay with Leo and his parents."

D He found a good price for a flight to Cape Town and a few days later he was on his way to South Africa. **(x)**
Finally he was there in Hout Bay and his holiday started. Daniel felt at home right away. He loved the climate, and he had all the same interests as his cousin Leo. Leo lived with his parents in a small house about ten minutes from the beach by car. 'The perfect place to be,' thought Daniel.
He sent his parents text messages every day and told them they needn't worry. **(x)**
One morning Leo borrowed his dad's car and they went surfing.

E After surfing for an hour, the boys were sitting on the sand. Over to his right, Daniel saw some strange clouds. As he watched, the sky went darker and darker over the sea.
"I'm so hungry!" Leo said. **(x)**
"Wait!" said Daniel as he took Leo's arm. Daniel saw that the waves were bigger now. Leo looked at the waves too.
Leo saw the clouds and suddenly knew what was going to happen. He took a deep breath and tried to think quickly. 'What happens if this storm hits the beach? Will we be OK?' **(x)**
He saw that Daniel was scared. "Stay cool, Daniel," he said. "Leave everything where it is and run for the car ... as fast as you can."
Thankfully Daniel was better at running than he was at surfing, and he didn't need Leo to tell him again. The boys got to the car as the rain started. **(x)**

F As soon as the rain stopped, the sun came out again. Daniel couldn't believe what had happened. "The sky is blue now and the sea is flat and perfect," shouted Daniel happily. "Even our things are still on the beach – all wet." **(x)**

1 **Match the headings to the right parts of the text (A–F). You don't need all the headings. There is an example (0.) at the beginning.**

0. School is over → A
1. The storm is over
2. Peaceful days in South Africa
3. What next?
4. What the parents said
5. Going on holiday with Leo
6. The weather changes

2 **Find the right places (x) in the text for the missing sentences. There is an example (0.) at the beginning.**

0. But first he needed a break. → line 4
1. He looked back at Daniel.
2. So much rain in five minutes – that was new for Daniel.
3. *Hout Bay is a peaceful place. No problems!* he wrote.
4. Then they had lunch on the beach.
5. The flight was great and his aunt met him at the airport.
6. "Let's get something to eat," Leo said, and started to get up.

D Text Production (Schreiben)

1 **Robin und seine Familie machen eine Safari im „Kruger National Park". Schreibe eine Geschichte auf Englisch, in der du alle Bilder berücksichtigst. Beginne wie folgt:**

The family was excited when their car arrived for the safari on the first day of their holiday in Kruger National Park. They …

Schreibe eine Geschichte von ungefähr 100 Wörtern auf ein gesondertes Blatt. Achte auf eine ansprechende äußere Form und eine gut lesbare Handschrift.

E Mediation (Sprachmittlung)

1 Situierung und Texte

Du träumst von einer Reise nach Südafrika mit deiner Familie. Du surfst im Internet und schaust nach Übernachtungsmöglichkeiten in Kapstadt. Lies die Beschreibungen aufmerksam.

Beschreibung der Unterkünfte

The Beach Hotel ★★★★★	**Happy Rhino Manor B&B**	**Lakeside View Hostel**
Our hotel is directly on the Waterfront and it has a view of the harbour, Table Mountain and the Atlantic Ocean. Our pool and wellness area are open to all our guests. All rooms have free Wi-Fi, air conditioning, flat screen TV, tea and coffee making facilities and an en-suite bathroom. Breakfast is included and you can also have lunch, afternoon tea and evening meals in our restaurant or grill, which both serve regional dishes.	All the rooms at our B&B have a balcony or terrace. Our pool and children's playground can be used by all our guests. We also organize cycling and hiking tours in the surrounding area. All rooms have free Wi-Fi, air conditioning, flat screen TV and an en-suite bathroom with a hairdryer. You can enjoy an exceptional breakfast in our breakfast room with a view of the surrounding mountains.	Our hostel offers perfect family rooms with wooden floors. All our rooms are non-smoking rooms. Pets are allowed. From here you can explore Cape Town and the surrounding area, which is great for cycling and fishing. Our outside pool can be used by all our guests. We have free Wi-Fi in the communal lounge and kitchen. Shared bathroom with bath and shower. There is a grill in the garden where the guests love to get together in the evenings.
30 km to Cape Town airport €1435: four nights, 2 adults + 2 children: 2 twin/double rooms	12 km from Waterfront and Robben Island ferry 13 km to Cape Town airport, free transfer available €684: four nights, 2 adults + 2 children: 1 family room	24 km from Waterfront and Robben Island ferry 20 km to Cape Town airport, free transfer available €375: four nights, 2 adults + 2 children: 1 family room

2 Aufgabe

Lies die Beschreibungen der drei Unterkünfte. In deiner Familie überlegt ihr, wo ihr am liebsten übernachten möchtet. Schreibe anschließend die Angaben (1-7), die in dem Dialog ergänzt werden sollen, in dein Heft.

	Lage
Mutter	Mein Favorit ist das Beach Hotel, weil es so zentral an der Waterfront liegt.
Vater	Ja, das stimmt. Außerdem hat man von dort einen guten Blick auf den Tafelberg, (1) ....
	Aktivitäten in und außerhalb des Hotels
Du	Hm, genau. Das Beach Hotel ist aber bestimmt nicht so passend für Kinder. Ich finde das Happy Rhino Manor B&B am besten, weil man dort viel machen kann. Alle Gäste dürfen (2) ..., und es gibt sogar ....
Deine Schwester	Wir sollten auf jeden Fall unsere Badesachen mitnehmen. Schließlich ist das Wetter ja in Südafrika viel sonniger und wärmer als bei uns. Mir gefällt das Lakeside View Hostel am besten. Vielleicht gibt es dort ja Hunde oder Katzen, weil (3) ....
	Flughafen/Transfer
Mutter	Wir werden doch unterwegs auch viele Tiere sehen. Aber immerhin ist das Hostel näher am Flughafen als das Beach Hotel.
Du	Ja, aber guck mal: Das Happy Rhino (4) ....
	Zimmerausstattung
Mutter	Ich glaube nicht, dass die paar Kilometer Unterschied ein Problem sind. Wir buchen ja ohnehin einen Mietwagen. Die Zimmer im Beach Hotel bieten gute Extras, wie kostenloses WLAN und Klimaanlage, und man kann sich auf dem Zimmer zum Trinken (5) ....
Deine Schwester	Schon, aber wir wollen ja nicht die ganze Zeit im Hotel sein. Wenn wir den ganzen Tag unterwegs sind, wäre doch ein einfacheres Zimmer auch in Ordnung.
	Preis
Vater	Also, das Beach Hotel ist mit Abstand (6) .... Und wir müssen noch die Kosten für die Flüge und den Mietwagen mit einkalkulieren!
Du	Warum einigen wir uns dann nicht auf einen Kompromiss und schicken eine Anfrage an das Happy Rhino Manor B&B? Das kostet für uns alle zusammen für vier Nächte (7) ....
Alle	Gute Idee, das machen wir!

That's the end of Test practice 3!

7 2,14 Unit 4 Intro

News from New Zealand

1 (SPEAKING) Talk about the photos.

Would New Zealand be an interesting place to visit? Say why or why not.

I think … because there is/are … in photo ….
Photo … shows that ….
Maybe ….
I would/wouldn't like (to) …

2 (READING) Read and take notes.

58/1–2

a) Write the information as notes:

- the capital
- industries
- the population and groups of people
- clubs and sport
- languages
- the 'Ring of Fire'

b) Check with a partner. Do you have the same information?

Am Ende dieser Unit kann ich ...
- Informationen über Neuseeland verstehen.
- über Jobmöglichkeiten und Fähigkeiten sprechen.
- einen Bericht über ein Praktikum schreiben.
- eine Geschichte über verschiedene Generationen verstehen.
- Informationen über einen Verein weitergeben.
- einen Film über Vulkane und Erdbeben verstehen.

New Zealand has many organizations with volunteers, and many young people are members of clubs. Rugby is a popular free-time activity and the national sport. The New Zealand rugby team is one of the best in the world.

The Maori people came to New Zealand from islands in the Pacific Ocean more than 700 years ago. Today about 15 % of the population say they are Maori. English and Maori are official languages in New Zealand.

New Zealand has amazing landscapes. It is part of the 'Ring of Fire'. This is an area around the Pacific Ocean where there are many volcanoes. Earthquakes often happen there too.

3 (LISTENING) **Listen to the radio interviews with young people.**

2,15

a) Copy the table in your exercise book. Listen and fill in the information.

Name:	Mason	Hazel
How old:		
Free-time activity:		
Why they like it:		

b) Talk about the free-time activities. Which would you like to do? Why or why not?

Ich kann Informationen über Neuseeland verstehen. ✔

Hier lerne ich, über Jobmöglichkeiten und Fähigkeiten zu sprechen.

Thinking about a career

1 (SPEAKING) Collect words about jobs and careers with a partner.

Think about:

where you can work | names of jobs | what you need when you apply | people at work

2 (READING) Read the dialogue and the form.

2,16

Liam is in year 10 at Newlands College in Wellington. He isn't sure about his future career so he has come to talk to Ms Waaka, the careers advisor at the school. He has completed a job suitability test.

Ms Waaka: I see you have completed the form. Thank you, Liam. Before we look at the results, what are you going to do next year?
Liam: I'm going to stay at school and try to get some work experience while I'm here. I'm not going to train as a mechanic in my dad's garage.
Ms Waaka: Well, it's a good plan to try different internships. I'm going to look at your test now. I see you find it easy to talk to people that you don't know. And when things go wrong, you usually stay calm. If someone is feeling sad, you can give them support. So you have good customer service and communication skills. But you don't like working with machines. Hm. Are you interested in sights and events in your town?
Liam: Yes, I am.
Ms Waaka: Tourism might be a good career for you. Have you ever thought about working in a tourist information centre?
Liam: Not really, but it sounds interesting.
Ms Waaka: If you stay at school, you can study for a National Certificate of Tourism. It's a good qualification. You'll have to take an exam at the end. We're going to have a careers day at the school at the beginning of July. A lot of companies and employers will be here with information about different jobs. The people from the tourist information centre are going to give a presentation. If I were you, I'd talk to them about an internship.
Liam: That sounds like a good idea. Well, thank you for your advice.
Ms Waaka: You're welcome. You can count on us if you need more help. Good luck, Liam.

B Job suitability test

Name: Liam Turner

1. I don't mind talking to people that I don't know.
   ☑ ☺ ☐ 😐 ☐ ☹
2. I am usually calm when things go wrong.
   ☑ ☺ ☐ 😐 ☐ ☹
3. If someone is feeling sad, I give them support.
   ☐ ☺ ☑ 😐 ☐ ☹
4. I like working with machines and tools.
   ☐ ☺ ☐ 😐 ☑ ☹

3 Right, wrong or not in the text? → M Peer correction, p.141

1. Liam wants to leave school in the summer.
2. He finds it easy to meet new people.
3. He also has good computer skills.
4. He has always wanted a job in tourism.
5. Ms Waaka will be at the careers day.
6. Liam can find out about internships there.

59/1

4 Work with words from the text.

a) Choose the right words to complete Liam's e-mail about his interview. → p.123

E-MAIL

Hi Ella,
I wanted to get some **information** • **advice** • **news** (1) about my career so I talked to Ms Waaka, the careers advisor. First I **completed** • **looked at** • **designed** (2) a job suitability test. Ms Waaka thinks I should study for a **question** • **qualification** • **quiz** (3) in tourism. Then I could work as an **interviewer** • **assistant** • **artist** (4) in a tourist information **building** • **centre** • **company** (5). They're going to have a **jobs** • **sports** • **careers** (6) day at the school in July. There will be a lot of **teams** • **companies** • **schools** (7) with information about jobs.
What about you? How did your interview go?
Bye,
Liam

b) Find the words in the text. Look at the lines.

1. How you feel when you are quiet or not excited (16–17)
2. What you give when you try to help somebody (17–19)
3. Another word for a test (30–31)
4. A person or company that gives you work and pays you for it (32–34)

5 Work with job words.

a) Match the jobs with what the people say. You don't need all the words.

chef | vet's assistant | hotel manager | hairdresser | check-in agent | mechanic | farmer | nurse

1. "It's great when I find out what's wrong with the car!"
2. "I sometimes have to tell people that their flight is late."
3. "I have to stay calm and help the doctor."
4. "I help people with their pets every day."
5. "I sometimes don't leave the restaurant before 1 a.m."
6. "We have guests from all around the world."

b) Write a sentence like the ones in a) for each of the jobs that you didn't need.

SPEAKING SKILLS

Wenn du das Wort für eine bestimmte Berufsbezeichnung oder Ausbildung auf Englisch nicht kennst, kannst du sie auch umschreiben. Sage: „It's a job where you …" oder „It's a kind of training that …"

6 (LISTENING) Listen to the dialogue between Liam and Ella.

2,17
59/2–3

Which three sentences are right?

1. Ella finds out about a job at the tourist information centre in Auckland.
2. The tourist information centre in Christchurch has a lot of international visitors.
3. Ms Waaka thinks Ella should work in tourism too.
4. Ella wants to work in her aunt's hairdressing salon.
5. Liam isn't sure about his career yet.

LISTENING SKILLS

Die Sprecherinnen und Sprecher in einem Dialog sagen oft nicht direkt, was sie denken und fühlen. Trotzdem kannst du erschließen, was gemeint ist. Oft musst du dafür mehrere Aussagen im Dialog kombinieren. Achte z. B. auf Formulierungen, die Zustimmung oder Ablehnung ausdrücken.

Language detectives → G 9, p.135

I'm going to try and get work experience next year.
I'm not going to train as a mechanic in my dad's garage.
We're going to have a careers day at the beginning of July.

Wenn du über Pläne für die Zukunft sprechen willst, verwendest du going to. Achte auf die Signalwörter!
Wie drückst du es im Deutschen oder in deiner Muttersprache aus, wenn du über Pläne sprichst?

7 Talk about plans. → M Bus stop, p.140

a) Make sentences about Ella and Liam's job plans. → ○ p.123

60/4

1. Ella (find out) about jobs as a hairdresser.
   Ella is going to find out about jobs as a hairdresser.
2. Liam (talk) to different employers next week.
3. Liam: I (apply) for jobs in tourism.
4. Liam (not work) with his dad.
5. Ella: I (train) in a hairdressing salon.
6. Ella and Liam (look) for jobs on the internet.
7. Ella and Liam (not leave) school next year.
8. Ella and Liam: We (visit) a careers day soon.

Remember the forms of 'to be'?
I am ....
He/She is ....
We are ....
They are ....

b) Write about your plans for these times. Write about two things that you are going to do and two things that you aren't going to do.

this afternoon | this evening | tomorrow | on Saturday | next week

8 (SPEAKING) Talk about plans with a partner.

What are your job plans? Look at the ideas.

A: I'm going to complete a job suitability test. And you?
B: Good idea. I'm going to do that too. / I'm not going to do that (I've already done that.) I'm (also) going to ....

complete a job suitability test
write my CV
speak to a careers advisor
find out about internships at ...
go to a careers day
apply for a job at ...

60/5

9 Write questions and find the answers.

a) Write questions about job plans. → p.123

1. Where / you / find out about jobs?
   Where are you going to find out about jobs?
2. What / Liam / do next year?
3. When / you / leave school?
4. Who / Liam / meet at the careers day?
5. When / you / write your CV?
6. Who / you / ask about your career?

Language → G 9, p.135
What are you going to do next year?

b) Match the answers to the questions in a). Which answer don't you need?

a. The careers advisor.
b. He wants to learn new things.
c. This afternoon.
d. At the careers day.
e. He's going to study for a National Certificate in Tourism.
f. Different companies.
g. Next year.

10 (TASK) A dialogue about jobs and qualities → V Jobs and qualities, p.152

61/6-7

a) Work with a partner. Copy the job suitability test into your exercise book and complete it for yourself.

1. I like working with people. ☺ 😐 ☹
2. I like working outside. ☺ 😐 ☹
3. I can listen to people and give them support. ☺ 😐 ☹
4. I like working with animals. ☺ 😐 ☹

b) Talk to your partner about the results. What kind of job do you think is best for you? What is best for your partner?

A: I like working with animals. I'm going to train as a vet's assistant.
B: But you like working outside ...

Maybe you could ... | ... might be a good career. | Why don't you ...? | ...

Ich kann über Jobmöglichkeiten und Fähigkeiten sprechen. ✓

Hier lerne ich, einen Bericht über ein Praktikum zu schreiben.

A job in retail?

1 (READING) Read the dialogue.

2,18

Some students from Newlands College are talking to the store manager of a supermarket in Wellington. They want to find out what it's like to work there. Later they are going to write a report.

Mr Roberts: Welcome everyone. My name is John Roberts. I'm going to talk to you about the exciting jobs in retail today. We offer jobs and apprenticeships in customer service, communication and IT. But before we start our tour, are there any questions?

Rose: Yes, I have a question. What do shop assistants do in their job?

Mr Roberts: Shop assistants do many different things. They help customers find the right products in the store and they work at the checkouts. Shop assistants also fill the shelves and help present the products.

Nikau: Can you tell us how a supermarket works?

Mr Roberts: Well, supermarkets buy their products from other local companies. These companies are called suppliers. Stores order large numbers of products from suppliers so that the prices are cheaper. Then the products are sold to customers.

Nikau: When did this store open?

Mr Roberts: It opened in 2008. It's one of the largest stores in Wellington. We have over 60,000 products – not only food, but also clothes and many other goods. But we work in the community too. We donate food to local charities to reduce food waste, for example.

Oliver: That's cool! How much food did you donate last year?

Mr Roberts: Well, last year we donated over NZ$3 million's worth of food.

Rose: Do you sell bread here?

Mr Roberts: Yes, we do. All our bread is made in the store.

Grace: Do you offer internships?

Mr Roberts: Yes, internships are offered here. You can apply for one in our office or you can visit us at the job fair next month. We're always looking for interns to help our fantastic team. We also offer summer jobs for students. You get a good salary and training is included.

Grace: Did you start your career here as a shop assistant?

Mr Roberts: Yes, I did. Although I've been at this company for ten years, I'll never forget what I learned in my first six months. Let's start our tour now.

2 Find the information in the text. Take notes under these headings. → M Peer correction, p.141

1. Different jobs at the company
2. When this store opened
3. The number of products
4. How the shop helps the community
5. Internships and summer jobs

62/1–2

3 What do they do?

a) Match the parts of the sentences. → p.124

1. The store manager is talking to
2. Stores order
3. The suppliers deliver
4. Shop assistants fill
5. Customers pay
6. The company donates

a. for products at the checkouts.
b. food to local charities.
c. products from suppliers.
d. products to the store.
e. students about jobs in retail.
f. the shelves every day.

b) Complete these sentences using the verbs and information in the text.

1. Companies which sell products to supermarkets .... (call)
2. Food, clothes and many other things .... (sell)
3. The supermarket's bread .... (make)
4. Apprenticeships, internships and summer jobs .... (offer)

Language → G 10, p.136
The products are sold to customers.

62/3

4 Choose the right meaning in German. → M Bus stop, p.140

1. Mr Roberts knows how supermarkets **work**.	a. (*v.*) arbeiten	b. (*v.*) funktionieren
2. He started his **career** ten years ago.	a. (*n.*) Karriere	b. (*n.*) Beruf
3. **Training** is included.	a. (*n.*, Sport) Training	b. (*n.*) Ausbildung
4. There's a job **fair** next month.	a. (*adj.*) fair, gerecht	b. (*n.*, Handel) Messe
5. Stores **order** large numbers of products.	a. (*n.*) Reihenfolge	b. (*v.*) bestellen
6. Let's start our **tour**.	a. (*n.*) Führung	b. (*n.*) Reise

STUDY SKILLS

Viele englische Wörter haben mehr als eine Bedeutung. Dein Wörterbuch gibt an, in welchem Zusammenhang (z. B. Schule, Sport) das Wort verwendet wird, und ob es sich um ein Nomen (n.), ein Verb (v.) oder ein Adjektiv (adj.) handelt. So kannst du das richtige Wort für das finden, über das du sprechen willst. Nimm nicht immer die erste Bedeutung, die dir das Wörterbuch anbietet!

62/4

5 (SOUNDS) Read, say and listen.

a) Make a chart in your exercise book and put the words into the right groups.

work | find | exciting | customer service | retail | price
waste | apply | internship | training | worth | donate

/ɜː/ learn	/eɪ/ day	/aɪ/ mine

2,19 b) Listen and check your answers.

Language detectives → G 1, p.127

This store opened in 2008.
Did you start your career as a shop assistant?
– Yes, I did.

Welche Zeitform ist das? Wann benutzt du sie? Welches Wort verwendest du, um Fragen und Kurzantworten zu bilden?

6 Talk about the first day of Grace's internship.

In the morning

learn about the company

After that

do office work for Mr Roberts

Then

help with different jobs

In the afternoon

phone three different people

Then

write four e-mails

After that

make two appointments

1. In the morning Grace learned about the company.
2. After that she ....

63/5 

7 Complete the questions about Grace's internship. → M Peer correction, p.141

a) Ask the questions with the right form. → ○ p.125

1. What — you — first? (do)
   What did you do first?
2. When — you — ? (start)
3. How — you — to work? (travel)
4. — you — with a computer? (work)
5. What — you — at lunchtime? (do)
6. When — you — the internship? (apply for)
7. — you — your internship? (enjoy)

b) Write Grace's answers to the questions. Use the pictures in Ex. 6 and the words below.

by bus • yes ... • go to café with other interns • six weeks ago • 9 a.m.

8 (SPEAKING) Ask your partner about last weekend.

63/6

A: Did you have a nice weekend?
B: Yes, thanks. / Yes, it was OK, thank you.
A: What did you do?
B: Well, I ... . Then I ... . I ... . And you?

Where did you go? | Who did you visit? | Did you stay long? | ...

watched | stayed | went to | ...

64/7

9 A report about a job fair

a) Read Oliver's report. Put in a suitable form of the word in brackets. → p.125

Last week I (1) visited (visit) a job fair at the Adelphi Hotel in Auckland. There (2) ___ (be) many companies at the fair. There were also a lot of young people who were (3) ___ (interest) in the companies. I wrote a list of questions before I (4) ___ (go) to the fair. I also (5) ___ (take) my CV with me. I talked to three employers and I want to apply for an (6) ___ (intern) with one of them. I stayed at the fair for about two (7) ___ (hour). It's the (8) ___ (good) way to find out about jobs.

b) Write the questions that Oliver's friend asked him after the job fair.

1. when – the job fair – start?
2. meet – other students from our school?
3. talk to – employers – from Wellington?
4. what – wear – to the fair?

10 (TASK) A report about an internship → V Talking about an internship, p.153

64/8

a) Think about your internship. Make notes:

Where did you do the internship?
When did you do it?
What did you do?
What did you learn?
What did you like most?

WRITING SKILLS

Es gibt verschiedene Möglichkeiten, deine Notizen zu ordnen. Du kannst dafür eine Mindmap oder eine Tabelle erstellen. Schreibe Stichwörter auf.

b) Use your notes from a) to write a draft of a report. Write about 80 words.

c) Check your draft. Use the checklist on page 145 and a dictionary. Then write your report on another page.

These phrases can help:
I worked with .... I helped .... I also ....
I learned about ....
... was great / interesting / ....
On the first day / At the end I felt ....

d) Read your reports in a group. Choose the best report. → M Writers' conference, p.143

Ich kann einen Bericht über ein Praktikum schreiben. ✓

The Whale Rider

1 Work with the photos. → M Think – pair – share, p.143

Look at the photos of the people in the story. Who is who? What do you think will happen?

2 (READING) Read the story.

2, 20

Kahu lives in Whangara, a Maori community on the New Zealand coast. She lives with her great-grandfather, Koro Apirana – she calls him 'Paka' – and Nani Flowers, her great-grandmother. Koro Apirana is the chief of a tribe that was founded by Paikea, the famous 'whale rider'. In the past the chief was always a man. But Kahu will be the next chief, and Koro Apirana doesn't think that a girl can do the job. Kahu's uncle, Rawiri, tells the story.

Two weeks after the beginning of the school holidays, Koro Apirana took the young boys from the school to the sea. It was early morning. He put them in his boat and went past the bay.
Koro Apirana began a prayer. He had a flat stone in his hand. Suddenly he threw it into the water.
"One of you must bring that stone back to me," Koro Apirana said. "Go now."
But the stone was too deep. Some of the boys were afraid. Others weren't able to swim so far down. Although they tried very hard, they couldn't do it.
Koro Apirana didn't look happy. "Okay, boys," he said. "Let's go home now."

When he got back home, Koro Apirana went to the bedroom. Slowly, he began to lament.
"Is something wrong with Koro?" Kahu asked.
We were sitting outside. "Is it because of the stone?"
"How did you know about that?" I asked.
"One of the boys told me," Kahu said. "I wish I could make Paka happy again." Her eyes looked sad.

The next morning Rawiri goes for a ride in his boat. Kahu and Nani Flowers come too.

We went past the bay and Kahu asked again about the stone.
"What stone?" Nani Flowers said.
So I told her. Nani wanted to see the place. We went out into the sea.

3 Work with the text.

a) Put the headings in the right order.

A A ride with Rawiri
B A stone and a fish for Paka
C Unhappy
D Some help for Kahu
E A test for the boys
F Is she okay?

b) Answer the questions with short answers.

1. Why did Koro test the boys?
2. Why was he unhappy?
3. How did Nani Flowers feel when Kahu jumped in?
4. Who is not ready at the end?
5. What do you think: Will Kahu become the chief of the tribe?

Kahu and her great-grandfather, Koro Apirana

Kahu's great-grandmother, Nani Flowers

"Well," Nani said. "No wonder those boys couldn't get it. This is deep."
Kahu said, "I'll get it."
She stood up and jumped.
Nani's mouth made a big 'O'. Then she shouted, "Oh, no! Go after her, Rawiri. Go."

Rawiri puts on a mask and jumps in. He sees Kahu swimming. Then Nani Flowers jumps in too.

"Where is she?" Nani Flowers shouted. "Oh, my Kahu!"
She took the mask and put it on. I pointed. Kahu was swimming slowly around the coral. She was looking for the stone, but she couldn't find it. Then a group of dolphins came towards her. They swam around Kahu and seemed to talk to her. The dolphins took her to another area of the reef. Kahu seemed to say, "Here?" and the dolphins seemed to nod. Suddenly Kahu moved. She picked something up, looked at it and went back to the dolphins. Slowly the girl and the dolphins moved towards us. When they were in the middle, Kahu stopped again. She kissed the dolphins goodbye. Then she picked up a crayfish.

When Kahu came up between us, Nani Flowers held her close.
"I'm okay, Nani," Kahu laughed. She showed the crayfish to us. "This is for Paka's tea, and you can give him back his stone." She put the stone in Nani Flowers' hands.
Nani Flowers looked at me quickly.
We got back into the small boat and she said, "Not a word about this to Koro Apirana."
I nodded. I looked back to the island and saw the carving of Paikea on his whale.

When we got to the beach, Nani Flowers said again, "Not a word, Rawiri. Not a word about the stone or our Kahu." She looked up at Paikea. "He's not ready yet," she said …

Adapted from: The Whale Rider by Witi Ihimaera, 2008.

4 Choose one of the tasks.

P 66/1–2 67/3–4

a) How did Kahu tell a friend about what happened? Write her story.
Start like this:

Paka was unhappy because …. So the next morning I …. When we got to the place I jumped … and …. I saw … and …. They helped …. I picked up … and …. …

OR

b) What other stories or films do you know where someone gets help from an animal? Research and give a short presentation.
Start like this: → M 1-minute-presentation, p.140

My story/film is ….
The animal is a …. It ….
It's exciting/interesting because …. …

Ich kann eine Geschichte über verschiedene Generationen verstehen. ✓

Joining a club

INTERNET

Home | What's new? | Gallery | Club history | Links

Auckland Hockey Club

We are a large sports club on Auckland's North Shore. We have more than 450 members.

Looking to play hockey next year? Register now!

Open training for girls and boys:
Tuesday, 12 March 5:30 – 6:45 p.m.
Girls' trials:
Sunday, 17 March 9:00 – 10:15 a.m.
Boys' trials:
Sunday, 17 March 10:30 a.m. – 12:00 p.m.

We provide hockey sticks if you don't have one, but please bring your own shoes and mouthguard. New players are welcome!
Fees: Youth players: NZ$ 250 per year; junior players: NZ$ 100 per year, due by 10 April

I started playing hockey here two years ago. Since then, I have made a lot of new friends. It wasn't always easy. I had to train hard to become a good player. Members have to help at events every month. It feels great to be part of a team and we have lots of fun together!

Leo, 14, member

At last year's summer fete we raised NZ$ 3,000 for our trip!

65/1

1 (MEDIATION) **Du möchtest wissen, was Jugendliche in Neuseeland in ihrer Freizeit gerne machen.**

Auf der Website eines Hockey-Clubs in Auckland findest du diese Informationen über das Vereinsleben. Ergänze die Lücken 1–7 mit Angaben auf Deutsch.

Der Auckland Hockey-Club ist ___ (1) am North Shore von Auckland. Wenn man ___ (2), muss man sich registrieren. Einen Hockeyschläger kann ___ (3). Schuhe und Mundschutz muss jeder ___ (4). Der ___ (5) beträgt NZ$ 100 oder NZ$ 250 und muss bis ___ (6). Mitglieder müssen einmal im Monat ___ (7).

CULTURE

Das Vereinsleben spielt in Neuseeland eine wichtige Rolle. Die ehrenamtlichen Mitarbeiter engagieren sich im Verein, da sie dort Freunde gewinnen und wertvolle Arbeitserfahrungen sammeln. Welche Vereine gibt es in deiner Umgebung?

Ich kann Informationen über einen Verein weitergeben. ✓

The natural violence of New Zealand

1 (SPEAKING) Describe the photo of New Zealand with a partner.

How is this part of New Zealand different from where you live?

This photo shows .... | mountains | the sea | beach | lake | ...

VIEWING SKILLS

In Dokumentarfilmen werden oft Grafiken und Computeranimationen verwendet. Diese können dir helfen, zu verstehen, worum es geht, auch wenn du nicht alle Wörter verstehst.

2 (VIEWING) Watch the film.

8

a) Choose the right answer.

1. New Zealand has mountains because there are **two** • **three** plates in the earth's crust under the country.
2. Mount Tongariro is a volcano on the **North Island** • **South Island**.
3. The North Island is famous for its **cold** • **hot** pools.
4. The film shows houses and roads after an earthquake in **Christchurch** • **Wellington**.
5. The earthquake happened in **2011** • **2016**.

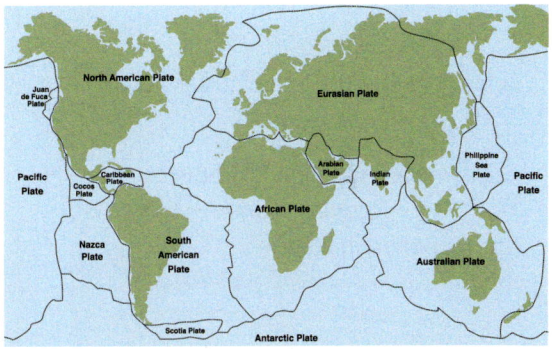

A map of the plates in the earth's crust

b) Watch the film again from 3:45. How do people in New Zealand help each other after an earthquake? Name three things from the film.

3 (SPEAKING) Talk about natural disasters.

Imagine you have to live without electricity for a few days. What problems will there be?

→ M Think – pair – share, p.143

I'll miss ...
I won't have ....
I won't be able to ....
... will be awful. / ... won't be so bad.

CULTURE

Die Menschen in Neuseeland sind gut auf Erdbeben vorbereitet. Viele von ihnen haben zusätzliches Wasser, Lebensmittel, Medikamente und Batterien zu Hause, damit sie einige Tage ohne Strom auskommen können. Nach einer Naturkatastrophe helfen ihnen diese Dinge wieder in ihren Alltag zurückzukehren.

Ich kann einen Film über Vulkane und Erdbeben verstehen. ✓

Checklist

Find more online: nd4r3a

Ich kann Informationen über Neuseeland verstehen.

New Zealand is about 1,000 miles (1,600 km) from Australia, its nearest neighbour. • Today about 15 % of the population say they are Maori.

68

Ich kann über Jobmöglichkeiten und Fähigkeiten sprechen.

I'm going to try to get some work experience. • When things go wrong, you usually stay calm

68

Ich kann einen Bericht über ein Praktikum schreiben.

Supermarkets buy their products from other local companies. • This store opened in 2008.

69

Ich kann eine Geschichte über verschiedene Generationen verstehen.

69

Ich kann Informationen über einen Verein weitergeben.

69

Ich kann einen Film über Vulkane und Erdbeben verstehen.

(UNIT TASK) A job interview

Stell dir vor, du hast dich im Auckland Zoo auf eine Stelle als Aushilfe beworben. Nun wurdest du zu einem Vorstellungsgespräch eingeladen. Bereite das Gespräch vor und führe es zusammen mit einer Partnerin oder einem Partner durch.

Zoo helper wanted!
Contact Matt Campbell at info@xyz.nz

Step 1

What's important when you're invited for a job interview?

Make a mind map.

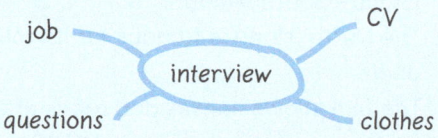

Step 2

Prepare for the role of the interviewer.

→ M Think – pair – share, p.143

Work in groups of four. Think of questions that the interviewer can ask.

- Have you ever worked with animals before?
- Why are you interested in this job?
- Can you tell us about your work experience/internship?
- Where did you hear about …?
- …

Step 3

Work with a partner. Agree on the five most important questions.

Choose five questions from Step 2 that are most important to you. Write them on cards.

Step 4

Prepare for the role of the applicant.

Think of your answers to the questions. Make notes.

1. *worked with animals? – No, but …*
2.

SPEAKING SKILLS

Es ist wichtig, sich bewusst zu machen, mit wem man spricht. Sei immer höflich und lächle. Rede deine Gesprächspartner mit „Mr …", „Ms …" oder „Mrs …" an. Sage nicht einfach nur „Hello". Vergiss nicht, dich am Ende des Gesprächs zu bedanken.

Step 5

Practise the interview with your partner.

Act the dialogue. Then change roles and act the dialogue again.

SPEAKING SKILLS

Wenn du eine Frage nicht verstehst, sei ehrlich. Sage, dass du die Frage nicht verstanden hast („I'm sorry, I didn't understand that.") oder bitte die Person darum, die Frage zu wiederholen („Could you say that again, please?").

Step 6

Act the interview in front of the class.

Step 7

Give feedback.

What was good about the interview? What could be better next time? Do you think that the applicant will get the job? → M Tip top, p.143

SPEAKING SKILLS

Wenn du zu einem Bewerbungsgespräch eingeladen wirst, sei pünktlich und trage angemessene Kleidung. Sei darauf vorbereitet, Fragen zum Job und zur Firma zu beantworten. Vergiss vor allem nicht, dein Handy auszuschalten.

More about New Zealand

1 (SPEAKING) Talk about photo 1 with a partner.

Look at the photo from New Zealand.
Think about these questions.

Where is the person? (Describe the place.)
What is the person doing?
What is he or she wearing?
What is the weather like?
How do you think the person feels?
Do you like to spend time in the mountains?
(Say why or why not.)

INFO

Die Neuseeländer werden auch als „Kiwis" bezeichnet. Der Kiwi ist eine in Neuseeland heimische Vogelart. Wie der australische Emu, kann der Kiwi nicht fliegen. Kiwis sind normalerweise nachtaktiv, deshalb ist es nicht einfach sie in freier Natur zu sehen. Die Vögel können 20 bis 30 Jahre alt werden.

2 Work with photos 2–5.

a) Match photos 2–5 with the headings A–F. There are more headings than you need.

A A young Maori at a festival
B Life in the city
C The 'All Blacks'
D On the road
E Farming in New Zealand
F Earthquake!

b) Talk with a partner. Describe the places and the people in the photos.

There's a … and a ….
He/She is ….They are ….

Applying for a job

Text 1: An ad

We make Kiwis' lives better every day.
Our supermarkets in Christchurch, Wellington and Auckland are looking for:

Young shop assistants
Apply to Joan Miller for jobs and internships with our company.

Text 2: An enquiry[1]

Dear Ms Miller,

I read your ad for young shop assistants on your website and I am very interested in an internship with your company. I live in Bavaria, Germany and will finish school this summer.
Could you please tell me more about this internship?
I look forward to hearing from you.

Yours sincerely,
Hannah Fischer

1 enquiry – *Anfrage*

Text 3: A form

Name: Hannah Fischer
Address: xxxxx
xxxxx
Germany
Phone: +49 987654321
E-Mail: xyz@xyz.de

Qualifications: Secondary leaving certificate

Skills: Good computer and communication skills; languages: German, English
Experience: Internship at a travel agent's

Text 4: A letter of application

1 (Your address)

2 (The person and address that you are writing to)
c/o Mr/Ms ...

(Date)

3 RE: Your ad for young shop assistants

4 Dear xxx,
I would like to apply for the job as a young shop assistant.
My first internship was at a travel agent's. During the internship I worked with customers and helped in the office. I liked the job very much.
I think I am qualified for this job because I have good communication skills and I enjoy working in a team. I am also flexible and I stay calm when things go wrong.
5 You will find more information in my CV. I look forward to hearing from you.
6 Yours sincerely,
(Your name)

Enclosed: CV

1 Work with the texts.

a) Take notes from the ad and the enquiry.

1. Where and what is/are the job(s)?
2. Who is interested and applies?
3. Who will get the enquiry?

b) Look at the form and the letter. Complete the sentences.

1. The person has done an internship ....
2. The person is qualified because ....
3. The person sends ... with the letter.

Durch eine Anfrage („enquiry") kannst du zeigen, dass du Interesse an dem Job oder dem Praktikum hast, und du kannst darin um weitere Informationen bitten. Das hilft dir zu entscheiden, ob du dich bewerben möchtest.

2 Copy and complete the form.

Copy and complete the form with your information. You can use the form on page 106 as a model.

Name: _____
Address: _____
_____
Phone: _____ **E-Mail:** _____
_____
Qualifications: _____
_____
Skills: _____
_____
Experience: _____
_____

Bevor du ein Formular ausfüllst, überlege dir, was du schreiben möchtest. Du musst keine vollständigen Sätze schreiben. Formuliere deine persönlichen Angaben so kurz wie möglich. Schaue dir das Geschriebene am Ende noch einmal genau an und überprüfe es auf Fehler.

72/1

3 Write a letter of application.

a) Write a letter of application in English for a job or internship you are interested in. Use the letter on page 106 as a model.

b) Show your letter to a partner. What tips can he or she give you?
→ M Tip top, p.143

Schreibe rechts oben deine Adresse (1): Straße, Postleitzahl, Stadt und Land. Schreibe links die Anschrift der Firma (2). c/o bedeutet „care of", d.h. diese Person erhält deine Bewerbung. Vergiss nicht, rechts das Datum zu schreiben. RE (3) bedeutet: „Reference" (Betreff). Verwende die Anrede (4) mit Mr oder Ms + Name.

Schreibe am Schluss, dass du dich auf eine Antwort freust (5). Schließe deine Bewerbung (6) mit „Yours sincerely", deiner Unterschrift und deinem Namen ab. Erwähne, wenn du z.B. deinen Lebenslauf hinzufügst.

Ein zweisprachiges Wörterbuch in Printform ist für die gesamte schriftliche Prüfung erlaubt.

A Listening Comprehension (Hörverstehen)

You will hear the recordings twice.

2, 21 **1** **Listen to Justine talking at a school in New Zealand. Write short answers. There is an example (0.) at the beginning.**

0. What is Justine going to talk about?
   – Project Jonah, a project that saves whales.
1. Where in Auckland does Justine work?
2. What does Justine do in her free time?
3. What did Justine do the first time she helped?
4. How long has Justine been a volunteer?
5. Give two examples that show how whales are intelligent animals.
6. What is the goal of Project Jonah?

2, 22 **2** **Listen to Justine. There is one mistake in each sentence. Write down the wrong word and the correct information. There is an example (0.) at the beginning.**

0. The first person with a question is a girl.
   girl → boy
1. They need more doctors to tell them about stranded whales.
2. You can visit an event at your school to raise money.
3. The girl with a question is wearing a blue skirt.
4. Justine says that some volunteers have been hurt.
5. Don't go near a whale's mouth.
6. Justine has got a podcast with more information.

B Use of English (Sprachgebrauch)

1 Read the text about the Maori. Choose the right word that fits in the sentence. There is an example (0.) at the beginning.

What do you know about the Maori?
Maori is the name of the (0) **person** • **people** who have lived in New Zealand the longest. They (1) **arrived** • **arrive** by canoe from islands in the Pacific Ocean. About 15 % of (2) **New Zealands'** • **New Zealand's** population say they are Maori.
Maori is one of the official languages in New Zealand. The Maori speak this special language and it is also (3) **taught** • **thought** in many schools. (4) **English** • **England** is also an official language in New Zealand.
Also (5) **famous** • **most famous** in New Zealand is the 'haka' dance. It is danced before the national team's rugby games and the players learn it (6) **easy** • **easily**. The players, who are really (7) **big** • **bigger**, are very serious when they do this dance.
Maori also love (8) **there** • **their** body art. You see it all around the world. People who (9) **have** • **had** this body art on their faces or arms look (10) **strong** • **strongly** but also scary.

2 Put the words in the right order to make sentences about the Sky Tower. There is an example (0.) at the beginning.

0. You can see the Sky Tower in Auckland
1. Because the floor is made of glass,
2. If the weather is good,
3. Many people came
4. We know the Sky Tower is very popular
5. The Sky Tower is 328 m high,
6. If you ever go to Auckland on 31st December,
7. The best attraction is the SkyJump,
8. If people do the SkyJump,

a) they can go up to 85 km/h.
b) when the Sky Tower opened on 3rd August 1997.
c) which you can do from the highest viewing platform.
d) which makes it the tallest building in New Zealand.
e) if there aren't any clouds.
f) visitors can look through it.
g) because it had more than 415,000 visitors last year.
h) you can see up to 82 kilometres into the distance.
i) don't miss the party at the top of the tower.

C Reading Comprehension (Leseverstehen)

Is there life after rugby?

As Jacob was lying in hospital, he kept thinking about last Saturday's rugby game. His team was winning and Jacob was brilliant. No wonder he was captain! Jacob heard everyone shout and cheer as he scored again and again. Then it happened. He couldn't remember what, but when he woke up, he hurt: hurt like he'd never hurt before. The doctor told him that he had injured his leg seriously.

Everyone visited him: his parents, his little brother, his friends and the whole rugby team. They all told Jacob what a fantastic player he was. He loved what they told him. But what he wanted to know was when he could start training again. Rugby was Jacob's life. And he was really good at it. Even the famous All Blacks were interested in him.

Then, on Tuesday, his dad came to visit him earlier than expected. The doctor was with him. They couldn't look Jacob in the eye. "I'm afraid I have some bad news," the doctor began. "We've done a lot of tests. You will get better, and in a few months walking and even running won't be a problem. But you can't play rugby ever again. If you have another accident like that, you will probably never walk again."

After the doctor left, Jacob's dad spoke to him. "Your mum and I talked lots before your accident. You play too much rugby and your school marks are getting worse. We want you to stop playing rugby too. You need to think about your future."

Jacob didn't understand. Never play rugby again? That couldn't be true!

"I know this is bad news for you, Jacob," his dad added. "But we will all help you."

Sometimes Jacob was angry, sometimes he was very sad. And it only got worse.

After a while he stopped talking to his visitors and he was happy when they left.

Then, one afternoon, his coach walked in.

"You want to stay here not talking to anyone? That's not what I've taught you. Let me tell you something. You fall down, you get back up. If you haven't learned that from the game, you haven't been listening. And you know what – life is the same."

"That's easy for you to say," Jacob said. "You're not the one whose whole future has been ruined!"

"You can't just give up," the coach said. "When you give up, you lose. I was talking to a friend who is really interested in you and what has happened. He wants you to finish school, with good marks, and he will give you a job. He is a sports doctor and he needs someone who knows rugby as well as you do to help him motivate injured players. You'll get special training, don't worry."

"Really? Someone wants to offer me a job?"

"Your situation has changed. Find out what's important to you in life and find a different way for yourself. Think about it, kid." And then the coach walked out of the door.

Jacob began to think ....

1 **Answer the questions using information from the text. Write short answers. There is an example (0.) at the beginning.**

0. When was Jacob hurt? last Saturday
1. Why were the All Blacks interested in Jacob?
2. What did the doctor and Jacob's dad tell him about playing rugby again?
3. How did Jacob feel after he heard the news?
4. What did the coach say about life?
5. What did the coach have for Jacob?

2 **Which line(s) in the text tell you these things? There is an example (0.) at the beginning. Which sentence tells you ...**

0. Jacob has had an accident. → lines 6–10
1. Jacob is a good rugby player.
2. Jacob loves playing rugby.
3. he is not doing as well at school as he used to.
4. Jacob's dad knew how he felt.
5. that Jacob was surprised he had a future.

D Text Production (Schreiben)

1 **Schreibe eine Geschichte auf Englisch, in der du das Bild und alle Angaben berücksichtigst. Beginne wie folgt:**

Not enough money!

Last Saturday I was at the supermarket and saw a group of students. They ...

supermarket to empty their pockets think about party decide pay

Schreibe eine Geschichte von ungefähr 100 Wörtern auf ein gesondertes Blatt. Achte auf eine ansprechende äußere Form und eine gut lesbare Handschrift.

E Mediation (Sprachmittlung)

1 Situierung und Text

Du bist im Internet auf Sarahs Blog gestoßen. Sie ist gerade auf einer dreiwöchigen Sprachreise in Neuseeland. Lies den Text aufmerksam durch. Als Übung für eine englische Klassenarbeit hat dein Freund Tim das Wichtigste aus dem Text auf Deutsch zusammengefasst und bittet dich, es nochmals durchzulesen.

INTERNET

My adventure has begun ...

This was my timetable when I left Germany:
11:30 (Saturday): left home town near Oberstdorf
13:45 (Saturday): arrived at Munich Airport
16:45 (Saturday): flight left Munich
23:00 (Saturday): arrived in Doha, Qatar (four-hour stopover)
4:45 (Monday): arrived in Auckland (17:45 (Sunday) German time)

Now that I am in New Zealand my everyday life will be in English – including this blog.

We flew over the sea, which was a beautiful colour as we came in to land. My guest family met me at the airport. They don't live far from the language school. I knew Auckland was bigger than where I live in Bavaria, but it made me speechless.

Today is Wednesday, and I woke up early, ready for my first day at the language school. The first three days will be great because we'll do a lot of excursions and the lessons only start next Monday. We had to be there at 9 and we met everyone in our class for the first time – there are only 15 of us! After that, we went to Viaduct Harbour to see the sights. I talked to Nicole from France and we have the same hobbies. Tomorrow we are going to the Auckland Museum to find out about the history of New Zealand and the Maori. On Friday we are going to climb on the Rangitoto volcano, and on Saturday there is a barbecue with the rest of the school at the beach. On Sunday I'm going to visit Hobbiton, where *The Lord of the Rings* (my favourite film) was filmed, with my guest family.

And next Monday the first real English language lessons are going to start. I think they will be fun as I have started talking to everyone in English already. It feels good.

I'll write more next week.
Sarah

2 Aufgabe

Lies den englischen Text sowie die Zusammenfassung auf Deutsch durch. Notiere die falschen Informationen in Tims deutscher Zusammenfassung in dein Heft. Schreibe anschließend stichpunktartig auf Deutsch die richtigen Informationen. Eine berichtigte Information (0.) ist bereits vorhanden.

Tims Zusammenfassung auf Deutsch:

Sarah hat ihre Heimatstadt am Samstag verlassen, um zum Münchner Flughafen zu fahren. Es dauerte über vier Stunden und ihr Flug ging um 16:45. Sie ist in Auckland um 4:45 deutscher Zeit gelandet.

Da sie nun in Neuseeland ist, wird sie nur ihren Blog auf Englisch schreiben.

Sie ist über das Meer geflogen und ihre Gastfamilie hat sie am Busbahnhof abgeholt. Obwohl Sarah wusste, dass Auckland richtig schön ist, war sie dann doch ganz sprachlos.

Am Donnerstag hatte sie ihren ersten Tag an der Sprachschule. In den ersten drei Tagen machen sie viele Ausflüge. Es sind nur 15 Studenten in Sarahs Klasse und sie kannten sich alle. Danach haben sie die Sehenswürdigkeiten am Hafen angeschaut. Sie hat sich mit Nicole aus Frankreich unterhalten. Sie haben beide die gleichen Haustiere. Am Donnerstag besucht die Klasse ein Museum über die Geschichte Neuseelands und die Maori. Am Freitag steigen sie auf den Vulkan Rangitoto, und am Samstag grillen sie mit den Gastfamilien am Strand. Am Sonntag besichtigt Sarah mit ihrer Gastfamilie Hobbiton, den Drehort von *Der Herr der Ringe*, da sie die Filme nicht kennt.

Nächsten Montag fängt der richtige Sprachunterricht an. Sie meinte, es wird Spaß machen, da sie noch nicht so richtig Englisch miteinander sprechen.

Es sind noch 10 falsche Informationen im Text. Notiere sie in dein Heft und berichtige sie.

0. Zeile 2: vier Stunden → zwei Stunden
1.

Unit 1, page 13

4 Work with adjectives from the text. → M Bus stop, p.140

a) Read what people at Uluru said. Put in the words.

disappointed | beautiful ✓ | modern | surprised | afraid | delicious

1. "Look at the evening sun on Uluru! It's beautiful!"
2. "Later we can eat some kangaroo meat. It's —— !"
3. "Tourists aren't allowed to climb Uluru. I was —— when I found out. ☹"
4. "It was my friend's birthday yesterday. She was —— when the guide gave her a small present!"
5. "Aboriginal people have a lot of traditions. But many have a —— lifestyle."
6. "Uluru is a safe place. You needn't be —— !"

Unit 1, page 14

6 Complete the story about Omeo, a tour guide at Uluru. → M Peer correction, p.141

a) Put in the right words.

visited ✓ | didn't play | went | tried | arrived | asked | was | sang

Last week a group of tourists from Germany (1) visited Uluru. They (2) a—— at three o'clock on Monday afternoon and they (3) w—— on a helicopter flight around the rock. It (4) w—— very exciting! After that they (5) a—— Omeo a lot of questions. They (6) s—— songs with Omeo in the evening, but he (7) d—— —— the didgeridoo for them. Later the tourists (8) t—— some delicious Aboriginal food.

Unit 1, page 14

7 Make the questions and find the right answers. → M Bus stop, p.140

a) Match the questions with the answers.

Friend:

1. When did you visit Uluru?
2. How long did you stay there?
3. Did you go on a walk around Uluru?
4. What did you like best?
5. How did you travel to Uluru?
6. Did you go on a helicopter tour?

Koa:

a. We went by plane.
b. Yes, we did. We walked for three hours!
c. No, we didn't. The flights are expensive.
d. We stayed for five days.
e. We went to the rock in September.
f. I liked the didgeridoo music best!

Unit 1, page 17

4 Work with the words. → M Think – pair – share, p.143

a) Make a mind map with the words and phrases.

a headache ✓ | take tablets ✓ | ill ✓ | a high temperature | drink tea | tired | stay in bed | the flu | a cold

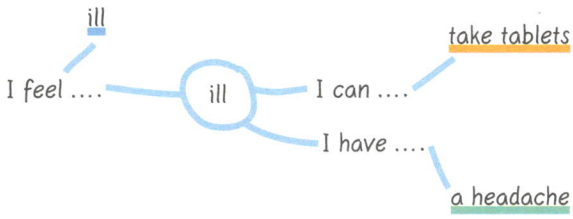

Unit 1, page 17

5 (SPEAKING) Make an appointment to see the doctor.

a) Put the phrases in the right order. Act the dialogue. The receptionist speaks first (3).
→ M Read and look up, p.142

Receptionist:	Patient:
1 Can you come today at 2:30 p.m.?	6 Thank you. Goodbye
2 No problem. Goodbye.	7 Yes, I can.
3 Hello. How can I help you?	8 Hogan. That's H-O-G-A-N.
4 Good. What was the name again?	9 Hello. My name is Mr Hogan. I would like to make an appointment. I think I have a high temperature.
5 OK, Mr Hogan. See you at 2:30 p.m.	

Unit 1, page 18

8 Write sentences about Penny. → M Bus stop, p.140

a) Complete the sentences.

1. If Penny goes to school on Monday, she — — cricket (play)
   If Penny goes to school on Monday, she will play cricket.
2. If she wants to talk, she — — her friends. (call)
3. They will have a barbecue too if they — longer. (stay)
4. Penny will work with her best friend if she — a project at school. (do)
5. If her dad isn't too busy, they — — surfing in a few weeks. (go)
6. She will take photos if she — her cousin in Sydney next month. (visit)
7. Her cousin will come to Canberra in December if she — time. (have)

Unit 2, page 39

5 Work with words for jobs. → M Peer correction, p.141

a) Match the sentence parts to say what the people do.

1. A computer programmer writes
2. A farmer produces
3. A tour guide shows
4. A virtual assistant does
5. A chef makes
6. A factory worker makes
7. A nurse looks after

a. meals in a restaurant.
b. car parts, for example.
c. food and keeps animals.
d. interesting sights to tourists.
e. office work for different people.
f. people who are ill.
g. computer programs.

Unit 2, page 40

7 Complete what Manjit says about his work.

a) Complete the sentences. Where do you need the -s? The underlined words can help you.

Manjit: I (1) work (work) between 40 and 65 hours every week. But I (2) —— (like) my job. I often (3) —— (listen) to music on the assembly line. Our boss (4) —— (visit) us most days. He (5) —— (work) in an office near the assembly line. He sometimes (6) —— (shout) at people when they (7) —— (arrive) late. Every Friday I (8) —— (finish) work at six o'clock. I (9) —— (go) home and the weekend (10) —— (start). No more work until Monday!

Unit 2, page 40

8 Complete the sentences about the others.

a) Choose the right answers.

1. Prisha: My father **lives** • **live** with me.
2. My father **don't work** • **doesn't work** any more.
3. Vibhu **works** • **work** for an IT company.
4. He **write** • **writes** programs with other workers.
5. They **don't repair** • **doesn't repair** computers.
6. Kashida **shows** • **show** tourists the Taj Mahal.
7. She **don't sell** • **doesn't sell** souvenirs.

Language → G 5, p.131

She likes … ☺
She doesn't like … ☹

Unit 2, page 43

3 Work with the text.

1,16

Deepali Chandra

What do Indian teenagers think?

By Deepali Chandra *20th August 2021*

1 The economy is growing fast in the big cities of India. But I wanted to find out about life in the country and on farms, where most people still live. What environmental problems do teenagers in Indian villages worry about? I spoke to Kyra, Tanvi and Moti, three teenagers from villages in different parts of India.

2 Kyra is a 16-year-old girl from a village in the north of India. She told me, "We need to make farming more sustainable so that we can grow food in the future too. There is a lot of pollution. We use fertilisers that help the crops to grow. But they are slowly damaging the soil. Another problem is that there are more people, so we need more food for them. We grow two or three different crops in the same field every year. This is not good for the soil. The crops don't grow well here."

3 I also spoke to Tanvi (15), from the east of the country. She said, "Villages in India don't have good sanitation. Many houses don't have bathrooms or toilets. People wash themselves and their clothes in rivers every day. Waste pollutes the soil and water."

4 Sixteen-year-old Moti is a boy from a village in Gujarat, in the west of India. "Our village doesn't have good drinking water," Moti said. "We have to walk to another village every day, so we use the water very carefully."

5 Indian villages have many problems. However, the situation is changing. Sustainable living is important for the young people there. Some villages have changed their crops, and this has helped the soil. Others have raised money for better sanitation and drinking water. What about where you live? What can you do to help the environment?

a) Answer the questions. You can use short answers.

1. What kind of problems did Deepali ask about?
2. What is the problem with fertilisers?
3. What can happen when there are two or three crops in the same year?
4. Why is bad sanitation a problem?
5. Why do they use water carefully in Moti's village?
6. What have some villages done to get better sanitation and drinking water?

Unit 2, page 43

4 Work with words from the text.

a) What is it? Choose the right answers.

1. People who are between 13 and 19 are **teenagers** • **teachers**.
2. A **village** • **valley** is a group of houses and other buildings in the country.
3. Farmers use **fertilisers** • **fields** to help plants to grow.
4. Water that is safe to drink is called **saving** • **drinking** water.
5. If farming is **sustainable** • **slow**, we will have food in the future too.
6. The **environment** • **economy** is another word for the world around us.

Unit 2, page 44

7 Write sentences about village life in India.

a) Use the words to write a sentence for each photo. Put the parts of the sentences in the right order.

1. The people have breakfast at home every day.

The people have breakfast **every day** • **at home**

They wash clothes **in the river** • **in the morning**

People work **very hard** • **every day**

They walk **to get drinking water** • **a long way**

Moti feeds the goats **on the farm** • **every evening**

Crops don't grow **in the soil** • **very well**

Unit 2, page 45

8 Deepali's blog → M Bus stop, p.140

a) Choose the right answers.

BLOG

Hi everyone!
Village life in India **is** • **are** (1) very different from in Europe. Most houses have chickens, so the people can get eggs **easy** • **easily** (2). They know each other **good** • **well** (3) and chat with **their** • **they** (4) neighbours.
Most people in villages **work** • **works** (5) on farms. Many **don't have** • **doesn't have** (6) drinking water so they have to **get** • **gets** (7) it from another village. Tomorrow **I talk** • **I'll talk** (8) to two other teenagers in Gujarat.
What do you like about where you live?
Bye,
Deepali

Unit 3, page 64

3 Work with the texts.

2,3

A INTERNET

Daily News | News | Sports | Lifestyle

Accident in Durban
10 Jan – A car hit a school bus with students yesterday. The accident happened in Umlazi, Durban, at about 1 p.m.
The bus driver was seriously injured. A student, Piet Jansen (16), and the car driver, Lunga Sekibo (23), a man from Cape Town, also had to go to hospital.
Police officer Riah Nkosi told us, "We don't know what caused the accident yet. The car was going very fast. The driver didn't have a driving licence," she added.
Phil Davidson, a tourist from the USA, saw the accident. "The car was going fast when it happened," Phil said. "The driver braked and the car skidded. It crashed into the bus."
The police are looking for more information about the accident.

B

Nicole: Jade. It's Nicole here. There's just been an accident and Piet has gone to hospital! I really hope he's OK! A car hit our bus while we were travelling to the cricket match. We were really looking forward to it. Cebile was showing me her new wallet when we heard an awful noise and then, bang! I still can't believe it! I really want to see you, Jade, but we have to go to the police station now. The police want all the details. Call me later, OK?

S.120

a) Match the parts of the sentences.

1. **Text A:** Piet and the two drivers were
2. Phil Davidson saw
3. Riah Nkosi is looking for
4. **Text B:** Nicole tells
5. Nicole and Cebile were
6. Jade should phone

a. more information.
b. Jade about the accident.
c. the car hit the bus.
d. Nicole later.
e. injured in the accident.
f. on the bus when it happened.

Unit 3, page 65

4 Work with words from the text. → M Bus stop, p.140

a) Complete the online comment about the report.

phones | accidents ✓ | brake | driving licence | skid | fast

Why are there so many car (1) accidents on South Africa's roads? We often read about people who drive without a (2) d— l—. Many drivers look at their (3) p— and go too (4) f—. Every day cars (5) s— and drivers have to (6) b— hard.

Unit 3, page 66

7 What did they do?

a) What did they do on the morning of the accident?

1. Piet **walks** • **walked** to school after breakfast. (walk)
2. Cebile and Nicole **talked** • **talk** at break. (talk)
3. They **meet** • **met** Piet in the cafeteria at lunchtime. (meet)
4. Nicole's phone **rang** • **is ringing** at 12:22 p.m. (ring)
5. She **doesn't hear** • **didn't hear** it. (not hear)
6. Phil **is leaving** • **left** his hotel at about 11:30 a.m. (leave)
7. He **didn't talk** • **doesn't talk** to his friend in the USA. (not talk)

Language → G 1, p.127
The accident happened yesterday.
Phil saw the accident.
The driver didn't have a driving licence.

Unit 3, page 67

10 Nicole is telling a friend about the accident. Complete her sentences.

a) Choose the right answers.

1. We were going to the cricket match when a car **crashed** • **was crashing** into the bus.
2. Cebile was showing me her new wallet when we **heard** • **were hearing** a loud bang.
3. The car driver was talking on his phone when the police **arrived** • **were arriving**.
4. While the police officer **talked** • **was talking** to the car driver, the witness came to help.
5. While I **sat** • **was sitting** in the police car, I sent a message to Jade.
6. While I **waited** • **was waiting** at the police station, my parents arrived.

Unit 3, page 69

2 Complete the sentences.

2,6

Miriam Makeba

Zackie Achmat

Kungawo: Hi everyone and welcome to our podcast about inspiring South Africans. With me now is Mia, who is going to tell us about her very special South African role model.

Mia: Yes, Kungawo. We've already talked about music on the show. My role model is the South African singer and songwriter Miriam Makeba.

Kungawo: Miriam Makeba? OK, tell us more.

Mia: Well, she became famous all around the world during apartheid. Life was hard for black people in South Africa at that time. They had to live in townships and many other places were for white people only. I admire Miriam Makeba because she fought against apartheid. The government took away her passport when she left South Africa. She couldn't go home.

Kungawo: That sounds awful!

Mia: Yes, it was. Her life has been an inspiration for a long time. She achieved a lot. What about you? Who do you admire?

Kungawo: My role model is Zackie Achmat.

Mia: Who's he?

Kungawo: Zackie Achmat is a South African film director. He fought against apartheid and has fought for gay and lesbian rights too. He has helped many South Africans with HIV and AIDS. He has made films about people who have the diseases.

Mia: HIV and AIDS have been serious problems in South Africa for many years.

Kungawo: That's right. There is medication for HIV, but at first it was very expensive. Zackie Achmat has been HIV-positive since 1990 but he didn't take medication right away. He fought for cheaper drugs. He only took medication in August 2003, when it was cheaper, and poorer people could pay for it too.

Mia: He was really brave. South Africans have achieved a lot since 1994 and before that.

Kungawo: Yes, there's a lot that this country can be proud of.

1. Mia's role model is a South African singer and songwriter.
2. During apartheid Miriam Makeba became famous ——.
3. Miriam Makeba couldn't go back to her country when the government ——.
4. Zackie Achmat's films are about ——.
5. At first medication for HIV ——.
6. Zackie Achmat was brave because he only took medication when ——.

Unit 3, page 69

3 Work with words from the text. → M Bus stop, p.140

a) Put the words into the right groups (nouns, verbs or adjectives).

brave | achieve | inspiration | sing | admire | proud | role model | singer | inspiring

Du kannst manchmal eine Silbe an den Anfang oder an das Ende eines Wortes stellen, um neue Wörter zu bilden.

Unit 3, page 70

7 How long have they done it? → M Peer correction, p.141

a) Make sentences with for or since.

1. Mia has been in Cape Town — two days.
   Mia has been in Cape Town for two days.
2. She has lived in her flat — January.
3. She has worked at a hairdressing salon — two years.
4. Her parents have been on holiday in Durban — last Friday.
5. Kungawo has shared a flat with his friend — six months.
6. He has worked at a large supermarket — November last year.
7. Kungawo and Mia have made podcasts together — they met.
8. Mia has been interested in music — a long time.

Mia, 18

Kungawo, 19

Unit 3, page 71

8 (SPEAKING) Ask a partner.

a) Ask your partner questions. → M Milling around, p.141

listen to South African music | meet a famous person | see a lion | organize a flea market | work with ... | ...

A: Have you ever listened to ...? B: Yes, I have./ No, I haven't. Have you ever met ...?
A: Yes, I have./ No, I haven't. Have you ever seen ...? ...

Language → G 8, p.134
Have you ever seen this film?
Yes, I have./ No, I haven't.

Unit 4, page 91

4 Work with words from the text.

a) Choose the right words to complete Liam's e-mail about his interview.

E-MAIL

Hi Ella,
I wanted to get some **advice** • **news** (1) about my career so I talked to Ms Waaka, the careers advisor. First I **completed** • **looked at** (2) a job suitability test. Ms Waaka thinks I should study for a **qualification** • **quiz** (3) in tourism. Then I could work as an **assistant** • **artist** (4) in a tourist information **building** • **centre** (5). They're going to have a **jobs** • **careers** (6) day at the school in July. There will be a lot of **companies** • **schools** (7) with information about jobs.
What about you? How did your interview go?
Bye,
Liam

Unit 4, page 92

7 Talk about plans. → M Bus stop, p.140

a) Choose the right forms of 'to be' and complete the sentences about Ella and Liam's job plans.

1. Ella — going to find out about jobs as a hairdresser.
   Ella is going to find out about jobs as a hairdresser.
2. Liam — going to talk to different employers next week.
3. Liam: I — going to apply for jobs in tourism.
4. Liam — (not) going to work with his dad.
5. Ella: I — going to train in a hairdressing salon.
6. Ella and Liam — going to look for jobs on the internet.
7. Ella and Liam — (not) going to leave school next year.
8. Ella and Liam: We — going to visit a careers day soon.

Remember the forms of 'to be'?
I am ....
He/She is ....
We are ....
They are ....

Unit 4, page 93

9 Write questions and find the answers.

a) Complete the questions about job plans.

1. Where — you — — find out about jobs?
   Where are you going to find out about jobs?
2. What — Liam — — do next year?
3. When — you — — leave school?
4. Who — Liam — — meet at the careers day?
5. When — you — — write your CV?
6. Who — you — — ask about your career?

Language → G 9, p.135
What are you going to do next year?

Unit 4, page 95

3 What do they do?

2,18

Some students from Newlands College are talking to the store manager of a supermarket in Wellington. They want to find out what it's like to work there. Later they are going to write a report.

Mr Roberts: Welcome everyone. My name is John Roberts. I'm going to talk to you about the exciting jobs in retail today. We offer jobs and apprenticeships in customer service, communication and IT. But before we start our tour, are there any questions?
Rose: Yes, I have a question. What do shop assistants do in their job?
Mr Roberts: Shop assistants do many different things. They help customers find the right products in the store and they work at the checkouts. Shop assistants also fill the shelves and help present the products.
Nikau: Can you tell us how a supermarket works?
Mr Roberts: Well, supermarkets buy their products from other local companies. These companies are called suppliers. Stores order large numbers of products from suppliers so that the prices are cheaper. Then the products are sold to customers.
Nikau: When did this store open?
Mr Roberts: It opened in 2008. It's one of the largest stores in Wellington. We have over 60,000 products – not only food, but also clothes and many other goods. But we work in the community too. We donate food to local charities to reduce food waste, for example.

Oliver: That's cool! How much food did you donate last year?
Mr Roberts: Well, last year we donated over NZ$3 million's worth of food.
Rose: Do you sell bread here?
Mr Roberts: Yes, we do. All our bread is made in the store.
Grace: Do you offer internships?
Mr Roberts: Yes, internships are offered here. You can apply for one in our office or you can visit us at the job fair next month. We're always looking for interns to help our fantastic team. We also offer summer jobs for students. You get a good salary and training is included.
Grace: Did you start your career here as a shop assistant?
Mr Roberts: Yes, I did. Although I've been at this company for ten years, I'll never forget what I learned in my first six months. Let's start our tour now.

a) Match the parts of the sentences.

1. The store manager is talking to students
2. Stores order products
3. The suppliers deliver products
4. Shop assistants fill the shelves
5. Customers pay for products
6. The company donates food

a. at the checkouts.
b. to local charities.
c. from suppliers.
d. to the store.
e. about jobs in retail.
f. every day.

Unit 4, page 96

7 Complete the questions about Grace's internship. → M Peer correction, p.141

a) Ask the questions with the right form.

1. What —— you —— first? (do)
   What did you do first?
2. When did you —— ? (start)
3. How did you —— to work? (travel)
4. Did you —— with a computer? (work)
5. What —— you —— at lunchtime? (do)
6. When —— you —— the internship? (apply for)
7. —— you —— your internship? (enjoy)

Unit 4, page 97

9 A report about a job fair

a) Read Oliver's report. Choose the right answer.

Last week I (1) **visited** • **visit** a job fair at the Adelphi Hotel in Auckland. There (2) **were** • **was** many companies at the fair. There were also a lot of young people who were (3) **interesting** • **interested** in the companies. I wrote a list of questions before I (4) **went** • **go** to the fair. I also (5) **have taken** • **took** my CV with me. I talked to three employers and I want to apply for an (6) **intern** • **internship** with one of them. I stayed at the fair for about two (7) **hour** • **hours**. It's the (8) **best** • **better** way to find out about jobs.

Grammar

Mit G sind die Grammatikkapitel gekennzeichnet und der Reihe nach durchnummeriert. Eine Übersicht über alle Themen findest du unten auf dieser Seite.

Beim Lupen-Symbol findest du Besonderheiten und Tipps.

(TEST YOURSELF)

Am Ende eines jeden Grammatikkapitels kannst du ausprobieren, ob du alles verstanden hast.
Die Lösungen dazu findest du auf S.137.

R = Revision (Wiederholung)

	Englisch	Deutsch	Beispiel	Seite
G1	**R:** simple past	einfache Vergangenheit	I went to Australia last year.	127
G2	**R:** will-future	Zukunft mit will	I hope we'll meet again.	128
G3	If-clauses I – with will-future – with can – with commands – with simple present	Bedingungssätze Typ I – mit will-future – mit can – mit Aufforderungen – mit simple present	If you stay in bed, you'll feel better soon.	129
G4	**R:** present progressive	Verlaufsform der Gegenwart	What are you doing?	130
G5	**R:** simple present	einfache Gegenwart	I don't work on Sundays.	131
G6	**R:** word order	Satzstellung	We work in the fields every day.	132
G7	past progressive – while and when	Verlaufsform der Vergangenheit – while und when	While I was talking to Sue, we heard a terrible noise.	133
G8	**R:** present perfect – for and since	Perfekt – for und since	Have you ever been to a charity concert? – I haven't been to a concert for years.	134
G9	**R:** going to-future	Zukunft mit going to	I'm not going to be a mechanic.	135
G10	**R:** passive voice – simple present – simple past	Passiv – einfache Gegenwart – einfache Vergangenheit	The island was hit by an earthquake.	136

Unit 1

G1 R: Die einfache Vergangenheit

Revision: The simple past

Um über Ereignisse zu sprechen, die in der Vergangenheit passiert und vorbei sind, verwendest du das **simple past.**

Signalwörter	
yesterday	gestern
last year	letztes Jahr
a week ago	vor einer Woche
in 2016	(im Jahr) 2016

Das **simple past** bildest du so:
Hänge die Endung **-ed** an das Verb.
Achte auf unregelmäßige Verben, z. B. do → **did**, get → **got**, go → **went**.
Eine Liste der unregelmäßigen Verben findest du auf den Seiten 138–139.

I **visited** Uluru last week.	Ich **habe** letzte Woche den Uluru **besucht**.
We **heard** some great music there.	Wir **haben** dort tolle Musik **gehört**.

Um zu sagen, was nicht passiert ist, setzt du **didn't** (= did not) vor das Verb.

I **didn't see** any tourists.	Ich **habe keine** Touristen **gesehen**.
Joe **didn't eat** kangaroo meat.	Joe **hat kein** Känguruflеisch **gegessen**.

Aussagen und Verneinungen mit **be** bildest du so:

I **was** in Sydney. I **wasn't** in Perth.	Ich **war** in Sydney. Ich **war nicht** in Perth.
The tour **was** fantastic.	Die Reise **war** fantastisch.
It **wasn't** dangerous at all.	Es **war** überhaupt **nicht** gefährlich.
The tourists **were** impressed.	Die Touristen **waren** beeindruckt.
They **weren't** disappointed.	Sie **waren nicht** enttäuscht.

Und so kannst du im **simple past** Fragen stellen und beantworten:

Did you **have** a good time in the outback?	Yes, I **did**.	No, I **didn't**.
When **did** you **meet** the Aboriginal people?	I **met** them last Saturday.	
Were you in Sydney too?	Yes, I **was**.	No, I **wasn't**.
Was the guide nice?	Yes, he **was**.	No, he **wasn't**.
Were the stories interesting?	Yes, they **were**.	No, they **weren't**.

(TEST YOURSELF) Choose the right verbs for the simple past. Give short answers to the questions in 3. and 7. (☺ = Yes. ☹ = No.)

1. Our family **has** • **had** a great time in Australia last summer.
2. We **don't climb** • **didn't climb** Uluru.
3. **Do** you **see** • **Did** you **see** any paintings? (☺)
4. What **ate** you • **did** you **eat** in the outback?
5. How long **do** you **stay** • **did** you **stay** at Uluru?
6. The weather **was** • **were** dry and hot.
7. **Was** • **Were** it dangerous? (☹)

G2 R: Die Zukunft mit will

Revision: The will-future

Mit dem **will-future** sprichst du über die Zukunft. Oft drückst du damit Hoffnungen, Wünsche und Vorhersagen aus. Dann beginnen diese Sätze mit **I hope**, **I think**, **I'm sure** oder **Maybe.**

Du bildest das will-future mit **will** oder **won't** und der **Grundform des Verbs**.

Häufig wird die Kurzform verwendet:

I will go → I ~~will~~ 'll go → I'll go

I ~~will not~~ won't go → I won't go

Achtung! Im Deutschen kann man über Zukünftiges mit der Zukunft oder der Gegenwart sprechen. Vergleiche: Ich rufe dich morgen an. / Ich werde dich morgen anrufen.

The weather **will be** fine next week.	Das Wetter **wird** nächste Woche gut (**werden**).
Maybe I'**ll go** to a lake with Pete.	Vielleicht **fahre** ich mit Pete an einen See.
I hope I'**ll get** a job quickly.	Ich hoffe, dass ich schnell einen Job **bekomme**.
Will the interview **be** outside?	**Wird** das Interview draußen **stattfinden**?
Yes, it **will.** / No, it **won't.**	Ja. / Nein.
I'm sure it **won't rain.**	Ich bin sicher, dass es **nicht regnen wird.**

Achtung! Verwechsle **will** (werden) nicht mit **want to** (wollen):

I **will buy** some souvenirs.	Ich **werde** ein paar Souvenirs **kaufen**.
I **want to buy** some souvenirs.	Ich **will** ein paar Souvenirs **kaufen**.

(TEST YOURSELF) Put the verbs in the will-future. Give short answers to the questions in 4. and 5. (☺ = Yes. ☹ = No.)

1. I hope I ___ (travel) to many countries.
2. Maybe I ___ (spend) a year in Australia after school.
3. I think I ___ (not start) working in July.
4. ___ the weather ___ (be) bad? (☹)
5. ___ your parents ___ (accept) your plans? (☺)
6. Where ___ you ___ (be) in ten years' time?
7. I'm sure I ___ (not become) a tour guide.
8. Where ___ you ___ (sleep) in the outback?

G3 Bedingungssätze Typ I

If-clauses I

If you see a sign like this in Australia, drive slowly.

If-Sätze benutzt man, um Bedingungen und Folgen auszudrücken. Im **if**-Satz steht das **simple present**, im Hauptsatz steht das **will-future**. Steht der **if**-Satz vorne, wird am Ende des **if**-Satzes ein Komma gesetzt. Steht der **if**-Satz hinter dem Hauptsatz, entfällt das Komma.

If I **feel** OK,	I'**ll come** with you.	Wenn es mir gut geht, komme ich mit.
If I **don't feel** better soon,	I'**ll go** to the doctor's.	Wenn es mir nicht bald besser geht, werde ich zum Arzt gehen.
If you **wear** warm clothes,	you **won't feel** cold.	Wenn du warme Sachen anziehst, wird dir nicht kalt werden.
I'**ll call** you	if I **have** time.	Ich rufe dich an, wenn ich Zeit habe.
We **won't come**	if you **are** ill.	Wir kommen nicht, wenn du krank bist.

Im Hauptsatz kann auch **can** oder **eine Aufforderung** stehen.
Sprichst du über **Fakten** oder **Tatsachen**, steht **simple present** im **if-Satz** und im Hauptsatz.

If you ask me, I **can help** you.	Wenn du mich fragst, **kann** ich dir **helfen**.
If you are not better by Monday, **go** to the doctor's!	Wenn es dir bis Montag nicht besser geht, **geh** zum Arzt! (Aufforderung)
If you want to buy special medicine, you **need** a prescription first.	Wenn du spezielle Medizin kaufen willst, **brauchst** du zuerst ein Rezept. (Fakt)

Diese Zeitenmuster sind in **if**-Sätzen Typ I möglich:

If-Satz:	+	Hauptsatz:
simple present		will-future oder can/can't
		Befehlsform
		simple present

(TEST YOURSELF) Complete the sentences.

1. If I meet Julia, I —— (talk) to her.
2. If you ask the doctor, she —— (can give) you a prescription.
3. If you don't feel well, —— (stay) at home!
4. You —— (not be) late if you leave now.
5. If Liz calls the doctor, she —— (can make) an appointment for tomorrow.
6. Don't go swimming if you still —— (feel) tired.

G4 R: Die Verlaufsform der Gegenwart

Revision: The present progressive

Mit dem **present progressive** kannst du sagen, was jemand gerade tut oder was im Augenblick passiert.

Aussagen im present progressive bildest du so: **am/are/is + Verb + ing.**

Signalwörter	
at the moment	im Moment
now	jetzt
Look, ...	Schau mal, ...
Listen, ...	Hör mal, ...

I'**m working** at the moment. I'll call you later.	Ich **arbeite** (gerade). Ich rufe dich später an.
The party is great. Everybody **is having** fun.	Die Party ist klasse. Jeder **hat** Spaß.

Achte auf die Schreibweise: write – writing, run – running, sit – sitting, swim – swimming

So verneinst du Sätze: **am not / are not / is not + Verb + -ing.**

Come in. I'**m not sleeping**.	Komm' herein. Ich **schlafe nicht**.
Lisa **isn't wearing** her new shoes today.	Lisa **trägt** heute **nicht** ihre neuen Schuhe.

Bei Fragen stellst du **am/are/is** an den Satzanfang. Ein Fragewort steht noch davor.

Are you **listening**?	**Hörst** du **zu**?
Yes, I **am**. / No, I'**m not**.	Ja./Nein.
What are you **doing** right now?	**Was machst** du (gerade)?
I'**m reading**.	Ich **lese** (gerade).
Who are you **talking to**?	**Mit wem sprichst** du (gerade)?

Du benutzt das **present progressive** auch, um ein Bild zu beschreiben. Zunächst beschreibst du, wen oder was du siehst ("I can see a/some/a lot of ..." oder: "There is/are ..."). Dann beschreibst du, was jemand tut. Du benutzt das **present progressive** für alle Handlungen, die im Bild zu sehen sind und für alles, was jemand **tut**.

Some people **are standing** around the fire.	Einige Leute **stehen** um ein Feuer herum.
They **are wearing** sports clothes.	Sie **tragen** Sportkleidung.
One woman **is talking** to another woman.	Eine Frau **spricht** mit einer anderen Frau.
It **is** cloudy, but it **isn't raining**.	Es **ist** bewölkt, aber es **regnet nicht**.

(TEST YOURSELF) Use the present progressive.

1. Where is Kate? – She ___ (sleep).
2. I ___ (make) lunch at the moment.
3. My parents ___ (not work) today.
4. ___ you ___ (have) fun?
5. Why ___ you ___ (not listen)?
6. Who ___ you ___ (write) to right now?

Unit 2

G5 R: Die einfache Gegenwart

Revision: The simple present

Du kennst schon das **simple present**. Du benutzt es, um einen Zustand zu beschreiben oder um zu sagen, dass etwas gewohnheitsmäßig, regelmäßig oder häufig geschieht. Du verwendest es auch für feste Termine in der Zukunft, z. B. bei Programmen, Fahrplänen, Stundenplänen usw.

Signalwörter	
every day	jeden Tag
always	immer
usually	normalerweise
often	oft
sometimes	manchmal
never	nie

He she, it, das **s** muss mit!

So bildest du das **simple present** mit **Vollverben**:

Aussagen	I **live** in Bavaria. My train **arrives** at 9 p.m.	Ich **lebe** in Bayern. Mein Zug **kommt** um 21 Uhr **an**.
Verneinte Aussagen	I **don't live** in the country. Ann **doesn't have** time. Some people **don't like** fish.	Ich **wohne nicht** auf dem Land. Ann **hat keine** Zeit. Manche Leute **mögen keinen** Fisch.
Fragen	**Do** you **work** on an assembly line? Yes, I **do**. / No, I **don't**. **Does** the company **have** a café? Yes, it **does**. / No, it **doesn't**. **Where do** you **live**?	**Arbeitest** du an einem Fließband? Ja. / Nein. **Hat** die Firma ein Café? Ja. / Nein. **Wo wohnst** du?

So bildest du das **simple present** mit **be**, z. B.:

Aussagen	I'**m** a vegetarian. Our customers **are** in Europe.	Ich **bin** Vegetarier/in. Unsere Kunden **sind** in Europa.
Verneinte Aussagen	I'**m not** a vegetarian. My job **isn't** boring.	Ich **bin nicht** Vegetarier/in. Meine Arbeit **ist nicht** langweilig.
Fragen	**Are** you happy? Yes, I **am**. / No, I'**m not**. **Where is** my bag?	**Bist** du / **Seid** ihr glücklich? Ja. / Nein. **Wo ist** meine Tasche?

(TEST YOURSELF) Choose the right verb. Write correct sentences.

1. I always **are** • **travel** • **live** to work by bus.
2. Sam never **work** • **works** • **likes** at home.
3. I **aren't** • **don't** • **am not** start work at 6 a.m.
4. My boss **is** • **are** • **don't** never late.
5. **Do** • **Does** • **Is** • he speak English?
6. Where **do** • **does** • **is** you work?

G6 R: Die Satzstellung mit Angaben des Ortes, der Zeit und der Art und Weise

Revision: Word order

Die wichtigste Satzstellungsregel im Englischen lautet: **Subjekt – Verb – Objekt**
Bei 2 Objekten steht das indirekte Objekt (Wem?) vor dem direkten Objekt (Wen? Was?).

Subjekt	Verb	Indirektes Objekt (Wem?)	Direktes Objekt (Wen? Was?)	
We	need		clean drinking water.	Wir brauchen sauberes Trinkwasser.
They	showed	us	their village.	Sie haben uns ihr Dorf gezeigt.

Eine weitere Satzstellungsregel lautet: **Ort vor Zeit** (place before time).

Subjekt	Verb	Objekt	Ort	Zeit	
I	can eat	lunch	at home	every day.	Ich kann jeden Tag zu Hause zu Mittag essen.

I want to work on a farm next summer.

Ortsangabe Zeitangabe

Die Regel **Ort vor Zeit** ist deshalb so wichtig, weil die Reihenfolge im Deutschen oft genau anders herum üblich ist. Vergleiche:
Ich möchte im nächsten Sommer (Zeit) auf einer Farm (Ort) arbeiten.

Adverbien der Art und Weise stehen meistens **am Ende** des Satzes, aber oft **vor** einer **Orts-** oder einer **Zeitangabe**. Das gilt auch für **Fragen**.

Kyra **told** her story **quietly**.	Kyra **hat** ihre Geschichte **ruhig erzählt**.
We **can get** fresh eggs **easily** every day.	Wir **können** jeden Tag **leicht** frische Eier **bekommen**.
She **drove** the van **carefully** yesterday.	Sie **hat** den Lieferwagen gestern **vorsichtig gefahren**.
Some crops **don't grow well** here.	Einige Feldfrüchte **wachsen** hier **nicht gut**.
Did you **sleep well** last night?	**Hast** du letzte Nacht **gut geschlafen**?

(TEST YOURSELF) Put the words in the right order.

1. need • in their houses • people • good sanitation
2. they • differently • crops • grow • in this soil
3. safely • the water • carried • Louisa • to her home
4. villagers in India • fresh milk • can get • at home • and eggs • easily
5. your friend • speak • does • well • English • ?
6. can we • the problem • easily • how • solve • ?

Unit 3

G7 Die Verlaufsform der Vergangenheit

The past progressive

While we were visiting the national park, we saw two elephants at a lake.

Mit dem **past progressive** drückst du aus, dass etwas in der Vergangenheit über einen **längeren Zeitraum** passierte. Im Deutschen sagt man etwa: Ich/Sie/Wir … war/waren (gerade) dabei, etwas zu tun. So bildest du Aussagen im **past progressive: was/were + Verb + -ing**

Yesterday I **was cleaning** my bike.	Gestern **habe** ich mein Rad **geputzt**./ … **war** ich **dabei**, mein Rad **zu putzen**.

Das **past progressive** beschreibt auch eine Handlung, die andauerte, als plötzlich eine neue eintrat (**simple past**). Solche Sätze bildest du mit **while** (= während) und **when** (= als).

While I **was walking**, my wallet **fell** out of my pocket. She **was working** at her desk **when** the accident **happened**.	**Während** ich (gerade) **gelaufen bin**, **ist** mein Geldbeutel aus der Tasche **gefallen**. Sie **hat** (gerade) an ihrem Schreibtisch **gearbeitet**, **als** der Unfall **passiert ist**.

While I was walking, (andauernde Handlung)

my wallet fell out of my pocket. (neues Ereignis)

Liefen in der Vergangenheit zwei Handlungen zur gleichen Zeit und gleich lange, wird für beide Handlungen das **past progressive** benutzt.

While I **was working** in the garden, Nick **was preparing** some food.	**Während** ich im Garten **gearbeitet habe**, **hat** Nick etwas zum Essen **vorbereitet**.

(TEST YOURSELF) Use the simple past or the past progressive.

1. I —— (wait) for the train when I got Dad's message.
2. What —— you —— (do) between 8 a.m and 10 a.m. yesterday?
3. Joe was running in the park when he suddenly —— (see) a rainbow.
4. While we —— (have) our garden party, it started (start) to rain heavily.

G8 R: Das Perfekt mit for und since

Revision: The present perfect with for and since

Wenn eine Handlung in der Vergangenheit beginnt und in der Gegenwart zu einem Ergebnis führt, verwendest du das **present perfect**:
have/haven't oder **has/hasn't** (bei he, she, it) + **3. Form** des Verbs (past participle).
Bei den meisten Verben hängst du für die 3. Form ein **-ed** an das Verb, z. B. help → help**ed**

Signalwörter	
already	schon
just	gerade
not ... yet	noch nicht
never	noch nie
ever (in Fragen)	jemals (in Fragen)
since	seit (Zeitpunkt)
for	seit (Zeitspanne)

Einige Verben haben unregelmäßige 3. Formen, z. B. be → **been**; write → **written**
Eine Liste der unregelmäßigen Verben findest du auf den Seiten 138–139.

I **have** just **tidied** my room.	Ich **habe** gerade mein Zimmer **aufgeräumt**.
The star **has** already **sung** in South Africa.	Der Star **hat** schon in Südafrika **gesungen**.
I **haven't been** to South Africa yet.	Ich **war** noch **nicht** in Südafrika.

Have you ever **met** a famous person?	Yes, I **have**.	No, I **haven't**.
Has your friend ever **been** on TV?	Yes, she **has**.	No, she **hasn't**.

Present perfect mit **for** (seit) und **since** (seit):
since verwendest du vor einem Zeitpunkt, z. B. **since** 6:00 a.m., **since** May, **since** I was young etc.
for verwendest du vor einer Zeitspanne, z. B. **for** one hour, **for** two years, **for** a long time etc.

I haven't seen Mia **since** Sunday.	Ich habe Mia **seit** Sonntag nicht gesehen.
I haven't seen Mia **for** a week.	Ich habe Mia **seit** einer Woche nicht gesehen.

(TEST YOURSELF) Put the verbs in the present perfect. Choose for or since where necessary.

1. I ___ already ___ (be) to South Africa a few times.
2. There ___ (be) serious problems with AIDS **since** • **for** many years.
3. Mia ___ (live) in South Africa **since** • **for** she was young.
4. South African people ___ (achieve) a lot **since** • **for** 1994.
5. ___ you ever ___ (listen) to South African music?
6. I ___ (not visit) the zoo **since** • **for** two years.

Unit 4

G9 R: Die Zukunft mit going to

Revision: The going to-future

Mit dem **going to-future** sagst du, was du in der Zukunft vorhast, planst, beabsichtigst zu tun. Aussagen im **going to-future** bildest du so: **am/are/is + going to + Verb**

I **am** (I'm) **going to apply** for a job.	Ich **werde** mich für einen Job **bewerben**.
You **are** (You're) **going to work** at a café.	Du **wirst** in einem Café **arbeiten**.
She **is** (She's) **going to fly** to New Zealand.	Sie **hat vor**, nach Neuseeland **zu fliegen**.
We **are** (We're) **going to meet** Luke.	Wir **werden** Luke **treffen**.
They **are** (They're) **going to see** a film.	Sie **planen**, sich einen Film **anzusehen**.

So bildest du verneinte Sätze im **going to-future**:

I **am** (I'm) **not going to fly** anywhere.	Ich **beabsichtige nicht**, irgendwo **hinzufliegen**.
He **is** (He's) **not going to work** as a vet.	Er **hat nicht vor**, als Tierarzt **zu arbeiten**.
They **are** (They're) **not going to meet**.	Sie **werden sich nicht treffen**.

Fragen im going to-future bildest du, indem du **am**, **are** oder **is an den Satzanfang** stellst. **Fragewörter** stehen noch davor am Satzanfang.

Are you **going to look for** a job on the internet?	**Wirst** du im Internet nach einem Job **suchen**?
Yes, I **am**. / No, I'm **not**.	Ja./Nein.
Is Nora **going to leave** Germany?	**Plant** Nora Deutschland **zu verlassen**?
Yes, she **is**. / No, she **isn't**.	Ja./Nein.
What are they **going to do** after school?	**Was werden** sie nach der Schule **tun**?
When are you **going to come back**?	**Wann planst** du **zurückzukommen**?

Aufgepasst bei Sätzen und Fragen mit dem Verb go!

I'm **going to go** to New Zealand.	Ich **habe vor**, nach Neuseeland **zu fahren**.
Are you **going to go** to New Zealand?	**Hast** du **vor**, nach Neuseeland **zu fahren**?
Yes, I **am**. / No, I'm **not**.	Ja./Nein.

(TEST YOURSELF) Put the verbs in the going to-future. Give short answers to the questions in 5. and 6. (☺ = Yes. ☹ = No.).

1. Both Sue and I ___ (write) our CVs soon.
2. We ___ (apply for) jobs in tourism.
3. I ___ (not work) in Germany.
4. What ___ you ___ (do) next summer?
5. ___ you ___ (go) to the next job fair? (☺)
6. ___ you ___ (visit) another country? (☹)

G10 R: Das Passiv

Revision: The passive voice (simple present and simple past)

Mit dem **Passiv** kannst du über eine Handlung Auskunft geben, ohne zu sagen, wer die Handlung ausführt. Im Vordergrund steht die Handlung.
Passivsätze gibt es wie Aktivsätze in allen Zeiten!

So bildest du das **Passiv** im **simple present**: **am/are/is + 3. Form** des Verbs (past participle)
Eine Liste der unregelmäßigen Verben findest du auf den Seiten 138–139.

Fish **is delivered** every day.	Fisch **wird** jeden Tag **geliefert**.
These goods **are sold** in Bavaria.	Diese Waren **werden** in Bayern **verkauft**.
The products **are presented** in a nice way.	Die Produkte **werden** schön **präsentiert**.

So bildest du das **Passiv** im **simple past**: **was/were + 3. Form** des Verbs (past participle)

The flight **was cancelled** ten minutes ago.	Der Flug **wurde** vor zehn Minuten **gestrichen**.
This T-shirt **was made** in Auckland.	Dieses T-Shirt **wurde** in Auckland **hergestellt**.
A lot of photos **were taken**.	Es **wurden** viele Fotos **gemacht**.
I **was born** in New Zealand.	Ich **wurde** in Neuseeland **geboren**.

Willst du in einem Passivsatz sagen, **wer** oder **was** die Handlung ausführt, ergänzt du sie, ihn oder es mit **by**.

My wallet **was found by** a young woman.	Mein Geldbeutel **wurde von** einer jungen Frau **gefunden**.
The island **was hit by** an earthquake.	Die Insel **wurde von** einem Erdbeben **getroffen**.

Aus vielen Aktivsätzen kannst du Passivsätze bilden.

Students	**write**	the report.	(Aktiv)
The report	**is written**	by students.	(Passiv)

(TEST YOURSELF) Choose the right words for the passive voice.

1. Food and drinks **is offered** • **are offered** on the train.
2. Fresh fruit **is bought** • **are bought** every day.
3. People who buy things **is called** • **are called** customers.
4. Fresh products **is often sold** • **were often sold** at markets.
5. Lots of goods **are delivered** • **were delivered** to Europe in 2019.
6. How much money **is donated** • **was donated** by the company last year?

Lösungen

TEST YOURSELF

G1

1. had
2. didn't climb
3. Did … see; Yes, I did.
4. did … eat
5. did … stay
6. was
7. Was; No, it wasn't.

G2

1. 'll/will travel
2. 'll/will spend
3. won't/will not start
4. Will … be; No, it won't.
5. Will … accept; Yes, they will.
6. will … be
7. won't/will not become
8. will … sleep

G3

1. 'll/will talk
2. can give
3. stay
4. won't/will not be
5. can make
6. feel

G4

1. 's/is sleeping
2. 'm/am making
3. aren't/are not working
4. Are … having
5. are … not/aren't … listening
6. are … writing

G5

1. travel
2. works
3. don't
4. is
5. Does
6. do

G6

1. People need good sanitation in their houses.
2. They grow crops differently in this soil.
3. Louisa carried the water to her home safely./ Louisa carried the water safely to her home.
4. Villagers in India can get fresh milk and eggs easily at home.
5. Does your friend speak English well?
6. How can we solve the problem easily?/ How easily can we solve the problem?

G7

1. was waiting
2. were … doing
3. saw
4. were having

G8

1. 've/have … been
2. have been, for
3. has lived, since
4. have achieved, since
5. Have … listened
6. haven't/have not visited, for

G9

1. are going to write
2. 're/are going to apply for
3. 'm/am not going to work
4. are … going to do
5. Are … going to go; Yes, I am.
6. Are … going to visit; No, I'm not.

G10

1. are offered
2. is bought
3. are called
4. were often sold
5. were delivered
6. was donated

List of irregular verbs

Hier findest du alle unregelmäßigen Verben, die im Buch vorkommen. Die Liste enthält jeweils alle drei Formen, auch wenn sie noch nicht alle in den Units vorgekommen sind.

infinitive	simple past	past participle	German
to be [bi:]	was, were [wɒz, wɜ:]	been [bi:n]	sein
to become [bɪˈkʌm]	became [bɪˈkeɪm]	become [bɪˈkʌm]	werden
to begin [bɪˈgɪn]	began [bɪˈgæn]	begun [bɪˈgʌn]	beginnen; anfangen
to break [breɪk]	broke [brəʊk]	broken [ˈbrəʊkn]	brechen
to bring [brɪŋ]	brought [brɔ:t]	brought [brɔ:t]	bringen; mitbringen
to build [bɪld]	built [bɪlt]	built [bɪlt]	bauen
to buy [baɪ]	bought [bɔ:t]	bought [bɔ:t]	kaufen
to catch [kætʃ]	caught [kɔ:t]	caught [kɔ:t]	fangen
to choose [tʃu:z]	chose [tʃəʊz]	chosen [ˈtʃəʊzn]	wählen; auswählen
to come [kʌm]	came [keɪm]	come [kʌm]	kommen
to cost [kɒst]	cost [kɒst]	cost [kɒst]	kosten
to cut [kʌt]	cut [kʌt]	cut [kʌt]	schneiden
to cut down [ˌkʌt ˈdaʊn]	cut down [ˌkʌt ˈdaʊn]	cut down [ˌkʌt ˈdaʊn]	fällen
to do [du:]	did [dɪd]	done [dʌn]	machen; tun
to drink [drɪŋk]	drank [dræŋk]	drunk [drʌŋk]	trinken
to drive [draɪv]	drove [drəʊv]	driven [ˈdrɪvn]	fahren; treiben
to eat [i:t]	ate [eɪt]	eaten [ˈi:tn]	essen
to fall [fɔ:l]	fell [fel]	fallen [ˈfɔ:ln]	fallen
to feed [fi:d]	fed [fed]	fed [fed]	füttern
to feel [fi:l]	felt [felt]	felt [felt]	fühlen; sich fühlen
to fight [faɪt]	fought [fɔ:t]	fought [fɔ:t]	kämpfen
to find [faɪnd]	found [faʊnd]	found [faʊnd]	finden
to fly [flaɪ]	flew [flu:]	flown [fləʊn]	fliegen
to forget [fəˈget]	forgot [fəˈgɒt]	forgotten [fəˈgɒtn]	vergessen
to get [get]	got [gɒt]	got [gɒt]	bekommen; werden
to give [gɪv]	gave [geɪv]	given [ˈgɪvn]	geben; schenken
to go [gəʊ]	went [went]	gone [gɒn]	gehen; fahren
to grow [grəʊ]	grew [gru:]	grown [grəʊn]	wachsen
to have [hæv]	had [hæd]	had [hæd]	haben; besitzen
to hear [hɪə]	heard [hɜ:d]	heard [hɜ:d]	hören
to hit [hɪt]	hit [hɪt]	hit [hɪt]	treffen; schlagen; anfahren
to hold [həʊld]	held [held]	held [held]	halten; festhalten
to hurt [hɜ:t]	hurt [hɜ:t]	hurt [hɜ:t]	verletzen; wehtun
to keep [ki:p]	kept [kept]	kept [kept]	halten; behalten
to know [nəʊ]	knew [nju:]	known [nəʊn]	kennen; wissen
to lead [li:d]	led [led]	led [led]	anführen; führen; leiten
to leave [li:v]	left [left]	left [left]	lassen; verlassen
to lose [lu:z]	lost [lɒst]	lost [lɒst]	verlieren

infinitive	simple past	past participle	German
to make [meɪk]	made [meɪd]	made [meɪd]	machen; tun; erstellen; herstellen
to mean [mi:n]	meant [ment]	meant [ment]	bedeuten; meinen
to meet [mi:t]	met [met]	met [met]	kennenlernen; treffen
to pay [peɪ]	paid [peɪd]	paid [peɪd]	bezahlen
to put [pʊt]	put [pʊt]	put [pʊt]	setzen; legen; stellen
to read [ri:d]	read [red]	read [red]	lesen; vorlesen
to ride [raɪd]	rode [rəʊd]	ridden ['rɪdn]	fahren; reiten
to ring [rɪŋ]	rang [ræŋ]	rung [rʌŋ]	klingeln; läuten
to run [rʌn]	ran [ræn]	run [rʌn]	laufen; rennen
to say [seɪ]	said [sed]	said [sed]	sagen; sprechen
to see [si:]	saw [sɔ:]	seen [si:n]	sehen
to sell [sel]	sold [səʊld]	sold [səʊld]	verkaufen
to send [send]	sent [sent]	sent [sent]	schicken; senden
to shake [ʃeɪk]	shook [ʃʊk]	shaken ['ʃeɪkn]	beben; zittern; schütteln
to shoot [ʃu:t]	shot [ʃɒt]	shot [ʃɒt]	erschießen; schießen
to sing [sɪŋ]	sang [sæŋ]	sung [sʌŋ]	singen
to sit [sɪt]	sat [sæt]	sat [sæt]	sitzen
to sleep [sli:p]	slept [slept]	slept [slept]	schlafen
to speak [spi:k]	spoke [spəʊk]	spoken ['spəʊkn]	sprechen
to spend [spend]	spent [spent]	spent [spent]	verbringen; ausgeben
to stand [stænd]	stood [stʊd]	stood [stʊd]	stehen
to swim [swɪm]	swam [swæm]	swum [swʌm]	schwimmen
to swing [swɪŋ]	swung [swʌŋ]	swung [swʌŋ]	schwingen; schwenken
to take [teɪk]	took [tʊk]	taken ['teɪkn]	nehmen; mitnehmen; dauern; brauchen
to teach [ti:tʃ]	taught [tɔ:t]	taught [tɔ:t]	unterrichten
to tell [tel]	told [təʊld]	told [təʊld]	erzählen; sagen
to think [θɪŋk]	thought [θɔ:t]	thought [θɔ:t]	denken; glauben
to throw [θrəʊ]	threw [θru:]	thrown [θrəʊn]	werfen
to understand [ˌʌndə'stænd]	understood [ˌʌndə'stʊd]	understood [ˌʌndə'stʊd]	verstehen
to wake up [ˌweɪk‿'ʌp]	woke up [ˌwəʊk‿'ʌp]	woken up [ˌwəʊkn‿'ʌp]	aufwachen; aufwecken
to wear [weə]	wore [wɔ:]	worn [wɔ:n]	anhaben; tragen
to win [wɪn]	won [wʌn]	won [wʌn]	gewinnen
to write [raɪt]	wrote [rəʊt]	written ['rɪtn]	schreiben

1-minute-presentation

Step 1
Nimm ein Blatt Papier im DIN-A4-Format quer und falte es so, dass das untere Drittel nach hinten wegknickt.

Step 2
Schreibe den Vortragstext auf die oberen zwei Drittel.

Step 3
Streiche nun die wichtigsten Stichpunkte im Text an. Notiere sie noch einmal auf dem unteren Drittel. Das ist dein Spickzettel.

Step 4
In deiner Präsentation verwendest du nur den Spickzettel. Wenn du steckenbleibst, darfst du ihn umknicken und kurz auf den Text oben schauen.

Bus stop
(Lerntempoduett)

Step 1
Bearbeite die Aufgabe zunächst allein.
Schreibe deine Lösungen auf.

Step 2
Wenn du fertig bist, gehe zum „bus stop". Entweder wartet dort schon jemand oder du wartest dort auf die nächste Person. Vergleicht und korrigiert eure Ergebnisse zu zweit.

Step 3
Gehe danach wieder zu deinem Platz zurück.
Bearbeite die nächste Aufgabe.

Dramatic reading
(Szenisches Lesen)

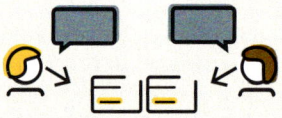

Step 1
Verteilt die Rollen innerhalb eurer Gruppe.

Step 2
Lies dir deinen Text lautlos oder ganz leise immer wieder vor, bis du ihn gut kennst.

Step 3
Übt euren Text in der Gruppe mit der Methode „Read and look up" (Seite 142).

Step 4
Überlegt euch, wie ihr euch in der Rolle fühlt und wie ihr euch bewegen würdet. Tragt euren Text so frei wie möglich vor.

Gallery walk
(Galerierundgang)

Step 1
Hängt nach eurer Gruppenarbeit eure Produkte gut sichtbar im Klassenzimmer auf.

Step 2
Eine „Expertin" oder ein „Experte" aus jeder Gruppe bleibt bei dem Produkt stehen und erklärt es den anderen. Der Rest der Gruppe geht im Klassenzimmer herum. Nach jedem Durchgang wechselt die Expertin oder der Experte.

Step 3
Seht euch die Produkte der anderen an und bewertet sie.

Step 4
Wertet im Anschluss eure Ergebnisse in der Klasse aus.

Milling around
(Marktplatz)

Step 1
Bearbeite die Aufgabe zunächst allein.

Step 2
Auf ein Zeichen von eurer Lehrerin oder eurem Lehrer steht ihr auf und geht durch den Raum. Vergesst nicht, die Aufgabe und einen Stift mitzunehmen.

Step 3
Wenn ein Signal ertönt, bleibt ihr stehen. Besprecht die Aufgabe mit der Person, die euch am nächsten steht.

Step 4
Beim nächsten Signal trennt ihr euch und geht weiter durch den Raum. Wiederholt den Vorgang.

Peer correction
(Partnerkontrolle)

Step 1
Bearbeite die Aufgabe zunächst allein.

Step 2
Tausche deine Lösungen mit einer Partnerin oder einem Partner. Kontrolliere seine oder ihre Lösungen.

Step 3
Vergleicht eure Lösungen und korrigiert sie dann gemeinsam.

Placemat
(Platzdeckchen)

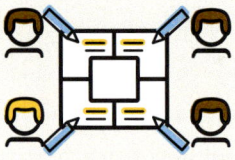

Step 1
Bildet Vierergruppen.

Step 2
Teilt ein großes Blatt Papier in fünf Bereiche ein.

Step 3
Setzt euch so hin, dass alle jeweils in eine Ecke des Blattes schreiben können.

Step 4
Jedes Gruppenmitglied denkt allein über das Thema nach und schreibt Ideen auf seinen Teil des Blattes.

Step 5
Tauscht euch über die Ideen aus. Einigt euch auf die besten Ideen und schreibt diese in die Mitte des Blattes.

Read and look up
(Lesen und Aufschauen)

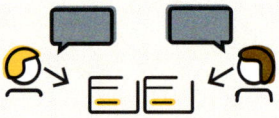

Step 1
Schaue auf deinen Text und präge dir die erste Zeile oder den ersten Satz ein. Schaue hoch und sprich deine Zeile / deinen Satz lautlos oder leise vor dich hin. Nimm dir die nächste Zeile / den nächsten Satz vor.

Step 2
Übe nun mit einer Partnerin oder einem Partner. Erzähle deinen Text, Zeile für Zeile oder Satz für Satz. Dazwischen schaust du immer wieder nach unten auf deinen Text.

Step 3
Wiederhole alles, bis es gut klappt. Überlege dir, wo du stehen und wie du dich bewegen willst.

Round robin
(Blitzlicht)

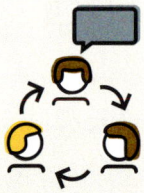

Step 1
Bildet Gruppen und setzt euch in einen Kreis.

Step 2
Jedes Gruppenmitglied überlegt sich kurz einen Satz, der seine persönliche Meinung zum Thema ausdrückt.

Step 3
Wenn alle bereit sind, sagen die Gruppenmitglieder der Reihe nach ihre Meinung. Die anderen Gruppenmitglieder dürfen die Sätze nicht kommentieren.

Think – pair – share

Step 1
Schreibe deine Ideen, Gedanken oder Lösungen zur Aufgabe auf.

Step 2
Tauscht euch zu zweit aus und besprecht eure Notizen.

Step 3
Präsentiert euer Ergebnis anderen Paaren oder der gesamten Klasse.

Tip top

Step 1
Sage zunächst, was dir gut gefallen hat – was „top" war.

Step 2
Sage nun, was noch nicht so gut war, und gib einen Tipp, was man noch verbessern könnte.

Writers' conference
(Schreibwerkstatt)

Step 1
Bildet Vierergruppen.

Step 2
Lest euch eure Sätze/Texte gegenseitig vor.

Step 3
Die Zuhörerinnen und Zuhörer sagen, was ihnen gefallen hat, und können Verbesserungsvorschläge machen.

Step 4
Jede Gruppe wählt den besten Text aus und liest ihn der Klasse vor.

Vocabulary tips

Du kennst schon einige Tipps und Tricks zum Vokabellernen.
Erinnerst du dich? Hier gibt es noch mehr Tipps.

Lerntipp: Wortfamilien

Beim ersten Anschauen eines neuen Wortes solltest du dir überlegen, ob es einen Anknüpfungspunkt an Wörter gibt, die du bereits kennst. Oft kann dir ein Wort aus der gleichen Wortfamilie helfen, die Bedeutung des neuen Wortes zu erschließen. Hier zwei Beispiele:

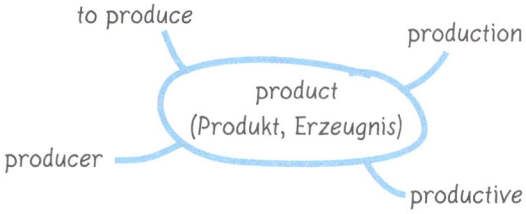

Lerntipp: Themenfelder

Lege dir zunächst verschiedene Themenfelder (z. B. Musik, Essen und Trinken, Umwelt) in deinem Heft oder digital an und schreibe alle Wörter auf, die du zum jeweiligen Themenfeld schon kennst. Versuche in Zukunft möglichst viele neue Wörter einem dieser Themenfelder zuzuordnen. Füge auch weitere Themenfelder hinzu.

Lerntipp: Die richtige Übersetzung im Wörterbuch finden

Wenn du ein Wort im Wörterbuch nachschlägst, findest du oft viele verschiedene Übersetzungen. Achte darauf, ob der Zusammenhang (z. B. Sport, Computer, Schule) im Eintrag mit angegeben ist. Dies kann dir helfen zu entscheiden, welche Übersetzung am besten passt. Bei jedem Eintrag im Wörterbuch findest du auch eine Angabe zur Wortart. Nomen werden mit n. (*noun*), Verben mit v. (*verb*) und Adjektive mit adj. (*adjective*) abgekürzt.

Lerntipp: Auf „falsche Freunde" („false friends") achten

Bei diesen Wörtern musst du aufpassen. Man kann sie leicht verwechseln.

German	English	English	German
also	so	also	auch
arm	poor	arm	Arm
Chef; Chefin	boss	chef	Koch; Küchenchef
Karte; Plan	map	card	Karte
Kunst (als Schulfach)	Art	type	Art; Sorte; Typ
Rock	skirt	rock	Fels; Stein
stehen	to stand	to stay	bleiben; übernachten
(zu etw.) werden	to become	to get	bekommen

Diese Checkliste kann dir helfen, Fehler zu vermeiden. Prüfe alle deine Texte damit. Du kannst auch ein „Fehlertagebuch" führen, in dem du deine eigenen häufigen Fehler aufschreibst. So bist du beim nächsten Mal sicherer.

- **Schreibung:**
  - ☐ *gh* wird meist nicht gesprochen. Vergiss es beim Schreiben nicht: z. B. **high**, **eight**
  - ☐ *k* kommt vor *t* so gut wie nie vor: z. B. **a**ctivity – **A**ktivität, **O**ctober – **O**ktober
  - ☐ *sh* kommt viel häufiger vor als *sch*: z. B. **sh**ip, **sh**oot
- **Gleiche Aussprache, unterschiedliche Schreibung:**
  - ☐ [iː] z. B. th**ree**, t**ea**, th**ese**, p**eo**ple, f**ie**ld
  - ☐ [uː] z. B. f**oo**d, fr**ui**t, to d**o**, fl**ew**, supermarket, barbe**cue**, b**eau**tiful
  - ☐ [eə] z. B. sh**are**, f**air**, c**are**ful
  - ☐ [aɪ] z. B. wh**ite**, s**igh**t, r**ide**
- **Achtung bei Kurzformen von *to be* und den Possessivpronomen:**
  - ☐ th**ey're** (Kurzform von *they are*) [ðeə]
    th**eir** (ihr, ihre) [ðeə]
  - ☐ it's (Kurzform von *it is*) [ɪts]
    its (sein) [ɪts]
  - ☐ you're (Kurzform von *you are*) [jɔː]
    your (dein; deine) [jɔː]
- **Gleiche Aussprache, unterschiedliche Schreibung und Bedeutung:**
  - ☐ [iː] z. B. to s**ee** – sehen, s**ea** – Meer
  - ☐ [uː] z. B. t**wo** – zwei, t**oo** – auch
- **Verdoppelung des Endkonsonanten:**
  - ☐ to sto**p** – sto**pp**ing, sto**pp**ed
  - ☐ to win – win**n**ing, win**n**er
- **y wird zu ie:**
  - ☐ in der 3. Person Singular und in der Vergangenheitsform: z. B.
    to wor**ry** – he wor**ries** – he wor**ried**
    aber: to bu**y** – she bu**ys**
  - ☐ im Plural: z. B. ci**ty** – ci**ties**,
    par**ty** – par**ties**; **aber**: bo**y** – bo**ys**
  - ☐ bei der Steigerung von Adjektiven:
    z. B. hap**py** – hap**pier** – (the) hap**piest**
- **Ähnlichkeiten in Schreibung und Aussprache zu deutschen Wörtern:**
  - ☐ **who** – wer; **where** – wo
- **Ähnlich und doch anders:**
  - ☐ Wortendung *-le*:
    z. B. tit**le** – Titel;
    mid**dle** – Mittel-
  - ☐ *ph* statt *f*:
    z. B. **ph**one – Telefon;
    photo – Foto
- **Großschreibung:**
  - ☐ Monatsnamen und Wochentage: z. B. January, Monday
  - ☐ Eigennamen und geografische Namen: z. B. Koa, Penny, the Brooks, the Taj Mahal, Cape Town, South Africa, Australia
- **Plural:**
  - ☐ Der Plural bekommt normalerweise ein *s*:
    z. B. friend – friend**s**, chair – chair**s**,
    film – film**s**
  - ☐ Endet ein Wort auf *s* oder *x*, wird *es* angehängt: z. B. bus – bus**es**,
    box – box**es**
  - ☐ Manche Wörter haben einen unregelmäßigen Plural:
    z. B. man – men, child – children,
    shelf – shelves, mouse – mice
- **Apostroph:**
  - ☐ bei Kurzformen:
    z. B. she is → she's;
    they are → they're
  - ☐ beim Genitiv-s: z. B. Matt's friend, Emma's family, the Jacksons' house, the children's games
- **Wörterbuch:**
  - ☐ Prüfe die Schreibung aller Wörter, bei denen du dir nicht ganz sicher bist, indem du sie im Wörterbuch nachschlägst.

Word bank: Talking about experiences → Find more online: mn28pj

Where I went

museum

concert

town/city

zoo

cathedral

gallery

theme park

airport

stadium

mountains

Useful phrases

Impressions I had

The building looked/was really ...
The ... was crowded/empty/busy/quiet/cheap/expensive.
I was surprised that ...
It was great/exciting/interesting to see ...
The journey was really long/short/interesting/boring.
Maybe I'll go again one day.
I won't go again.

Things I found out

... was built in ...
... is the oldest/smallest/largest ...
I found out that ... came from/was born in/died in/visited ... in ...
... takes place every year/month/week/day.
I learned that ...
The guide told us about ...
Did you know that ...?

Word bank: Talking about being ill → Find more online: mn28pj

Being ill

I feel ...
ill.
sick.
weak.
tired.
a bit hot.

I have ...
a bad headache.
a high temperature.
a cold.
stomach ache.
a sore throat.
backache.

My head/foot/back/throat/arm/leg/stomach/ankle ... really hurts.

Giving advice

You should ...
go to the doctor's.
take some medicine/tablets.
go to the pharmacy.
stay in bed.
drink lots of water/tea.
do as the doctor says.
go back to the doctor if you don't feel better.

You shouldn't ...
do any sport for a week.
go to the party on Friday.
meet everyone in the snack bar.
stay up late.

Useful phrases

If you drink lots of water, you'll feel better.
If you take your medicine, you'll get better quicker.
If you stay in bed, you'll get more sleep.
You'll feel better if you sleep a lot.
Why don't you call me, and I'll come around and visit you?
Maybe you could call your mum and she could pick you up?
If you don't get better, you'll have to go back to the doctor.

Word bank: Presenting a company

→ Find more online: mn28pj

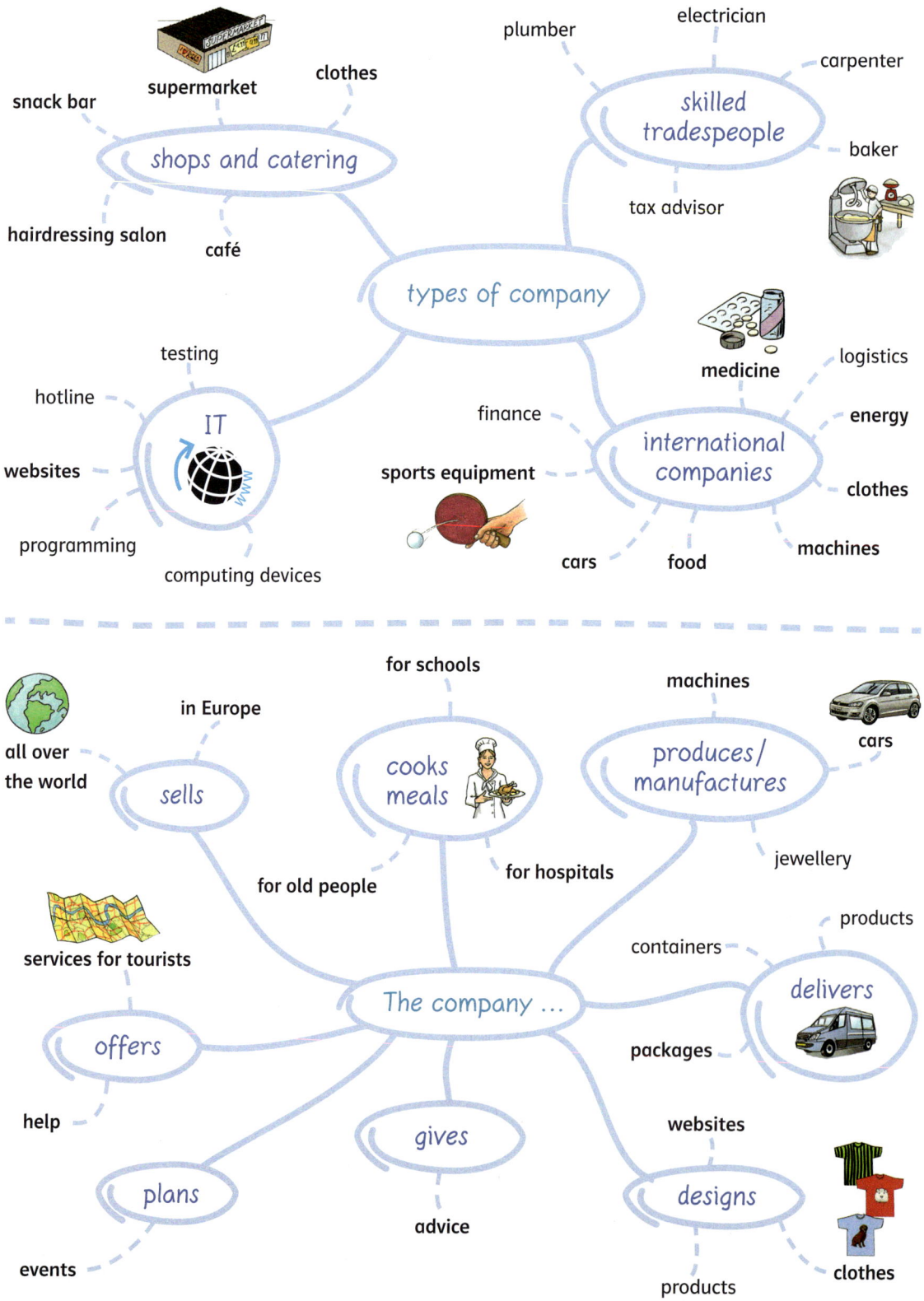

Word bank: Sustainable living

→ Find more online: mn28pj

sustainable living

What I can do

- eat more vegetarian food and less meat
- install solar panels on the roof
- reduce consumption
- take my own bags when I go shopping
- buy products that aren't in lots of packaging
- recycle as much as possible
- use public transport or my bike more often
- turn off electrical devices when I don't need them

What governments can do

- build more wind farms
- advise people about saving energy
- increase the price of flights
- research new ways of recycling
- make public transport cheaper
- improve public transport

Word bank: Talking about an accident

→ Find more online: mn28pj

What police officers say

What is your name, address and phone number?

What is your date of birth?

What did you see?

What time did the accident happen?

Who was involved?
How many cars / people were in the accident?
What happened (next)?

Can you explain that in more detail, please?

Are you sure about that?

I see. / Really. / Interesting.

Thank you for your help.

We will get in touch if we have any more questions.

What witnesses say

My name is ..., my address is ... and phone number ...

My date of birth is ...

First ...
Then ...
After that ...
I think that ...

I arrived at ...
I think the accident happened ... minutes before I arrived.

There was (a car) and (three) people in the accident.

The car / cyclist / van didn't stop / was going too fast.

Yes, I am.
I think so.
I'm not really sure now.

You're welcome.

No problem.

Word bank: Describing a role model → Find more online: mn28pj

Personal qualities

confident	I admire people who are confident in front of others.
considerate	People who put others first are considerate.
determined	Someone who gets what they want is determined.
enthusiastic	If you are enthusiastic you can get lots of people to help you.
generous	Generous people do a lot to help charities.
happy	It makes people happy to help others.
helpful	If you ask a helpful person, they will always help you.
honest	Honest people tell the truth.
kind	Kind people always have time for other people.
nervous	He is nervous but doesn't show it.
polite	You are polite if you say please and thank you to others.
proud	She is very proud of who she is.
reliable	Reliable people are known for being there when you need them.
respectful	I look up to people who are respectful to everyone.
tolerant	I admire people who are tolerant.
self-confident	Self-confident people post pictures on social media.
strong	In hard situations you have to be strong.

Useful phrases

I admire ... because he/she ...
I follow ... because he/she ...
I read that ...
I saw pictures of ...
... is known for ...
... helps homeless/sick/... people/animals.
... raised lots of money for charities.
... always has time for ...

Word bank: **Jobs and qualities** → Find more online: mn28pj

Jobs

with customers
baker Bäcker/-in
butcher Fleischer/-in; Metzger/-in
hairdresser Friseur/-in
salesperson Verkäufer/-in

working outside
animal keeper Tierpfleger/-in
bricklayer Maurer/-in
firefighter Feuerwehrmann/-frau
(landscape) gardener (Landschafts)Gärtner/-in

helping people
dentist's **assistant** Zahnarzthelfer/-in
nursery teacher Erzieher/-in
police officer Polizist/-in
speech therapist Logopäde/Logopädin

working with hands
carpenter Schreiner/-in; Tischler/-in
mechanic Mechaniker/-in
metalworker Metallbauer/-in
vehicle painter Fahrzeuglackierer/-in

being creative
chef Koch/Köchin
florist Florist/-in
media designer Mediengestalter/-in

working with computers
computer programmer Programmierer/-in
engineer Ingenieur/-in
office worker Büroarbeiter/-in

Qualities needed

creative
patient
flexible
well-organized
responsible
confident
good at listening to others
stay calm in difficult situations
like working outside
prefer **working in an office/inside**
can work in a team
good with one's hands

Word bank: Talking about an internship → Find more online: mn28pj

Useful phrases

The thing I liked best was ...
I'd like to try ... in the future.
I'd like to learn about ...
I don't think I'll ... again.
It helped me decide (not) to ...
I was surprised that ...
I didn't know that ...

Vocabulary

Das Vocabulary enthält alle neuen Wörter und Wendungen. Die Reihenfolge ist wie im Buch.

Die Wortliste ist in drei Spalten aufgeteilt:

Links findest du das englische Wort mit der Lautschrift in Klammern. (Die Lautschrift wird ganz unten auf jeder Seite im *Dictionary* erklärt.)

In der mittleren Spalte steht die deutsche Übersetzung.

Rechts findest du Beispielsätze, Hinweise und Tipps, die dir beim Lernen helfen.

Die **fett** gedruckten Wörter musst du lernen.

Symbole und Abkürzungen:

👄	Achtung Aussprache!	sth	something
✎	Achtung Schreibweise!	sb	somebody
↔	ist das Gegenteil von	*(sg)*	Einzahl (Singular)
→	ist verwandt mit	*(pl)*	Mehrzahl (Plural)
=	entspricht	R	ähnlich wie im Russischen
		T	ähnlich wie im Türkischen

Die *Word bank*-Seiten (S.146 bis 153) helfen dir, die *Task*-Aufgaben in den *Units* zu bearbeiten. Du findest dort nützlichen individuellen Wortschatz zum Thema der *Unit*, der dir hilft, über deine eigene Situation zu sprechen oder zu schreiben. Diese Wörter findest du auch im *Dictionary*.

Wenn du ein Wort nicht weißt und im Wörterbuch nachschlagen willst, schau auf den *Dictionary*-Seiten ab S.172 nach. Oder bei den *Instructions* auf S.221.

Zoom in – A world language

p. 8	**billion** [ˈbɪliən]	Milliarde	R биллион
	official language [əˌfɪʃl ˈlæŋgwɪdʒ]	Amtssprache	There are 22 **official languages** in India.
	majority [məˈdʒɒrəti]	Mehrheit; Mehrzahl	The **majority** of people speak English.
	speaker [ˈspiːkə]	Sprecher; Sprecherin; Redner; Rednerin	**speaker** → to speak
	(software) program [(ˌsɒfweə) ˈprəʊgræm]	(Software)Programm	His team writes **software programs**.
	half *(sg)* [hɑːf], **halves** *(pl)* [hɑːvz]	(die) Hälfte	**Half** of the population speaks English.
	competition [ˌkɒmpəˈtɪʃn]	Wettbewerb	James won the **competition**.
p. 9	to **communicate** [kəˈmjuːnɪkeɪt]	kommunizieren; sich verständigen	I can **communicate** in English.

English-speaking [ˌɪŋglɪʃˈspiːkɪŋ]	englischsprachig	The UK is an **English-speaking** country.
international [ˌɪntəˈnæʃnl]	international	Achtung Aussprache!
business [ˈbɪznɪs]	Geschäftswelt; Geschäft	English is the language of international **business**.
to **give** [gɪv]	halten	I have to **give** a presentation next week.
task [tɑːsk]	Aufgabe; Auftrag	They have to do these **tasks** in English.

Unit 1 Around Australia

p. 10	**around** [əˈraʊnd]	unterwegs (in)	This book is called '**Around** Australia'.

Intro

	G'day! (= Good day!) [gəˈdaɪ]	Hi!; Hallo!; Tag!	This is how you say hello in Australia.
	to **begin** [bɪˈgɪn]	beginnen; anfangen	In Australia, spring **begins** in September.
	Australian [ɒsˈtreɪliən]	Australier; Australierin; australisch	**Australian** → Australia
	creature [ˈkriːtʃə]	Lebewesen; Kreatur; Geschöpf	Lots of **creatures** live near the coast.
p. 11	to **break** [breɪk], **broke** [brəʊk], **broken** [ˈbrəʊkn]	brechen; zerbrechen; kaputt machen	Australia **broke** away from Antarctica.
	koala [kəʊˈɑːlə]	Koala	R коала T koala
	kangaroo [ˌkæŋgrˈuː]	Känguru	R кенгуру T kanguru
	Aboriginal people [æbəˌrɪdʒnl ˈpiːpl]	die Aborigines	**Aboriginal people** have been in Australia for over 50,000 years.
	British [ˈbrɪtɪʃ]	britisch	She drives a **British** car.
	settler [ˈsetlə]	Siedler; Siedlerin	The **settlers** came from the east.
	to **kill** [kɪl]	töten	They **killed** thousands of Aboriginal people.
	to **struggle** [ˈstrʌgl]	kämpfen; ringen; sich anstrengen; Mühe haben	They **struggled** for their independence.
	right [raɪt]	Recht	Aboriginal people wanted the same **rights**.
	flat [flæt]	flach; eben; platt	When the land is **flat** you can see far.
	the outback [ðiˈ aʊtbæk]	das Outback *(australisches Hinterland)*	Kangaroos live in **the outback**.
	long [lɒŋ]	*hier:* weit	They live a **long** way away from each other.

Topic 1

p. 12	**rock** [rɒk]	Fels; Stein	
	Aboriginal [ˌæbəˈrɪdʒnl]	Aborigine-; zur Aborigine-Kultur gehörend	Koa saw some **Aboriginal** dances.
	tribe [traɪb]	Stamm; Volksstamm	Koa's father is from an Aboriginal **tribe**.
	lifestyle [ˈlaɪfstaɪl]	Lebensstil; Lebensart; Lebensweise	the way you live your life
	disappointed [ˌdɪsəˈpɔɪntɪd]	enttäuscht	Some tourists were **disappointed**.
	helicopter [ˈhelɪkɒptə]	Helikopter; Hubschrauber	There are **helicopter** flights over Uluru.
	didgeridoo [ˌdɪdʒriˈduː]	Didgeridoo *(australisches Musikinstrument)*	Many Aboriginal people play the **didgeridoo**.
	colourful [ˈkʌləfl]	bunt	
	dot [dɒt]	Punkt	There is a **dot** in the website address.
	painting [ˈpeɪntɪŋ]	Gemälde	There were lots of **paintings** on the wall.
	afraid [əˈfreɪd]	ängstlich	A star is never **afraid**.
	giant [dʒaɪənt]	Riesen-; riesig	We saw **giant** creatures in the zoo.
	to **think of** [ˈθɪŋk‿əv]	davon halten	So what did you **think of** it?
	delicious [dɪˈlɪʃəs]	lecker; köstlich	Achtung Aussprache!
	to **learn** [lɜːn]	erfahren; herausfinden	They **learned** that a boy died in the fire.

Das kenne ich schon

adjectives for talking about experiences

afraid [əˈfreɪd]	ängstlich	excited [ɪkˈsaɪtɪd]	aufgeregt; begeistert
boring [ˈbɔːrɪŋ]	langweilig	exciting [ɪkˈsaɪtɪŋ]	spannend; aufregend
confident [ˈkɒnfɪdnt]	selbstsicher; selbstbewusst; sicher	happy [ˈhæpi]	glücklich
delicious [dɪˈlɪʃəs]	lecker; köstlich	interesting [ˈɪntrəstɪŋ]	interessant
disappointed [ˌdɪsəˈpɔɪntɪd]	enttäuscht	sad [sæd]	traurig
		surprised [səˈpraɪzd]	überrascht
		worried [ˈwʌrɪd]	beunruhigt; besorgt

Topic 2

p. 16	**receptionist** [rɪˈsepʃnɪst]	Arzthelfer; Arzthelferin	I told the **receptionist** my name.
	appointment [əˈpɔɪntmənt]	Termin	I've got an **appointment** at 9 o'clock.
	list [lɪst]	Liste	I can't find you in our **list** of patients.
	patient [ˈpeɪʃnt]	Patient; Patientin	The **patient** said he had a bad cold.

to **register** [ˈredʒɪstə]	sich registrieren lassen; sich eintragen; sich anmelden	You will have to **register** with us.
medical record [ˌmedɪkl ˈrekɔːd]	Krankenakte	We need your **medical records**.
ill [ɪl]	krank; schlecht	I feel really **ill** today.
Oh dear. [ˌəʊ ˈdɪə]	Oje.	**Oh dear.** What happened?
What's the matter? [ˌwɒts ðə ˈmætə]	Was ist los?; Was hast du?	You look ill. **What's the matter?**
high temperature [ˌhaɪ ˈtemprətʃə]	Fieber	Penny has a **high temperature**.
to **catch sth** [kætʃ]	*hier:* sich etw. einfangen *(medizinisch)*	Penny has **caught a cold**.
flu [fluː]	Grippe	A lot of people have had the **flu**.
to **be afraid** [biː əˈfreɪd]	befürchten	I'**m afraid** you've caught the flu.
to **get better** [ˌget ˈbetə]	sich wieder besser fühlen; sich verbessern	You'll **get better** soon.
prescription [prɪˈskrɪpʃn]	Rezept *(für Arzneimittel)*	Here is a **prescription** for some tablets.
medicine [ˈmedsn]	Medikamente; Medizin	This **medicine** will help you.
to **take** [teɪk]	*hier:* einnehmen	Don't forget to **take** your medicine.
tablet [ˈtæblət]	Tablette	Have you got any headache **tablets**, please?
pharmacy [ˈfɑːməsi]	Apotheke	Take the prescription to the **pharmacy**.
You're welcome. [jɔː ˈwelkəm]	Gern geschehen.	Thanks. – **You're welcome.**
Get well soon! [ˌget wel ˈsuːn]	Gute Besserung!	Goodbye and **get well soon**!

Das kenne ich schon

at the doctor's

receptionist [rɪˈsepʃnɪst]	Arzthelfer; Arzthelferin
patient [ˈpeɪʃnt]	Patient; Patientin
doctor [ˈdɒktə]	Arzt; Ärztin
nurse [nɜːs]	Krankenpfleger; Krankenschwester
appointment [əˈpɔɪntmənt]	Termin
medical record [ˌmedɪkl ˈrekɔːd]	Krankenakte
prescription [prɪˈskrɪpʃn]	Rezept *(für Arzneimittel)*
medicine [ˈmedsn]	Medikamente; Medizin
tablet [ˈtæblət]	Tablette
pharmacy [ˈfɑːməsi]	Apotheke
ill [ɪl]	krank; schlecht
flu [fluː]	Grippe
cold [kəʊld]	Erkältung
tired [ˈtaɪəd]	müde
high temperature [ˌhaɪ ˈtemprətʃə]	Fieber
headache [ˈhedeɪk]	Kopfweh; Kopfschmerzen
to be sick [biː ˈsɪk]	sich übergeben
to take [teɪk], took [tʊk], taken [ˈteɪkn]	*hier:* einnehmen
to catch sth [kætʃ]	*hier:* sich etw. einfangen *(medizinisch)*
to hurt [hɜːt], hurt [hɜːt], hurt [hɜːt]	verletzen; wehtun
to register [ˈredʒɪstə]	sich registrieren lassen; sich eintragen; sich anmelden
Get well soon! [ˌget wel ˈsuːn]	Gute Besserung!

Text

p. 20	**danger** [ˈdeɪndʒə]	Gefahr	**danger** → dangerous
	reef [riːf]	Riff	R риф T resif
	coral [ˈkɒrəl]	Koralle	R коралл
	climate change [ˈklaɪmət ˌtʃeɪndʒ]	Klimawandel	**Climate change** is dangerous.
	bleaching [ˈbliːtʃɪŋ]	Bleichen; Ausbleichen	Coral **bleaching** is a problem.
	temperature [ˈtemprətʃə]	Temperatur	R температура
	alga *(sg)* [ˈælgə], **algae** *(pl)* [ˈældʒiː]	Alge	Warm water kills the **algae** on the coral.
	area [ˈeəriə]	Fläche; Bereich	Large **areas** of the reef have already died.
	oil spill [ˈɔɪl ˌspɪl]	Ölteppich; Ölpest	**Oil spills** cause a lot of damage.
	to **recover** [rɪˈkʌvə]	sich erholen	It will take years for the reef to **recover**.
	government [ˈgʌvnmənt]	Regierung	✎ Achtung Schreibweise! gover<u>n</u>ment
	law [lɔː]	Gesetz	The government has made new **laws**.
	however [haʊˈevə]	jedoch	**However**, I still don't like him.
	alone [əˈləʊn]	allein	**alone** ↔ together
	may [meɪ]	können; dürfen	The reef **may** die soon.

	completely [kəmˈpliːtli]	völlig	That's **completely** wrong!
p. 21	**department** [dɪˈpɑːtmənt]	Abteilung	Let's go to the shoe **department**.
	energy [ˈenədʒi]	Energie; Kraft	We have to save more **energy**.
	GPO [ˌdʒiː piː ˈəʊ]	Hauptpostamt	Sydney's **GPO** building is very beautiful.
	to **protest** [prəˈtest]	protestieren	I **protested** against the new law.
	destruction [dɪˈstrʌkʃn]	Zerstörung	Can we stop the **destruction** of the reef?

Film

wide [waɪd]	breit; groß	**manta ray** [ˈmæntə ˌreɪ]	Teufelsrochen
whale shark [ˈweɪl ˌʃɑːk]	Walhai	**full of** [ˈfʊl‿əv]	voller
saltwater crocodile [sɔːltˌwɔːtə ˈkrɒkədaɪl]	Salzwasserkrokodil	**as much as** [əz ˈmʌtʃəz]	bis zu
dolphin [ˈdɒlfɪn]	Delfin	**real** [rɪəl]	echt; richtig; wirklich

Speaking skills

p. 28	**corner** [ˈkɔːnə]	Ecke	There's a TV in the **corner** of the room.
	at the bottom [æt ðə ˈbɒtəm]	unten	The sea is **at the bottom** of the picture.
	at the top [æt ðə ˈtɒp]	oben	The sky is **at the top**.

Unit 2 Exploring India

Intro

p. 36	**slum** [slʌm]	Slum; Elendsviertel	Millions of poor people live in **slums**.
	Indian [ˈɪndiən]	Inder; Inderin; indisch	Most **Indians** speak English.
p. 37	to **lead** [liːd], **led** [led], **led** [led]	anführen; führen; leiten	A president **leads** a country.
	protest [ˈprəʊtest]	Protest; Demonstration	**protest** → to protest
	the British [ðə ˈbrɪtɪʃ]	die Briten	There were protests against **the British**.
	independent [ˌɪndɪˈpendənt]	unabhängig	India is an **independent** country now.
	environmental [ɪnˌvaɪrnˈmentl]	Umwelt-	**environmental** → environment
	pollution [pəˈluːʃn]	Verschmutzung	There are problems with **pollution**.
	waste [weɪst]	Abfall	**waste** = rubbish
	arranged marriage [əˌreɪndʒd ˈmærɪdʒ]	arrangierte Hochzeit	There are many **arranged marriages** in India.
	wedding [ˈwedɪŋ]	Hochzeit	There was a big party after the **wedding**.

several [ˈsevrl]	mehrere; einige; verschiedene	**several** = three or more, but not many

Topic 1

p. 38 **computer programmer** [kəmˌpjuːtə ˈprəʊgræmə]	Programmierer; Programmiererin	My sister is a **computer programmer**.
IT (Information Technology) [ˌaɪˈtiː (ɪnfəˌmeɪʃn tekˈnɒlədʒi)]	Informatik; Informationstechnik	Vibhu works for a big **IT** company.
to **solve** [sɒlv]	lösen	I like **solving** difficult problems.
to **enjoy + -ing** [ɪnˈdʒɔɪ … ɪŋ]	mögen; Gefallen finden an; genießen; genießen, … zu tun	I **enjoy** listening to music.
tour guide [ˈtʊə ˌgaɪd]	Reiseleiter; Reiseleiterin	Our **tour guide** knew a lot about India.
prince [prɪns]	Prinz	Achtung Schreibweise! prin<u>ce</u>
assembly line [əˈsembli ˌlaɪn]	Fließband	Manjit works on the **assembly line**.
to **make** [meɪk]	*hier:* herstellen	The company **makes** car parts.
goods *(pl only)* [gʊdz]	Waren; Güter	My parents sell **goods** in a small shop.
machine [məˈʃiːn]	Maschine; Automat	The **machines** were very loud.
true [truː]	wahr; richtig	It is **true** that he is leaving her.
virtual [ˈvɜːtʃuəl]	virtuell	I'm a **virtual** assistant and work online.
office [ˈɒfɪs]	Büro	My dad works in an **office** in London.

Das kenne ich schon

world of work

to communicate [kəˈmjuːnɪkeɪt]	kommunizieren; sich verständigen	office [ˈɒfɪs]	Büro
to finish [ˈfɪnɪʃ]	beenden; fertig machen; erledigen; enden; aufhören	assembly line [əˈsembli ˌlaɪn]	Fließband
to help [help]	helfen	machine [məˈʃiːn]	Maschine; Automat
to organize [ˈɔːgənaɪz]	organisieren	working hours *(pl)* [ˈwɜːkɪŋ ˌaʊəz]	Arbeitszeit
to sell [sel], sold [səʊld], sold [səʊld]	verkaufen	customer [ˈkʌstəmə]	Kunde; Kundin
to solve [sɒlv]	lösen	phone call [ˈfəʊn ˌkɔːl]	Telefonanruf; Anruf
to start [stɑːt]	anfangen; beginnen; starten	reservation [ˌrezəˈveɪʃn]	Reservierung
outside [ˌaʊtˈsaɪd]	außen; draußen; im Freien	(software) program [(ˌsɒfweə) ˈprəʊgræm]	(Software)Programm
		e-mail [ˈiːmeɪl]	E-Mail

Das kenne ich schon

phrases with -ing

to be good at + -ing [bi: ˈgʊd‿ət ...ɪŋ]	gut sein in; gut sein bei	to hate + -ing [ˌheɪt ˈ...ɪŋ]	hassen; nicht mögen
can't stand + -ing [ˌkɑ:nt ˈstænd ...ɪŋ]	nicht ausstehen können; nicht ertragen	to like + -ing [ˌlaɪk ˈ...ɪŋ]	mögen; gerne tun
to enjoy + -ing [ˌɪndʒɔɪ ˈ...ɪŋ]	mögen; Gefallen finden an; genießen; genießen, … zu tun	to look forward to + -ing [ˌlʊk ˈfɔ:wəd tə ...ɪŋ]	sich freuen auf

Topic 2

p. 42	**teenager** [ˈti:nˌeɪdʒə]	Teenager; Jugendlicher; Jugendliche	**Teenagers** in India must work hard.
	economy [ɪˈkɒnəmi]	Wirtschaft	R экономия
	to **grow** [grəʊ], **grew** [gru:], **grown** [grəʊn]	wachsen; anbauen; züchten; ziehen	The economy is **growing** very fast.
	year-old [ˌjɪər‿ˈəʊld]	-jährig; Jahre alt	My **2-year-old** sister sleeps a lot.
	farming [ˈfɑ:mɪŋ]	Landwirtschaft; Ackerbau	**farming** → farm, farmer
	sustainable [səˈsteɪnəbl]	nachhaltig	Farming needs to be more **sustainable**.
	fertiliser [ˈfɜ:tɪlaɪzə]	Dünger	**Fertilisers** cause pollution of the fields.
	crop [krɒp]	Feldfrucht; Ernte	**Crops** are the plants that farmers grow.
	to **damage** [ˈdæmɪdʒ]	beschädigen; schaden	The fire **damaged** a lot of houses.
	soil [sɔɪl]	Boden; Erde	Fertilisers pollute the **soil**.
	sanitation [ˌsænɪˈteɪʃn]	sanitäre Anlagen	Some villages don't have good **sanitation**.
	toilet [ˈtɔɪlət]	Toilette	
	to **pollute** [pəˈlu:t]	verschmutzen; verunreinigen	**to pollute** → pollution
	drinking [ˈdrɪŋkɪŋ]	Trink-	Everyone needs clean **drinking** water.
	living [ˈlɪvɪŋ]	Lebensweise; Wohnen; Leben	**living** → to live

Das kenne ich schon

living in the country

animal [ˈænɪml]	Tier	crop [krɒp]	Feldfrucht; Ernte
farm [fɑ:m]	Bauernhof	plant [plɑ:nt]	Pflanze
farmer [fɑ:mə]	Bauer; Bäuerin; Landwirt; Landwirtin	to grow [grəʊ], grew [gru:], grown [grəʊn]	wachsen; anbauen; züchten; ziehen
farming [ˈfɑ:mɪŋ]	Landwirtschaft; Ackerbau	to feed [fi:d], fed [fed], fed [fed]	füttern
village [ˈvɪlɪdʒ]	Dorf	fertiliser [ˈfɜ:tɪlaɪzə]	Dünger
field [fi:ld]	Feld	pollution [pəˈlu:ʃn]	Verschmutzung
soil [sɔɪl]	Erde; Boden		

Text

p. 46	**certainly** [ˈsɜːtnli]	auf jeden Fall; offensichtlich; sicher	He **certainly** likes her.
	lawyer [ˈlɔɪə]	Anwalt; Anwältin; Jurist; Juristin	Gandhi became a **lawyer**.
	non-violent [ˌnɒnˈvaɪəlnt]	friedlich; gewaltfrei	Gandhi believed in **non-violent** protest.
	to **break the law** [ˌbreɪk ðə ˈlɔː]	gegen das Gesetz verstoßen	Gandhi wasn't afraid to **break the law**.
	prison [ˈprɪzn]	Gefängnis	He's in **prison**. 
	soul [səʊl]	Seele	Mahatma means 'great **soul**'.
p. 47	**salt** [sɔːlt]	Salz	I like **salt** on my chips.
	peaceful [ˈpiːsfl]	friedlich	Gandhi was a **peaceful** man.
	to **join** [dʒɔɪn]	sich anschließen; beitreten	Come and **join** our team.
	march [mɑːtʃ]	Marsch; Kundgebung	Gandhi organized non-violent **marches**.
	unfortunately [ʌnˈfɔːtʃnətli]	leider; unglücklicherweise	**Unfortunately**, there was a lot of violence.
	Hindu [ˈhɪnduː]	Hindu; hinduistisch	Gandhi was a **Hindu**.
	to **respect** [rɪˈspekt]	respektieren	I love and **respect** animals.
	religion [rɪˈlɪdʒn]	Religion	Gandhi respected other **religions**.
	extremist [ɪkˈstriːmɪst]	Extremist; Extremistin	Achtung Aussprache!

Das kenne ich schon

protests

march [mɑːtʃ]	Marsch; Kundgebung	to lead [liːd], led [led], led [led]	anführen; führen; leiten
non-violent [ˌnɒnˈvaɪəlnt]	friedlich; gewaltfrei	violence *(no pl)* [ˈvaɪəlns]	Gewalt
protest [ˈprəʊtest]	Protest; Demonstration	prison [ˈprɪzn]	Gefängnis
to protest [prəˈtest]	protestieren		
to fight [faɪt]	kämpfen; (sich) streiten		

Film

feed [fiːd]	ernähren	delivery service [dɪˈlɪvri ˌsɜːvɪs]	Lieferdienst

Writing skills

p. 54	**in time** [ɪn ˈtaɪm]	rechtzeitig; pünktlich	I hope we'll be there **in time**.
	crazy [ˈkreɪzi]	verrückt	Look at her! She is **crazy**!
	sacred [ˈseɪkrɪd]	heilig	In India cows are **sacred**.

Unit 3 Discover South Africa

p. 62	to **discover** [dɪˈskʌvə]	entdecken	Let's **discover** the world.
	South Africa [ˌsaʊθ‿ˈæfrɪkə]	Südafrika	**South Africa** is a beautiful country.

Intro

	parliament [ˈpɑːləmənt]	Parlament	Achtung Schreibweise! parliament
	African [ˈæfrɪkən]	afrikanisch; aus Afrika; Afrikaner; Afrikanerin	T Afrikalı
	apartheid *(no pl)* [əˈpɑːtaɪt]	Apartheid	**Apartheid** started in the early 1940s.
	to **separate** [ˈsepreɪt]	trennen	Achtung Schreibweise! separate
	township [ˈtaʊnʃɪp]	Township *(ehemalige Wohnsiedlungen für die schwarze Bevölkerung in Südafrika)*; Armutsviertel	Poor people live in **townships**.
	to **end** [end]	enden; beenden; aufhören	Classes **ended** at 2:30 p.m. on Friday.
p. 63	**South African** [ˌsaʊθ‿ˈæfrɪkən]	Südafrikaner; Südafrikanerin; südafrikanisch; aus Südafrika	**South African** → South Africa
	high school [ˈhaɪ ˌskuːl]	High School *(weiterführende Schule, Oberstufe)*	He didn't finish **high school**.
	rich [rɪtʃ]	reich	Some people in South Africa are very **rich**.
	electricity [ˌelɪkˈtrɪsəti]	Strom; Elektrizität	A lot of houses don't have **electricity**.
	safari [səˈfɑːri]	Safari	Achtung Aussprache!
	lion [ˈlaɪən]	Löwe	
	elephant [ˈelɪfənt]	Elefant	
	buffalo *(sg)* [ˈbʌfləʊ], **buffaloes** *(pl)* [ˈbʌfləʊz]	Büffel	We saw **buffaloes** at the zoo.
	square [skweə]	Quadrat-	It has an area of 1,100 **square** kilometres.

Topic 1

p. 64	to **hit** [hɪt]	*hier:* anfahren; rammen	The car **hit** the bus.
	to **injure** [ˈɪndʒə]	verletzen	Piet was **injured** in the accident.
	driving licence [ˈdraɪvɪŋ ˌlaɪsns]	Führerschein	You need a **driving licence** to drive a car.
	to **add** [æd]	hinzufügen	"I'll come back later", she **added**.

to **brake** [breɪk]	bremsen	The car **braked** but it was too late.
to **skid** [skɪd]	schleudern; schlittern	The car **skidded** and hit the bus.
to **crash** [kræʃ]	krachen	The car **crashed** into the bus.
wallet ['wɒlɪt]	Brieftasche; Geldbeutel; Geldbörse	Oh no! I forgot my **wallet**!
bang [bæŋ]	peng; Knall	There was a noise and then, **bang**!
police station [pə'liːs ˌsteɪʃn]	Polizeirevier; Polizeiwache	We all had to go to the **police station**.
detail ['diːteɪl]	Detail; Einzelheit	T detay

Das kenne ich schon

road accidents

road accident ['rəʊdˌæksɪdnt]	Verkehrsunfall	detail ['diːteɪl]	Detail; Einzelheit
accident ['æksɪdnt]	Unfall	hospital ['hɒspɪtl]	Krankenhaus
fast [fɑːst]	schnell	to injure ['ɪndʒə]	verletzen
to hit [hɪt], hit [hɪt], hit [hɪt]	anfahren; rammen	to drive [draɪv], drove [drəʊv], driven ['drɪvn]	fahren
to brake [breɪk]	bremsen	driver ['draɪvə]	Fahrer; Fahrerin
to skid [skɪd]	schleudern; schlittern	driving licence ['draɪvɪŋ ˌlaɪsns]	Führerschein
to crash [kræʃ]	krachen	damage ['dæmɪdʒ]	Schäden; Schaden; Beschädigung
witness ['wɪtnəs]	Zeuge; Zeugin	to damage ['dæmɪdʒ]	schaden; beschädigen
bang [bæŋ]	peng; Knall	news [njuːz]	Nachricht(en)
police station [pə'liːs ˌsteɪʃn]	Polizeirevier; Polizeiwache	newspaper ['njuːsˌpeɪpə]	Zeitung
police officer [pə'liːsˌɒfɪsə]	Polizeibeamter; Polizeibeamtin		

Topic 2

p. 68	**role model** ['rəʊl ˌmɒdl]	Vorbild	Miriam Makeba is Mia's **role model**.
	podcast ['pɒdkɑːst]	Podcast	I got the new **podcast** last night.
	inspiring [ɪn'spaɪərɪŋ]	inspirierend; anregend	The programme is about **inspiring** people.
	songwriter ['sɒŋˌraɪtə]	Songschreiber; Songschreiberin; Liedermacher; Liedermacherin	She's a **songwriter** – she writes songs.
	to **admire** [əd'maɪə]	bewundern	I don't know who I **admire** most.
	inspiration [ˌɪnspɪ'reɪʃn]	Inspiration; Eingebung	Achtung Aussprache!
	to **achieve** [ə'tʃiːv]	erreichen; erfolgreich sein; leisten; vollbringen	Miriam Makeba **achieved** a lot.
	director [dɪ'rektə]	Regisseur; Regisseurin	Zackie Achmat is a famous film **director**.
	gay [geɪ]	homosexuell; schwul; Schwuler	He's **gay**. He loves men.

lesbian [ˈlezbiən]	homosexuell; lesbisch; Lesbe	She is **lesbian** and loves women.
HIV [ˌeɪtʃaɪˈviː]	HIV; HI-Virus; HIV-	There is more information about **HIV** today.
AIDS [eɪdz]	Aids *(erworbene Immunabwehrschwäche)*	He has helped many people with **AIDS**.
disease [dɪˈziːz]	Krankheit	This new **disease** is very dangerous.
medication [ˌmedɪˈkeɪʃn]	Medikament; Arznei; Arzneimittel	Medicine and tablets are **medication**.
at first [ət ˈfɜːst]	zuerst; zunächst	I wasn't happy **at first**, then it was OK.
right away [ˌraɪt‿əˈweɪ]	sofort; gleich	He didn't take medication **right away**.
drug [drʌg]	Medikament; Arznei; Arzneimittel	He fought for cheaper **drugs**.
only [ˈəʊnli]	*hier:* erst	He **only** took medication much later.
to **pay** [peɪ]	bezahlen	Poorer people couldn't **pay** for it.

Das kenne ich schon

for – since

for [fɔː]	seit	since [sɪns]	seit
for two years [fə ˈtuː ˌjɪəz]	seit zwei Jahren	since 2020 [sɪns ˈtwentitwenti]	seit 2020
for three hours [fə ˈθriː ˌaʊəz]	seit drei Stunden	since last year [ˌsɪns ˈlɑːst jɪə]	seit letztem Jahr
for a long time [fər‿ə ˈlɒŋ taɪm]	seit Langem	since I was born [sɪns‿aɪ wəz ˈbɔːn]	seit meiner Geburt
for many years [fə ˈmæni ˌjɪəz]	seit vielen Jahren	since 3 o'clock [sɪns ˌθriː əˈklɒk]	seit 3 Uhr

Text

p. 72	**unemployed** [ˌʌnɪmˈplɔɪd]	arbeitslos	**unemployed** → employee
	organization [ˌɔːgnaɪˈzeɪʃn]	Organisation	**organization** → organize
	to **cut down** [ˌkʌt ˈdaʊn]	fällen	Our workers **cut down** trees.
	to **control** [kənˈtrəʊl]	kontrollieren	The workers **control** the area.
	to **be in charge (of)** [biː ˌɪn ˈtʃɑːdʒ (əv)]	leiten; zuständig sein (für); die Verantwortung tragen (für)	Shaka would like to **be in charge of** the office.
	guitar [gɪˈtɑː]	Gitarre	
	a bit [ə ˈbɪt]	ein bisschen	At first, I was **a bit** worried.
	fortunately [ˈfɔːtʃnətli]	zum Glück	**fortunately** ↔ unfortunately
	Afrikaans [ˌæfrɪˈkɑːns]	Afrikaans *(Sprache in Südafrika)*	Keeya speaks English and **Afrikaans**.
p. 73	**Sesotho** [sɪˈsuːtuː]	Sesotho *(Sprache in Südafrika)*	I speak the **Sesotho** language at home.
	kindergarten [ˈkɪndəˌgɑːtn]	Kindergarten	✎ Achtung Schreibweise: kindergarten

preschool [pri:ˈsku:l]	Vorschul-; Vorschule	Do you remember your **preschool** teacher?
to **do handicrafts** [ˌdu: ˈhændikra:fts]	basteln	I **do handicrafts** in my free time.
a week [ə ˈwi:k]	in der Woche; pro Woche	I have school five days **a week**.
medical insurance [ˌmedɪkl‿ɪnˈʃʊərns]	Krankenversicherung	My family doesn't have **medical insurance**.
hope [həʊp]	Hoffnung	**hope** → to hope

Film

baboon [bəˈbu:n]	Pavian	flower [ˈflaʊə]	Blume

Mediation skills

p. 80	**distance** [ˈdɪstns]	Entfernung; Distanz	Find out the **distance** from A to B.
	gate [geɪt]	Tor	
	emergency [ɪˈmɜ:dʒnsi]	Notfall	Help! It's an **emergency**.
	to **disturb** [dɪˈstɜ:b]	stören; belästigen	Never **disturb** the animals.
	as long as [əz ˈlɒŋ‿əz]	solange; sofern	**As long as** we're together, we'll be safe.
	to **follow** [ˈfɒləʊ]	befolgen; folgen	**to follow** → follower
	rule [ru:l]	Regel	We must follow the **rules**.
	situation [ˌsɪtjuˈeɪʃn]	Situation	This was a very dangerous **situation**.
p. 81	**nature** [ˈneɪtʃə]	Natur	The ranger likes **nature** very much.
	could [kʊd]	könnte	**Could** you open the window, please?
	to **repeat** [rɪˈpi:t]	wiederholen	Could you **repeat** it, please?
	to **explain** [ɪkˈspleɪn]	erklären	Could you **explain** that again, please?

Unit 4 News from New Zealand

p. 88	**New Zealand** [ˌnju: ˈzi:lənd]	Neuseeland	**New Zealand** is near Australia.

Intro

careers [kəˈrɪəz]	Berufs-	**careers** → career
advisor [ədˈvaɪzə]	Berater; Beraterin	**advisor** → advice
a third [ə ˈθɜ:d]	ein Drittel	**A third** of my class is boys.
industry [ˈɪndəstri]	Industriezweig; Gewerbe	Achtung Aussprache!

p. 89	**volunteer** [ˌvɒlənˈtɪə]	Freiwilliger; Freiwillige; ehrenamtlicher Helfer; ehrenamtliche Helferin	**Volunteers** help people and don't get any money.
	member [ˈmembə]	Mitglied	The **members** of my family live together.
	club [klʌb]	Verein	R клуб
	free-time [ˌfriːˈtaɪm]	Freizeit-	Rugby is a popular **free-time** activity.
	Maori [ˈmaʊri]	Maori-; maorisch; Maori	R маори T Maori
	people [ˈpiːpl]	*hier:* Volk	What do you know about the Maori **people**?
	landscape [ˈlændskeɪp]	Landschaft	New Zealand has amazing **landscapes**.
	volcano *(sg)* [vɒlˈkeɪnəʊ], **volcanoes** *(pl)* [vɒlˈkeɪnəʊz]	Vulkan	R вулкан T volkan 

Topic 1

p. 90	**form** [fɔːm]	Formular	The careers advisor looked at Liam's **form**.
	future [ˈfjuːtʃə]	zukünftig; Zukunfts-	Liam isn't sure about his **future** career.
	Ms [mɪz]	Frau *(Anrede)*	Our teacher is called **Ms** Miller.
	to **complete** [kəmˈpliːt]	ausfüllen; machen	He **completed** the form online.
	suitability [ˌsuːtəˈbɪləti]	Eignungs-; Eignung; Tauglichkeit	The **suitability** test was useful.
	test [test]	Test; Klassenarbeit	Who likes class **tests**?
	result [rɪˈzʌlt]	Ergebnis	You can find the **results** here.
	work experience [ˈwɜːkˌɪkˌspɪəriəns]	Berufserfahrung; Praktikum	Liam wants to get some **work experience**.
	mechanic [mɪˈkænɪk]	Mechaniker; Mechanikerin	Liam doesn't want to become a **mechanic**.
	garage [ˈgærɑːʒ]	Kfz-Werkstatt; Tankstelle; Garage	Mechanics work in **garages**.
	to **go wrong** [ˌgəʊ ˈrɒŋ]	schiefgehen	When things **go wrong**, I don't get angry.
	calm [kɑːm]	ruhig; friedlich	I was **calm** when I spoke to the police.
	support [səˈpɔːt]	Unterstützung; Hilfe	My parents give me lots of **support**.
	communication [kəˌmjuːnɪˈkeɪʃn]	Kommunikation	**communication** → to communicate
	might [maɪt]	könnte	We **might** see a wild animal.
	tourist information centre [ˌtʊərɪst ɪnfəˈmeɪʃn ˌsentə]	Touristeninformation	Where's the **Tourist Information Centre**?
	to **study (for) sth** [ˈstʌdi (fə)]	(auf einen Abschluss) studieren; (für) etw. lernen	You can **study for a certificate** at school.
	certificate [səˈtɪfɪkət]	Zertifikat; Bescheinigung; Urkunde; Zeugnis	✎ Achtung Schreibweise! certificate

to **take an exam** [ˌteɪk ˌən ˌɪgˈzæm]	eine Prüfung schreiben; ein Examen schreiben	You'll have to **take an exam** at the end.
careers day [kəˈrɪəz ˌdeɪ]	Berufsinformationstag	There's a **careers day** at school next week.
employer [ɪmˈplɔɪə]	Arbeitgeber; Arbeitgeberin	**employer** → employee
to **count on sb** [ˌkaʊnt ˈɒn]	sich auf jmdn. verlassen	You can **count on us**.
to **mind sth** [maɪnd]	etwas gegen etw. haben; einem etwas ausmachen	I don't **mind** hard work.
tool [tuːl]	Werkzeug; Gerät	

Das kenne ich schon

careers advice

career [kəˈrɪə]	Laufbahn; Karriere; Beruf	to take an exam [ˌteɪk ˌən ˌɪgˈzæm]	eine Prüfung schreiben; ein Examen schreiben
careers [kəˈrɪəz]	Berufs-	certificate [səˈtɪfɪkət]	Zertifikat; Bescheinigung; Urkunde; Zeugnis
advice [ədˈvaɪs]	Rat; Ratschlag	qualification [ˌkwɒlɪfɪˈkeɪʃn]	Ausbildung; Qualifikation; Abschluss; Schulabschluss
advisor [ədˈvaɪzə]	Berater; Beraterin	future [ˈfjuːtʃə]	Zukunft
careers day [kəˈrɪəz ˌdeɪ]	Berufsinformationstag	company [ˈkʌmpəni]	Unternehmen; Firma; Gesellschaft
to complete [kəmˈpliːt]	ausfüllen; machen	employer [ɪmˈplɔɪə]	Arbeitgeber; Arbeitgeberin
suitability [ˌsuːtəˈbɪləti]	Eignungs-, Eignung; Tauglichkeit	training [ˈtreɪnɪŋ]	Ausbildung; Training
test [test]	Test; Klassenarbeit		
result [rɪˈzʌlt]	Ergebnis		

Topic 2

p. 94	**retail** [ˈriːteɪl]	Einzelhandel	Would you like a job in **retail**?
	report [rɪˈpɔːt]	Bericht	The students are going to write a **report**.
	apprenticeship [əˈprentɪʃɪp]	Ausbildung; Lehre	I will do an **apprenticeship** after school.
	shop assistant [ˈʃɒp ˌəˌsɪstnt]	Verkäufer; Verkäuferin	The **shop assistant** gave me my things.
	product [ˈprɒdʌkt]	Produkt; Erzeugnis	Achtung Aussprache!
	checkout [ˈtʃekaʊt]	Kasse	Please pay at the **checkouts**.
	to **fill** [fɪl]	füllen; befüllen	I **fill** the shelves and make them look nice.
	to **present** [prɪˈzent]	präsentieren	**to present** → presentation
	to **work** [wɜːk]	funktionieren	I can't call you, my phone doesn't **work**.
	supplier [səˈplaɪə]	Zulieferer; Anbieter	We get our products from local **suppliers**.
	to **order** [ˈɔːdə]	bestellen	The supermarket **ordered** more fish.
	to **open** [ˈəʊpn]	eröffnen	The supermarket **opened** in 2008.

community [kəˈmjuːnəti]	Gemeinde; Gemeinschaft	Many **communities** don't have enough money.
to **donate** [dəˈneɪt]	spenden; stiften	We **donate** food to local charities.
to **reduce** [rɪˈdjuːs]	reduzieren; vermindern; verringern	We must **reduce** the rubbish in our cities.
worth of [ˈwɜːθ‿əv]	im Wert von	We gave NZ$3 million's **worth of** food.
intern [ˈɪntɜːn]	Praktikant; Praktikantin	**intern** → internship
to **be included** [biː ɪnˈkluːdɪd]	mit enthalten sein; inbegriffen sein	A picnic lunch **is included** in the trip.
although [ɔːlˈðəʊ]	obwohl	**Although** she was slow, she wasn't late.

Das kenne ich schon

in a supermarket

to sell [sel], sold [səʊld], sold [səʊld]	verkaufen	checkout [ˈtʃekaʊt]	Kasse
retail [ˈriːteɪl]	Einzelhandel	customer service [ˌkʌstəmə ˈsɜːvɪs]	Kundenbetreuung; Kundendienst; Kundenservice
shop [ʃɒp]	Laden; Geschäft	supplier [səˈplaɪə]	Zulieferer; Anbieter
shop assistant [ˈʃɒp‿əˌsɪstnt]	Verkäufer; Verkäuferin	to deliver [dɪˈlɪvə]	liefern; ausliefern
to fill [fɪl]	füllen; befüllen	product [ˈprɒdʌkt]	Produkt; Erzeugnis
shelf *(sg)* [ʃelf], shelves *(pl)* [ʃelvz]	Regal; Regalbrett	customer [ˈkʌstəmə]	Kunde; Kundin
to pack [pæk]	einpacken; packen	to buy [baɪ], bought [bɔːt], bought [bɔːt]	kaufen
bag [bæg]	Tasche; Tüte		

Text

p. 98	**rider** [ˈraɪdə]	Reiter; Reiterin	**rider** → to ride
	great- [greɪt]	Ur-	My **great**-grandfather ist very old.
	grandmother [ˈgræn‿mʌðə]	Großmutter	**grandmother** = grandma
	chief [tʃiːf]	Häuptling	The leader of a group or tribe.
	to **found** [faʊnd]	gründen; begründen	The city was **founded** in 1718.
	bay [beɪ]	Bucht	
	prayer [preə]	Gebet	Say a **prayer** for me on Sunday.
	deep [diːp]	tief	The stone was too **deep**.
	to **try hard** [ˌtraɪ ˈhɑːd]	sich anstrengen	I always **try hard** in my class tests.
	to **get back** [ˌget ˈbæk]	zurückkommen; zurückgehen	When he **got back** home, he felt very sad.

to **lament** [lə'ment]	klagen	Paka **lamented** very loudly in his room.
because of [bɪ'kɒz‿əv]	wegen	I was late **because of** the weather.
to **wish** [wɪʃ]	wünschen	I **wish** every day was Saturday.
out [aʊt]	hinaus	And then we went **out** into the sea.
p. 99 **wonder** ['wʌndə]	Wunder	No **wonder** the boys couldn't get it.
to **stand up** [ˌstænd‿'ʌp]	aufstehen	He **stood up** and left the room.
mask [mɑ:sk]	Maske	R маска T maske
to **point** [pɔɪnt]	zeigen	**Point** to the cake you would like.
dolphin ['dɒlfɪn]	Delfin	R дельфин
towards [tə'wɔ:dz]	auf … zu; in Richtung	We were walking **towards** the station.
to **seem** [si:m]	scheinen	Kahu **seemed** to talk to the dolphins.
to **nod** [nɒd]	nicken	The dolphins seemed to **nod**.
to **pick up** [ˌpɪk‿'ʌp]	aufheben	The man **picked up** something.
to **kiss** [kɪs]	küssen	I would never **kiss** him.
crayfish ['kreɪfɪʃ]	Languste; Flusskrebs	
close [kləʊs]	fest	They held each other **close**.
carving ['kɑ:vɪŋ]	Schnitzerei	The king got a **carving** as a present.

Das kenne ich schon

conjunctions

after ['ɑ:ftə]	nachdem	if [ɪf]	wenn; falls; ob
although [ɔ:l'ðəʊ]	obwohl	since [sɪns]	seit; seitdem
and [ænd]	und	so [səʊ]	also; deshalb
because [bɪ'kɒz]	weil; da	so that [səʊ 'ðæt]	damit; sodass
before [bɪ'fɔ:]	bevor; vorher; zuvor	until [ʌn'tɪl]	bis
but [bʌt]	aber	when [wen]	als; wenn
however [haʊ'evə]	jedoch	while [waɪl]	während

Das kenne ich schon

phrasal verbs

to ask about [ˌɑːskˌəˈbaʊt]	fragen nach; sich erkundigen nach	to get out [ˌgetˌˈaʊt]	aussteigen; herauskommen
to cut down [ˌkʌt ˈdaʊn]	fällen	to get up [ˌgetˌˈʌp]	aufstehen
to drive off [ˌdraɪvˌˈɒf]	wegfahren	to look after [ˌlʊkˌˈɑːftə]	aufpassen auf; hüten; sich kümmern um
to fall off [ˌfɔːlˌˈɒf]	stürzen von; herunterfallen; hinunterfallen	to look at [ˈlʊkˌət]	anschauen
to find out [ˌfaɪndˌˈaʊt]	herausfinden	to rely on [rɪˈlaɪ ɒn]	sich verlassen auf; vertrauen auf
to get in [ˌgetˌˈɪn]	einsteigen	to stand for [ˈstænd fə]	stehen für
		to take out [ˌteɪkˌˈaʊt]	hinausbringen

Film

natural [ˈnætʃrl]	Natur-; natürlich	pool [puːl]	Tümpel

Writing skills

p. 106 **Kiwi** [ˈkiːwiː]	Kiwi *(Kosename für Neuseeländer)*	People from New Zealand are also called **Kiwis**.
enquiry [ɪnˈkwaɪəri]	Anfrage	How do I write an **enquiry**?
c/o [siːˈəʊ]	bei	**c/o** Ms Miller
RE [riː]	Betr.	**RE**: Your ad for shop assistants
qualified [ˈkwɒlɪfaɪd]	qualifiziert	**qualified** → qualification
enclosed [ɪnˈkləʊzd]	beigefügt; anbei	My certificates and CV are **enclosed**.

Dictionary

Die Abkürzungen geben an, wo das Wort zum ersten Mal vorkommt.
Verwendete Abkürzungen und Zeichen:

U = Unit
* = unregelmäßige Verben

I = Band 1 II = Band 2 III = Band 3 IV = Band 4
V U1, 27 = Band 5, Unit 1, S.27
<V U1, 19> = nur zum Nachschlagen, gehört nicht zum Lernwortschatz

A

a [ə] ein; eine I
a bit [ə 'bɪt] ein bisschen V U3, 72
a few [ə 'fju:] ein paar; einige; wenige IV
a little (bit) [ə 'lɪtl (bɪt)] ein (kleines) bisschen; ein (klein) wenig II
a lot [ə 'lɒt] viel; sehr I
a lot of [ə 'lɒt‿əv] viel; viele; eine Menge I
a week [ə 'wi:k] in der Woche; pro Woche V U3, 73
a year [ə 'jɪə] pro Jahr; im Jahr IV
a/one hundred ['hʌndrəd] hundert; einhundert I
a/one thousand ['θaʊznd] tausend; eintausend II
a.m. [ˌeɪ'em] vormittags *(Uhrzeit)* III
*to be **able** to (do sth) [bi: 'eɪbl tə] (etw. tun) können; (zu etw.) fähig sein *(Ersatzform für can)* IV
Aboriginal [ˌæbə'rɪdʒnl] Aborigine-; zur Aborigine-Kultur gehörend V U1, 12
Aboriginal people [æbəˌrɪdʒnl 'pi:pl] die Aborigines V U1, 11
about [ə'baʊt] über I; ungefähr; circa; etwa II; an III; wegen IV
to hang about [ˌhæŋ‿ə'baʊt] herumhängen I
out and about [ˌaʊt‿ən‿ə'baʊt] unterwegs III
above [ə'bʌv] über; oberhalb II
accent ['æksnt] Akzent III
accident ['æksɪdnt] Unfall I
road accident ['rəʊd‿ˌæksɪdnt] Verkehrsunfall <V U3, 64>
to **achieve** [ə'tʃi:v] erreichen; erfolgreich sein; leisten; vollbringen V U3, 68
across [ə'krɒs] über II
to **act** [ækt] spielen; mitspielen III
acting workshop ['æktɪŋ ˌwɜ:kʃɒp] Schauspielworkshop III
activity [æk'tɪvəti] Aktivität I
actor ['æktə] Schauspieler; Schauspielerin; Darsteller; Darstellerin III
to **add** [æd] hinzufügen V U3, 64
address [ə'dres] Adresse IV
adjective ['ædʒɪktɪv] Adjektiv; Eigenschaftswort <III>
to **admire** [əd'maɪə] bewundern V U3, 68
adventure [əd'ventʃə] Abenteuer; Erlebnis III
adverb ['ædvɜ:b] Adverb <IV>
adverb of manner [ˌædvɜ:b‿əv 'mænə] Adverb der Art und Weise <IV>
ad(vert) (= advertisement) ['æd(vɜ:t) (əd'vɜ:tɪsmənt)] Werbung; Anzeige III
advice [əd'vaɪs] Rat; Ratschlag III
to **advise** sb [əd'vaɪz] jmdn. beraten; jmdm. (etw.) raten <V U2, 149>
advisor [əd'vaɪzə] Berater; Beraterin V U4, 88
tax advisor ['tæks‿ədˌvaɪzə] Steuerberater; Steuerberaterin <V U2, 148>
afraid [ə'freɪd] ängstlich V U1, 12
to be afraid [bi: ə'freɪd] befürchten V U1, 16
I'm afraid [aɪm‿ə'freɪd] leider IV
African ['æfrɪkən] afrikanisch; aus Afrika; Afrikaner; Afrikanerin V U3, 62
African American [ˌæfrɪkən‿ə'merɪkən] Afroamerikaner; Afroamerikanerin IV
South African [ˌsaʊθ‿'æfrɪkən] Südafrikaner; Südafrikanerin; südafrikanisch; aus Südafrika V U3, 63
Afrikaans [ˌæfrɪ'kɑ:ns] Afrikaans *(Sprache in Südafrika)* V U3, 72
after ['ɑ:ftə] nach I; nachdem IV
after that [ˌɑ:ftə 'ðæt] danach I
afternoon [ˌɑ:ftə'nu:n] Nachmittag I
again [ə'gen] noch einmal; wieder I
against [ə'genst] gegen III
check-in **agent** [ˌtʃekɪn 'eɪdʒnt] Check-in-Mitarbeiter; Check-in-Mitarbeiterin IV
travel **agent** ['trævl‿eɪdʒnt] Reisebürokaufmann; Reisebürokauffrau IV
travel **agent's** ['trævl‿eɪdʒnts] Reisebüro IV
ago [ə'gəʊ] vor II
to **agree** (on) [ə'gri: (ɒn)] sich einigen (auf) <V U4, 103>
to **agree** (with) [ə'gri: (wɪð)] zustimmen; einer Meinung sein (mit) II
AIDS [eɪdz] Aids *(erworbene Immunabwehrschwäche)* V U3, 68
air [eə] Luft III
airport ['eəpɔ:t] Flughafen IV
Alaskan [ə'læskən] alaskisch; Alaska- IV
alga *(sg)* ['ælgə], **algae** *(pl)* ['ældʒi:] Alge V U1, 20
all [ɔ:l] alle; ganz I
all of ['ɔ:l‿əv] ganz II

all over [ˌɔːl ˈəʊvə] in ganz; überall II
all around the world [ɔːl ˌəˌraʊnd ðə ˈwɜːld] in aller Welt II
All the best, [ɔːl ðə ˈbest] Alles Gute II
of all the states [əv ˈɔːl ðə ˌsteɪts] von allen Staaten IV
all-day [ˈɔːldeɪ] Ganztages- III
allergy [ˈælədʒi] Allergie <V U3, 74>
alligator [ˈælɪgeɪtə] Alligator II
*to be **allowed** to (do sth) [biː əˈlaʊd tə] (etw. tun) dürfen IV
almost [ˈɔːlməʊst] fast; beinahe <V U3, 76>
alone [əˈləʊn] allein V U1, 20
alphabet [ˈælfəbet] Alphabet <I>
alphabetical [ˌælfəˈbetɪkl] alphabetisch <II>
already [ɔːlˈredi] schon; bereits III
also [ˈɔːlsəʊ] auch I
although [ɔːlˈðəʊ] obwohl V U4, 94
always [ˈɔːlweɪz] immer I; schon immer III
amazing [əˈmeɪzɪŋ] erstaunlich; unglaublich; toll II
American [əˈmerɪkən] amerikanisch; Amerikanisch; aus Amerika; Amerikaner; Amerikanerin II
African American [ˌæfrɪkən əˈmerɪkən] Afroamerikaner; Afroamerikanerin IV
American football [əˌmerɪkən ˈfʊtbɔːl] American Football II
Native American [ˌneɪtɪv əˈmerɪkən] Ureinwohner Amerikas; Ureinwohnerin Amerikas; Indianer; Indianerin; indianisch III
an [æn] ein; eine I
and [ænd] und I
angry [ˈæŋgri] wütend; zornig; verärgert; böse II
animal [ˈænɪml] Tier I
animal rescue shelter [ˌænɪml ˈreskjuː ˌʃeltə] Tierheim I
ankle [ˈæŋkl] Fußgelenk; Fußknöchel <V U1, 147>
announcement [əˈnaʊnsmənt] Durchsage; Ankündigung <II>
annoyed [əˈnɔɪd] verärgert IV
another [əˈnʌðə] ein anderer; noch ein; andere IV
answer [ˈɑːnsə] Antwort II
to **answer** [ˈɑːnsə] antworten; beantworten II
any [ˈeni] irgendwelche; irgendeine I
not … any more [ˌnɒt … eni ˈmɔː] nicht mehr III
not … any [ˌnɒt … eni] kein; keine III
anybody [ˈeniˌbɒdi] irgendjemand; jemand; jeder III
anyone [ˈeniwʌn] irgendjemand; irgendeiner IV
anything [ˈeniθɪŋ] etwas; irgendetwas III
not … anything [nɒt … ˈeniθɪŋ] nichts III
Anything else? [ˌeniθɪŋ ˈels] Darf es sonst noch etwas sein? I
apartheid *(no pl)* [əˈpɑːtaɪt] Apartheid V U3, 62
apartment *(AE)* [əˈpɑːtmənt] Wohnung; Apartment IV
app [æp] App IV
apple [ˈæpl] Apfel I
applicant [ˈæplɪkənt] Bewerber; Bewerberin <V U4, 103>
application [ˌæplɪˈkeɪʃn] Bewerbung IV
letter of application [ˌletər əv æplɪˈkeɪʃn] Bewerbungsschreiben IV
to **apply** (for) [əˈplaɪ (fə)] sich bewerben (für/um) IV
appointment [əˈpɔɪntmənt] Termin V U1, 16
apprenticeship [əˈprentɪʃɪp] Ausbildung; Lehre V U4, 94
April [ˈeɪprl] April I
area [ˈeəriə] Gebiet; Gegend; Areal IV; Fläche; Bereich V U1, 20
argument [ˈɑːgjəmənt] Auseinandersetzung; Streit II
arm [ɑːm] Arm II
around [əˈraʊnd] um … herum II; durch; um III ; unterwegs (in) V U1, 10; vorbei <V U1, 147>
to walk around [ˌwɔːk əˈraʊnd] umherlaufen; herumlaufen <I>
arranged marriage [əˌreɪndʒd ˈmærɪdʒ] arrangierte Hochzeit V U2, 37
arrival [əˈraɪvl] Ankömmling IV
to **arrive** [əˈraɪv] ankommen I
Art [ɑːt] Kunst I
article [ˈɑːtɪkl] Artikel; Bericht *(in einer Zeitung)* <V U1, 20>
artist [ˈɑːtɪst] Künstler; Künstlerin III
as [æz] wie; als II
… as well as … [əz ˈwel əz] sowohl … als auch … II
as … as [əz … əz] so … wie III
as long as [əz ˈlɒŋ əz] solange; sofern V U3, 80
as much as [əz ˈmʌtʃ əz] bis zu <V U1, 23>
to **ask** [ɑːsk] fragen I
to ask about [ˈɑːsk əˌbaʊt] fragen nach; sich erkundigen nach II
to ask for [ˈɑːsk fɔː] bitten um <III>
to ask the way [ˌɑːsk ðə ˈweɪ] nach dem Weg fragen <II>
aspect [ˈæspekt] Aspekt; Gesichtspunkt; Blickwinkel <IV>
assembly line [əˈsembli ˌlaɪn] Fließband V U2, 38
assistant [əˈsɪstnt] Verkäufer; Verkäuferin I; Helfer; Helferin; Assistent; Assistentin; Mitarbeiter; Mitarbeiterin IV
shop assistant [ˈʃɒp əˌsɪstnt] Verkäufer; Verkäuferin V U4, 94
at [æt] zu; in; an; auf; um; bei I
at first [ət ˈfɜːst] zuerst; zunächst V U3, 68
at home [ət ˈhəʊm] zu Hause; daheim I
at night [ət ˈnaɪt] nachts IV
at school [ət ˈskuːl] in der Schule I
at the back (of) [ət ðə ˈbæk (ɒv)] hinten (in) <III>
at the bottom [æt ðə ˈbɒtəm] unten V U1, 28
at the doctor's [ət ðə ˈdɒktəz] beim Arzt II
at the end [ˌət ði ˈend] am Ende II
at the moment [ət ðə ˈməʊmənt] im Moment; momentan II
at the same time [ət ðə seɪm ˈtaɪm] gleichzeitig; nebenher II

at the seaside [ət ðə 'si:saɪd] am Meer I
at the top [æt ðə 'tɒp] oben V U1, 28
ate [eɪt] simple past von *to eat* II
attic ['ætɪk] Dachboden I
August ['ɔ:gəst] August I
aunt [ɑ:nt] Tante I
Australian [ɒs'treɪliən] Australier; Australierin; australisch V U1, 10
autumn ['ɔ:təm] Herbst II
available [ə'veɪləbl] erhältlich; verfügbar IV
to **avoid** [ə'vɔɪd] aus dem Weg gehen; vermeiden; meiden; ausweichen IV
away [ə'weɪ] weg; entfernt II
to be a long way away [bi: ə 'lɒŋ ˌweɪ ə'weɪ] weit weg sein II
right away [ˌraɪt ə'weɪ] sofort; gleich V U3, 68
awesome ['ɔ:səm] großartig; toll; beeindruckend III
awful ['ɔ:fl] schrecklich; furchtbar I

B

baboon [bə'bu:n] Pavian <V U3, 75>
back [bæk] Rücken <V U1, 147>
at the back (of) [ət ðə 'bæk (ɒv)] hinten (in) <III>
back [bæk] zurück II
to get back [ˌget 'bæk] zurückkommen; zurückgehen V U4, 98
backache ['bækeɪk] Rückenschmerzen <V U1, 147>
background ['bækgraʊnd] Hintergrund III
bacon ['beɪkn] Speck I
bad [bæd] schlecht I; schlimm II
That's too bad. [ˌðæts tu: 'bæd] Schade! II
bag [bæg] Tasche; Tüte; Sack I
bagpipes *(pl)* ['bægpaɪps] Dudelsack III
baker ['beɪkə] Bäcker; Bäckerin <V U2, 148>
balcony ['bælkəni] Balkon I
ball [bɔ:l] Ball I; Kugel III
cannon ball ['kænən ˌbɔ:l] Kanonenkugel III
banana [bə'nɑ:nə] Banane I
band [bænd] Band; Musikgruppe II
bang [bæŋ] peng; Knall V U3, 64
snack **bar** ['snæk ˌbɑ:] Imbissstube; Café I
barbecue ['bɑ:bɪkju:] Grill; Grillfest I
to **bark** [bɑ:k] bellen II
base [beɪs] Base; Mal III
baseball ['beɪsbɔ:l] Baseball III
basic ['beɪsɪk] grundlegend <III>
basket ['bɑ:skɪt] Basketballkorb; Korb III
basketball ['bɑ:skɪtbɔ:l] Basketball II
bat [bæt] Fledermaus I
bathroom ['bɑ:θrʊm] Bad(ezimmer) II
batter ['bætə] Schlagmann; Schlagfrau III
bay [beɪ] Bucht V U4, 98
*to **be** [bi:] sein I
to be a long way away [bi: ə 'lɒŋ ˌweɪ ə'weɪ] weit weg sein II
to be able to (do sth) [bi: 'eɪbl tə] (etw. tun) können; (zu etw.) fähig sein *(Ersatzform für can)* IV
to be afraid [bi: ə'freɪd] befürchten V U1, 16
to be allowed to (do sth) [bi: ə'laʊd tə] (etw. tun) dürfen IV
to be born [bi: 'bɔ:n] geboren werden IV
to be fed up (with) [bi: ˌfed 'ʌp (wɪð)] die Nase voll haben (von) III
to be fun [bi: 'fʌn] Spaß machen; witzig sein II
to be going to do sth [bi: ˌgəʊɪŋ tə 'du:] etw. tun werden III
to be good at [bi: 'gʊd ət] gut sein in; gut sein bei I
to be homesick [bi: 'həʊmsɪk] Heimweh haben IV
to be in charge (of) [bi: ˌɪn 'tʃɑ:dʒ (əv)] leiten; zuständig sein (für); die Verantwortung tragen (für) V U3, 72
to be included [bi: ɪn'klu:dɪd] mit enthalten sein; inbegriffen sein V U4, 94
to be interested in [bi: 'ɪntrəstɪd ɪn] interessiert sein an; sich interessieren für III
to be involved [bi: ɪn'vɒlvd] sich beteiligen; sich engagieren <V U3, 150>
to be known [bi: 'nəʊn] bekannt sein <V U3, 151>
to be late [bi: 'leɪt] zu spät kommen II
to be lucky [bi: 'lʌki] Glück haben II
to be scared [bi: 'skeəd] Angst haben I
to be sick [bi: 'sɪk] sich übergeben I
beach [bi:tʃ] Strand I
bear [beə] Bär II
grizzly bear ['grɪzli ˌbeə] Grizzlybär IV
beautiful ['bju:tɪfl] schön; hübsch; wunderschön III
became [bɪ'keɪm] simple past von *to become* II
because [bɪ'kɒz] weil; da I
because of [bɪ'kɒz əv] wegen V U4, 98
*to **become** [bɪ'kʌm] (zu etw.) werden II
bed [bed] Bett I
bed and breakfast (B & B) [ˌbed ən 'brekfəst] Frühstückspension III
to go to bed [ˌgəʊ tə 'bed] ins Bett gehen I
bedroom ['bedrʊm] Kinderzimmer; Schlafzimmer II
been [bi:n] past participle von *to be* III
before [bɪ'fɔ:] vor; bevor II; vorher; zuvor III
before [bɪ'fɔ:] bevor <I>
began [bɪ'gæn] simple past von *to begin* V U4, 98
*to **begin** [bɪ'gɪn] beginnen; anfangen V U1, 10
beginning [bɪ'gɪnɪŋ] Anfang; Beginn II
behind [bɪ'haɪnd] hinter I
to **believe** [bɪ'li:v] glauben II
bell [bel] Glocke II
below [bɪ'ləʊ] unten <IV>
best [best] am besten; beste; am liebsten II
All the best, [ɔ:l ðə 'best] Alles Gute II

Best wishes, [ˌbest ˈwɪʃɪz] Viele Grüße; Alles Gute! I
better [ˈbetə] besser II
to get better [ˌget ˈbetə] sich wieder besser fühlen; sich verbessern V U1, 16
between [bɪˈtwiːn] zwischen III
big [bɪg] groß I
big wheel [ˌbɪg ˈwiːl] Riesenrad II
bike [baɪk] Fahrrad I
to go bike riding [ˌgəʊ ˈbaɪk ˌraɪdɪŋ] Fahrrad fahren II
billion [ˈbɪliən] Milliarde V ZI, 8
Biology [baɪˈɒlədʒi] Biologie I
bird [bɜːd] Vogel IV
early bird [ˈɜːli ˌbɜːd] Frühaufsteher; Frühaufsteherin <V U3, 76>
date of **birth** [ˌdeɪt ˌəv ˈbɜːθ] Geburtsdatum IV
birthday [ˈbɜːθdeɪ] Geburtstag I
biscuit [ˈbɪskɪt] Keks III
a **bit** [ə ˈbɪt] ein bisschen V U3, 72
black [blæk] schwarz I
blackboard [ˈblækbɔːd] Tafel I
blanket [ˈblæŋkɪt] Decke; Bettdecke; Wolldecke IV
bleaching [ˈbliːtʃɪŋ] Bleichen; Ausbleichen V U1, 20
blog [blɒg] Blog; Internettagebuch I
blue [bluː] blau I
boarding card [ˈbɔːdɪŋ ˌkɑːd] Bordkarte IV
boarding time [ˈbɔːdɪŋ ˌtaɪm] Einsteigezeit IV
boat [bəʊt] Boot; Schiff IV
body [ˈbɒdi] Leiche; Körper IV
book [bʊk] Buch; Heft I
exercise book [ˈeksəsaɪz ˌbʊk] Übungsheft I
to **book** [bʊk] buchen; reservieren III
boom [buːm] Donner; Boom IV
Boom! [buːm] Bum! IV
border [ˈbɔːdə] Grenze IV
bored [bɔːd] gelangweilt <V U4, 153>
boring [ˈbɔːrɪŋ] langweilig I
*to be **born** [biː ˈbɔːn] geboren werden IV
borough [ˈbʌrə] Stadtteil; Bezirk IV
to **borrow** [ˈbɒrəʊ] (sich) ausleihen II
boss [bɒs] Boss; Chef; Chefin III
both [bəʊθ] beide IV
a **bottle** of [ə ˈbɒtl̩ əv] eine Flasche … II
at the **bottom** [æt ðə ˈbɒtəm] unten V U1, 28
bought [bɔːt] simple past von *to buy* I; past participle von *to buy* III
to **bounce** [baʊns] prellen; hüpfen III
box [bɒks] Box; Kiste; Schachtel I
telephone box [ˈtelɪfəʊn ˌbɒks] Telefonzelle II
boy [bɔɪ] Junge; Bub I
bracket [ˈbrækɪt] Klammer <V U1, 14>
to **brake** [breɪk] bremsen V U3, 64
brave [breɪv] mutig; tapfer III
bread [bred] Brot I
break [breɪk] Pause I
*to **break** [breɪk] brechen; zerbrechen; kaputt machen V U1, 11
to break the law [ˌbreɪk ðə ˈlɔː] gegen das Gesetz verstoßen V U2, 46
breakfast [ˈbrekfəst] Frühstück I
bed and breakfast (B & B) [ˌbed ˌən ˈbrekfəst] Frühstückspension III
to have breakfast [ˌhæv ˈbrekfəst] frühstücken I
bricklayer [ˈbrɪkleɪə] Maurer; Maurerin <V U4, 152>
bridge [brɪdʒ] Brücke II
*to **bring** [brɪŋ] mitbringen; bringen II
British [ˈbrɪtɪʃ] britisch V U1, 11
the British [ðə ˈbrɪtɪʃ] die Briten V U2, 37
brochure [ˈbrəʊʃə] Broschüre; Prospekt III
broke [brəʊk] simple past von *to break* V U1, 11
broken [ˈbrəʊkn] past participle von *to break* V U1, 11
brother [ˈbrʌðə] Bruder I
brought [brɔːt] simple past von *to bring* II
brown [braʊn] braun I
buffalo *(sg)* [ˈbʌfləʊ], **buffaloes** *(pl)* [ˈbʌfləʊz] Büffel V U3, 63
*to **build** [bɪld] bauen II
building [ˈbɪldɪŋ] Gebäude; Bauwerk II
built [bɪlt] simple past von *to build* II
burger [ˈbɜːgə] Hamburger I
bus [bʌs] Bus I
on the bus [ˌɒn ðə ˈbʌs] im Bus II
business [ˈbɪznɪs] Geschäftswelt; Geschäft V ZI, 9
busy [ˈbɪzi] beschäftigt I; belebt; voller Menschen <V U1, 146>
a busy day [ə ˌbɪzi ˈdeɪ] ein ausgefüllter Tag II
but [bʌt] aber I
butcher [ˈbʊtʃə] Fleischer; Fleischerin; Metzger; Metzgerin <V U4, 152>
butter [ˈbʌtə] Butter I
*to **buy** [baɪ] kaufen I
by [baɪ] von; an; neben III; bis <V U4, 100>
by (train) [baɪ (treɪn)] mit (dem Zug) I
Bye. [baɪ] Tschüss. I

C

c/o [siːˈəʊ] bei V U4, 106
caber [ˈkeɪbə] Baumstamm III
caber toss [ˈkeɪbə ˌtɒs] Baumstammwerfen III
cable car [ˈkeɪbl̩ ˌkɑː] seilgezogene Straßenbahn; Seilbahn IV
café [ˈkæfeɪ] Café III
cafeteria [kæfəˈtɪəriə] Cafeteria; Mensa I
cage [keɪdʒ] Käfig II
cake [keɪk] Kuchen I
calculator [ˈkælkjəleɪtə] Taschenrechner I
phone **call** [ˈfəʊn ˌkɔːl] Telefonanruf; Anruf I
to **call** [kɔːl] anrufen; rufen; nennen III
caller [ˈkɔːlə] Anrufer; Anruferin <II>
calm [kɑːm] ruhig; friedlich V U4, 90
came [keɪm] simple past von *to come* I
camp [kæmp] Camp; Lager III
*to go **camping** [ˌgəʊ ˈkæmpɪŋ] campen gehen; zelten gehen III
campsite [ˈkæmpsaɪt] Campingplatz; Zeltplatz III
can [kæn] können I; Dose IV
can't [kɑːnt] nicht können I
I can't wait [aɪ ˌkɑːnt ˈweɪt] ich kann es kaum erwarten III

Canadian [kə'neɪdiən] Kanadier; Kanadierin; kanadisch; aus Kanada IV
canal [kə'næl] Kanal III
cannon ['kænən] Kanone III
cannon ball ['kænən ˌbɔ:l] Kanonenkugel III
canoe [kə'nu:] Kanu IV
canoeing [kə'nu:ɪŋ] Kanufahren I
capital (city) ['kæpɪtl (ˌsɪti)] Hauptstadt I
captain ['kæptɪn] Kapitän; Kapitänin; Mannschaftsführer; Mannschaftsführerin II
caption ['kæpʃn] Bildunterschrift; Untertitel <III>
car [kɑ:] Auto I
card [kɑ:d] Karte III
boarding card ['bɔ:dɪŋ ˌkɑ:d] Bordkarte IV
*to take **care** of [ˌteɪk 'keər ˌəv] sich kümmern um; sorgen für <V U2, 48>
career [kə'rɪə] Laufbahn; Karriere; Beruf IV
careers [kə'rɪəz] Berufs- V U4, 88
careers day [kə'rɪəz ˌdeɪ] Berufsinformationstag V U4, 90
careful ['keəfl] vorsichtig; sorgfältig III
caretaker ['keəˌteɪkə] Hausmeister; Hausmeisterin I
Caribbean [ˌkærɪ'bi:ən] Karibe; Karibin; karibisch IV
carnival ['kɑ:nɪvl] Karneval; Fasching I
carpenter ['kɑ:pntə] Schreiner; Schreinerin; Tischler; Tischlerin <V U2, 148>
carpet ['kɑ:pɪt] Teppich II
carving ['kɑ:vɪŋ] Schnitzerei V U4, 99
castle ['kɑ:sl] Burg; Schloss III
cat [kæt] Katze I
*to **catch** [kætʃ] fangen II
to catch (bus/train) [kætʃ (bʌs/treɪn)] nehmen (Bus/Zug); bekommen (Bus/Zug) III
to catch sth [kætʃ] sich etw. einfangen *(medizinisch)* V U1, 16
catering ['keɪtrɪŋ] Gastronomie; Verpflegung <V U2, 148>
cathedral [kə'θi:drl] Kathedrale; Dom <V U1, 146>
caught [kɔ:t] simple past von *to catch* II; past participle von *to catch* V U1, 16
to **cause** [kɔ:z] verursachen; auslösen IV
cave [keɪv] Höhle IV
to **celebrate** ['seləbreɪt] feiern III
cent [sent] Cent *(Währung)* III
center *(AE)* ['sentə] Zentrum; Mitte; Center III
centre ['sentə] Zentrum; Mitte; Center III
city centre [ˌsɪti 'sentə] Stadtzentrum; Stadtmitte II
shopping centre ['ʃɒpɪŋ ˌsentə] Einkaufszentrum I
sports centre ['spɔ:ts ˌsentə] Sportzentrum I
century ['senʃri] Jahrhundert IV
certainly ['sɜ:tnli] auf jeden Fall; offensichtlich; sicher V U2, 46
certificate [sə'tɪfɪkət] Zertifikat; Bescheinigung; Urkunde; Zeugnis V U4, 90
secondary school leaving certificate ['sekndri sku:l ˌli:vɪŋ sə'tɪfɪkət] mittlerer Schulabschluss; Realschulabschluss IV
chain [tʃeɪn] Kette III
chair [tʃeə] Stuhl I
champion ['tʃæmpiən] Gewinner; Gewinnerin; Sieger; Siegerin <I>
chance [tʃɑ:ns] Möglichkeit; Chance; Gelegenheit III
change [tʃeɪndʒ] Wechselgeld I
climate change ['klaɪmət ˌtʃeɪndʒ] Klimawandel V U1, 20
to **change** [tʃeɪndʒ] verändern; ändern; wechseln II; umsteigen III
chant [tʃɑ:nt] Sprechgesang <I>
charades [ʃə'rɑ:dz] Scharaden <II>
*to be in **charge** (of) [bi: ˌɪn 'tʃɑ:dʒ (əv)] leiten; zuständig sein (für); die Verantwortung tragen (für) V U3, 72
charity ['tʃærɪti] Wohltätigkeitsorganisation; Stiftung; wohltätige Zwecke; Wohltätigkeits- II
chart [tʃɑ:t] Tabelle; Diagramm <I>
to **chat** [tʃæt] chatten; plaudern II
cheap [tʃi:p] günstig; billig II
to **check** [tʃek] überprüfen; kontrollieren II
check-in agent [ˌtʃekɪn 'eɪdʒnt] Check-in-Mitarbeiter; Check-in-Mitarbeiterin IV
checklist ['tʃeklɪst] Checkliste <I>
checkout ['tʃekaʊt] Kontrolle <I>; Kasse V U4, 94
cheerleader ['tʃɪəˌli:də] Cheerleader; Cheerleaderin III
cheerleading ['tʃɪəˌli:dɪŋ] Cheerleading III
cheese [tʃi:z] Käse I
chef [ʃef] Koch; Küchenchef II
chicken ['tʃɪkɪn] Hähnchen; Huhn I
chicken fried rice ['tʃɪkɪn ˌfraɪd 'raɪs] gebratener Reis mit Hühnerfleisch II
chief [tʃi:f] Häuptling V U4, 98
children *(pl)* ['tʃɪldrn] Kinder I
chimpanzee [ˌtʃɪmpn'zi:] Schimpanse II
Chinese [tʃaɪ'ni:z] chinesisch; Chinesisch; aus China; Chinese; Chinesin II
chips *(pl)* [tʃɪps] Pommes frites I
chocolate ['tʃɒklət] Schokolade I
*to **choose** [tʃu:z] wählen; auswählen III
chorus ['kɔ:rəs] Refrain <I>
chose [tʃəʊz] simple past von *to choose* III
chosen ['tʃəʊzn] past participle von *to choose* III
Christmas ['krɪsməs] Weihnachten I
Merry Christmas! [ˌmeri 'krɪsməs] Frohe Weihnachten! I
church [tʃɜ:tʃ] Kirche II
cinema ['sɪnəmə] Kino I
citizen ['sɪtɪzn] Staatsbürger; Staatsbürgerin; Staatsangehöriger; Staatsangehörige IV
city ['sɪti] Stadt; Großstadt I
city centre [ˌsɪti 'sentə] Stadtzentrum; Stadtmitte II
class [klɑ:s] Klasse I; Unterricht; Unterrichtsstunde; Kurs IV

classmate ['klɑ:smeɪt] Klassenkamerad; Klassenkameradin; Mitschüler; Mitschülerin <IV>
classroom ['klɑ:srʊm] Klassenzimmer I
to **clean** [kli:n] sauber machen; putzen II
to **clear up** [ˌklɪər ˈʌp] aufräumen <V U4, 153>
clear [klɪə] klar; deutlich III
climate ['klaɪmət] Klima IV
climate change ['klaɪmət ˌtʃeɪndʒ] Klimawandel V U1, 20
to **climb** [klaɪm] besteigen; klettern; erklettern; steigen II
clock [klɒk] Uhr II
o'clock [ə'klɒk] Uhr *(Zeitangabe bei vollen Stunden)* I
to **close** [kləʊz] zumachen; schließen I
close [kləʊs] fest V U4, 99
closed [kləʊzd] geschlossen I
clothes *(pl only)* [kləʊðz] Kleider; Kleidung I
cloud [klaʊd] Wolke II
cloudy ['klaʊdi] bewölkt; wolkig II
club [klʌb] Klub; Treff; Schul-AG I; Verein V U4, 89
clue [klu:] Hinweis; Spur I
coal mine ['kəʊl ˌmaɪn] Kohlenbergwerk; Kohlengrube III
coast [kəʊst] Küste III
coat [kəʊt] Jacke I
cola ['kəʊlə] Cola I
cold [kəʊld] kalt I; Erkältung; Kälte II
collar ['kɒlə] Halsband I
to **collect** [kə'lekt] sammeln <I>
collection [kə'lekʃn] Sammlung III
colony ['kɒləni] Kolonie IV
color *(AE)* ['kʌlə] Farbe III
colour ['kʌlə] Farbe I
colourful ['kʌləfl] bunt V U1, 12
*to **come** [kʌm] kommen I
come [kʌm] past participle von *to come* <IV>
comic ['kɒmɪk] Comic(heft) II
comment ['kɒment] Kommentar IV
to **comment** (on) ['kɒment (ɒn)] kommentieren IV
to **communicate** [kə'mju:nɪkeɪt] kommunizieren; sich verständigen V ZI, 9
communication [kəˌmju:nɪ'keɪʃn] Kommunikation V U4, 90
community [kə'mju:nəti] Gemeinde; Gemeinschaft V U4, 94
company ['kʌmpəni] Unternehmen; Firma; Gesellschaft II
comparative [kəm'pærətɪv] Komparativ <IV>
to **compare** [kəm'peə] vergleichen <I>
comparison [kəm'pærɪsn] Vergleich <IV>
competition [ˌkɒmpə'tɪʃn] Wettbewerb V ZI, 8
to **complain** [kəm'pleɪn] sich beschweren; sich beklagen IV
to **complete** [kəm'pli:t] vervollständigen <I>; ausfüllen; machen V U4, 90
completely [kəm'pli:tli] völlig V U1, 20
computer [ˌkəm'pju:tə] Computer I
computer programmer [kəmˌpju:tə 'prəʊgræmə] Programmierer; Programmiererin V U2, 38
computing [ˌkəm'pju:tɪŋ] Computer- <V U2, 148>
concert ['kɒnsət] Konzert I
working **conditions** *(pl only)* ['wɜ:kɪŋ kənˌdɪʃnz] Arbeitsbedingungen <V U4, 153>
confident ['kɒnfɪdnt] selbstsicher; selbstbewusst; sicher IV
Congratulations! [kənˌgrætʃə'leɪʃnz] Glückwunsch! II
staying **connected** [ˌsteɪɪŋ kə'nektɪd] in Verbindung bleiben III
considerate [kən'sɪdrət] rücksichtsvoll; aufmerksam <V U3, 151>
consumption [kən'sʌmpʃn] Verbrauch; Konsum <V U2, 149>
contact ['kɒntækt] Kontakt I
to **contact** ['kɒntækt] kontaktieren; sich in Verbindung setzen <V U2, 50>
container [kən'teɪnə] Container; Behälter; Behältnis <V U2, 148>
content ['kɒntent] Inhalt <V U2, 51>
continent ['kɒntɪnənt] Kontinent; Erdteil II
to **control** [kən'trəʊl] kontrollieren V U3, 72
cook [kʊk] Koch; Köchin <V U2, 48>
to **cook** [kʊk] kochen II
cookie *(AE)* ['kʊki] Keks III
cooking ['kʊkɪŋ] Kochen; Koch- II
cool [ku:l] cool; super I
to **copy** ['kɒpi] abschreiben; kopieren <III>
copyright ['kɒpiraɪt] Copyright; Urheberrecht IV
coral ['kɒrəl] Koralle V U1, 20
corn [kɔ:n] Mais; Korn; Getreide IV
corner ['kɔ:nə] Ecke V U1, 28
to **correct** [kə'rekt] verbessern; richtigstellen; korrigieren II
correct [kə'rekt] richtig; korrekt <I>
*to **cost** [kɒst] kosten III
cost [kɒst] simple past, past participle von *to cost* III
costume ['kɒstju:m] Kostüm I
could [kʊd] könnte V U3, 81; konnte III
to **count on sb** [ˌkaʊnt ˈɒn] sich auf jmdn. verlassen V U4, 90
country ['kʌntri] Land; ländliche Gegend I
home country [ˌhəʊm 'kʌntri] Heimat; Heimatland IV
of **course** [əv 'kɔ:s] natürlich; selbstverständlich II
cousin ['kʌzn] Cousin; Cousine II
cow [kaʊ] Kuh III
to **crash** [kræʃ] krachen V U3, 64
crayfish ['kreɪfɪʃ] Languste; Flusskrebs V U4, 99
crazy ['kreɪzi] verrückt V U2, 54
creative [kri'eɪtɪv] kreativ <V U4, 152>
creature ['kri:tʃə] Lebewesen; Kreatur; Geschöpf V U1, 10
cricket ['krɪkɪt] Kricket II
saltwater **crocodile** [sɔ:ltˌwɔ:tə 'krɒkədaɪl] Salzwasserkrokodil <V U1, 23>
crop [krɒp] Feldfrucht; Ernte V U2, 42
crowded ['kraʊdɪd] überfüllt <V U1, 146>
crowded with people [ˌkraʊdɪd wɪð 'pi:pl] voller Leute <V U3, 76>
crown jewels *(pl)* [ˌkraʊn 'dʒu:əlz] Kronjuwelen II
crust [krʌst] Kruste; Rinde IV

culture ['kʌltʃə] Kultur III
a **cup** of [ə 'kʌp‿əv] eine Tasse … II
current ['kʌrnt] Strömung III
customer ['kʌstəmə] Kunde; Kundin I
customer service [ˌkʌstəmə 'sɜ:vɪs] Kundenbetreuung; Kundendienst; Kundenservice IV
*to **cut** down [ˌkʌt 'daʊn] fällen V U3, 72
CV (curriculum vitae) [ˌsi:'vi: (kəˌrɪkjələm'vi:taɪ)] Lebenslauf IV
cyclist ['saɪklɪst] Radfahrer; Radfahrerin <V U3, 150>

D

dad [dæd] Papa; Vati I
daily routine [ˌdeɪli ru:'ti:n] Alltag <V U2, 40>
damage ['dæmɪdʒ] Schäden; Schaden; Beschädigung IV
to **damage** ['dæmɪdʒ] beschädigen; schaden V U2, 42
dance [dɑ:ns] Tanz III
square dance ['skweə ˌdɑ:ns] Squaredance *(amerikanischer Volkstanz)* II
to **dance** [dɑ:ns] tanzen I
dancer ['dɑ:nsə] Tänzer; Tänzerin I
dancing ['dɑ:nsɪŋ] Tanz; Tanzen III
danger ['deɪndʒə] Gefahr V U1, 20
dangerous ['deɪndʒrəs] gefährlich III
dark [dɑ:k] dunkel I
date [deɪt] Datum; Zeitpunkt IV
date of birth [ˌdeɪt‿əv 'bɜ:θ] Geburtsdatum IV
daughter ['dɔ:tə] Tochter I
day [deɪ] Tag I
a busy day [ə ˌbɪzi 'deɪ] ein ausgefüllter Tag II
careers day [kə'rɪəz ˌdeɪ] Berufsinformationstag V U4, 90
lucky day [ˌlʌki 'deɪ] Glückstag II
one day ['wʌn deɪ] eines Tages I
sports day ['spɔ:ts ˌdeɪ] Sportfest II
dead [ded] tot IV
Oh **dear**. [ˌəʊ 'dɪə] Oje. V U1, 16
Dear …, [dɪə] Liebe(r) …, *(Anrede in Briefen)* I; Sehr geehrte(r) …, IV
December [dɪ'sembə] Dezember I
to **decide** [dɪ'saɪd] (sich) entscheiden; beschließen III
decision [dɪ'sɪʒn] Entscheidung IV
decoration [ˌdek'reɪʃn] Dekoration; Schmuck <V U1, 25>
deep [di:p] tief V U4, 98
defining relative clause [dɪˌfaɪnɪŋ 'relətɪv ˌklɔ:z] notwendiger Relativsatz <IV>
definition [ˌdefɪ'nɪʃn] Definition <V U2, 43>
delayed [dɪ'leɪd] verspätet IV
delicious [dɪ'lɪʃəs] lecker; köstlich V U1, 12
to **deliver** [dɪ'lɪvə] liefern; ausliefern IV
delivery [dɪ'lɪvri] Lieferung; Auslieferung; Zustellung <V U4, 153>
delivery service [dɪ'lɪvri ˌsɜ:vɪs] Lieferdienst <V U2, 49>
dentist ['dentɪst] Zahnarzt; Zahnärztin <V U4, 152>
to **depart** [dɪ'pɑ:t] abfliegen; abfahren IV
department [dɪ'pɑ:tmənt] Abteilung V U1, 21
to **describe** [dɪ'skraɪb] beschreiben <III>
design [dɪ'zaɪn] Design; Gestaltung; Entwurf II
DT (Design Technology) [ˌdi:'ti: (dɪˌzaɪn tek'nɒlədʒi)] Technik I
to **design** [dɪ'zaɪn] konstruieren; entwerfen; gestalten; entwickeln IV
desk [desk] Schreibtisch; Tisch II
to **destroy** [dɪ'strɔɪ] zerstören IV
destruction [dɪ'strʌkʃn] Zerstörung V U1, 21
detail ['di:teɪl] Detail; Einzelheit V U3, 64
detective [dɪ'tektɪv] Detektiv; Detektivin I
determined [dɪ'tɜ:mɪnd] entschlossen; entschieden; zielstrebig <V U3, 151>
device [dɪ'vaɪs] Gerät; Vorrichtung <V U2, 148>
dialogue ['daɪəlɒg] Dialog; Gespräch II
diameter [daɪ'æmɪtə] Durchmesser II
diamond ['daɪəmənd] Diamant <II>
diary ['daɪəri] Tagebuch I
dictionary ['dɪkʃnri] Wörterbuch <II>
did [dɪd] simple past von *to do* I
didgeridoo [ˌdɪdʒri'du:] Didgeridoo *(australisches Musikinstrument)* V U1, 12
to **die** [daɪ] sterben III
difference ['dɪfrns] Unterschied <IV>
different ['dɪfrnt] verschieden; unterschiedlich; anders I; andere III
difficult ['dɪfɪklt] schwierig; schwer; kompliziert III
dinner ['dɪnə] Mittagessen; Abendessen I
direct speech [dɪˌrekt 'spi:tʃ] direkte Rede <V U3, 76>
directions *(pl)* [dɪ'rekʃnz] Wegbeschreibung; Anweisungen <III>
giving directions [ˌgɪvɪŋ dɪ'rekʃnz] eine Wegbeschreibung geben; Anweisungen geben <II>
director [dɪ'rektə] Regisseur; Regisseurin V U3, 68
dirty ['dɜ:ti] dreckig; schmutzig I
to **disagree** [ˌdɪsə'gri:] anderer Meinung sein; nicht einverstanden sein IV
disappointed [ˌdɪsə'pɔɪntɪd] enttäuscht V U1, 12
to **discover** [dɪ'skʌvə] entdecken V U3, 62
disease [dɪ'zi:z] Krankheit V U3, 68
to empty the **dishwasher** [ˌemti ðə 'dɪʃwɒʃə] die Spülmaschine ausräumen II
to load the **dishwasher** [ˌləʊd ðə 'dɪʃwɒʃə] die Spülmaschine einräumen II
distance ['dɪstns] Entfernung; Distanz V U3, 80
to **disturb** [dɪ'stɜ:b] stören; belästigen V U3, 80
*to **do** [du:] machen; tun I
to do handicrafts [ˌdu: 'hændikrɑ:fts] basteln V U3, 73
to do homework [ˌdu: 'həʊmwɜ:k] Hausaufgabe(n) machen I
to do magic [ˌdu: 'mædʒɪk] zaubern II
doctor ['dɒktə] Arzt; Ärztin II

at the doctor's [ət ðə ˈdɒktəz] beim Arzt II
dog [dɒg] Hund I
dollar ($) [ˈdɒlə] Dollar *(amer. Währungseinheit)* IV
dolphin [ˈdɒlfɪn] Delfin V U4, 99
don't sing [ˌdəʊnt ˈsɪŋ] singe nicht; singt nicht I
to **donate** [dəˈneɪt] spenden; stiften V U4, 94
done [dʌn] past participle von *to do* III
door [dɔː] Tür II
doorbell [ˈdɔːbel] Türklingel I
dot [dɒt] Punkt V U1, 12
down [daʊn] hinunter; herunter III
draft [drɑːft] Entwurf <II>
drama [ˈdrɑːmə] Theater-; Drama; Schauspielerei III
drank [dræŋk] simple past von *to drink* II
*to **draw** [drɔː] zeichnen <I>
dream [driːm] Traum I
dress [dres] Kleid I
fancy dress [ˌfænsi ˈdres] Kostüm; Verkleidung I
drink [drɪŋk] Getränk I
*to **drink** [drɪŋk] trinken II
drinking [ˈdrɪŋkɪŋ] Trink- V U2, 42
*to **drive** [draɪv] fahren; treiben IV
to drive off [ˌdraɪv ˈɒf] wegfahren IV
driving licence [ˈdraɪvɪŋ ˌlaɪsns] Führerschein V U3, 64
driven [ˈdrɪvn] past participle von *to drive* IV
driver [ˈdraɪvə] Fahrer; Fahrerin IV
drove [drəʊv] simple past von *to drive* IV
drug [drʌg] Droge IV; Medikament; Arznei; Arzneimittel V U3, 68
dry [draɪ] trocken II
DT (Design Technology) [ˌdiːˈtiː (dɪˌzaɪn tekˈnɒlədʒi)] Technik I
due [djuː] fällig <V U4, 100>
during [ˈdʒʊərɪŋ] bei; während IV
DVD [ˌdiːviːˈdiː] DVD I

E

e.g. (= for example) [ˌiːˈdʒiː] z. B. (= zum Beispiel) <II>
each [iːtʃ] jede <I>
each one [ˌiːtʃ ˈwʌn] jedes <IV>
each other [ˌiːtʃˈʌðə] einander; sich; gegenseitig III
early [ˈɜːli] früh II
early bird [ˈɜːli ˌbɜːd] Frühaufsteher; Frühaufsteherin <V U3, 76>
earth [ɜːθ] Welt; Erde III
earthquake [ˈɜːθkweɪk] Erdbeben IV
east [iːst] Ost-; Osten III
easy [ˈiːzi] einfach; leicht I
*to **eat** [iːt] essen I
economy [ɪˈkɒnəmi] Wirtschaft V U2, 42
education [ˌedʒʊˈkeɪʃn] Ausbildung; Erziehung; Bildung IV
efficient [ɪˈfɪʃnt] effizient; leistungsfähig IV
egg [eg] Ei I
Eid [iːd] *muslimisches Fest* I
eight [eɪt] acht I
eighteen [ˌeɪˈtiːn] achtzehn I
eighty [ˈeɪti] achtzig I
not … **either** [nɒt … ˈaɪðə] auch nicht III
electrical [ɪˈlektrɪkl] Elektro- <V U2, 149>
electrician [ˌelɪkˈtrɪʃn] Elektriker; Elektrikerin <V U2, 148>
electricity [ˌelɪkˈtrɪsəti] Strom; Elektrizität V U3, 63
elephant [ˈelɪfənt] Elefant V U3, 63
eleven [ɪˈlevn] elf I
e-mail [ˈiːmeɪl] E-Mail II
emergency [ɪˈmɜːdʒnsi] Notfall V U3, 80
emotion [ɪˈməʊʃn] Gefühl; Emotion <V U3, 76>
employee [ɪmˈplɔɪiː] Mitarbeiter; Mitarbeiterin; Arbeitnehmer; Arbeitnehmerin; Angestellter; Angestellte IV
employer [ɪmˈplɔɪə] Arbeitgeber; Arbeitgeberin V U4, 90
to **empty** the dishwasher [ˌemti ðə ˈdɪʃwɒʃə] die Spülmaschine ausräumen II
empty [ˈemti] leer <V U1, 146>
enclosed [ɪnˈkləʊzd] beigefügt; anbei V U4, 112
end [end] Ende; Schluss II
at the end [ˌət ði ˈend] am Ende II
end-of-term [ˌend ˌəv ˈtɜːm] Schuljahresabschluss <I>
to **end** [end] enden; beenden; aufhören V U3, 62
ending [ˈendɪŋ] Ende; Schluss <III>
energy [ˈenədʒi] Energie; Kraft V U1, 21
search **engine** [ˈsɜːtʃˌendʒɪn] Suchmaschine <IV>
engineer [ˌendʒɪˈnɪə] Ingenieur; Ingenieurin; Techniker; Technikerin II
English [ˈɪŋglɪʃ] Englisch I; englisch; aus England III
English-speaking [ˌɪŋglɪʃˈspiːkɪŋ] englischsprachig V Z1, 9
the English [ði ˈɪŋglɪʃ] die Engländer III
to **enjoy** [ɪnˈdʒɔɪ] genießen; Gefallen finden an IV
to enjoy + -ing [ɪnˈdʒɔɪ …ɪŋ] mögen; Gefallen finden an; genießen; genießen, … zu tun V U2, 38
to enjoy oneself [ɪnˈdʒɔɪ wʌnˌself] Spaß haben; sich amüsieren IV
enough [ɪˈnʌf] genug; genügend III
enquiry [ɪnˈkwaɪəri] Anfrage V U4, 106
enthusiastic [ɪnˌθjuːziˈæstɪk] enthusiastisch; begeistert <V U3, 151>
entry [ˈentri] Eintrag; Eintritt <II>
environment [ɪnˈvaɪrnmənt] Umwelt; Umgebung II
environmental [ɪnˌvaɪrnˈmentl] Umwelt- V U2, 37
episode [ˈepɪsəʊd] Folge; Episode IV
equipment [ɪˈkwɪpmənt] Ausrüstung; Zubehör; Ausstattung <III>
to **escape** [ɪˈskeɪp] entkommen; fliehen; entfliehen; flüchten IV
euro [ˈjʊərəʊ] Euro *(Währung)* III
European [ˌjʊərəˈpiːən] Europäer; Europäerin; europäisch; aus Europa III
evening [ˈiːvnɪŋ] Abend I
in the evening [ɪn ðiˈiːvnɪŋ] abends I
event [ɪˈvent] Veranstaltung; Ereignis II

ever ['evə] schon einmal; jemals; überhaupt III
every ['evri] jede I; alle II
everyone ['evriwʌn] alle; jeder; zusammen II
everything ['evriθɪŋ] alles II
everywhere ['evriweə] überallhin; überall II
exam [ɪg'zæm] Prüfung; Examen V U4, 90
to take an exam [ˌteɪk‿ənˌɪg'zæm] eine Prüfung schreiben; ein Examen schreiben V U4, 90
example [ɪg'zɑ:mpl] Beispiel III
for example [fərˌɪg'zɑ:mpl] zum Beispiel III
excited [ɪk'saɪtɪd] aufgeregt; begeistert II
exciting [ɪk'saɪtɪŋ] spannend; aufregend I
Excuse me. [ɪk'skju:z mi] Entschuldigung. II
exercise ['eksəsaɪz] Übung I
exercise book ['eksəsaɪz ˌbʊk] Übungsheft I
exhibition [ˌeksɪ'bɪʃn] Ausstellung III
expensive [ɪk'spensɪv] teuer I
experience [ɪk'spɪəriəns] Erfahrung; Erlebnis IV
work experience ['wɜ:k‿ɪkˌspɪəriəns] Berufserfahrung; Praktikum V U4, 90
experiment [ɪk'sperɪmənt] Versuch; Experiment II
to **explain** [ɪk'spleɪn] erklären V U3, 81
to **explore** [ɪk'splɔ:] erkunden; erforschen IV
expression [ɪk'spreʃn] Ausdruck; Wendung; Äußerung <IV>
extra ['ekstrə] zusätzlich <IV>
extremist [ɪk'stri:mɪst] Extremist; Extremistin V U2, 47
eye [aɪ] Auge I

F

face [feɪs] Gesicht I
face painting ['feɪs peɪntɪŋ] Schminken II
fact [fækt] Fakt; Tatsache II
factory ['fæktri] Fabrik; Werk III
fair [feə] Fest; Messe; Jahrmarkt II; fair; gerecht IV
fall *(AE)* [fɔ:l] Herbst III
*to **fall** [fɔ:l] fallen; hinfallen I
to fall off [ˌfɔ:l‿'ɒf] von etw. stürzen; herunterfallen; hinunterfallen II
to fall out [ˌfɔ:l‿'aʊt] herausfallen III
fallen ['fɔ:lən] past participle von *to fall* III
family ['fæmli] Familie I
family tree [ˌfæmli 'tri:] Familienstammbaum <I>
famous ['feɪməs] berühmt I
fan [fæn] Fan I
fancy dress [ˌfænsi 'dres] Kostüm; Verkleidung I
fantastic [fæn'tæstɪk] fantastisch; großartig II
far [fɑ:] weit II
farm [fɑ:m] Bauernhof I
wind farm ['wɪnd ˌfɑ:m] Windpark <V U2, 149>
farmer ['fɑ:mə] Bauer; Bäuerin; Landwirt; Landwirtin I
farming ['fɑ:mɪŋ] Landwirtschaft; Ackerbau V U2, 42
fashion ['fæʃn] Mode IV
fast [fɑ:st] schnell II
father ['fɑ:ðə] Vater I
favorite *(AE)* ['feɪvrɪt] Lieblings- III
favourite ['feɪvrɪt] Lieblings- I
feature story ['fi:tʃə ˌstɔ:ri] Leitartikel; Sonderbericht <V U3, 76>
February ['februri] Februar I
fed [fed] simple past von *to feed* I
*to be **fed** up (with) [bi: ˌfed‿'ʌp (wɪð)] die Nase voll haben (von) III
fee [fi:] Gebühr <V U4, 100>
*to **feed** [fi:d] füttern I; ernähren <V U2, 49>
feedback ['fi:dbæk] Rückmeldung; Feedback <I>
*to **feel** [fi:l] (sich) fühlen II; sich anfühlen III
feeling ['fi:lɪŋ] Gefühl <II>
fell [fel] simple past von *to fall* I
felt [felt] simple past von *to feel* II; past participle von *to feel* III
fence [fens] Zaun <V U4, 153>
fertiliser ['fɜ:tɪlaɪzə] Dünger V U2, 42
festival ['festɪvl] Festival; Fest III
fete [feɪt] Fest <V U4, 100>
a **few** [ə 'fju:] ein paar; einige; wenige IV
science **fiction** [ˌsaɪəns 'fɪkʃn] Science-Fiction I
field ['fi:ld] Spielfeld; Feld; Gebiet III
playing field ['pleɪɪŋ ˌfi:ld] Sportplatz II
fifteen [ˌfɪf'ti:n] fünfzehn I
fifty ['fɪfti] fünfzig I
*to **fight** [faɪt] kämpfen; (sich) streiten II
figure ['figə] Figur; Gestalt II
to **fill** [fɪl] füllen; befüllen V U4, 94
to fill in [ˌfɪl‿'ɪn] eintragen; ausfüllen <II>
film [fɪlm] Film I
finance ['faɪnæns] Finanzen <V U2, 148>
*to **find** [faɪnd] finden; herausfinden I
to find out [ˌfaɪnd‿'aʊt] herausfinden IV; erkundigen <I>
fine [faɪn] gut; in Ordnung; schön I
I'm fine. [ˌaɪm 'faɪn] Mir geht es gut. I
to **finish** ['fɪnɪʃ] fertigstellen; vervollständigen I; beenden; fertig machen; erledigen; enden; aufhören II
fire [faɪə] Feuer III
firefighter ['faɪəˌfaɪtə] Feuerwehrmann; Feuerwehrfrau <V U4, 152>
first ['fɜ:st] zuerst; als Erstes II; erste I
at first [ət 'fɜ:st] zuerst; zunächst V U3, 68
the first time [ðə fɜ:st 'taɪm] das erste Mal I
first-aid [ˌfɜ:st'eɪd] Erste-Hilfe- IV
fish *(sg)* [fɪʃ], **fish** *(pl)* [fɪʃ] Fisch I
*to go **fishing** [ˌgəʊ 'fɪʃɪŋ] angeln gehen; fischen gehen IV
fit [fɪt] fit III
five [faɪv] fünf I
flag [flæg] Flagge; Fahne IV
flat [flæt] Wohnung I; flach; eben; platt V U1, 11
flea [fli:] Floh I
flea market ['fli: ˌmɑ:kɪt] Flohmarkt I
flew [flu:] simple past von *to fly* II
flexible ['fleksɪbl] flexibel IV

flight [flaɪt] Flug IV
Have a good flight! [ˌhæv‿ə ɡʊd ˈflaɪt] Guten Flug! IV
floor [flɔː] Stockwerk; Etage II
florist [ˈflɒrɪst] Florist; Floristin <V U4, 152>
flower [ˈflaʊə] Blume <V U3, 75>
flu [fluː] Grippe V U1, 16
*to **fly** [flaɪ] fliegen II
flyer [ˈflaɪə] Flyer; Faltblatt <III>
flying [ˈflaɪɪŋ] Fliegen III
to **follow** [ˈfɒləʊ] befolgen; folgen V U3, 80
follower [ˈfɒləʊə] Follower; Folgerin; Anhänger; Anhängerin IV
food [fuːd] Essen; Lebensmittel I
foot *(sg)* [fʊt], **feet** *(pl)* [fiːt] Fuß II
on foot [ɒn ˈfʊt] zu Fuß I
football [ˈfʊtbɔːl] Fußball I
American football [əˌmerɪkən ˈfʊtbɔːl] American Football II
for [fɔː] für I; seit IV
for example [fər‿ɪgˈzɑːmpl] zum Beispiel III
for the 200th time [fə‿ðə ˈtuː hʌndrədθ ˌtaɪm] zum 200. Mal III
foreground [ˈfɔːɡraʊnd] Vordergrund III
forever [fəˈrevə] für immer; ewig IV
*to **forget** [fəˈget] vergessen II
forgot [fəˈɡɒt] simple past von *to forget* II
form [fɔːm] Form <I>; Formular V U4, 90
fortunately [ˈfɔːtʃnətli] zum Glück V U3, 72
forty [ˈfɔːti] vierzig I
to look **forward** to (+ -ing) [ˌlʊk ˈfɔːwəd tə] sich freuen auf IV
fought [fɔːt] simple past von *to fight* II
to **found** [faʊnd] gründen; begründen V U4, 98
found [faʊnd] simple past von *to find* II; past participle von *to find* III
lost and found notice [ˌlɒst‿ən ˈfaʊnd ˌnəʊtɪs] Suchplakat; Aushang III
four [fɔː] vier I
fourteen [ˌfɔːˈtiːn] vierzehn I
free [friː] kostenlos; frei III
free time [ˌfriː ˈtaɪm] Freizeit I
free-time [ˌfriːˈtaɪm] Freizeit- V U4, 89
freeze frame [ˈfriːz ˌfreɪm] Standbild <II>
French [frenʃ] französisch; Französisch; aus Frankreich IV
Friday [ˈfraɪdeɪ] Freitag I
chicken **fried** rice [ˈtʃɪkɪn ˌfraɪd ˈraɪs] gebratener Reis mit Hühnerfleisch II
friend [frend] Freund; Freundin I
to make friends [ˌmeɪk ˈfrendz] Freundschaft(en) schließen II
friendly [ˈfrendli] freundlich; sympathisch IV
frisbee [ˈfrɪzbi] Frisbee; Frisbeescheibe I
from [frɒm] aus; von I
in **front** [ɪn ˈfrʌnt] vorn II
in **front** of [ɪn ˈfrʌnt‿əv] vor; davor I
fruit [fruːt] Obst; Frucht I
full of [ˈfʊl‿əv] voller <V U1, 23>
fun [fʌn] Spaß; Freude I; lustig; spaßig; amüsant III
to be fun [biː ˈfʌn] Spaß machen; witzig sein II
funny [ˈfʌni] merkwürdig; komisch; lustig I
future [ˈfjuːtʃə] Zukunft IV; zukünftig; Zukunfts- V U4, 90

G

G'day! (= Good day!) [ɡəˈdaɪ] Hi!; Hallo!; Tag! V U1, 10
gallery [ˈɡælri] Galerie <V U1, 146>
game [ɡeɪm] Spiel I
gap [ɡæp] Lücke; Spalt <II>
garage [ˈɡærɑːʒ] Kfz-Werkstatt; Tankstelle; Garage V U4, 90
garden [ˈɡɑːdn] Garten I
gardener [ˈɡɑːdnə] Gärtner; Gärtnerin <V U2, 48>
gate [ɡeɪt] Gate; Flugsteig IV; Tor V U3, 80
gave [ɡeɪv] simple past von *to give* I
gay [ɡeɪ] homosexuell; schwul; Schwuler V U3, 68
generous [ˈdʒenrəs] großzügig <V U3, 151>
German [ˈdʒɜːmən] Deutsch I; Deutscher; Deutsche; deutsch; aus Deutschland II
*to **get** [ɡet] bekommen; werden; kommen I; holen; bringen IV
to get back [ˌɡet ˈbæk] zurückkommen; zurückgehen V U4, 98
to get better [ˌɡet ˈbetə] sich wieder besser fühlen; sich verbessern V U1, 16
to get in [ˌɡet‿ˈɪn] einsteigen IV
to get in touch [ˌɡet‿ɪn ˈtʌtʃ] in Verbindung treten (mit); kontaktieren <V U3, 150>
to get into [ˌɡet‿ˈɪntə] bilden <I>
to get lost [ˌɡet ˈlɒst] verloren gehen; sich verirren IV
to get off [ˌɡet‿ˈɒf] aussteigen II
to get on sth [ˌɡet‿ˈɒn] in etw. steigen; in etw. einsteigen IV
to get out [ˌɡet‿ˈaʊt] aussteigen; herauskommen IV
to get up [ˌɡet‿ˈʌp] aufstehen I
to get used to (sth) [ˌɡet ˈjuːst tə] sich gewöhnen an (etw.) IV
Get well soon! [ˌɡet wel ˈsuːn] Gute Besserung! V U1, 16
ghost [ɡəʊst] Geist; Gespenst IV
giant [dʒaɪənt] Riesen-; riesig V U1, 12
girl [ɡɜːl] Mädchen I
*to **give** [ɡɪv] geben; schenken I; halten V Z1, 9
giving directions [ˌɡɪvɪŋ dɪˈrekʃnz] eine Wegbeschreibung geben; Anweisungen geben <II>
given [ˈɡɪvn] past participle von *to give* IV
glove [ɡlʌv] Handschuh II
*to **go** [ɡəʊ] gehen; fahren I; hinkommen <IV>
to go bike riding [ˌɡəʊ ˈbaɪk ˌraɪdɪŋ] Fahrrad fahren II
to go camping [ˌɡəʊ ˈkæmpɪŋ] campen gehen; zelten gehen III
to go fishing [ˌɡəʊ ˈfɪʃɪŋ] angeln gehen; fischen gehen IV
to go on [ˌɡəʊ‿ˈɒn] weitergehen <III>
to go rafting [ˌɡəʊ ˈrɑːftɪŋ] raften gehen III

to go skating [ˌgəʊ ˈskeɪtɪŋ] inline-skaten gehen; Schlittschuhlaufen gehen II
to go surfing [ˌgəʊ ˈsɜːfɪŋ] surfen gehen III
to go swimming [ˌgəʊ ˈswɪmɪŋ] schwimmen gehen I
to go tandem bike riding [ˌgəʊ ˈtændəm ˌbaɪk raɪdɪŋ] Tandem fahren II
to go to bed [ˌgəʊ tə ˈbed] ins Bett gehen I
to go together [ˌgəʊ təˈgeðə] zusammenpassen <III>
to go wrong [ˌgəʊ ˈrɒŋ] schiefgehen V U4, 90

goal [gəʊl] Tor; Treffer; Ziel III
goalpost [ˈgəʊlpəʊst] Torpfosten; Torstange III
goat [gəʊt] Ziege III
gold [gəʊld] Gold; golden; Gold- III
gone [gɒn] past participle von *to go* III
good [gʊd] gut I
to be good at [biː ˈgʊd‿ət] gut sein in; gut sein bei I
Good luck! [ˌgʊd ˈlʌk] Alles Gute!; Viel Glück! IV
Have a good flight! [ˌhæv‿ə gʊd ˈflaɪt] Guten Flug! IV
Goodbye. [gʊdˈbaɪ] Auf Wiedersehen.; Servus. I
goods *(pl only)* [gʊdz] Waren; Güter V U2, 38
got [gɒt] simple past von *to get* I; past participle von *to get* IV
government [ˈgʌvnmənt] Regierung V U1, 20
GPO [ˌdʒiː piː ˈəʊ] Hauptpostamt V U1, 21
GPS (Global Positioning System) [ˌdʒiːpiːˈes] GPS *(ein satellitengestütztes System zur weltweiten Positionsbestimmung)* I
grade *(AE)* [greɪd] Klasse; Jahrgangsstufe; Note II
grammar [ˈgræmə] Grammatik <I>
grandfather [ˈgræn,faːðə] Großvater II
grandma [ˈgrænmaː] Oma I
grandmother [ˈgræn,mʌðə] Großmutter V U4, 98
grandparents *(pl)* [ˈgræn,peərnts] Großeltern II
great [greɪt] großartig; toll I; groß; riesig III
great- [greɪt] Ur- V U4, 98
great-great-grandad [ˌgreɪtgreɪt ˈgrændæd] Ururopa I
green [griːn] grün I
greenhouse [ˈgriːnhaʊs] Gewächshaus; Treibhaus <V U2, 48>
to **greet** [griːt] begrüßen; grüßen <V U3, 71>
grew [gruː] simple past von *to grow* V U2, 42
grey [greɪ] grau I
grizzly bear [ˈgrɪzli ˌbeə] Grizzlybär IV
group [gruːp] Gruppe IV
*to **grow** [grəʊ] wachsen; anbauen; züchten; ziehen V U2, 42
grown [grəʊn] past participle von *to grow* V U2, 42
to **guess** [ges] überlegen; raten; erraten I
Guess what? [ges ˈwɒt] Stellt euch vor!; Stell dir vor! II
guest [gest] Gast IV
guide [gaɪd] Führer; Führerin IV
tour guide [ˈtʊə ˌgaɪd] Reiseleiter; Reiseleiterin V U2, 38
guinea pig [ˈgɪni ˌpɪg] Meerschweinchen II
guitar [gɪˈtaː] Gitarre V U3, 72
gun [gʌn] Pistole; Schusswaffe; Waffe IV

H

had [hæd] simple past von *to have* I; past participle von *to have* IV
hairdresser [ˈheəˌdresə] Friseur; Friseurin IV
hairdressing salon [ˈheədresɪŋ ˌsælɒn] Friseursalon IV
half *(sg)* [haːf], **halves** *(pl)* [haːvz] (die) Hälfte V ZI, 8
half [haːf] halb III
half past (seven) [ˌhaːf ˈpaːst (ˌsevn)] halb (acht) II
half a million [ˌhaːf‿ə ˈmɪljən] eine halbe Million III
Halloween [ˌhæləʊˈiːn] Halloween I
hammer [ˈhæmə] Hammer III
hammer throwing [ˈhæmə ˌθrəʊɪŋ] Hammerwerfen III
hamster [ˈhæmstə] Hamster I
hand [hænd] Hand II
*to do **handicrafts** [ˌduː ˈhændikraːfts] basteln V U3, 73
*to **hang** about [ˌhæŋ‿əˈbaʊt] herumhängen I
to **happen** [ˈhæpn] passieren; geschehen II; vorkommen; sich ereignen IV
That's what happened. [ˌðæts wɒt ˈhæpnd] Das ist passiert. II
happy [ˈhæpi] glücklich I; froh; fröhlich IV
hard [haːd] hart; schwer; schwierig II
to try hard [ˌtraɪ ˈhaːd] sich anstrengen V U4, 98
hat [hæt] Mütze; Hut II
to **hate** [heɪt] hassen; nicht mögen I
*to **have** [hæv] haben; besitzen; essen; trinken I
to have (got) to [ˈhæv (gɒt) tə] müssen II
to have a party [ˌhæv‿ə ˈpaːti] eine Party feiern I
to have breakfast [ˌhæv ˈbrekfəst] frühstücken I
to have got [hæv ˈgɒt] haben; besitzen II
to have to [ˈhæv tə] müssen II
Have a good flight! [ˌhæv‿ə gʊd ˈflaɪt] Guten Flug! IV
he [hiː] er I
head [hed] Kopf II
headache [ˈhedeɪk] Kopfweh; Kopfschmerzen II
heading [ˈhedɪŋ] Überschrift <I>
headline [ˈhedlaɪn] Überschrift <V U3, 76>
healthy [ˈhelθi] gesund III
*to **hear** [hɪə] hören II
to hear about [ˌhɪər‿əˈbaʊt] erfahren von; hören von IV
heard [hɜːd] simple past von *to hear* II; past participle von *to hear* IV
hearing [ˈhɪərɪŋ] Gehör II

heavy [ˈhevi] schwer; stark; schwierig III
height [haɪt] Höhe II
held [held] simple past von *to hold* II
helicopter [ˈhelɪkɒptə] Helikopter; Hubschrauber V U1, 12
Hello. [həˈləʊ] Hallo. I
helmet [ˈhelmət] Helm I
help [help] Hilfe I
helpful [ˈhelpfl] hilfreich; hilfsbereit <V U3, 151>
to **help** [help] helfen I
helper [ˈhelpə] Helfer; Helferin <V U4, 102>
her [hɜː] ihr I; sie II
here [hɪə] hier I; hierhin; hierher III
Here you are. [ˌhɪə juˈɑː] Bitte schön. I
hers [hɜːz] ihre III
herself [həˈself] sich selbst; sich; selbst IV
Hi. [haɪ] Hi.; Hallo. I
high [haɪ] hoch; groß II
high school [ˈhaɪ ˌskuːl] High School *(weiterführende Schule, Oberstufe)* V U3, 63
high temperature [ˌhaɪ ˈtemprətʃə] Fieber V U1, 16
junior high school [ˌdʒuːniə ˈhaɪ skuːl] Junior Highschool *(Mittelschule in den USA, in der Regel Klassenstufe 7–9)* II
hill [hɪl] Berg; Hügel IV
him [hɪm] ihm; ihn II
himself [hɪmˈself] sich; selbst; sich selbst IV
Hindi [ˈhɪndiː] Hindi *(Sprache in Indien)* <V ZI, 8>
Hindu [ˈhɪnduː] Hindu; hinduistisch V U2, 47
his [hɪz] sein I; seine III
Hispanic [hɪˈspænɪk] Hispanoamerikaner; Hispanoamerikanerin; hispanisch IV
history [ˈhɪstri] Geschichte <V U4, 100>
*to **hit** [hɪt] schlagen; treffen III; anfahren; rammen V U3, 64
hit [hɪt] simple past, past participle von *to hit* III
HIV [ˌeɪtʃaɪˈviː] HIV; HI-Virus; HIV- V U3, 68
hobby [ˈhɒbi] Hobby II
hockey [ˈhɒki] Eishockey; Hockey IV
ice hockey [ˈaɪs ˌhɒki] Eishockey IV
*to **hold** [həʊld] halten; festhalten II; abhalten <V U1, 25>
hole [həʊl] Loch I
holiday [ˈhɒlədeɪ] Ferien; Urlaub II
holiday *(AE)* [ˈhɒlədeɪ] Feiertag IV
home [həʊm] Zuhause; Heim; nach Hause I; Startseite <V U4, 100>
at home [ət ˈhəʊm] zu Hause; daheim I
home country [ˌhəʊm ˈkʌntri] Heimat; Heimatland IV
homeless [ˈhəʊmləs] obdachlos <V U3, 151>
*to be **homesick** [biː ˈhəʊmsɪk] Heimweh haben IV
homework [ˈhəʊmwɜːk] Hausaufgabe(n) I
to do homework [ˌduː ˈhəʊmwɜːk] Hausaufgabe(n) machen I
honest [ˈɒnɪst] ehrlich <V U3, 151>
to **hoover** [ˈhuːvə] staubsaugen II
hope [həʊp] Hoffnung V U3, 73
to **hope** (for) [həʊp (fə)] hoffen (auf) II
horse [hɔːs] Pferd I
horse riding [ˈhɔːs ˌraɪdɪŋ] Reiten I
hospital [ˈhɒspɪtl] Krankenhaus II
hostel [ˈhɒstl] Herberge; Hostel II
hot [hɒt] heiß I
hot dog [ˈhɒt ˌdɒg] Hotdog II
hotel [həˈtel] Hotel IV
hotline [ˈhɒtlaɪn] Hotline <V U2, 148>
hour [aʊə] Stunde II
hours *(pl)* [ˈaʊəz] Zeiten IV
working hours *(pl)* [ˈwɜːkɪŋ ˌaʊəz] Arbeitszeit IV
visiting hours *(pl)* [ˈvɪzɪtɪŋ ˌaʊəz] Besuchszeiten <V U3, 74>
house [haʊs] Haus I
how [haʊ] wie I
How are you? [ˌhaʊˈɑː jə] Wie geht es dir? I
How can I help you? [ˌhaʊ kæn aɪ ˈhelp juː] Was kann ich für euch/dich tun? I
How much (is/are) …? [ˌhaʊ ˈmʌtʃ (ɪz/ɑː)] Wie viel (kostet/kosten) …? I
How old are you? [haʊˈəʊld ə juː] Wie alt bist du? I
how to … [ˈhaʊ tə] wie man … IV
however [haʊˈevə] jedoch V U1, 20
a/one **hundred** [ˈhʌndrəd] hundert; einhundert I
hungry [ˈhʌŋgri] hungrig I
treasure **hunt** [ˈtreʒə ˌhʌnt] Schnitzeljagd; Schatzsuche II
hurling [ˈhɜːlɪŋ] Hurling *(ähnliche Sportart wie Hockey)* III
hurricane [ˈhʌrɪkən] Hurrikan; Orkan; Wirbelsturm IV
*to **hurt** [hɜːt] verletzen; wehtun II
hurt [hɜːt] simple past von *to hurt* II; verletzt III; past participle von *to hurt* <V U3, 74>
husky [ˈhʌski] Husky *(Schlittenhunderasse)* IV

I

I [aɪ] ich I
I can't find … [aɪ kɑːnt ˈfaɪnd] ich kann … nicht finden I
I can't wait [aɪ ˌkɑːnt ˈweɪt] ich kann es kaum erwarten III
I don't mind. [aɪ ˌdəʊnt ˈmaɪnd] Es macht nichts. IV
I don't know. [ˌaɪ dəʊnt ˈnəʊ] Ich weiß (es) nicht! I
I wouldn't like (to) … [aɪ ˈwʊdnt laɪk (tə)] ich möchte nicht …; ich würde nicht gerne … I
I'm afraid [aɪmˈəˈfreɪd] leider IV
I'm sorry. [aɪm ˈsɒri] Es tut mir leid.; Entschuldigung. II
I'd (= I would) [aɪd] ich würde; ich hätte gern I
I'd like (to) … (= I would like to) [aɪd ˈlaɪk (tə)] ich möchte …; ich würde gerne … I
I'd love (to) … (= I would love to) [aɪd ˈlʌv (tə)] ich würde sehr gern …; ich hätte gern … IV
I'm fine. [ˌaɪm ˈfaɪn] Mir geht es gut. I
ice cream [ˌaɪs ˈkriːm] Eis; Eiscreme II
ice hockey [ˈaɪs ˌhɒki] Eishockey IV
idea [aɪˈdɪə] Idee I
if [ɪf] wenn; falls; ob IV

ill [ɪl] krank; schlecht V U1, 16
to **imagine** [ɪˈmædʒɪn] sich vorstellen <II>
immigrant [ˈɪmɪgrənt] Einwanderer; Einwanderin; Immigrant; Immigrantin IV
important [ɪmˈpɔːtnt] wichtig III
impossible [ɪmˈpɒsəbl] unmöglich IV
impression [ɪmˈpreʃn] Eindruck <V U1, 146>
to **improve** [ɪmˈpruːv] verbessern <V U2, 149>
in [ɪn] im; in; auf; am I; bei; an IV
in front [ɪn ˈfrʌnt] vorn II
in the middle of [ɪn ðə ˈmɪdl‿əv] mitten in II
in a park [ɪn‿ə ˈpɑːk] im Park I
in front of [ɪn ˈfrʌnt‿əv] vor; davor I
in the evening [ɪn ðiˈ‿iːvnɪŋ] abends I
in the north of [ˌɪn ðə ˈnɔːθ‿əv] im Norden von III
in time [ɪn ˈtaɪm] rechtzeitig; pünktlich V U2, 54
*to be **included** [biː ɪnˈkluːdɪd] mit enthalten sein; inbegriffen sein V U4, 94
to **increase** [ɪnˈkriːs] erhöhen <V U2, 149>
independence [ˌɪndɪˈpendəns] Unabhängigkeit IV
independent [ˌɪndɪˈpendənt] unabhängig V U2, 37
Indian [ˈɪndiən] Inder; Inderin; indisch V U2, 36
indoor [ˌɪnˈdɔː] Hallen-; Innen- III
industry [ˈɪndəstri] Industrie III; Industriezweig; Gewerbe V U4, 88
tourist industry [ˈtʊərɪst‿ˌɪndəstri] Tourismus IV
information [ˌɪnfəˈmeɪʃn] Information(en) II
to **injure** [ˈɪndʒə] verletzen V U3, 64
inside cover [ˌɪnsaɪd ˈkʌvə] Umschlaginnenseite <II>
inspiration [ˌɪnspɪˈreɪʃn] Inspiration; Eingebung V U3, 68
inspiring [ɪnˈspaɪərɪŋ] inspirierend; anregend V U3, 68
to **install** [ɪnˈstɔːl] installieren <V U2, 149>
medical **insurance** [ˌmedɪkl‿ɪnˈʃʊərns] Krankenversicherung V U3, 73
interest [ˈɪntrəst] Interesse IV
*to be **interested** in [biː ˈɪntrəstɪd‿ɪn] interessiert sein an; sich interessieren für III
interesting [ˈɪntrəstɪŋ] interessant I
intern [ˈɪntɜːn] Praktikant; Praktikantin V U4, 94
international [ˌɪntəˈnæʃnl] international V Z1, 9
internet [ˈɪntənet] Internet I
to surf the internet [ˌsɜːf ðiˈ ˈɪntənet] im Internet surfen <III>
internship [ˈɪntɜːnʃɪp] Praktikum; Berufspraktikum IV
interview [ˈɪntəvjuː] Interview; Befragung; Gespräch IV
job interview [ˈdʒɒb ˌɪntəvjuː] Vorstellungsgespräch <IV>
to **interview** [ˈɪntəvjuː] befragen; interviewen <II>
interviewer [ˈɪntəvjuːə] Interviewer; Interviewerin; Befrager; Befragerin IV
into [ˈɪntu] in; in … hinein II
intro [ˈɪntrəʊ] Auftakt; Einführung <I>
to **introduce** sb to sb [ˌɪntrəˈdjuːs] jmdn. jmdm. vorstellen III
introduction [ˌɪntrəˈdʌkʃn] Einleitung; Einführung <III>; Vorstellung <V U1, 24>
Inuit [ˈɪnuɪt] Inuit *(Ureinwohner Kanadas)* IV
invitation [ˌɪnvɪˈteɪʃn] Einladung I
to **invite** [ɪnˈvaɪt] einladen II
*to be **involved** [biː ɪnˈvɒlvd] sich beteiligen; sich engagieren <V U3, 150>
Irish [ˈaɪrɪʃ] irisch; Irisch; aus Irland III
is [ɪz] ist I
Is something wrong? [ɪz ˈsʌmθɪŋ rɒŋ] Stimmt etwas nicht? II
island [ˈaɪlənd] Insel IV
it [ɪt] es; er; sie I; ihn; ihm II
it's (= it is) [ɪts] es ist I
It's ten pounds. [ɪts ˌten ˈpaʊndz] Es kostet zehn Pfund. I
IT (Information Technology) [ˌaɪˈtiː (ɪnfəˌmeɪʃn tekˈnɒlədʒi)] Informatik; Informationstechnik V U2, 38
Italian [ɪˈtæliən] italienisch; Italienisch; Italiener; Italienerin IV
item [ˈaɪtəm] Ding; Artikel; Gegenstand IV
its [ɪts] sein; ihr I

J

January [ˈdʒænjuri] Januar I
Japanese [ˌdʒæpnˈiːz] japanisch; Japanisch; aus Japan; Japaner; Japanerin IV
jeans *(pl)* [dʒiːnz] Jeans I
crown **jewels** *(pl)* [ˌkraʊn ˈdʒuːəlz] Kronjuwelen II
jewellery [ˈdʒuːəlri] Schmuck <V U2, 148>
job [dʒɒb] Job I; Aufgabe; Tätigkeit III
job ad [ˈdʒɒb æd] Stellenanzeige <IV>
job interview [ˈdʒɒb ˌɪntəvjuː] Vorstellungsgespräch <IV>
to **join** [dʒɔɪn] sich anschließen; beitreten V U2, 47
journey [ˈdʒɜːni] Fahrt; Reise III
juice [dʒuːs] Saft I
July [dʒʊˈlaɪ] Juli I
long **jump** [ˈlɒŋ ˌdʒʌmp] Weitsprung II
to **jump** [dʒʌmp] springen III
June [dʒuːn] Juni I
junior [ˈdʒuːniə] Nachwuchs- <V U4, 100>
junior high school [ˌdʒuːniə ˈhaɪ skuːl] Junior Highschool *(Mittelschule in den USA, in der Regel Klassenstufe 7–9)* II
just [dʒʌst] gerade (eben); soeben; einfach; nur III
just for fun [ˌdʒʌst fə ˈfʌn] nur (so) zum Spaß <I>

K

kangaroo [ˌkæŋgrˈuː] Känguru V U1, 11
kayak [ˈkaɪæk] Kajak IV
kayaking [ˈkaɪækɪŋ] Kajakfahren IV
*to **keep** [kiːp] halten II
to keep away [ˌkiːp‿əˈweɪ] fernhalten IV
to keep in touch [ˌkiːp ɪn ˈtʌtʃ] in Kontakt bleiben II

to keep sb prisoner [ˌkiːp ˈprɪznə] jmdn. gefangen halten IV
keeper [ˈkiːpə] Pfleger; Pflegerin <V U4, 152>
kept [kept] simple past von *to keep* II; past participle von *to keep* IV
key [kiː] Schlüssel III
to **kick** [kɪk] schießen; treten III
kid [kɪd] Kind I
to **kill** [kɪl] töten V U1, 11
kilo (kg, kilogram) [ˈkɪləʊ] Kilo (kg, Kilogramm) I
kilometre (km) [kɪˈlɒmɪtə] Kilometer (km) IV
kilt [kɪlt] Kilt; Schottenrock III
kind [kaɪnd] Art; Sorte II; freundlich; nett <V U3, 151>
kindergarten [ˈkɪndəˌgɑːtn] Kindergarten V U3, 73
king [kɪŋ] König II
newspaper **kiosk** [ˈnjuːspeɪpə ˌkiːɒsk] Zeitungsstand II
to **kiss** [kɪs] küssen V U4, 99
kitchen [ˈkɪtʃɪn] Küche II
Kiwi [ˈkiːwiː] Kiwi *(Kosename für Neuseeländer)* V U4, 106
knew [njuː] simple past von *to know* IV
to **knock** sb off sth [ˌnɒk … ˈɒf] jmdn. von etw. stoßen IV
*to **know** [nəʊ] wissen; kennen I
I don't know. [ˌaɪ dəʊnt ˈnəʊ] Ich weiß (es) nicht! I
*to be **known** [biː ˈnəʊn] bekannt sein <V U3, 151>
koala [kəʊˈɑːlə] Koala V U1, 11

L

to **label** [ˈleɪbl] beschriften <II>
ladder [ˈlædə] Leiter I
lady [ˈleɪdi] Frau; Dame IV
lake [leɪk] See IV
to **lament** [ləˈment] klagen V U4, 98
lamp [læmp] Lampe II
to **land** [lænd] landen IV
landmark [ˈlænmɑːk] Wahrzeichen IV
landscape [ˈlændskeɪp] Landschaft V U4, 89
language [ˈlæŋgwɪdʒ] Grammatik <I>; Sprache IV
official language [əˌfɪʃl ˈlæŋgwɪdʒ] Amtssprache V ZI, 8
lantern [ˈlæntən] Laterne II
laptop [ˈlæptɒp] Laptop I
large [lɑːdʒ] groß II
to **last** [lɑːst] dauern; andauern II
last [lɑːst] letzte I
late [leɪt] (zu) spät II
to be late [biː ˈleɪt] zu spät kommen II
later [ˈleɪtə] später I
to **laugh** [lɑːf] lachen II
law [lɔː] Gesetz V U1, 20
to break the law [ˌbreɪk ðə ˈlɔː] gegen das Gesetz verstoßen V U2, 46
to mow the **lawn** [ˌməʊ ðə ˈlɔːn] den Rasen mähen <V U4, 153>
lawyer [ˈlɔɪə] Anwalt; Anwältin; Jurist; Juristin V U2, 46
*to **lead** [liːd] anführen; führen; leiten V U2, 37
leader [ˈliːdə] Leiter; Leiterin III
to **learn** [lɜːn] lernen II; erfahren; herausfinden V U1, 12
*to **leave** [liːv] verlassen; lassen; abfahren; weggehen II; vergessen; hinterlassen III; abfliegen; gehen IV
leaving [ˈliːvɪŋ] Abschieds- II
led [led] simple past, past participle von *to lead* V U2, 37
left [left] links; simple past von *to leave* II; übrig; past participle von *to leave* III
on the left [ɒn ðə ˈleft] links; auf der linken Seite II
leg [leg] Bein II
lesbian [ˈlezbiən] homosexuell; lesbisch; Lesbe V U3, 68
less [les] weniger III
lesson [ˈlesn] Schulstunde; Unterricht I
let's (= let us) [lets] lass(t) uns I
letter [ˈletə] Buchstabe; Brief; Schreiben IV
letter of application [ˌletər ˌəv ˌæplɪˈkeɪʃn] Bewerbungsschreiben IV
driving **licence** [ˈdraɪvɪŋ ˌlaɪsns] Führerschein V U3, 64
to **lie** [laɪ] lügen IV
life *(sg)* [laɪf], **lives** *(pl)* [laɪvz] Leben II
lifestyle [ˈlaɪfstaɪl] Lebensstil; Lebensart; Lebensweise V U1, 12
lift [lɪft] Aufzug II
to **like** [laɪk] mögen; gernhaben I
like + -ing [ˌlaɪk ˈ…ɪŋ] … gerne I
like [laɪk] wie I; als ob IV
like this [laɪk ˈðɪs] so; auf diese Weise <I>
line [laɪn] Linie III; Zeile <IV>
assembly line [əˈsembli ˌlaɪn] Fließband V U2, 38
zip line [ˈzɪp ˌlaɪn] Seilrutsche III
link [lɪŋk] Link; Verbindung <V U4, 100>
lion [ˈlaɪən] Löwe V U3, 63
mountain lion [ˈmaʊntɪn ˌlaɪən] Puma II
list [lɪst] Liste V U1, 16
shopping list [ˈʃɒpɪŋ ˌlɪst] Einkaufszettel I
to **listen** (to) [ˈlɪsn (tə)] anhören; hören; zuhören I
listening [ˈlɪsnɪŋ] Hörverstehen <I>
listening skills [ˈlɪsnɪŋ ˌskɪlz] Fertigkeit Hören <I>
little [ˈlɪtl] klein I
a little (bit) [ə ˈlɪtl (bɪt)] ein (kleines) bisschen; ein (klein) wenig II
to **live** [lɪv] wohnen; leben I
living [ˈlɪvɪŋ] Lebensweise; Wohnen; Leben V U2, 42
living room [ˈlɪvɪŋ ˌrʊm] Wohnzimmer II
to **load** the dishwasher [ˌləʊd ðə ˈdɪʃwɒʃə] die Spülmaschine einräumen II
local [ˈləʊkl] örtlich; lokal; hiesig II
location [ləʊˈkeɪʃn] Ort <V U1, 24>
locked [lɒkt] abgeschlossen I
logistics [ləˈdʒɪstɪks] Logistik <V U2, 148>
lonely [ˈləʊnli] einsam III
long [lɒŋ] lang III; weit V U1, 11
as long as [əz ˈlɒŋ ˌəz] solange; sofern V U3, 80
to be a long way away [biː ə ˈlɒŋ ˌweɪ əˈweɪ] weit weg sein II
long jump [ˈlɒŋ ˌdʒʌmp] Weitsprung II

longer ['lɒŋgə] länger I
to **look** [lʊk] schauen; aussehen; sehen; nachschauen I
to look after [ˌlʊk‿'ɑ:ftə] aufpassen auf; hüten; sich kümmern um II
to look at ['lʊk‿ət] anschauen I
to look for ['lʊk fə] suchen (nach) IV
to look forward to (+ -ing) [ˌlʊk 'fɔ:wəd tə] sich freuen auf IV
to look to do sth ['lʊk ˌtə] etw. planen <V U4, 100>
to look up to sb [ˌlʊk‿'ʌp tə] zu jmdm. aufschauen; jmdn. bewundern <V U3, 151>
*to **lose** [lu:z] verlieren II
lost [lɒst] simple past von *to lose* II; past participle von *to lose* III
to get lost [ˌget 'lɒst] verloren gehen; sich verirren IV
lost and found notice [ˌlɒst‿ən 'faʊnd ˌnəʊtɪs] Suchplakat; Aushang III
a **lot** [ə 'lɒt] viel; sehr I
a **lot** of [ə 'lɒt‿əv] viel; viele; eine Menge I
lots of ['lɒts‿əv] jede Menge; viel; viele I
loud [laʊd] laut I
Love, [lʌv] Liebe Grüße; Herzliche Grüße I
to **love** [lʌv] lieben; gern mögen I
I'd love (to) … (= I would love to) [aɪd 'lʌv (tə)] ich würde sehr gern …; ich hätte gern … IV
Good **luck**! [ˌgʊd 'lʌk] Alles Gute!; Viel Glück! IV
lucky ['lʌki] glücklich; Glück bringend II
to be lucky [bi:‿'lʌki] Glück haben II
lucky day [ˌlʌki 'deɪ] Glückstag II
lunch [lʌnʃ] Mittagessen I
lunchtime ['lʌnʃtaɪm] Mittagspause; Mittagszeit I

M

machine [mə'ʃi:n] Maschine; Automat V U2, 38
made [meɪd] simple past von *to make* II; past participle von *to make* III
magazine [ˌmægə'zi:n] Zeitschrift IV
*to do **magic** [ˌdu: 'mædʒɪk] zaubern II
magician [mə'dʒɪʃn] Zauberkünstler; Zauberkünstlerin II
main [meɪn] wichtigste <III>
majority [mə'dʒɒrəti] Mehrheit; Mehrzahl V ZI, 8
*to **make** [meɪk] erstellen; basteln; machen; tun I; bilden; ausmachen <II>; herstellen V U2, 38
to make friends [ˌmeɪk 'frendz] Freundschaft(en) schließen II
to make reservations [ˌmeɪk rezə'veɪʃnz] reservieren IV
to make up [ˌmeɪk‿'ʌp] erfinden; sich ausdenken <V U2, 41>
mall [mɔ:l] Einkaufspassage; Einkaufszentrum II
man *(sg)* [mæn], **men** *(pl)* [men] Mann I
manager ['mænɪdʒə] Manager; Managerin; Geschäftsführer; Geschäftsführerin IV
manta ray ['mæntə ˌreɪ] Teufelsrochen <V U1, 23>
to **manufacture** [ˌmænjə'fæktʃə] fertigen; herstellen <V U2, 148>
many ['meni] viele I
Maori ['maʊri] Maori-; maorisch; Maori V U4, 89
map [mæp] Karte; Plan II
March [mɑ:tʃ] März I
march [mɑ:tʃ] Marsch; Kundgebung V U2, 47
market ['mɑ:kɪt] Markt I
flea market ['fli: ˌmɑ:kɪt] Flohmarkt I
arranged **marriage** [əˌreɪndʒd 'mærɪdʒ] arrangierte Hochzeit V U2, 37
mask [mɑ:sk] Maske V U4, 99
match [mætʃ] Spiel; Match I
to **match** [mætʃ] zuordnen <I>
to match sth [mætʃ] zu etw. passen <V U2, 50>
Math *(AE)* [mæθ] Mathe; Mathematik III
Maths [mæθs] Mathe I
What's the **matter**? [ˌwɒts ðə 'mætə] Was ist los?; Was hast du? V U1, 16
May [meɪ] Mai I
may [meɪ] können; dürfen V U1, 20
maybe ['meɪbi] vielleicht II
me [mi:] ich; mich; mir I
meal [mi:l] Essen; Mahlzeit II
*to **mean** [mi:n] bedeuten; meinen IV
meaning ['mi:nɪŋ] Bedeutung <III>
meant [ment] simple past, past participle von *to mean* IV
meat [mi:t] Fleisch IV
mechanic [mɪ'kænɪk] Mechaniker; Mechanikerin V U4, 90
medal ['medl] Medaille II
media ['mi:diə] Medien <II>
media designer ['mi:diə dɪˌzaɪnə] Mediengestalter; Mediengestalterin <V U4, 152>
social media [ˌsəʊʃl 'mi:diə] soziale Medien III
mediation [ˌmi:di'eɪʃn] Sprachmittlung <I>
mediation skills [ˌmi:di'eɪʃn ˌskɪlz] Fertigkeit Sprachmittlung <I>
medical insurance [ˌmedɪkl‿ɪn'ʃʊərns] Krankenversicherung V U3, 73
medical record [ˌmedɪkl 'rekɔ:d] Krankenakte V U1, 16
medication [ˌmedɪ'keɪʃn] Medikament; Arznei; Arzneimittel V U3, 68
medicine ['medsn] Medikamente; Medizin V U1, 16
*to **meet** [mi:t] kennenlernen; treffen I; (sich) treffen II
meeting ['mi:tɪŋ] Besprechung; Meeting <V U4, 153>
member ['membə] Mitglied V U4, 89
menu ['menju:] Menu; Speisekarte <V U2, 48>
Merry Christmas! [ˌmeri 'krɪsməs] Frohe Weihnachten! I
mess [mes] Durcheinander; Unordnung I
message ['mesɪdʒ] Nachricht; SMS II
messenger ['mesɪndʒə] Kurier; Kurierin; Bote; Botin IV
met [met] simple past von *to meet* II
metal ['metl] Metall-; metallen III

metalworker ['metlwɜ:kə] Metallbauer; Metallbauerin <V U4, 152>
meter *(AE)* ['mi:tə] Meter III
metre ['mi:tə] Meter II
middle ['mɪdl] Mitte III
in the middle of [ɪn ðə 'mɪdl‿əv] mitten in II
might [maɪt] könnte V U4, 90
mild [maɪld] mild II
mile [maɪl] Meile III
million ['mɪljən] Million I
half a million [ˌhɑ:f‿ə 'mɪljən] eine halbe Million III
mind map ['maɪnd ˌmæp] Wörternetz <I>
to **mind** sth [maɪnd] etwas gegen etw. haben; einem etwas ausmachen V U4, 90
Never mind. [ˌnevə 'maɪnd] Macht nichts.; Schon gut.; Mach dir nichts draus. II
coal **mine** ['kəʊl ˌmaɪn] Kohlenbergwerk; Kohlengrube III
mine [maɪn] meine III
minute ['mɪnɪt] Minute I
to **miss** [mɪs] verpassen; vermissen II
Miss [mɪs] Frau *(Anrede)* IV
missing ['mɪsɪŋ] fehlend; verschwunden <V U2, 37>
mistake [mɪ'steɪk] Fehler <V U1, 11>
model ['mɒdl] Vorlage; Muster <I>
role model ['rəʊl ˌmɒdl] Vorbild V U3, 68
modern ['mɒdn] modern I
mom *(AE)* [mɒm] Mama III
at the **moment** [ət ðə 'məʊmənt] im Moment; momentan II
Monday ['mʌndeɪ] Montag I
money ['mʌni] Geld I
to raise money [ˌreɪz 'mʌni] Geld sammeln; Geld aufbringen II
month [mʌnθ] Monat II
moose *(sg)* [mu:s], **moose** *(pl)* [mu:s] Elch IV
more [mɔ:] mehr; weitere II
more often [mɔ:r‿'ɒfn] häufiger; öfter IV
morning ['mɔ:nɪŋ] Morgen; Vormittag I
this morning [ðɪs 'mɔ:nɪŋ] heute Morgen II
most [məʊst] die meisten; die Mehrheit; am meisten III
mother ['mʌðə] Mutter I
to **motivate** ['məʊtɪveɪt] anspornen; motivieren III
mountain ['maʊntɪn] Berg II
mountain lion ['maʊntɪn ˌlaɪən] Puma II
mouse *(sg)* [maʊs], **mice** *(pl)* [maɪs] Maus I
mouth [maʊθ] Mund II
mouthguard ['maʊθgɑ:d] Mundschutz <V U4, 100>
to **move** [mu:v] umziehen II; (sich) bewegen; ziehen IV
movement ['mu:vmənt] Bewegung IV
movie *(AE)* ['mu:vi] Film III
to **mow** the lawn [ˌməʊ ðə 'lɔ:n] den Rasen mähen <V U4, 153>
Mr ['mɪstə] Herr *(Anrede)* I
Mrs ['mɪsɪz] Frau *(Anrede)* I
Ms [mɪz] Frau *(Anrede)* V U4, 90
much [mʌtʃ] viel I
as much as [əz 'mʌtʃ‿əz] bis zu <V U1, 23>
mud [mʌd] Schlamm; Matsch I
muffin ['mʌfɪn] Muffin II
multicultural [ˌmʌlti'kʌltʃrl] multikulturell IV
mum [mʌm] Mama; Mutti I
museum [mju:'zi:əm] Museum II
music ['mju:zɪk] Musik I
Muslim ['mʊzlɪm] Muslim; Muslimin I
must [mʌst] müssen II
my [maɪ] mein I
My name is … [maɪ 'neɪm‿ɪz] Ich heiße … I
myself [maɪ'self] mich; selbst III; mir; mich selbst IV

N

name [neɪm] Name I
to **name** [neɪm] benennen <I>
narrator [nə'reɪtə] Erzähler; Erzählerin I
nation ['neɪʃn] Volk; Nation; Land; Staat III
national ['næʃnl] National-; national III
national park [ˌnæʃnl 'pɑ:k] Nationalpark III
nationality [ˌnæʃn'æləti] Nationalität; Staatsangehörigkeit IV
native ['neɪtɪv] eingeboren; einheimisch <V ZI, 8>
Native American [ˌneɪtɪv‿ə'merɪkən] Ureinwohner Amerikas; Ureinwohnerin Amerikas; Indianer; Indianerin; indianisch III
natural ['nætʃrl] Natur-; natürlich <V U4, 101>
nature ['neɪtʃə] Natur V U3, 81
near [nɪə] in der Nähe von I; nah II
nearly ['nɪəli] fast; beinahe II
neck [nek] Hals; Nacken II
to **need** [ni:d] brauchen I
to need to ['ni:d ˌtə] müssen III
negative ['negətɪv] negativ <IV>
neighbour ['neɪbə] Nachbar; Nachbarin I
nervous ['nɜ:vəs] nervös; aufgeregt <V U3, 151>
netball ['netbɔ:l] Korbball I
never ['nevə] nie; niemals II
Never mind. [ˌnevə 'maɪnd] Macht nichts.; Schon gut.; Mach dir nichts draus. II
new [nju:] neu I
news [nju:z] Nachricht(en); Neuigkeit(en) II
newspaper ['nju:sˌpeɪpə] Zeitung III
newspaper kiosk ['nju:speɪpə ˌki:ɒsk] Zeitungsstand II
next [nekst] nächste I; als Nächstes II
next to ['nekst tə] neben I
nice [naɪs] schön; nett I
Nice to meet you. [ˌnaɪs tə 'mi:t ju:] Schön, dich kennenzulernen. I
night [naɪt] Nacht I
at night [ət 'naɪt] nachts IV
nine [naɪn] neun I
nineteen [ˌnaɪn'ti:n] neunzehn I
ninety ['naɪnti] neunzig I
no [nəʊ] kein; keine; nein I
no one ['nəʊ wʌn] niemand I
nobody ['nəʊbədi] niemand II
to **nod** [nɒd] nicken V U4, 99
noise [nɔɪz] Geräusch I
noisy ['nɔɪzi] laut III
non- [nɒn] nicht- <V ZI, 8>

non-violent [ˌnɒnˈvaɪəlnt] friedlich; gewaltfrei V U2, 46
north [nɔːθ] Norden; Nord- III
in the north of [ˌɪn ðə ˈnɔːθ‿əv] im Norden von III
nose [nəʊz] Nase II
not [nɒt] nicht I
not … any [ˌnɒt … eni] kein; keine III
not … any more [ˌnɒt … eni ˈmɔː] nicht mehr III
not … anything [nɒt … ˈeniθɪŋ] nichts III
not … either [nɒt … ˈaɪðə] auch nicht III
not … yet [nɒt … ˈjet] noch nicht III
note [nəʊt] Notiz; Zettel; Nachricht <V U1, 13>
notes *(pl)* [nəʊts] Notizen <I>
to take notes [ˌteɪk ˈnəʊts] sich Notizen machen <I>
nothing [ˈnʌθɪŋ] nichts II
lost and found **notice** [ˌlɒst‿ən ˈfaʊnd ˌnəʊtɪs] Suchplakat; Aushang III
noun [naʊn] Nomen; Hauptwort <V U3, 69>
November [nəˈvembə] November I
now [naʊ] jetzt; nun I
number [ˈnʌmbə] Zahl; Nummer I; Anzahl <V ZI, 8>
nurse [nɜːs] Krankenpfleger; Krankenschwester IV
nursery teacher [ˈnɜːsri ˌtiːtʃə] Erzieher; Erzieherin <V U4, 152>

O

o'clock [əˈklɒk] Uhr *(Zeitangabe bei vollen Stunden)* I
occasionally [əˈkeɪʒnli] gelegentlich III
ocean [ˈəʊʃn] Ozean <V U3, 78>
October [ɒkˈtəʊbə] Oktober I
odd one out [ˌɒd wʌn‿ˈaʊt] das Wort, das nicht in die Gruppe passt <I>
of [ɒv] von I; mit; vor; aus III
of course [əv ˈkɔːs] natürlich; selbstverständlich II
of all the states [əv‿ˈɔːl ðə ˌsteɪts] von allen Staaten IV
to turn **off** [ˌtɜːn‿ˈɒf] abschalten; ausschalten <V U2, 149>
to knock sb **off** sth [ˌnɒk … ˈɒf] jmdn. von etw. stoßen IV
to **offer** [ˈɒfə] bieten; anbieten IV
office [ˈɒfɪs] Büro V U2, 38
police **officer** [pəˈliːs‿ˌɒfɪsə] Polizeibeamter; Polizeibeamtin I
official [əˈfɪʃl] offiziell <IV>
official language [əˌfɪʃl ˈlæŋgwɪdʒ] Amtssprache V ZI, 8
often [ˈɒfn] oft; häufig II
more often [mɔːr‿ˈɒfn] häufiger; öfter IV
oh [əʊ] Null *(bei Uhrzeiten und Telefonnummern)* III
Oh dear. [ˌəʊ ˈdɪə] Oje. V U1, 16
oil [ɔɪl] Öl II
oil spill [ˈɔɪl ˌspɪl] Ölteppich; Ölpest V U1, 20
OK (okay) [əʊˈkeɪ] okay I
old [əʊld] alt I
on [ɒn] auf; an; am I; mit II
to put on [ˌpʊt‿ˈɒn] anziehen II
to try on [ˌtraɪ ˈɒn] anprobieren II
on foot [ɒn ˈfʊt] zu Fuß I
on Saturdays [ɒn ˈsætədeɪz] samstags I
on the bus [ˌɒn ðə ˈbʌs] im Bus II
on the left [ɒn ðə ˈleft] links; auf der linken Seite II
on the right [ɒn ðə ˈraɪt] rechts; auf der rechten Seite II
on TV [ɒn ˌtiːˈviː] im Fernsehen III
once [wʌns] einmal; einst II
once upon a time [ˌwʌns əpɒn‿ə ˈtaɪm] es war einmal II
one [wʌn] eins; ein I
a/one hundred [ˈhʌndrəd] hundert; einhundert I
a/one thousand [ˈθaʊznd] tausend; eintausend II
each one [ˌiːtʃ ˈwʌn] jedes <IV>
no one [ˈnəʊ wʌn] niemand I
one day [ˈwʌn deɪ] eines Tages I
one(s) [wʌn(z)] *Platzhalter für ein Nomen* III
online [ˌɒnˈlaɪn] online; Online- II
only [ˈəʊnli] nur I; erst V U3, 68
to **open** [ˈəʊpn] öffnen; aufmachen I; eröffnen V U4, 94
open [ˈəʊpn] geöffnet I; offen <V U4, 100>
opportunity [ˌɒpəˈtjuːnəti] Chance; Möglichkeit; Gelegenheit IV
opposite [ˈɒpəzɪt] Gegenteil <I>; gegenüber II
or [ɔː] oder I
orange [ˈɒrɪndʒ] orange; Orange I
order [ˈɔːdə] Reihenfolge <I>
word order [ˈwɜːd‿ˌɔːdə] Wortstellung; Satzstellung <II>
to **order** [ˈɔːdə] bestellen V U4, 94
organization [ˌɔːgnaɪˈzeɪʃn] Organisation V U3, 72
to **organize** [ˈɔːgnaɪz] organisieren I
other [ˈʌðə] andere II
each other [ˌiːtʃ‿ˈʌðə] einander; sich; gegenseitig III
others [ˈʌðəz] anderen II
our [aʊə] unser I
ours [aʊəz] unsere III
ourselves [ˌaʊəˈselvz] uns; selbst; uns selbst IV
out [aʊt] hinaus V U4, 98
out and about [ˌaʊt‿ən‿əˈbaʊt] unterwegs III
out of … [ˈaʊt‿əv] aus … heraus I
the **outback** [ðiˈaʊtbæk] das Outback *(australisches Hinterland)* V U1, 11
outdoors [ˌaʊtˈdɔːz] im Freien <V U2, 48>
outside [ˌaʊtˈsaɪd] außerhalb; außen; draußen; im Freien II
oval [ˈəʊvl] oval; eiförmig III
over [ˈəʊvə] vorbei <II>; über; herüber; drüben III
all over [ˌɔːl‿ˈəʊvə] in ganz; überall II
to turn over [ˌtɜːn ˈəʊvə] umkippen; (sich) umdrehen III
to **own** [əʊn] besitzen III
own [əʊn] eigene II

P

p.m. [ˌpiːˈem] nachmittags *(Uhrzeit)* III
to **pack** [pæk] packen; einpacken III
package [ˈpækɪdʒ] Paket IV
packaging [ˈpækɪdʒɪŋ] Verpackung <V U2, 149>
page [peɪdʒ] Seite <I>

to **paint** [peɪnt] bemalen; malen; streichen II
painting ['peɪntɪŋ] Gemälde V U1, 12
face painting ['feɪs peɪntɪŋ] Schminken II
wall painting ['wɔ:l peɪntɪŋ] Wandmalerei II
pair [peə] Paar <II>
solar **panel** [ˌsəʊlə 'pænl] Sonnenkollektor <V U2, 149>
paper ['peɪpə] Papier III
parade [pə'reɪd] Parade; Umzug; Prozession IV
parents *(pl)* ['peərnts] Eltern I
park [pɑ:k] Park I
national park [ˌnæʃnl 'pɑ:k] Nationalpark III
theme park ['θi:m ˌpɑ:k] Freizeitpark II
parliament ['pɑ:ləmənt] Parlament V U3, 62
part [pɑ:t] Teil; Rolle II
to take part (in) [ˌteɪk 'pɑ:t (ɪn)] mitmachen (bei); teilnehmen (an) II
partner ['pɑ:tnə] Partner; Partnerin I
party ['pɑ:ti] Party; Feier I
to have a party [ˌhæv‿ə 'pɑ:ti] eine Party feiern I
to **pass** on [ˌpɑ:s‿ɒn] weitergeben <V U3, 81>
passenger ['pæsndʒə] Passagier; Passagierin IV
passive voice ['pæsɪv ˌvɔɪs] Passiv <IV>
passport ['pɑ:spɔ:t] Pass; Reisepass IV
past [pɑ:st] vorbei (an) I; nach *(bei Uhrzeitangaben)* II; Vergangenheit III
half past (seven) [ˌhɑ:f 'pɑ:st (ˌsevn)] halb (acht) II
quarter to/past ['kwɔ:tə tə/pɑ:st] Viertel vor/nach II
patient ['peɪʃnt] Patient; Patientin V U1, 16; geduldig <V U2, 51>
*to **pay** [peɪ] bezahlen V U3, 68
PE (Physical Education) [ˌpi:'i: (ˌfɪzɪkl edʒʊ'keɪʃn)] Sportunterricht I
peaceful ['pi:sfl] friedlich V U2, 47
pen [pen] Stift; Füller I
pencil ['pensl] Bleistift I
penfriend ['penfrend] Brieffreund; Brieffreundin III
people ['pi:pl] Leute; Menschen I; Volk V U4, 89
Aboriginal people [æbəˌrɪdʒnl 'pi:pl] die Aborigines V U1, 11
per [pɜ:] pro <V U4, 100>
percent (%) [pə'sent] Prozent III
present **perfect** [ˌpreznt 'pɜ:fɪkt] das Perfekt <III>
person *(sg)* ['pɜ:sn] Mensch; Person II
persons *(pl)* ['pɜ:sns] Leute; Menschen II
pet [pet] Haustier I
pharmacist ['fɑ:məsɪst] Apotheker; Apothekerin <V U1, 22>
pharmacy ['fɑ:məsi] Apotheke V U1, 16
phone [fəʊn] Telefon; Handy I
phone call ['fəʊn ˌkɔ:l] Telefonanruf; Anruf I
to **phone** [fəʊn] anrufen; telefonieren II
photo ['fəʊtəʊ] Foto I
to take photos (of) [ˌteɪk 'fəʊtəʊz (əv)] Fotos machen; fotografieren II
phrase [freɪz] Wortverbindung; Satzteil; Satz; Redewendung <III>
to **pick** up [ˌpɪk‿'ʌp] abholen <V U1, 147>; aufheben V U4, 99
picnic ['pɪknɪk] Picknick I
picture ['pɪktʃə] Bild I
picture-based ['pɪktʃəbeɪst] bildbezogen <III>
a **piece** of [ə 'pi:s‿əv] ein Stück … II
pier [pɪə] Pier II
pink [pɪŋk] pink; rosa I
pizza ['pi:tsə] Pizza I
place [pleɪs] Platz; Stelle; Ort I
to take place [ˌteɪk 'pleɪs] stattfinden <V U1, 146>
plan [plæn] Plan IV
to **plan** [plæn] planen IV
plane [pleɪn] Flugzeug IV
planner ['plænə] Kalender; Planer II
plant [plɑ:nt] Pflanze III
to **plant** [plɑ:nt] pflanzen <V U4, 153>
plate [pleɪt] Teller; (Kontinental-) Platte IV
play [pleɪ] Theaterstück III
to **play** [pleɪ] spielen I
player ['pleɪə] Spieler; Spielerin II
playground ['pleɪgraʊnd] Schulhof; Pausenhof; Spielplatz I
playing field ['pleɪɪŋ ˌfi:ld] Sportplatz II
please [pli:z] bitte I
plum [plʌm] Pflaume I
plumber ['plʌmə] Installateur; Installateurin; Klempner; Klempnerin <V U2, 148>
podcast ['pɒdkɑ:st] Podcast V U3, 68
poem ['pəʊɪm] Gedicht III
point [pɔɪnt] Punkt III
to **point** [pɔɪnt] zeigen V U4, 99
police [pə'li:s] Polizei IV
police officer [pə'li:s‿ɒfɪsə] Polizeibeamter; Polizeibeamtin I
police station [pə'li:s ˌsteɪʃn] Polizeirevier; Polizeiwache V U3, 64
polite [pə'laɪt] höflich <V U3, 151>
to **pollute** [pə'lu:t] verschmutzen; verunreinigen V U2, 42
pollution [pə'lu:ʃn] Verschmutzung V U2, 37
pool [pu:l] Tümpel <V U4, 101>
swimming pool ['swɪmɪŋ ˌpu:l] Schwimmbad I
poor [pɔ:] arm IV
pop [pɒp] Pop *(Musik)* II
popular ['pɒpjələ] beliebt III
population *(no pl)* [ˌpɒpjə'leɪʃn] Bevölkerung; Einwohner; Einwohnerzahl IV
positive ['pɒzətɪv] positiv III
possible ['pɒsəbl] möglich <V U2, 149>
post [pəʊst] Post; Beitrag <V U1, 12>
to **post** [pəʊst] posten; online stellen III
postcard ['pəʊskɑ:d] Postkarte I
poster ['pəʊstə] Poster II
pot [pɒt] Topf III
potato *(sg)* [pə'teɪtəʊ], **potatoes** *(pl)* [pə'teɪtəʊz] Kartoffel IV
pound (£) [paʊnd] Pfund *(brit. Währungseinheit)* I
practice ['præktɪs] Training; Übung I
to **practise** ['præktɪs] üben; trainieren <II>
prayer [preə] Gebet V U4, 98

to **prefer** [prɪˈfɜː] bevorzugen; vorziehen <V U4, 152>
to **prepare** [prɪˈpeəˌ] vorbereiten <IV>
preschool [priːˈskuːl] Vorschul-; Vorschule V U3, 73
prescription [prɪˈskrɪpʃn] Rezept *(für Arzneimittel)* V U1, 16
present [ˈpreznt] Geschenk I
present perfect [ˌpreznt ˈpɜːfɪkt] das Perfekt <III>
present progressive [ˌpreznt prəˈgresɪv] Verlaufsform der Gegenwart <II>
to **present** [prɪˈzent] präsentieren V U4, 94
presentation [ˌprezn̩ˈteɪʃn] Präsentation; Referat; Vortrag III
presentation skills [ˌprezn̩ˈteɪʃn ˌskɪlz] Fertigkeit Präsentieren <III>
presenter [prɪˈzentə] Moderator; Moderatorin <V U1, 25>
president [ˈprezɪdnt] Präsident; Präsidentin III
pretty [ˈprɪti] hübsch II
price [praɪs] Preis I
primary school [ˈpraɪmri ˌskuːl] Grundschule IV
prince [prɪns] Prinz V U2, 38
prison [ˈprɪzn] Gefängnis V U2, 46
prisoner [ˈprɪznə] Gefangener; Gefangene IV
to keep sb prisoner [ˌkiːp ˈprɪznə] jmdn. gefangen halten IV
prize [praɪz] Preis; Gewinn II
probably [ˈprɒbəbli] wahrscheinlich IV
problem [ˈprɒbləm] Problem I
procession [prəˈseʃn] Umzug; Festzug II
to **produce** [prəˈdjuːs] erzeugen; herstellen; anbauen IV
product [ˈprɒdʌkt] Produkt; Erzeugnis V U4, 94
profile [ˈprəʊfaɪl] Profil; Steckbrief III
(software) **program** [(ˌsɒfweə) ˈprəʊgræm] (Software)Programm V ZI, 8
programme [ˈprəʊgræm] Sendung; Programm III
computer **programmer** [kəmˌpjuːtə ˈprəʊgræmə] Programmierer; Programmiererin V U2, 38
programming [ˈprəʊgræmɪŋ] Programmieren <V U2, 148>
present **progressive** [ˌpreznt prəˈgresɪv] Verlaufsform der Gegenwart <II>
project [ˈprɒdʒekt] Projekt II
to **protect** [prəˈtekt] schützen III
protest [ˈprəʊtest] Protest; Demonstration V U2, 37
to **protest** [prəˈtest] protestieren V U1, 21
proud (of) [praʊd (əv)] stolz (auf) IV
to **prove** [pruːv] beweisen IV
to **provide** [prəˈvaɪd] bereitstellen; bieten; versorgen <V U4, 100>
public transport [ˌpʌblɪk ˈtrænspɔːt] öffentliche Verkehrsmittel III
to **pull** [pʊl] ziehen I
pullover [ˈpʊləʊvə] Pullover I
to **push** [pʊʃ] schieben I
stone **put** [ˈstəʊn ˌpʊt] Steinstoßen III
*to **put** [pʊt] setzen; legen; stellen I; bringen; stecken II
to put in [ˌpʊtˌ ˈɪn] einsetzen <I>
to put into [ˌpʊt ˈɪntə] eingeben (in) <IV>
to put on [ˌpʊtˌ ˈɒn] anziehen II
put [pʊt] simple past von *to put* I

Q

qualification [ˌkwɒlɪfɪˈkeɪʃn] Ausbildung; Qualifikation; Abschluss; Schulabschluss IV
qualified [ˈkwɒlɪfaɪd] qualifiziert V U4, 112
quality [ˈkwɒləti] Eigenschaft; Qualität; Merkmal <V U4, 93>
quantity [ˈkwɒntəti] Menge <IV>
quarter to/past [ˈkwɔːtə tə/pɑːst] Viertel vor/nach II
queen [kwiːn] Königin II
question [ˈkwestʃən] Frage I
queue [kjuː] Warteschlange II
quick [kwɪk] schnell IV
quiet [kwaɪət] leise; ruhig; still II
quite [kwaɪt] ziemlich; ganz; völlig II
quiz [kwɪz] Rätsel <I>; Quiz; Ratespiel IV

R

rabbit [ˈræbɪt] Kaninchen I
raccoon [rəˈkuːn] Waschbär I
race [reɪs] Wettrennen; Rennen; Wettlauf II
sack race [ˈsæk ˌreɪs] Sackhüpfen II
radio [ˈreɪdiəʊ] Radio III
raffle [ˈræfl] Gewinnspiel; Tombola II
raft [rɑːft] Raft; Floß III
rafting [ˈrɑːftɪŋ] Rafting III
to go rafting [ˌgəʊ ˈrɑːftɪŋ] raften gehen III
railway [ˈreɪlweɪ] Eisenbahn; Bahn IV
railway station [ˈreɪlweɪ ˌsteɪʃn] Bahnhof IV
to **rain** [reɪn] regnen I
rainbow [ˈreɪnbəʊ] Regenbogen III
rainy [ˈreɪni] regnerisch II
to **raise** [reɪz] sammeln; aufbringen <V U4, 100>
to raise money [ˌreɪz ˈmʌni] Geld sammeln; Geld aufbringen II
ran [ræn] simple past von *to run* II
rang [ræŋ] simple past von *to ring* II
ranger *(AE)* [ˈreɪndʒə] Ranger; Rangerin IV
rap [ræp] Rap I
rapid [ˈræpɪd] Stromschnelle III
rarely [ˈreəli] selten III
RE [riː] Betr. V U4, 106
*to **read** [riːd] lesen; vorlesen II
read [red] simple past von *to read* II
reading [ˈriːdɪŋ] Lesen <I>; Lesung <V U1, 24>
reading skills [ˈriːdɪŋ ˌskɪlz] Fertigkeit Lesen <I>
ready [ˈredi] bereit; fertig I
real [rɪəl] echt; richtig; wirklich <V U1, 23>
really [ˈrɪəli] wirklich; eigentlich I
reason [ˈriːzn] Grund <V U3, 71>
*to **rebuild** [ˌriːˈbɪld] wiederaufbauen IV
receptionist [rɪˈsepʃnɪst] Empfangschef; Empfangsdame IV; Arzthelfer; Arzthelferin V U1, 16

medical record [ˌmedɪkl ˈrekɔːd] Krankenakte V U1, 16
to **record** [rɪˈkɔːd] aufnehmen; aufzeichnen <I>
to **recover** [rɪˈkʌvə] sich erholen V U1, 20
to **recycle** [ˌriːˈsaɪkl] recyceln; wiederverwerten <V U2, 149>
recycling [ˌriːˈsaɪklɪŋ] Recycling; Wiederaufbereitung <V U2, 149>
red [red] rot I
to **reduce** [rɪˈdjuːs] reduzieren; vermindern; verringern V U4, 94
reef [riːf] Riff V U1, 20
reference [ˈrefrns] Referenz; Arbeitszeugnis; Empfehlung IV
reflexive pronoun [rɪˌfleksɪv ˈprəʊnaʊn] Reflexivpronomen <IV>
reggae [ˈregeɪ] Reggae *(Musik)* IV
to **register** [ˈredʒɪstə] sich registrieren lassen; sich eintragen; sich anmelden V U1, 16
registration [ˌredʒɪˈstreɪʃn] Überprüfung der Anwesenheit I
reliable [rɪˈlaɪəbl] verlässlich; zuverlässig; vertrauenswürdig IV
religion [rɪˈlɪdʒn] Religion V U2, 47
to **rely** (on) [rɪˈlaɪ (ɒn)] sich verlassen (auf); vertrauen (auf) IV
to **remember** [rɪˈmembə] sich erinnern (an); sich merken III
to **repair** [rɪˈpeə] reparieren IV
to **repeat** [rɪˈpiːt] wiederholen V U3, 81
report [rɪˈpɔːt] Bericht V U4, 94
to **report** [rɪˈpɔːt] berichten <III>
request [rɪˈkwest] Anfrage IV
animal **rescue** shelter [ˌænɪml ˈreskjuː ˌʃeltə] Tierheim I
research [rɪˈsɜːtʃ] Recherche; Forschung <IV>
to **research** [rɪˈsɜːtʃ] recherchieren; erforschen; untersuchen <V U4, 99>
reservation [ˌrezəˈveɪʃn] Reservat; Reservierung III
to make reservations [ˌmeɪk rezəˈveɪʃnz] reservieren IV
respectful [rɪˈspektfl] respektvoll <V U3, 151>
to **respect** [rɪˈspekt] respektieren V U2, 47
responsible [rɪsˈpɒnsəbl] verantwortungsvoll; verantwortlich <V U4, 152>
rest [rest] Rest II
restaurant [ˈrestrɒnt] Restaurant II
result [rɪˈzʌlt] Ergebnis V U4, 90
retail [ˈriːteɪl] Einzelhandel V U4, 94
return ticket [rɪˈtɜːn ˌtɪkɪt] Hin- und Rückfahrkarte III
rhyme [raɪm] Reim <III>
to **rhyme** [raɪm] (sich) reimen <III>
rice [raɪs] Reis II
chicken fried rice [ˈtʃɪkɪn ˌfraɪd ˈraɪs] gebratener Reis mit Hühnerfleisch II
rich [rɪtʃ] reich V U3, 63
Richter scale *(no pl)* [ˈrɪktə ˌskeɪl] Richterskala IV
ride [raɪd] Fahrt; Fahrgeschäft; Ritt II
*to **ride** [raɪd] fahren; reiten I
rider [ˈraɪdə] Reiter; Reiterin V U4, 98
horse **riding** [ˈhɔːs ˌraɪdɪŋ] Reiten I
right [raɪt] Recht V U1, 11
right [raɪt] richtig; korrekt I; rechts; rechte II; okay <V U3, 74>
right away [ˌraɪtəˈweɪ] sofort; gleich V U3, 68
on the right [ɒn ðə ˈraɪt] rechts; auf der rechten Seite II
You're right. [jɔːˈraɪt] Du hast recht. I
*to **ring** [rɪŋ] klingeln; läuten I
river [ˈrɪvə] Fluss I
road [rəʊd] Straße I
road accident [ˈrəʊd ˌæksɪdnt] Verkehrsunfall <V U3, 64>
road train [ˈrəʊd ˌtreɪn] Fernlastzug <V U1, 26>
rock [rɒk] Fels; Stein V U1, 12
rock climbing [ˈrɒk ˌklaɪmɪŋ] Klettern I
rocket [ˈrɒkɪt] Rakete III
role [rəʊl] Rolle <V U1, 19>
role model [ˈrəʊl ˌmɒdl] Vorbild V U3, 68
role play [ˈrəʊl ˌpleɪ] Rollenspiel <I>
roller coaster [ˈrəʊlə ˌkəʊstə] Achterbahn II
roof [ruːf] Dach III
room [ruːm] Zimmer; Raum I
root word [ˌruːt ˈwɜːd] Grundwort; Stammwort <IV>
daily **routine** [ˌdeɪli ruːˈtiːn] Alltag <V U2, 40>
rubber [ˈrʌbə] Radiergummi I
rubbish [ˈrʌbɪʃ] Müll; Abfall I
rugby [ˈrʌgbi] Rugby III
rule [ruːl] Regel V U3, 80
ruler [ˈruːlə] Lineal I
*to **run** [rʌn] laufen; rennen; fahren II
to run away [ˌrʌnəˈweɪ] weglaufen II
Russian [ˈrʌʃn] Russisch; russisch; aus Russland; Russe; Russin IV

S

sack race [ˈsæk ˌreɪs] Sackhüpfen II
sacred [ˈseɪkrɪd] heilig V U2, 54
sad [sæd] traurig I
safari [səˈfɑːri] Safari V U3, 63
safe [seɪf] sicher; ungefährlich; in Sicherheit; unversehrt IV
said [sed] simple past von *to say* I; past participle von *to say* III
salad [ˈsæləd] Salat I
salary [ˈsælri] Gehalt IV
salesperson [ˈseɪlzˌpɜːsn] Verkäufer; Verkäuferin <V U4, 152>
hairdressing **salon** [ˈheədresɪŋ ˌsælɒn] Friseursalon IV
salt [sɔːlt] Salz V U2, 47
saltwater crocodile [sɔːltˌwɔːtə ˈkrɒkədaɪl] Salzwasserkrokodil <V U1, 23>
the **same** [ðə ˈseɪm] der gleiche; derselbe; gleich; genauso II
at the same time [ət ðə seɪm ˈtaɪm] gleichzeitig; nebenher II
sandwich [ˈsænwɪdʒ] Sandwich; belegtes Brot I
sang [sæŋ] simple past von *to sing* II
sanitation [ˌsænɪˈteɪʃn] sanitäre Anlagen V U2, 42
sat [sæt] simple past, past participle von *to sit* IV
Saturday [ˈsætədeɪ] Samstag I
on Saturdays [ɒn ˈsætədeɪz] samstags I
to **save** [seɪv] retten; sparen II
saw [sɔː] simple past von *to see* I

saxophone ['sæksəfəʊn] Saxofon I
*to **say** [seɪ] nennen; sagen; nachsprechen; sprechen I; aussprechen III
Richter **scale** *(no pl)* ['rɪktə ˌskeɪl] Richterskala IV
to **scan** [skæn] nach Details durchsuchen; scannen <III>
to **scare** [skeə] erschrecken <II>
*to be **scared** [bi: 'skeəd] Angst haben I
scarf *(sg)* [skɑ:f], **scarves** *(pl)* [skɑ:vz] Schal; Tuch II
scary ['skeəri] unheimlich; gruselig; beängstigend I
scene [si:n] Szene <II>
scenery ['si:nri] Kulissen; Bühnenbild III
school [sku:l] Schule I
at school [ət 'sku:l] in der Schule I
high school ['haɪ ˌsku:l] High School *(weiterführende Schule, Oberstufe)* V U3, 63
junior high school [ˌdʒu:niə 'haɪ sku:l] Junior Highschool *(Mittelschule in den USA, in der Regel Klassenstufe 7–9)* II
primary school ['praɪmri ˌsku:l] Grundschule IV
school trip [ˌsku:l 'trɪp] Klassenfahrt; Schulausflug II
secondary school ['sekndri ˌsku:l] weiterführende Schule; Mittelschule IV
science ['saɪəns] Naturwissenschaft; Wissenschaft III
science fiction [ˌsaɪəns 'fɪkʃn] Science-Fiction I
to **score** [skɔ:] erzielen III
Scottish ['skɒtɪʃ] schottisch; aus Schottland III
scratch [skrætʃ] Kratzer IV
screenshot ['skri:nʃɒt] Bildschirmfoto <IV>
sea [si:] Meer I
search [sɜ:tʃ] Recherche; Suche <IV>
search engine ['sɜ:tʃˌendʒɪn] Suchmaschine <IV>
to **search** [sɜ:tʃ] suchen <V U2, 41>
at the **seaside** [ət ðə 'si:saɪd] am Meer I
season ['si:zn] Jahreszeit; Saison II
seat [si:t] Sitzplatz; Sitz III
Take a seat. [ˌteɪkˌə 'si:t] Setz dich.; Setzen Sie sich.; Nimm Platz.; Nehmen Sie Platz. IV
second ['sekənd] Sekunde <I>; zweite II; zweit- IV
secondary school ['sekndri ˌsku:l] weiterführende Schule; Mittelschule IV
secondary school leaving certificate ['sekndri sku:l ˌli:vɪŋ sə'tɪfɪkət] mittlerer Schulabschluss; Realschulabschluss IV
second-hand [ˌsekn'hænd] gebraucht; secondhand; aus zweiter Hand I
*to **see** [si:] sehen I
See you. ['si: ˌju:] Wir sehen uns.; Bis bald.; Tschüss. II
See you soon. [ˌsi: ˌju: 'su:n] Bis bald. I
to see sb [si:] jmdn. empfangen <V U3, 74>
to **seem** [si:m] scheinen V U4, 99
seen [si:n] past participle von *to see* III
self-confident [ˌself'kɒnfɪdnt] selbstsicher; selbstbewusst <V U3, 151>
selfie ['selfi] Selfie IV
*to **sell** [sel] verkaufen I
*to **send** [send] schicken; senden I
sense [sens] Sinn; Bedeutung IV
sense of smell [ˌsensˌəv 'smel] Geruchssinn IV
sent [sent] simple past von *to send* I
sentence ['sentəns] Satz <I>
to **separate** ['sepreɪt] trennen V U3, 62
Sepedi [se'peədi] Nord-Sotho *(Sprache in Südafrika)* <V U3, 79>
September [sep'tembə] September I
series *(no pl)* ['sɪəri:z] Serie IV
serious ['sɪəriəs] ernst; schwer II
service ['sɜ:vɪs] Dienst; Service <V U2, 148>
customer service [ˌkʌstəmə 'sɜ:vɪs] Kundenbetreuung; Kundendienst; Kundenservice IV
delivery service [dɪ'lɪvri ˌsɜ:vɪs] Lieferdienst <V U2, 49>
Sesotho [sɪ'su:tu:] Sesotho *(Sprache in Südafrika)* V U3, 73
Setswana [se'tswɑ:nə] Setswana *(Sprache in Südafrika)* <V U3, 79>
settler ['setlə] Siedler; Siedlerin V U1, 11
seven ['sevn] sieben I
seventeen [ˌsevn'ti:n] siebzehn I
seventy ['sevnti] siebzig I
several ['sevrl] mehrere; einige; verschiedene V U2, 37
*to **shake** [ʃeɪk] beben; zittern; schütteln IV
shaken ['ʃeɪkn] past participle von *to shake* IV
shamrock ['ʃæmrɒk] Kleeblatt III
to **share** [ʃeə] teilen III
shark [ʃɑ:k] Hai I
whale shark ['weɪl ˌʃɑ:k] Walhai <V U1, 23>
she [ʃi:] sie I
sheep *(sg)* [ʃi:p], **sheep** *(pl)* [ʃi:p] Schaf I
shelf *(sg)* [ʃelf], **shelves** *(pl)* [ʃelvz] Regal; Regalbrett II
animal rescue **shelter** [ˌænɪml 'reskju: ˌʃeltə] Tierheim I
ship [ʃɪp] Schiff I
shirt [ʃɜ:t] Hemd; Shirt I
shoe [ʃu:] Schuh I
shook [ʃʊk] simple past von *to shake* IV
*to **shoot** [ʃu:t] schießen; erschießen IV
shop [ʃɒp] Geschäft; Laden I
shop assistant ['ʃɒpˌəˌsɪstnt] Verkäufer; Verkäuferin V U4, 94
sports shop ['spɔ:ts ˌʃɒp] Sportgeschäft II
shopping ['ʃɒpɪŋ] Einkaufen I
shopping centre ['ʃɒpɪŋ ˌsentə] Einkaufszentrum I
shopping list ['ʃɒpɪŋ ˌlɪst] Einkaufszettel I
short [ʃɔ:t] kurz II
shorts *(pl)* [ʃɔ:ts] Shorts; kurze Hose II
shot [ʃɒt] simple past, past participle von *to shoot* IV
should [ʃʊd] sollte III
to **shout** [ʃaʊt] rufen; schreien I
show [ʃəʊ] Show; Aufführung I
*to **show** [ʃəʊ] zeigen II
sick [sɪk] krank <V U1, 147>

to be sick [bi: 'sɪk] sich übergeben I
side [saɪd] Seite II
sight [saɪt] Sehenswürdigkeit II
sign [saɪn] Schild; Zeichen; Anzeichen IV
to **sign** [saɪn] unterschreiben; unterzeichnen <V U3, 74>
to **signal** ['sɪgnl] blinken IV
silly ['sɪli] albern II
simple past [ˌsɪmpl 'pɑ:st] einfache Vergangenheit <II>
simple present [ˌsɪmpl 'preznt] einfache Gegenwart; Präsens <II>
since [sɪns] seit; seitdem IV
Yours **sincerely**, [ˌjɔ:z sɪn'sɪəli] Mit freundlichen Grüßen IV
*to **sing** [sɪŋ] singen I
don't sing [ˌdəʊnt 'sɪŋ] singe nicht; singt nicht I
singer ['sɪŋə] Sänger; Sängerin I
single ticket [ˌsɪŋgl 'tɪkɪt] einfache Fahrkarte III
sister ['sɪstə] Schwester I
*to **sit** [sɪt] sitzen IV
to sit (down) [ˌsɪt ('daʊn)] sich setzen; sich hinsetzen I
site [saɪt] Seite *(im Internet)* <IV>
situation [ˌsɪtju'eɪʃn] Situation V U3, 80
six [sɪks] sechs I
sixteen [ˌsɪk'sti:n] sechzehn I
sixty ['sɪksti] sechzig I
size [saɪz] Größe II
to **skate** [skeɪt] inlineskaten; Schlittschuh laufen II
skateboard ['skeɪtbɔ:d] Skateboard I
skater ['skeɪtə] Skater; Skaterin I
*to go **skating** [ˌgəʊ 'skeɪtɪŋ] inlineskaten gehen; Schlittschuhlaufen gehen II
to **skid** [skɪd] schleudern; schlittern V U3, 64
skill [skɪl] Fertigkeit; Geschick; Kenntnis; Fähigkeit IV
skilled [skɪld] qualifiziert; ausgebildet; Fach- <V U2, 148>
to **skim** [skɪm] überfliegen <III>
skirt [skɜ:t] Rock III
sky [skaɪ] Himmel IV
slave [sleɪv] Sklave; Sklavin IV
slave trader ['sleɪv ˌtreɪdə] Sklavenhändler; Menschenhändler IV
sled [sled] Schlitten IV
sleep [sli:p] Schlaf <V U1, 147>
*to **sleep** [sli:p] schlafen II
slept [slept] simple past von *to sleep* II
slow [sləʊ] langsam IV
slum [slʌm] Slum; Elendsviertel V U2, 36
small [smɔ:l] klein I
smell [smel] Geruch; Duft IV
sense of smell [ˌsens ˌəv 'smel] Geruchssinn IV
*to **smell** [smel] riechen <V U3, 77>
smoke [sməʊk] Rauch IV
smurf [smɜ:f] Schlumpf I
snack bar ['snæk ˌbɑ:] Imbissstube; Café I
snow [snəʊ] Schnee II
snowboard ['snəʊbɔ:d] Snowboard I
snowy ['snəʊi] schneereich; verschneit II
so [səʊ] also; deshalb I; so; dermaßen II
so that [səʊ 'ðæt] damit; sodass IV
soccer *(AE)* ['sɒkə] Fußball II
social media [ˌsəʊʃl 'mi:diə] soziale Medien III
software ['sɒfweə] Software IV
soil [sɔɪl] Boden; Erde V U2, 42
solar panel [ˌsəʊlə 'pænl] Sonnenkollektor <V U2, 149>
sold [səʊld] simple past von *to sell* II; past participle von *to sell* V U4, 94
to **solve** [sɒlv] lösen V U2, 38
some [sʌm] etwas; einige; ein paar I
somebody ['sʌmbədi] jemand I
someone ['sʌmwʌn] jemand; irgendjemand III
something ['sʌmθɪŋ] etwas I
sometimes ['sʌmtaɪmz] manchmal I
son [sʌn] Sohn IV
song [sɒŋ] Lied I
songwriter ['sɒŋˌraɪtə] Songschreiber; Songschreiberin; Liedermacher; Liedermacherin V U3, 68
soon [su:n] bald II
See you soon. [ˌsi: ˌju: 'su:n] Bis bald. I
sore throat [ˌsɔ: 'θrəʊt] Halsschmerzen <V U1, 147>
Sorry. ['sɒri] Tut mir leid.; Entschuldigung. I
I'm sorry. [aɪm 'sɒri] Es tut mir leid.; Entschuldigung. II
to **sort** [sɔ:t] sortieren <IV>
soul [səʊl] Seele V U2, 46
sound [saʊnd] Laut; Geräusch; Ton <I>
to **sound** [saʊnd] klingen III
source [sɔ:s] Quelle <V ZI, 8>
South African [ˌsaʊθ ˌ'æfrɪkən] Südafrikaner; Südafrikanerin; südafrikanisch; aus Südafrika V U3, 63
south [saʊθ] Süd-; Süden III
southern ['sʌðən] südlich; Süd-; Südstaaten- IV
souvenir [ˌsu:vn'ɪə] Souvenir; Andenken II
space [speɪs] Raumfahrt; Weltraum III
Spanish ['spænɪʃ] spanisch; Spanisch; aus Spanien IV
*to **speak** [spi:k] sprechen I
English-speaking [ˌɪŋglɪʃ'spi:kɪŋ] englischsprachig V ZI, 9
speaker ['spi:kə] Sprecher; Sprecherin; Redner; Rednerin V ZI, 8
speaking ['spi:kɪŋ] Sprechen <I>
speaking skills ['spi:kɪŋ ˌskɪlz] Fertigkeit Sprechen <I>
special ['speʃl] besonders; speziell I
direct **speech** [dɪˌrekt 'spi:tʃ] direkte Rede <V U3, 76>
speech therapist ['spi:tʃ ˌθerəpɪst] Logopäde; Logopädin <V U4, 152>
*to **spell** [spel] buchstabieren <V U3, 65>
spelling ['spelɪŋ] Rechtschreibung I
*to **spend** [spend] verbringen *(Zeit)*; ausgeben *(Geld)* II
spent [spent] simple past von *to spend* II
oil **spill** ['ɔɪl ˌspɪl] Ölteppich; Ölpest V U1, 20
spoke [spəʊk] simple past von *to speak* V U2, 42
*to **spoken** ['spəʊkn] past participle von *to speak* <V U3, 79>
sport [spɔ:t] Sport III
sports *(pl only)* [spɔ:ts] Sportarten I

sports centre ['spɔ:ts ˌsentə] Sportzentrum I
sports day ['spɔ:ts ˌdeɪ] Sportfest II
sports shop ['spɔ:ts ˌʃɒp] Sportgeschäft II
spring [sprɪŋ] Frühling II
to **spy** [spaɪ] sehen I
square [skweə] Quadrat- V U3, 63
square dance ['skweə ˌdɑ:ns] Squaredance *(amerikanischer Volkstanz)* II
stadium ['steɪdiəm] Stadion I
stage [steɪdʒ] Bühne II
stall [stɔ:l] Stand; Bude I
*to **stand** [stænd] stehen II
can't stand + -ing [ˌkɑ:nt 'stænd … ɪŋ] etw. nicht ausstehen können; etw. nicht ertragen III
to stand for ['stænd fə] stehen für III
to stand up [ˌstænd‿'ʌp] aufstehen V U4, 99
star [stɑ:] Star I
start [stɑ:t] Anfang; Beginn; Start <I>
to **start** [stɑ:t] anfangen; beginnen; starten I
state [steɪt] Bundesstaat; Staat III
of all the states [əv‿'ɔ:l ðə ˌsteɪts] von allen Staaten IV
statement ['steɪtmənt] Aussage <IV>
station ['steɪʃn] Station; Bahnhof; Haltestelle III
police station [pə'li:s ˌsteɪʃn] Polizeirevier; Polizeiwache V U3, 64
railway station ['reɪlweɪ ˌsteɪʃn] Bahnhof IV
train station ['treɪn ˌsteɪʃn] Bahnhof <III>
statue ['stætʃu:] Statue IV
to **stay** [steɪ] bleiben; übernachten I
to stay up [ˌsteɪ 'ʌp] aufbleiben <V U1, 147>
staying connected [ˌsteɪɪŋ kə'nektɪd] in Verbindung bleiben III
steamboat ['sti:mbəʊt] Dampfer; Dampfschiff IV
step [step] Schritt; Stufe II
stick [stɪk] Schläger; Stock III
still [stɪl] noch; immer noch II
stock [stɒk] Bestand <V U4, 153>
stomach ['stʌmək] Magen; Bauch <V U1, 147>
stomachache ['stʌmək‿eɪk] Bauchweh; Bauchschmerzen <V U1, 147>
stone [stəʊn] Stein III
stone put ['stəʊn ˌpʊt] Steinstoßen III
stood [stʊd] simple past von *to stand* II
stop [stɒp] Haltestelle; Halt II
to **stop** [stɒp] beenden; aufhören; anhalten II
store *(AE)* [stɔ:] Laden; Geschäft III
storm [stɔ:m] Sturm I
story ['stɔ:ri] Geschichte I
feature story ['fi:tʃə ˌstɔ:ri] Leitartikel; Sonderbericht <V U3, 76>
straight on [streɪt‿'ɒn] geradeaus II
strawberry ['strɔ:bri] Erdbeere I
street [stri:t] Straße I
stress [stres] Betonung <V U1, 13>
strong [strɒŋ] stark III; stabil IV
to **struggle** ['strʌgl] kämpfen; ringen; sich anstrengen; Mühe haben V U1, 11
*to be **stuck** [bi: 'stʌk] feststecken; stecken bleiben I
student ['stju:dnt] Schüler; Schülerin I
study skills [ˌstʌdi 'skɪlz] Fertigkeit Lern- und Arbeitstechniken <I>
to **study** (for) sth ['stʌdi (fə)] (auf einen Abschluss) studieren; (für) etw. lernen V U4, 90
subject ['sʌbdʒɪkt] Schulfach I; Betreff III
successful [sək'sesfl] erfolgreich IV
suddenly ['sʌdnli] plötzlich; auf einmal I
suitability [ˌsu:tə'bɪləti] Eignungs-; Eignung; Tauglichkeit V U4, 90
suitable ['su:təbl] geeignet; passend <V U3, 65>
suitcase ['su:tkeɪs] Koffer IV
summer ['sʌmə] Sommer II
sun [sʌn] Sonne II
Sunday ['sʌndeɪ] Sonntag I
sunny ['sʌni] sonnig II
superlative [su:'pɜ:lətɪv] Superlativ <IV>
supermarket ['su:pəˌmɑ:kɪt] Supermarkt I
supplier [sə'plaɪə] Zulieferer; Anbieter V U4, 94
supplies *(pl)* [sə'plaɪz] Vorräte IV
support [sə'pɔ:t] Unterstützung; Hilfe V U4, 90
sure [ʃɔ:] sicher II
to **surf** the internet [ˌsɜ:f ðɪ 'ɪntənet] im Internet surfen <III>
surfing ['sɜ:fɪŋ] Surfen; Wellenreiten; Surf- IV
to go surfing [ˌgəʊ 'sɜ:fɪŋ] surfen gehen III
surprise [sə'praɪz] Überraschung III
surprised [sə'praɪzd] überrascht II
survey ['sɜ:veɪ] Umfrage <III>
sustainable [sə'steɪnəbl] nachhaltig V U2, 42
swam [swæm] simple past von *to swim* IV
sweet [swi:t] Süßigkeit; Bonbon I
*to **swim** [swɪm] schwimmen I
*to go **swimming** [ˌgəʊ 'swɪmɪŋ] schwimmen gehen I
swimming pool ['swɪmɪŋ ˌpu:l] Schwimmbad I
*to **swing** [swɪŋ] schwingen; schwenken III
sword [sɔ:d] Schwert III
swung [swʌŋ] simple past, past participle von *to swing* III
symbol ['sɪmbl] Symbol III

T

table ['teɪbl] Tisch; Tabelle <I>
tablet ['tæblət] Tablette V U1, 16
tail [teɪl] Schwanz I
*to **take** [teɪk] mitnehmen; nehmen I; hinbringen II; dauern; brauchen III; einnehmen V U1, 16
to take an exam [ˌteɪk‿ən‿ɪg'zæm] eine Prüfung schreiben; ein Examen schreiben V U4, 90
to take care of [ˌteɪk 'keər‿əv] sich kümmern um; sorgen für <V U2, 48>
to take notes [ˌteɪk 'nəʊts] sich Notizen machen <I>
to take out [ˌteɪk‿'aʊt] hinausbringen II

to take part (in) [ˌteɪk ˈpɑːt (ɪn)] mitmachen (bei); teilnehmen (an) II
to take photos (of) [ˌteɪk ˈfəʊtəʊz (əv)] Fotos machen; fotografieren II
to take place [ˌteɪk ˈpleɪs] stattfinden <V U1, 146>
to take the dog for a walk [ˌteɪk ðə dɒg fɔːr‿ə ˈwɔːk] den Hund ausführen I
to take turns [ˌteɪk ˈtɜːnz] sich abwechseln <I>
Take a seat. [ˌteɪk‿ə ˈsiːt] Setz dich.; Setzen Sie sich.; Nimm Platz.; Nehmen Sie Platz. IV
taken [ˈteɪkn] past participle von *to take* III
talent [ˈtælənt] Talent; Begabung I
talk [tɔːk] Vortrag; Gespräch; Unterhaltung <III>
to **talk** (to) [tɔːk (tə)] reden (mit); sprechen (mit) I
tall [tɔːl] hoch; groß II
tandem [ˈtændəm] Tandem II
task [tɑːsk] Aufgabe; Auftrag V Z1, 9
to **taste** [teɪst] schmecken <V U2, 48>
taught [tɔːt] simple past, past participle von *to teach* IV
tax advisor [ˈtæks‿ədˌvaɪzə] Steuerberater; Steuerberaterin <V U2, 148>
tea [tiː] Tee; Abendessen I
*to **teach** [tiːtʃ] lehren; beibringen; unterrichten IV
teacher [ˈtiːtʃə] Lehrer; Lehrerin I
team [tiːm] Mannschaft; Team; Gruppe I
technology [tekˈnɒlədʒi] Technik; Technologie III
DT (Design Technology) [ˌdiːˈtiː (dɪˌzaɪn tekˈnɒlədʒi)] Technik I
teddy [ˈtedi] Teddybär I
teen [tiːn] Jugend-; Teenager; Teenagerin; Jugendlicher; Jugendliche II
teenager [ˈtiːnˌeɪdʒə] Teenager; Jugendlicher; Jugendliche V U2, 42
telephone box [ˈtelɪfəʊn ˌbɒks] Telefonzelle II
television [ˈtelɪvɪʒn] Fernsehen; Fernseher III
*to **tell** [tel] erzählen; sagen I
to tell sb to do sth [ˈtel tə ˌduː] jmdm. etw. auftragen III
temperature [ˈtemprətʃə] Temperatur V U1, 20
high temperature [ˌhaɪ ˈtemprətʃə] Fieber V U1, 16
ten [ten] zehn I
tennis [ˈtenɪs] Tennis I
tent [tent] Zelt II
test [test] Test; Klassenarbeit V U4, 90
to **test** [test] testen; prüfen II
testing [ˈtestɪŋ] Testen <V U2, 148>
text [tekst] Text <I>
than [ðæn] als II
thank you [ˈθæŋk ju] Dankeschön <V U1, 25>
Thank you. [ˈθæŋk ju] Danke. I
Thank you very much. [ˌθæŋk ju veri ˈmʌtʃ] Vielen Dank.; Herzlichen Dank. <V U1, 22>
thankful [ˈθæŋkfl] dankbar IV
Thanks. [θæŋks] Danke. I
Thanksgiving [ˌθæŋksˈgɪvɪŋ] Erntedankfest IV
that [ðæt] das; dieses; jene I; dass II; der; die III
after that [ˌɑːftə ˈðæt] danach I
so that [səʊ ˈðæt] damit; sodass IV
that's why [ˈðæts waɪ] deshalb; deswegen II
That's too bad. [ˌðæts tuː ˈbæd] Schade! II
the [ðə] die; der; das I
theater *(AE)* [ˈθɪətə] Theater III
theatre [ˈθɪətə] Theater III
their [ðeə] ihr I
theirs [ðeəz] ihre III
them [ðem] sie *(Pl.)* I; ihnen II
theme [θiːm] Thema; Motto <I>
theme park [ˈθiːm ˌpɑːk] Freizeitpark II
themselves [ðəmˈselvz] sich; selbst; sie selbst III; sich selbst IV
then [ðen] dann; danach I
there [ðeə] da; dort; dorthin; dahin I
there are [ðeər‿ˈɑː] da sind; es gibt I
there's (= there is) [ðeəz] da ist; dort ist; es gibt I
these [ðiːz] diese II
they [ðeɪ] sie *(Pl.)* I
thing [θɪŋ] Sache; Ding I
*to **think** [θɪŋk] denken; glauben II; überlegen <IV>
to think about [ˌθɪŋk‿əˈbaʊt] nachdenken über; sich überlegen; denken an III
to think of [ˈθɪŋk‿əv] denken an/über; sich einfallen lassen; sich ausdenken III; davon halten V U1, 12
third [θɜːd] dritte II
a **third** [ə ˈθɜːd] ein Drittel V U4, 88
thirteen [θɜːˈtiːn] dreizehn I
thirty [ˈθɜːti] dreißig I
this [ðɪs] das; dies I
this morning [ðɪs ˈmɔːnɪŋ] heute Morgen II
like this [laɪk ˈðɪs] so; auf diese Weise <I>
those [ðəʊz] jene II
thought [θɔːt] simple past von *to think* II; past participle von *to think* III
a/one **thousand** [ˈθaʊznd] tausend; eintausend II
three [θriː] drei I
threw [θruː] simple past von *to throw* II
throat [θrəʊt] Hals <V U1, 147>
sore throat [ˌsɔː ˈθrəʊt] Halsschmerzen <V U1, 147>
through [θruː] durch III
*to **throw** [θrəʊ] werfen II
Thursday [ˈθɜːzdeɪ] Donnerstag I
ticket [ˈtɪkɪt] Ticket; Eintrittskarte; Fahrschein II
return ticket [rɪˈtɜːn ˌtɪkɪt] Hin- und Rückfahrkarte III
single ticket [ˌsɪŋgl ˈtɪkɪt] einfache Fahrkarte III
to **tidy** [ˈtaɪdi] aufräumen; in Ordnung bringen II
tidy [ˈtaɪdi] ordentlich <II>
time [taɪm] Zeit; Uhrzeit; Mal I
at the same time [ət ðə seɪm ˈtaɪm] gleichzeitig; nebenher II
boarding time [ˈbɔːdɪŋ ˌtaɪm] Einsteigezeit IV
free time [ˌfriː ˈtaɪm] Freizeit I
for the 200th time [fə‿ðə ˈtuː hʌndrədθ ˌtaɪm] zum 200. Mal III

timeline

in time [ɪn ˈtaɪm] rechtzeitig; pünktlich V U2, 54
the first time [ðə fɜːst ˈtaɪm] das erste Mal I
timeline [ˈtaɪmˌlaɪn] Zeitstrahl <V U2, 47>
timetable [ˈtaɪmˌteɪbl] Stundenplan I; Fahrplan III
tip [tɪp] Tipp; Ratschlag <I>
tired [ˈtaɪəd] müde I
title [ˈtaɪtl] Titel; Überschrift <I>
to [tuː] zu; nach; in I; um zu; an II; auf; bei; bis III; für IV
quarter to/past [ˈkwɔːtə tə/pɑːst] Viertel vor/nach II
today [təˈdeɪ] heute I
together [təˈgeðə] zusammen I
to go together [ˌgəʊ təˈgeðə] zusammenpassen <III>
toilet [ˈtɔɪlət] Toilette V U2, 42
told [təʊld] simple past von *to tell* I; past participle von *to tell* III
tolerant [ˈtɒlrnt] tolerant <V U3, 151>
tomato *(sg)* [təˈmɑːtəʊ], **tomatoes** *(pl)* [təˈmɑːtəʊz] Tomate I
tomorrow [təˈmɒrəʊ] morgen II
too [tuː] auch; zu I
took [tʊk] simple past von *to take* II
tool [tuːl] Werkzeug; Gerät V U4, 90
tooth *(sg)* [tuːθ], **teeth** *(pl)* [tiːθ] Zahn II
top [tɒp] Spitze; oberer Teil; oberes Ende II; Top- <V ZI, 8>
at the top [æt ðə ˈtɒp] oben V U1, 28
topic [ˈtɒpɪk] Thema IV
topic-based [ˈtɒpɪkbeɪst] themenbezogen <IV>
torch [tɔːtʃ] Taschenlampe I
caber **toss** [ˈkeɪbə ˌtɒs] Baumstammwerfen III
*to get in **touch** [ˌgetˌɪn ˈtʌtʃ] in Verbindung treten (mit); kontaktieren <V U3, 150>
*to keep in **touch** [ˌkiːp ɪn ˈtʌtʃ] in Kontakt bleiben II
tour [tʊə] Tour; Führung; Reise III
tour guide [ˈtʊə ˌgaɪd] Reiseleiter; Reiseleiterin V U2, 38
tourism [ˈtʊərɪzm] Tourismus IV
tourist [ˈtʊərɪst] Tourist; Touristin II
tourist industry [ˈtʊərɪstˌɪndəstri] Tourismus IV
tourist information centre [ˌtʊərɪst ɪnfəˈmeɪʃn ˌsentə] Touristeninformation V U4, 90
towards [təˈwɔːdz] auf … zu; in Richtung V U4, 99
tower [ˈtaʊə] Turm II
town [taʊn] Stadt I
twin town [ˌtwɪn ˈtaʊn] Partnerstadt III
townhouse [ˈtaʊnhaʊs] Reihenhaus III
township [ˈtaʊnʃɪp] Township *(ehemalige Wohnsiedlungen für die schwarze Bevölkerung in Südafrika)*; Armutsviertel V U3, 62
slave **trader** [ˈsleɪv ˌtreɪdə] Sklavenhändler; Menschenhändler IV
tradespeople [ˈtreɪdspiːpl] Handwerker *(Pl.)* <V U2, 148>
tradition [trəˈdɪʃn] Tradition III
traffic [ˈtræfɪk] Verkehr III
train [treɪn] Zug I
train station [ˈtreɪn ˌsteɪʃn] Bahnhof <III>
to **train** [treɪn] trainieren; eine Ausbildung machen; ausbilden IV
trainer [ˈtreɪnə] Turnschuh II
training [ˈtreɪnɪŋ] Ausbildung; Training IV
tram [træm] Straßenbahn I
transport [ˈtrænspɔːt] Verkehr; Transport II
public transport [ˌpʌblɪk ˈtrænspɔːt] öffentliche Verkehrsmittel III
to **transport** [trænˈspɔːt] transportieren; befördern IV
travel agent [ˈtrævlˌeɪdʒnt] Reisebürokaufmann; Reisebürokauffrau IV
travel agent's [ˈtrævlˌeɪdʒnts] Reisebüro IV
to **travel** [ˈtrævl] fahren; reisen II
treasure hunt [ˈtreʒə ˌhʌnt] Schnitzeljagd; Schatzsuche II
tree [triː] Baum I
trial [ˈtraɪəl] Probe; Probe- <V U4, 100>
tribe [traɪb] Stamm; Volksstamm V U1, 12
trick [trɪk] Kunststück; Trick I; Streich II
trip [trɪp] Ausflug; Fahrt; Reise I
school trip [ˌskuːl ˈtrɪp] Klassenfahrt; Schulausflug II
true [truː] richtig; wahr V U2, 38
trumpet [ˈtrʌmpɪt] Trompete II
truth [truːθ] Wahrheit IV
to **try** [traɪ] versuchen; probieren; ausprobieren III
to try hard [ˌtraɪ ˈhɑːd] sich anstrengen V U4, 98
to try on [ˌtraɪ ˈɒn] anprobieren II
T-shirt [ˈtiːʃɜːt] T-Shirt II
tsunami [tsʊˈnɑːmi] Tsunami *(durch Seebeben ausgelöste Flutwelle)* IV
Tuesday [ˈtjuːzdeɪ] Dienstag I
turkey [ˈtɜːki] Truthahn; Pute IV
Turkish [ˈtɜːkɪʃ] türkisch; Türkisch; aus der Türkei IV
Your **turn.** [ˌjɔː ˈtɜːn] Du bist dran. <V U3, 81>
to **turn** [tɜːn] abbiegen II
to turn off [ˌtɜːnˌˈɒf] abschalten; ausschalten <V U2, 149>
to turn over [ˌtɜːn ˈəʊvə] umkippen; (sich) umdrehen III
Turn the music down. [ˌtɜːn ðə mjuːzɪk ˈdaʊn] Mach die Musik leiser. I
*to take **turns** [ˌteɪk ˈtɜːnz] sich abwechseln <I>
tutorial [tjuːˈtɔːriəl] Tutorial; Anleitung IV
TV [ˌtiːˈviː] Fernseher I; Fernseh-; Fernsehen IV
on TV [ɒn ˌtiːˈviː] im Fernsehen III
to watch TV [ˌwɒtʃ tiːˈviː] fernsehen I
twelve [twelv] zwölf I
twenty [ˈtwenti] zwanzig I
twenty-one [ˌtwentiˈwʌn] einundzwanzig I
twin town [ˌtwɪn ˈtaʊn] Partnerstadt III
two [tuː] zwei I
type [taɪp] Sorte; Art; Typ <III>
typical [ˈtɪpɪkl] typisch; charakteristisch <I>

U

uncle [ˈʌŋkl] Onkel I
under [ˈʌndə] unter I
underground [ˈʌndəgraʊnd] U-Bahn I

underlined [ˌʌndəˈlaɪnd] unterstrichen <III>
*to **understand** [ˌʌndəˈstænd] verstehen II
understood [ˌʌndəˈstʊd] simple past von *to understand* II
unemployed [ˌʌnɪmˈplɔɪd] arbeitslos V U3, 72
unfortunately [ʌnˈfɔːtʃnətli] leider; unglücklicherweise V U2, 47
unhappy [ʌnˈhæpi] unglücklich; traurig II
uniform [ˈjuːnɪfɔːm] Uniform I
unit [ˈjuːnɪt] Lektion; Kapitel <I>
until [ʌnˈtɪl] bis III
up [ʌp] hinauf; oben; hoch II
to stand up [ˌstænd ˈʌp] aufstehen V U4, 99
update [ˈʌpdeɪt] aktuelle Information; Update; Aktualisierung IV
to **upload** [ʌpˈləʊd] hochladen II
US [ˌjuːˈes] US-amerikanisch III
us [ʌs] uns; wir II
to **use** [juːz] benutzen; verwenden; nehmen; nutzen III
to get used to (sth) [ˌget ˈjuːst tə] sich gewöhnen an (etw.) IV
useful [ˈjuːsfl] nützlich; hilfreich; brauchbar III
usually [ˈjuːʒli] normalerweise; gewöhnlich II

V

vacation *(AE)* [vəˈkeɪʃn] Urlaub; Ferien III
valley [ˈvæli] Tal III
van [væn] Lieferwagen; Transporter IV
vegetable (veg) [ˈvedʒtəbl (vedʒ)] Gemüse IV
vegetarian [ˌvedʒɪˈteəriən] Vegetarier; Vegetarierin I; vegetarisch <V U2, 149>
vehicle painter [ˈvɪəkl ˌpeɪntə] Fahrzeuglackierer; Fahrzeuglackiererin <V U4, 152>
verb [vɜːb] Verb <II>
very [ˈveri] sehr I
vet [vet] Tierarzt; Tierärztin IV
video [ˈvɪdiəʊ] Video III
viewing [ˈvjuːɪŋ] Hör-/Sehverstehen <I>
viewing skills [ˈvjuːɪŋ ˌskɪlz] Fertigkeit Hör-/Sehverstehen <I>
village [ˈvɪlɪdʒ] Dorf I
violence *(no pl)* [ˈvaɪələns] Gewalt IV
virtual [ˈvɜːtʃuəl] virtuell V U2, 38
visit [ˈvɪzɪt] Besuch III
to **visit** [ˈvɪzɪt] besuchen I
visiting hours *(pl)* [ˈvɪzɪtɪŋ ˌaʊəz] Besuchszeiten <V U3, 74>
visitor [ˈvɪzɪtə] Besucher; Besucherin II
vocabulary [vəˈkæbjəlri] Vokabular; Wortschatz <IV>
volcano *(sg)* [vɒlˈkeɪnəʊ], **volcanoes** *(pl)* [vɒlˈkeɪnəʊz] Vulkan V U4, 89
volunteer [ˌvɒlənˈtɪə] Freiwilliger; Freiwillige; ehrenamtlicher Helfer; ehrenamtliche Helferin V U4, 89

W

to **wait** (for) [weɪt (fə)] warten (auf) II
*to **wake** up [ˌweɪk ˈʌp] aufwachen; erwachen; aufwecken III
walk [wɔːk] Wanderung; Spaziergang I
to **walk** [wɔːk] laufen; gehen; zu Fuß gehen IV
to walk around [ˌwɔːk əˈraʊnd] umherlaufen; herumlaufen <I>
wall [wɔːl] Wand; Mauer II
wall painting [ˈwɔːl peɪntɪŋ] Wandmalerei II
wallet [ˈwɒlɪt] Brieftasche; Geldbeutel; Geldbörse V U3, 64
to **want** (to) [wɒnt (tə)] wollen; mögen I
wanted [ˈwɒntɪd] gesucht <V U4, 102>
wardrobe [ˈwɔːdrəʊb] Kleiderschrank II
warehouse [ˈweəhaʊs] Lager; Lagerhalle; Depot <V U4, 153>
warm [wɔːm] warm II
warm-up [ˈwɔːmʌp] Aufwärmtraining; Aufwärmen II
was [wɒz] simple past von *to be* I
wash [wɒʃ] Wäsche II
to **wash** [wɒʃ] (sich) waschen; spülen II
waste [weɪst] Abfall V U2, 37
to **watch** [wɒtʃ] anschauen; ansehen I; zuschauen; zusehen; beobachten II
to watch TV [ˌwɒtʃ tiːˈviː] fernsehen I
water [ˈwɔːtə] Wasser I
wave [weɪv] Welle III
wax [wæks] Wachs II
way [weɪ] Weg I; Art und Weise III
to ask the way [ˌɑːsk ðə ˈweɪ] nach dem Weg fragen <II>
to be a long **way** away [biː ə ˈlɒŋ ˌweɪ əˈweɪ] weit weg sein II
we [wiː] wir I
weak [wiːk] schwach <V U1, 147>
*to **wear** [weə] tragen; anhaben I
weather [ˈweðə] Wetter; Witterung II
website [ˈwebsaɪt] Website; Internetseite III
wedding [ˈwedɪŋ] Hochzeit V U2, 37
Wednesday [ˈwenzdeɪ] Mittwoch I
week [wiːk] Woche I
a week [ə ˈwiːk] in der Woche; pro Woche V U3, 73
weekend [ˈwiːkend] Wochenende I
welcome (to) [ˈwelkəm (tə)] willkommen (bei/in) I
You're welcome. [jɔː ˈwelkəm] Gern geschehen. V U1, 16
well [wel] gut II
Well, … [wel] Na ja, …; Also … II
… as well as … [əz ˈwel əz] sowohl … als auch … II
Well done! [ˌwel ˈdʌn] Gut gemacht! II
well-organized [ˈwelˌɔːgnaɪzd] gut organisiert <V U4, 152>
Welsh [welʃ] Walisisch; walisisch; aus Wales III
went [went] simple past von *to go* I
were [wɜː] simple past von *to be* I
west [west] Westen; West- III
wet [wet] nass I
whale [weɪl] Wal IV
whale shark [ˈweɪl ˌʃɑːk] Walhai <V U1, 23>
whale-watching [ˈweɪlˌwɒtʃɪŋ] Walbeobachtungs- IV
what [wɒt] was; welche I

What about …? [ˌwɒt‿əˈbaʊt] Und …?; Was ist mit …? II
What colour is …? [ˌwɒt ˈkʌlər‿ɪz] Welche Farbe hat …? I
What time is it? [ˌwɒt ˈtaɪm‿ɪz‿ɪt] Wie viel Uhr ist es?; Wie spät ist es? I
What's the matter? [ˌwɒts ðə ˈmætə] Was ist los?; Was hast du? V U1, 16
What's the weather like? [ˌwɒts ðə ˈweðə laɪk] Wie ist das Wetter? II
What's your name? [ˌwɒts jə ˈneɪm] Wie heißt du? I
wheel [wiːl] Rad II
big wheel [ˌbɪg ˈwiːl] Riesenrad II
wheelchair [ˈwiːltʃeə] Rollstuhl I
when [wen] wann I; wenn; als II
where [weə] wo; wohin; woher I
Where are you from? [ˌweər‿ə ju ˈfrɒm] Woher kommst du? I
which [wɪtʃ] welche; was II; das; der; die III
while [waɪl] während IV
white [waɪt] weiß I
who [huː] wer I; die; der; das III
whose [huːz] wessen <III>
why [waɪ] warum I
that's why [ˈðæts waɪ] deshalb; deswegen II
wide [waɪd] breit; groß <V U1, 23>
wild [waɪld] wild IV
wilderness [ˈwɪldənəs] Wildnis IV
will [wɪl] werden II
*to **win** [wɪn] siegen; gewinnen I
wind [wɪnd] Wind I
wind farm [ˈwɪnd ˌfɑːm] Windpark <V U2, 149>
window [ˈwɪndəʊ] Fenster I
windy [ˈwɪndi] windig II
winner [ˈwɪnə] Sieger; Siegerin; Gewinner; Gewinnerin I
winter [ˈwɪntə] Winter I
Best **wishes**, [ˌbest ˈwɪʃɪz] Viele Grüße; Alles Gute! I
to **wish** [wɪʃ] wünschen V U4, 98
with [wɪð] mit I; bei II
without [wɪˈðaʊt] ohne II
witness [ˈwɪtnəs] Zeuge; Zeugin IV
wizard [ˈwɪzəd] Zauberer II
woke up [ˌwəʊk‿ˈʌp] simple past von *to wake up* III
woken up [ˌwəʊkn‿ˈʌp] past participle von *to wake up* III
wolf *(sg)* [wʊlf], **wolves** *(pl)* [wʊlvz] Wolf II
woman *(sg)* [ˈwʊmən], **women** *(pl)* [ˈwɪmɪn] Frau I
won [wʌn] simple past von *to win* II; past participle von *to win* III
won't (= will not) [wəʊnt] nicht werden II
wonder [ˈwʌndə] Wunder V U4, 99
wood [wʊd] Holz I; Wald IV
woof [wʊf] wau I
wool [wʊl] Wolle I
word [wɜːd] Wort II
root word [ˌruːt ˈwɜːd] Grundwort; Stammwort <IV>
word order [ˈwɜːd‿ˌɔːdə] Wortstellung; Satzstellung <II>
wore [wɔː] simple past von *to wear* I
work [wɜːk] Arbeit II
work experience [ˈwɜːk‿ɪkˌspɪəriəns] Berufserfahrung; Praktikum V U4, 90
to **work** [wɜːk] arbeiten I; funktionieren V U4, 94
worker [ˈwɜːkə] Arbeiter; Arbeiterin; Angestellter; Angestellte IV
working conditions *(pl)* [ˈwɜːkɪŋ kənˌdɪʃnz] Arbeitsbedingungen <V U4, 153>
working hours *(pl)* [ˈwɜːkɪŋ ˌaʊəz] Arbeitszeit IV
workshop [ˈwɜːkʃɒp] Workshop; Seminar III
acting workshop [ˈæktɪŋ ˌwɜːkʃɒp] Schauspielworkshop III
world [wɜːld] Welt I
all around the world [ɔːl‿əˌraʊnd ðə ˈwɜːld] in aller Welt II
worried [ˈwʌrid] beunruhigt; besorgt II
to **worry** [ˈwʌri] sich Sorgen machen I
Don't worry. [ˌdəʊnt ˈwʌri] Mach dir keine Sorgen. I
worse [wɜːs] schlechter; schlimmer II
worst [wɜːst] schlimmste; schlechteste II
worth [wɜːθ] wert V U4, 94
worth of [ˈwɜːθ‿əv] im Wert von V U4, 94
would [wʊd] würde(n) <IV>
I wouldn't like (to) … [aɪ ˈwʊdnt laɪk (tə)] ich möchte nicht …; ich würde nicht gerne … I
I'd (= I would) [aɪd] ich würde; ich hätte gern I
I'd love (to) … (= I would love to) [aɪd ˈlʌv (tə)] ich würde sehr gern …; ich hätte gern … IV
Would you like (to) …? [ˌwʊd jə ˈlaɪk (tə)] Möchtest du …?; Würdest du gern …? I
Wow! [waʊ] Wow!; Toll! I
wrecked [rekt] demoliert; zerstört; zertrümmert IV
*to **write** [raɪt] schreiben I
writer [ˈraɪtə] Verfasser; Verfasserin; Schriftsteller; Schriftstellerin <V U3, 76>
writing [ˈraɪtɪŋ] Schreiben <I>
writing skills [ˈraɪtɪŋ ˌskɪlz] Fertigkeit Schreiben <II>
wrong [rɒŋ] falsch I
to go wrong [ˌgəʊ ˈrɒŋ] schiefgehen V U4, 90
wrote [rəʊt] simple past von *to write* II

X

Xhosa [ˈkɔːsə] Xhosa *(Sprache in Südafrika)* <V U3, 79>
Xitsonga [ksiˈtsɒŋgə] Xitsonga *(Sprache in Südafrika)* <V U3, 79>

Y

year [jɪə] Klasse; Jahrgangsstufe; Jahr I
year-old [ˌjɪər‿ˈəʊld] -jährig; Jahre alt V U2, 42
yellow [ˈjeləʊ] gelb I
yes [jes] ja I
yesterday [ˈjestədeɪ] gestern I
yet [jet] schon III
not … yet [nɒt … ˈjet] noch nicht III
you [juː] du; Sie; ihr; dich; euch; dir; Ihnen I

You're welcome. [jɔː ˈwelkəm] Gern geschehen. VU1, 16
young [jʌŋ] jung II
your [jɔː] dein; euer; Ihr I
yours [jɔːz] deine; eure; Ihre III
Yours sincerely, [ˌjɔːz sɪnˈsɪəli] Mit freundlichen Grüßen IV
Yours, [jɔːz] Dein *(Grußformel in Briefen oder E-Mails)* II
yourself [jɔːˈself] dich; selbst III; dir; dir selbst; sich; sich selbst IV
yourselves [jɔːˈselvz] selbst; euch; euch selbst; sich; Sie sich; Sie sich selbst IV
youth [juːθ] Jugend- I

Z

zero [ˈzɪərəʊ] null I
zip line [ˈzɪp ˌlaɪn] Seilrutsche III
zoo [zuː] Zoo; Tierpark IV
to **zoom** in [ˈzuːm‿ɪn] heranzoomen <I>
Zulu [ˈzuːluː] Zulu *(Sprache in Südafrika)* <VU3, 79>

Boys' names

Daku [dɑːˈkuː] VU1, 15
John [dʒɒn] VU4, 94
Koa [kəʊˈɑː] VU1, 12
Koro [ˈkɒrəʊ] VU4, 98
Krish [krɪʃ] VU2, 37
Kungawo [kʌngəˈwəʊ] VU3, 68
Leo [ˈliːəʊ] <VU4, 100>
Liam [ˈliːəm] VU4, 88
Lunga [ˈlʌŋgə] VU3, 64
Manjit [mænˈdʒɪt] VU2, 38
Mason [ˈmeɪsn] VU4, 89
Matt [mæt] <VU4, 102>
Moti [ˈmɒti] VU2, 42
Nikau [ˈnɪkəʊ] VU4, 94
Oliver [ˈɒlɪvə] VU4, 94
Omeo [ˈɔːmiəʊ] VU1, 14
Paka [ˈpʌkə] VU4, 98
Peter [ˈpiːtə] VU1, 11
Phil [fɪl] VU3, 64
Piet [pit] VU3, 64
Rawiri [rəˈwiːri] VU4, 98
Robert [ˈrɒbət] VU1, 21
Sanjay [ˈsændʒeɪ] <VU2, 48>
Shaka [ˈʃækə] VU3, 72
Tanvi [ˈtænvi] VU2, 42
Uuka [ˈjuːkə] VU3, 73
Vibhu [vɪbˈhuː] VU2, 38

Girls' names

Amahle [əˈmɑːlə] VU3, 73
Amita [əˈmiːtə] VU2, 37
Barbara [ˈbɑːbrə] VU1, 21
Bertha [ˈbɜːθə] VU3, 72
Cathy [ˈkæθi] VU3, 65
Cebile [ˈsebɪlə] VU3, 64
Chandran [ˈtʃændrn] VU2, 54
Deepali [ˈdiːpəli] VU2, 42
Ella [ˈelə] VU4, 91
Hazel [ˈheɪzl] VU4, 89
Jasmine [ˈdʒæzmɪn] <VU2, 48>
Joan [dʒəʊn] VU4, 106
Julia [ˈdʒuːliə] <VU1, 24>
Kahu [kəˈhuː] VU4, 98
Kashida [kæˈʃiːdə] VU2, 38
Keeya [ˈkiːjə] VU3, 72
Kyra [ˈkaɪrə] VU2, 42
Nani [ˈnɑːni] VU4, 98
Nicole [nɪˈkəʊl] VU3, 64
Penny [ˈpeni] VU1, 10
Prisha [ˈprɪʃə] VU2, 38
Riah [ˈriːə] VU3, 64
Rose [rəʊz] VU4, 94
Sophia [səˈfiːə] VU3, 71

Surnames

Apirana [æpɪˈrɑːnə] VU4, 98
Campbell [ˈkæmbl] <VU4, 102>
Chandra [ˈtʃændrə] VU2, 42
Davidson [ˈdeɪvɪdsn] VU3, 64
Flowers [ˈflaʊəz] VU4, 98
Hogan [ˈhəʊgn] VU1, 17
Jansen [ˈjɑnsn] VU3, 64
Nkosi [nəˈkɒsi] VU3, 64
Phillips [ˈfɪlɪps] VU1, 21
Robson [ˈrɒbsn] VU1, 16
Sekibo [səˈkiːbəʊ] VU3, 64
Singh [sɪŋ] VU2, 54
Thompson [ˈtɒmsn] VU1, 21
Waaka [ˈwækə] VU4, 90
Watkins [ˈwɒtkɪnz] VU1, 16

Place names

Africa [ˈæfrɪkə] Afrika II
Agra [ˈɑːgrə] *Ort in Indien* VU2, 38
America [əˈmerɪkə] Amerika III
Antarctica [ænˈtɑːktɪkə] Antarktis II
Auckland [ˈɔːkləɪnd] *Stadt in Neuseeland* VU4, 88
Australia [ɒsˈtreɪliə] Australien I
Bangalore [ˌbæŋgəˈlɔː] *Großstadt in Indien* VU2, 38
Bavaria [bəˈveəriə] Bayern I
Bloemfontein [ˈbluːmfɒnteɪn] *Hauptstadt Südafrikas* VU3, 62
Brisbane [ˈbrɪzbən] *Großstadt in Australien* VU1, 21
Britain [ˈbrɪtn] Großbritannien II
The **British Isles** [ðə ˌbrɪtɪʃ ˈaɪlz] die Britischen Inseln III
Cambridge [ˈkeɪmbrɪdʒ] *Stadt in Ostengland* <VU2, 48>
Canada [ˈkænədə] Kanada I
Canberra [ˈkænbrə] *Hauptstadt von Australien* VU1, 10
The **Cape of Good Hope** [ðə ˌkeɪp‿əv gʊd ˈhəʊp] Kap der Guten Hoffnung <VU3, 78>
Cape Town [ˈkeɪp ˌtaʊn] Kapstadt *(Hauptstadt Südafrikas)* VU3, 62
Christchurch [ˈkraɪsˌtʃɜːtʃ] *Stadt in Neuseeland* VU4, 92
Cuba [ˈkjuːbə] Kuba IV
Durban [ˈdɜːbən] *Stadt in Südafrika* VU3, 64
Eastern Cape [ˈiːstn ˌkeɪp] Ostcap VU3, 73
England [ˈɪŋgləɪnd] England I
Europe [ˈjʊərəp] Europa II
France [frɑːns] Frankreich IV
Germany [ˈdʒɜːməni] Deutschland I
Great Britain [ˌgreɪt ˈbrɪtn] Großbritannien I
Gujarat [ˌgʊdʒəˈrɑːt] *indischer Bundesstaat* VU2, 42
India [ˈɪndiə] Indien I
Ireland [ˈaɪələnd] Irland III
Istanbul [ˌɪstænˈbʊl] *Großstadt in der Türkei* I
Italy [ˈɪtli] Italien IV
Jamaica [dʒəˈmeɪkə] Jamaika II
Johannesburg [dʒəˈhænɪsbɜːg] *Großstadt in Südafrika* VU3, 73

Klerksdorp ['klerksdɔ:p] *Stadt in Südafrika* V U3, 72
London ['lʌndən] *Hauptstadt von England* I
Makhanda [mə'kændə] *Stadt in Südafrika* V U3, 73
Manchester ['mæntʃɪstə] *Stadt in Nordengland* II
Mexico ['meksɪkəʊ] Mexiko IV
Moscow ['mɒskəʊ] Moskau I
Mumbai [ˌmʌm'baɪ] *Großstadt in Indien* V U2, 36
New Delhi [ˌnju: 'deli] Neu-Delhi V U2, 36
New Zealand [ˌnju: 'zi:lənd] Neuseeland V U4, 88
North Shore [ˌnɔ:θ 'ʃɔ:] *Region in Neuseeland* <V U4, 100>
Northern Ireland [ˌnɔ:ðn‿'aɪələnd] Nordirland III
Perth [pɜ:θ] *Stadt in Australien* V U1, 12
Poland ['pəʊlənd] Polen II
Porbandar ['pɔ:bəndɑ:] *Stadt in Indien* V U2, 46
Pretoria [prɪ'tɔ:riə] *Hauptstadt Südafrikas* V U3, 62
The **Republic of Ireland** [ðə rɪˌpʌblɪk‿əv‿'aɪələnd] Irland III
Russia ['rʌʃə] Russland I
Sanand ['sænənd] *Ort in Indien* V U2, 38
Scotland ['skɒtlənd] Schottland I
South Africa [ˌsaʊθ‿'æfrɪkə] Südafrika V U3, 62
Soweto [səʊ'wetəʊ] *Stadt in Südafrika* V U3, 73
Sydney ['sɪdni] *Stadt in Australien* V U1, 10
Thailand ['taɪlænd] **Thailand** I
Turkey ['tɜ:ki] Türkei I
UK (United Kingdom) [ˌju:'keɪ (ju:ˌnaɪtɪd 'kɪŋdəm)] Vereinigtes Königreich von Großbritannien und Nordirland II
Umlazi [ʊm'lɑ:zi] *Stadtteil von Durban* V U3, 64
United States [ju:ˌnaɪtɪd'steɪts] Vereinigte Staaten II
USA (United States of America) [ˌju:es'eɪ (ju:ˌnaɪtɪd ˌsteɪts‿əv ə'merɪkə)] USA (Vereinigte Staaten von Amerika) I
Wales [weɪlz] Wales III
Wellington ['welɪŋtən] *Stadt in Neuseeland* V U4, 88
Whangara ['wɒngɑ:rə] *Ort in Neuseeland* V U4, 98

Other names

Zackie **Achmat** [ˌzæki 'ækmet] *südafrikanischer Regisseur* V U3, 68
ACT [ˌeɪ si: 'ti:] *Abkürzung für das Territorium um Canberra* V U1, 21
Adelphi Hotel [ə'delfi ˌhəʊtel] *Hotelname* V U4, 97
All Blacks [ˌɔ:l 'blæks] *neuseeländisches Rugby-Team* <V U4, 106>
Auckland Hockey Club [ˌɔ:kləɪnd 'hɒki ˌklʌb] *Name eines Hockeyvereins* <V U4, 100>
Cape Town Cycle Tour [keɪp ˌtaʊn 'saɪkl ˌtʊə] *Name eines Radrennens* <V U3, 78>
Daily News [ˌdeɪli 'nju:z] *Zeitungsname* V U3, 64
Darwin Road [ˌdɑ:wɪn 'rəʊd] *Straßenname* V U1, 16
Mahatma **Gandhi** [məˌhɑ:tmə 'gændi] *indischer Freiheitskämpfer* V U2, 37
Mohandas **Gandhi** [məˌhændəs 'gændi] *Geburtsname von Mahatma Gandhi* V U2, 46
Great Barrier Reef [ˌgreɪt ˌbæriə 'ri:f] *Korallenriff vor der Küste Australiens* V U1, 10
Mika **Hensing** [ˌmaɪkə 'hensɪŋ] *Verfasserin* <V U3, 76>
Holi ['hɒli] *Name eines indischen Festes* V U2, 37
Kakadu National Park [ˌkækədu: ˌnæʃnl 'pɑ:k] *Nationalpark in Australien* <V U1, 23>
Kruger National Park [ˌkru:gə ˌnæʃnl 'pɑ:k] *Nationalpark in Südafrika* V U3, 63
Miriam **Makeba** [ˌmɪriəm mə'keɪbə] *südafrikanische Sängerin* V U3, 68
Martens Place [ˌmɑ:tnz 'pleɪs] *Straßenname* V U1, 21
Mount Tongariro [maʊnt 'tɒŋgəri:rəʊ] *Berg in Neuseeland* <V U4, 101>
National Certificate of Tourism [ˌnæʃnl səˌtɪfɪkət‿ev 'tʊərɪzm] *Zertifikat der neuseeländischen Tourismusbranche* V U4, 90
Nelson **Mandela** [ˌnelsn mæn'delə] *Präsident von Südafrika (1994–1999)* V U3, 62
Newlands College [ˌnju:lənz 'kɒlɪdʒ] *Name einer Hochschule* V U4, 90
Ningaloo Reef [ˌnɪngəlu:'ri:f] Ningaloo-Riff <V U1, 23>
North Island ['nɔ:θ ˌaɪlənd] Nordinsel <V U4, 101>
Pacific Ocean [pəˌsɪfɪk‿'əʊʃn] Pazifischer Ozean V U4, 89
Paikea ['paɪkjə] *Urahn von Neuseeland* V U4, 98
QLD [ˌkju: el 'dɪ:] *Abkürzung für Queensland* V U1, 21
Ring of Fire [ˌrɪŋ‿əv 'faɪə] Pazifischer Feuerring *(Vulkangürtel und Erdbebengebiet bei Neuseeland)* V U4, 89
Salt March [ˌsɔ:lt 'mɑ:tʃ] Salzmarsch *(Protestmarsch)* V U2, 46
School of the Air [ˌsku:l‿əv ði 'eə] *Fernunterricht in Australien* V U1, 11
South Island ['saʊθ ˌaɪlənd] Südinsel <V U4, 101>
Sydney Harbour Bridge [ˌsɪdni ˌhɑ:bə 'brɪdʒ] *ein Wahrzeichen von Sydney* <V U1, 26>
Table Mountain ['teɪbl ˌmaʊntɪn] Tafelberg V U3, 62
Taj Mahal [ˌtɑ:dʒ mə'hɑ:l] *Grabmoschee in Indien* V U2, 36
The Whale Rider [ðə ˌweɪl 'raɪdə] Whalerider *(Roman über ein Maorimädchen)* V U4, 98
Tshepong Hospital [ˌʃi:pɒŋ 'hɒspɪtl] *Krankenhaus in Südafrika* V U3, 72
Uluru [u:'lu:ru:] Uluru = Ayers Rock *(heiliger Berg der Aborigines)* V U1, 12
Working for Water [ˌwɜ:kɪŋ fə 'wɔ:tə] *südafrikanisches Umweltprogramm* V U3, 72
World Cup [ˌwɜ:ld 'kʌp] Weltmeisterschaft <V U3, 78>
Karen **Zoid** [ˌkærn 'zɔɪd] *Sängerin* V U3, 71

A

abbiegen to turn II
Abend evening I
Abendessen dinner; tea I
abends in the evening I
Abenteuer adventure III
aber but I
abfahren to leave II; to depart IV
Abfall rubbish I; waste V U2, 37
abfliegen to depart; to leave IV
abgeschlossen locked I
die **Aborigines** Aboriginal people V U1, 11
Aborigine- Aboriginal V U1, 12
zur Aborigine-Kultur gehörend Aboriginal V U1, 12
Abschieds- leaving II
Abschluss qualification IV
Abteilung department V U1, 21
acht eight I
Achterbahn roller coaster II
achtzehn eighteen I
achtzig eighty I
Ackerbau farming V U2, 42
Adresse address IV
Afrikaans *(Sprache in Südafrika)* Afrikaans V U3, 72
Afrikaner African V U3, 62
Afrikanerin African V U3, 62
afrikanisch African V U3, 62
Afroamerikaner African American IV
Afroamerikanerin African American IV
Aids *(erworbene Immunabwehrschwäche)* AIDS V U3, 68
Aktivität activity I
Aktualisierung update IV
aktuelle Information update IV
Akzent accent III
Alaska- Alaskan IV
alaskisch Alaskan IV
albern silly II
alle all I; everyone; every II
von allen Staaten of all the states IV
allein alone V U1, 20
alles everything II
Alles Gute Best wishes, I; All the best, II
Alligator alligator II
als as; than; when II
als Nächstes next II
als ob like IV
also so I
Also … Well, … II
alt old I
am in; on I
am Ende at the end II
Amerikaner American II
Amerikanerin American II
Amerikanisch American II
amerikanisch American II
Amtssprache official language V ZI, 8
amüsant fun III
sich **amüsieren** to enjoy oneself IV
an on; at I; to II; about; by III; in IV
anbauen to produce IV; to grow V U2, 42
anbei enclosed V U4, 112
anbieten to offer IV
Anbieter supplier V U4, 94
andauern to last II
Andenken souvenir II
andere other II; different III; another IV
anderen others II
ein anderer another IV
anderer Meinung sein to disagree IV
ändern to change II
anders different I
anfahren to hit V U3, 64
Anfang beginning II
anfangen to start I
Anfrage request IV; enquiry V U4, 106
sich **anfühlen** to feel III
anführen to lead V U2, 37
angeln gehen to go fishing IV
Angestellte worker; employee IV
Angestellter worker; employee IV
Angst haben to be scared I
ängstlich afraid V U1, 12
anhaben to wear I
anhalten to stop II
Anhänger follower IV
Anhängerin follower IV
anhören to listen (to) I
ankommen to arrive I
Ankömmling arrival IV
sanitäre **Anlagen** sanitation V U2, 42
Anleitung tutorial IV
sich **anmelden** to register V U1, 16
anprobieren to try on II
anregend inspiring V U3, 68
Anruf phone call I
anrufen to phone II; to call III
anschauen to look at; to watch I
sich **anschließen** to join V U2, 47
ansehen to watch I
anspornen to motivate III
sich **anstrengen** to struggle V U1, 11; to try hard V U4, 98
Antwort answer II
antworten to answer II
Anwalt lawyer V U2, 46
Anwältin lawyer V U2, 46
Anzeichen sign IV
Anzeige ad(vert) (= advertisement) III
anziehen to put on II
Apartheid apartheid *(no pl)* V U3, 62
Apartment apartment *(AE)* IV
Apfel apple I
Apotheke pharmacy V U1, 16
App app IV
April April I
Arbeit work II
arbeiten to work I
Arbeiter worker IV
Arbeiterin worker IV
Arbeitgeber employer V U4, 90
Arbeitgeberin employer V U4, 90
Arbeitnehmer employee IV
Arbeitnehmerin employee IV
arbeitslos unemployed V U3, 72
Arbeitszeit working hours *(pl)* IV
Arbeitszeugnis reference IV
Areal area IV
Arm arm II
arm poor IV
Armutsviertel township V U3, 62
Art kind II
Art und Weise way III
Artikel item IV
Arznei medication; drug V U3, 68
Arzneimittel medication; drug V U3, 68
Arzt doctor II
Arzthelfer receptionist V U1, 16
Arzthelferin receptionist V U1, 16
Ärztin doctor II
Assistent assistant IV
Assistentin assistant IV
auch too; also I
auch nicht not … either III

auf in; on; at I; to III
auf einmal suddenly I
Auf Wiedersehen. Goodbye. I
auf … zu towards V U4, 99
auf der linken Seite on the left II
auf der rechten Seite on the right II
auf jeden Fall certainly V U2, 46
Geld **aufbringen** to raise money II
Aufführung show I
Aufgabe job III; task V ZI, 9
aufgeregt excited II
aufheben to pick up V U4, 99
aufhören to finish; to stop II; to end V U3, 62
aufmachen to open I
aufpassen auf to look after II
aufräumen to tidy II
aufregend exciting I
aufstehen to get up I; to stand up V U4, 99
Auftrag task V ZI, 9
jmdm. etw. **auftragen** to tell sb to do sth III
aufwachen to wake up III
Aufwärmen warm-up II
Aufwärmtraining warm-up II
aufwecken to wake up III
Aufzug lift II
Auge eye I
August August I
aus from I; of III
aus dem Weg gehen to avoid IV
ausbilden to train IV
Ausbildung training; qualification; education IV; apprenticeship V U4, 94
eine Ausbildung machen to train IV
Ausbleichen bleaching V U1, 20
sich **ausdenken** to think of III
Auseinandersetzung argument II
Ausflug trip I
den Hund **ausführen** to take the dog for a walk I
ausfüllen to complete V U4, 90
ausgeben *(Geld)* to spend II
ein **ausgefüllter** Tag a busy day II
Aushang lost and found notice III
(sich) **ausleihen** to borrow II
ausliefern to deliver IV
auslösen to cause IV
einem etwas **ausmachen** to mind sth V U4, 90
ausprobieren to try III
die Spülmaschine **ausräumen** to empty the dishwasher II
aussehen to look I
außen outside II
außerhalb outside II
aussprechen to say III
etw. nicht **ausstehen** können can't stand + -ing III
aussteigen to get off II; to get out IV
Ausstellung exhibition III
Australier Australian V U1, 10
Australierin Australian V U1, 10
australisch Australian V U1, 10
auswählen to choose III
ausweichen to avoid IV
Auto car I
Automat machine V U2, 38

B

Bad(ezimmer) bathroom II
Bahn railway IV
Bahnhof station III; railway station IV
bald soon II
Balkon balcony I
Ball ball I
Banane banana I
Band band II
Bär bear II
Base base III
Baseball baseball III
Basketball basketball II
Basketballkorb basket III
basteln to make II; to do handicrafts V U3, 73
bauen to build II
Bauer farmer I
Bäuerin farmer I
Bauernhof farm I
Baum tree I
Baumstamm caber III
Baumstammwerfen caber toss III
Bauwerk building II
beängstigend scary I
beantworten to answer II
beben to shake IV
bedeuten to mean IV
Bedeutung sense IV
beeindruckend awesome III
beenden to finish; to stop II; to end V U3, 62
befolgen to follow V U3, 80
befördern to transport IV
Befrager interviewer IV
Befragerin interviewer IV
Befragung interview IV
befüllen to fill V U4, 94
befürchten to be afraid V U1, 16
Begabung talent I
begeistert excited II
Beginn beginning II
beginnen to start I; to begin V U1, 10
begründen to found V U4, 98
bei at I; with II; to III; in; during IV; c/o V U4, 106
beibringen to teach IV
beide both IV
beigefügt enclosed V U4, 112
Bein leg II
beinahe nearly II
Beispiel example III
zum Beispiel for example III
beitreten to join V U2, 47
sich **beklagen** to complain IV
bekommen to get I
bekommen (Bus/Zug) to catch (bus/train) III
belästigen to disturb V U3, 80
beliebt popular III
bellen to bark II
bemalen to paint II
benutzen to use III
beobachten to watch II
Berater advisor V U4, 88
Beraterin advisor V U4, 88
Bereich area V U1, 20
bereit ready I
bereits already III
Berg mountain II; hill IV
Bericht report V U4, 94
Beruf career IV
Berufs- careers V U4, 88
Berufserfahrung work experience V U4, 90
Berufsinformationstag careers day V U4, 90
Berufspraktikum internship IV
berühmt famous I
beschädigen to damage V U2, 42

Beschädigung damage IV
beschäftigt busy I
Bescheinigung certificate V U4, 90
beschließen to decide III
sich **beschweren** to complain IV
besitzen to have I; to have got II; to own III
besonders special I
besorgt worried II
besser better II
sich wieder **besser** fühlen to get better V U1, 16
Gute **Besserung**! Get well soon! V U1, 16
beste best II
am besten best II
besteigen to climb II
bestellen to order V U4, 94
Besuch visit III
besuchen to visit I
Besucher visitor II
Besucherin visitor II
Betr. RE V U4, 106
Betreff subject III
Bett bed I
ins Bett gehen to go to bed I
Bettdecke blanket IV
beunruhigt worried II
Bevölkerung population *(no pl)* IV
bevor before II
(sich) **bewegen** to move IV
Bewegung movement IV
beweisen to prove IV
sich **bewerben** (für/um) to apply (for) IV
Bewerbung application IV
Bewerbungsschreiben letter of application IV
bewölkt cloudy II
bewundern to admire V U3, 68
bezahlen to pay V U3, 68
Bezirk borough IV
bieten to offer IV
Bild picture I
Bildung education IV
billig cheap II
Biologie Biology I
bis until; to III
Bis bald. See you soon. I; See you. II
ein **bisschen** a bit V U3, 72
ein (kleines) **bisschen** a little (bit) II
bitte please I
Bitte schön. Here you are. I
blau blue I
bleiben to stay I
in Verbindung bleiben staying connected III
stecken bleiben to be stuck I
Bleichen bleaching V U1, 20
Bleistift pencil I
blinken to signal IV
Blog blog I
Boden soil V U2, 42
Bonbon sweet I
Boom boom IV
Boot boat IV
Bordkarte boarding card IV
böse angry II
Boss boss III
Bote messenger IV
Botin messenger IV
Box box I
brauchbar useful III
brauchen to need I; to take III
braun brown I
brechen to break V U1, 11
bremsen to brake V U3, 64
Brief letter IV
Brieffreund penfriend III
Brieffreundin penfriend III
Brieftasche wallet V U3, 64
bringen to bring II; to get IV
die **Briten** the British V U2, 37
britisch British V U1, 11
Broschüre brochure III
Brot bread I
belegtes Brot sandwich I
Brücke bridge II
Bruder brother I
Bub boy I
Buch book I
buchen to book III
Buchstabe letter IV
Bucht bay V U4, 98
Bude stall I
Bühne stage II
Bühnenbild scenery III
Bundesstaat state III
bunt colourful V U1, 12
Burg castle III
Büro office V U2, 38
Bus bus I
Butter butter I

C

Café snack bar I; café III
Cafeteria cafeteria I
Camp camp III
campen gehen to go camping III
Campingplatz campsite III
Cent *(Währung)* cent III
Center centre; center *(AE)* III
Chance chance III; opportunity IV
chatten to chat II
Check-in-Mitarbeiter check-in agent IV
Check-in-Mitarbeiterin check-in agent IV
Cheerleader cheerleader III
Cheerleaderin cheerleader III
Cheerleading cheerleading III
Chef boss III
Chefin boss III
Chinese Chinese II
Chinesin Chinese II
Chinesisch Chinese II
chinesisch Chinese II
circa about II
Cola cola I
Comic(heft) comic II
Computer computer I
cool cool I
Copyright copyright IV
Cousin cousin II
Cousine cousin II

D

da there; because I
Dach roof III
Dachboden attic I
daheim at home I
dahin there I
Dame lady IV
damit so that IV
Dampfer steamboat IV
Dampfschiff steamboat IV
danach then; after that I
dankbar thankful IV
Danke. Thanks.; Thank you. I
dann then I
Darsteller actor III

Darstellerin actor III
das the; this; that I; which; who III
dass that II
Datum date IV
dauern to last II; to take III
davor in front of I
Decke blanket IV
dein your I
Dein *(Grußformel in Briefen oder E-Mails)* Yours, II
deine yours III
Delfin dolphin V U4, 99
demoliert wrecked IV
Demonstration protest V U2, 37
denken to think II
denken an to think about III
denken an/über to think of III
der the I; which; that; who III
dermaßen so II
derselbe the same II
deshalb so I
Design design II
Detail detail V U3, 64
Detektiv detective I
Detektivin detective I
deutlich clear III
Deutsch German I
deutsch German II
Deutsche German II
Deutscher German II
Dezember December I
Dialog dialogue II
dich you I; yourself III
Didgeridoo *(australisches Musikinstrument)* didgeridoo V U1, 12
die the I; which; that; who III
Dienstag Tuesday I
dies this I
diese these II
dieses that I
Ding thing I; item IV
dir you I; yourself IV
dir selbst yourself IV
Distanz distance V U3, 80
Dollar *(amer. Währungseinheit)* dollar ($) IV
Donner boom IV
Donnerstag Thursday I
Dorf village I
dort there I
dorthin there I
Dose can IV
Drama drama III
draußen outside II
dreckig dirty I
drei three I
dreißig thirty I
dreizehn thirteen I
dritte third II
ein **Drittel** a third V U4, 88
Droge drug IV
drüben over III
du you I
Dudelsack bagpipes *(pl)* III
Duft smell IV
Dünger fertiliser V U2, 42
dunkel dark I
durch around; through III
Durcheinander mess I
Durchmesser diameter II
dürfen may V U1, 20
(etw. tun) dürfen to be allowed to (do sth) IV

E

eben flat V U1, 11
Ecke corner V U1, 28
effizient efficient IV
ehrenamtliche Helferin volunteer V U4, 89
ehrenamtlicher Helfer volunteer V U4, 89
Ei egg I
eiförmig oval III
eigene own II
eigentlich really I
Eignung suitability V U4, 90
Eignungs- suitability V U4, 90
ein one; a; an I
ein bisschen a bit V U3, 72
ein paar a few IV
einander each other III
eine a; an I
einfach easy I; just III
einfache Fahrkarte single ticket III
die einfachste the least difficult III
sich **einfallen** lassen to think of III
sich etw. **einfangen** *(medizinisch)* to catch sth V U1, 16
Eingebung inspiration V U3, 68
einhundert a/one hundred I
einige some I; a few IV; several V U2, 37
Einkaufen shopping I
Einkaufspassage mall II
Einkaufszentrum shopping centre I; mall II
Einkaufszettel shopping list I
einladen to invite II
Einladung invitation I
einmal once II
schon einmal ever III
einnehmen to take V U1, 16
einpacken to pack III
die Spülmaschine **einräumen** to load the dishwasher II
eins one I
einsam lonely III
einst once II
einsteigen to get in IV
in etw. einsteigen to get on sth IV
Einsteigezeit boarding time IV
eintausend a/one thousand II
sich **eintragen** to register V U1, 16
Eintrittskarte ticket II
einundzwanzig twenty-one I
nicht **einverstanden** sein to disagree IV
Einwanderer immigrant IV
Einwanderin immigrant IV
Einwohner population *(no pl)* IV
Einwohnerzahl population *(no pl)* IV
Einzelhandel retail V U4, 94
Einzelheit detail V U3, 64
Eis ice cream II
Eiscreme ice cream II
Eisenbahn railway IV
Eishockey ice hockey; hockey IV
Elch moose IV
Elefant elephant V U3, 63
Elektrizität electricity V U3, 63
Elendsviertel slum V U2, 36
elf eleven I
Eltern parents *(pl)* I
E-Mail e-mail II
Empfangschef receptionist IV
Empfangsdame receptionist IV
Empfehlung reference IV
Ende end II
am Ende at the end II
oberes Ende top II
enden to finish II; to end V U3, 62

Energie energy V U1, 21
die **Engländer** the English III
Englisch English I
englisch English III
englischsprachig English-speaking V ZI, 9
entdecken to discover V U3, 62
entfernt away II
Entfernung distance V U3, 80
entfliehen to escape IV
mit **enthalten** sein to be included V U4, 94
entkommen to escape IV
(sich) **entscheiden** to decide III
Entscheidung decision IV
Entschuldigung. Sorry. I; I'm sorry.; Excuse me. II
enttäuscht disappointed V U1, 12
entwerfen to design IV
entwickeln to design IV
Entwurf design II
Episode episode IV
er it; he I
Erdbeben earthquake IV
Erdbeere strawberry I
Erde earth III; soil V U2, 42
Erdteil continent II
sich **ereignen** to happen IV
Ereignis event II
erfahren to learn V U1, 12
erfahren von to hear about IV
Erfahrung experience IV
erfolgreich successful IV
erfolgreich sein to achieve V U3, 68
erforschen to explore IV
Ergebnis result V U4, 90
erhältlich available IV
sich **erholen** to recover V U1, 20
sich **erinnern** (an) to remember III
Erkältung cold II
erklären to explain V U3, 81
erklettern to climb II
erkunden to explore IV
sich **erkundigen** nach to ask about II
Erlebnis adventure III; experience IV
erledigen to finish II
ernst serious II
Ernte crop V U2, 42
Erntedankfest Thanksgiving IV
eröffnen to open V U4, 94
erraten to guess I
erreichen to achieve V U3, 68
erschießen to shoot IV
erst only V U3, 68
erstaunlich amazing II
erste first I
das erste Mal the first time I
Erste-Hilfe- first-aid IV
als **Erstes** first II
etw. nicht **ertragen** can't stand + -ing III
erwachen to wake up III
erzählen to tell I
Erzähler narrator I
Erzählerin narrator I
erzeugen to produce IV
Erzeugnis product V U4, 94
Erziehung education IV
erzielen to score III
es it I
Es macht nichts. I don't mind. IV
Es tut mir leid. I'm sorry. II
es war einmal once upon a time II
Essen food I; meal II
essen to eat; to have I
Etage floor II
etwa about II
etwas something; some I; anything III
euch you I; yourselves IV
euch selbst yourselves IV
euer your I
eure yours III
Euro *(Währung)* euro III
Europäer European III
Europäerin European III
europäisch European III
ewig forever IV
Examen exam V U4, 90
ein Examen schreiben to take an exam V U4, 90
Experiment experiment II
Extremist extremist V U2, 47
Extremistin extremist V U2, 47

F

Fabrik factory III
(zu etw.) **fähig** sein *(Ersatzform für can)* to be able to (do sth) IV
Fähigkeit skill IV
fahren to go; to ride I; to run; to travel II; to drive IV
Fahrrad fahren to go bike riding II
Tandem fahren to go tandem bike riding II
Fahrer driver IV
Fahrerin driver IV
Fahrgeschäft ride II
einfache **Fahrkarte** single ticket III
Fahrplan timetable III
Fahrrad bike I
Fahrrad fahren to go bike riding II
Fahrschein ticket II
Fahrt trip I; ride II; journey III
fair fair IV
Fakt fact II
auf jeden **Fall** certainly V U2, 46
fallen to fall I
fällen to cut down V U3, 72
falls if IV
falsch wrong I
Familie family I
Fan fan I
fangen to catch II
fantastisch fantastic II
Farbe colour I; color *(AE)* III
Fasching carnival I
fast nearly II
Februar February I
Feier party I
feiern to celebrate III
eine Party feiern to have a party I
Feiertag holiday *(AE)* IV
Feld field III
Feldfrucht crop V U2, 42
Fels rock V U1, 12
Fenster window I
Ferien holiday II; vacation *(AE)* III
fernhalten to keep away IV
Fernseh- TV IV
Fernsehen television III; TV IV
im Fernsehen on TV III
fernsehen to watch TV I
Fernseher TV I; television III
fertig ready I
fertig machen to finish II
Fertigkeit skill IV
fertigstellen to finish I
Fest fair II; festival III
fest close V U4, 99
festhalten to hold II

Festival festival III
feststecken to be stuck I
Festzug procession II
Feuer fire III
Fieber high temperature V U1, 16
Figur figure II
Film film I; movie *(AE)* III
finden to find I
Gefallen finden an to enjoy IV
Gefallen finden an to enjoy + -ing V U2, 38
Firma company II
Fisch fish I
fischen gehen to go fishing IV
fit fit III
flach flat V U1, 11
Fläche area V U1, 20
Flagge flag IV
eine **Flasche** … a bottle of II
Fledermaus bat I
Fleisch meat IV
flexibel flexible IV
Fliegen flying III
fliegen to fly II
fliehen to escape IV
Fließband assembly line V U2, 38
Floh flea I
Flohmarkt flea market I
Floß raft III
flüchten to escape IV
Flug flight IV
Guten Flug! Have a good flight! IV
Flughafen airport IV
Flugsteig gate IV
Flugzeug plane IV
Fluss river I
Flusskrebs crayfish V U4, 99
Folge episode IV
Follower follower IV
Followerin follower IV
Formular form V U4, 90
Foto photo I
Fotos machen to take photos (of) II
fotografieren to take photos (of) II
Frage question I
fragen to ask I
fragen nach to ask about II
Französisch French IV
französisch French IV
Frau woman I; lady IV
Frau *(Anrede)* Mrs I; Miss IV; Ms V U4, 90
frei free III
im **Freien** outside II
Freitag Friday I
Freiwillige volunteer V U4, 89
Freiwilliger volunteer V U4, 89
Freizeit free time I
Freizeit- free-time V U4, 89
Freizeitpark theme park II
Freude fun I
sich **freuen** auf to look forward to (+ -ing) IV
Freund friend I
Freundin friend I
freundlich friendly IV
Freundschaft(en) schließen to make friends II
friedlich non-violent V U2, 46; peaceful V U2, 47; calm V U4, 90
Frisbee frisbee I
Frisbeescheibe frisbee I
Friseur hairdresser IV
Friseurin hairdresser IV
Friseursalon hairdressing salon IV
froh happy IV
Frohe Weihnachten! Merry Christmas! I
fröhlich happy IV
Frucht fruit I
früh early II
Frühling spring II
Frühstück breakfast I
frühstücken to have breakfast I
Frühstückspension bed and breakfast (B & B) III
(sich) **fühlen** to feel II
sich wieder besser fühlen to get better V U1, 16
führen to lead V U2, 37
Führer guide IV
Führerin guide IV
Führerschein driving licence V U3, 64
Führung tour III
füllen to fill V U4, 94
Füller pen I
fünf five I
fünfzehn fifteen I
fünfzig fifty I
funktionieren to work V U4, 94
für for I; to IV
für immer forever IV
furchtbar awful I
Fuß foot II
zu Fuß on foot I
zu Fuß gehen to walk IV
Fußball football I; soccer *(AE)* II
füttern to feed I

G

ganz all I; all of; quite II
in ganz all over II
Ganztages- all-day III
Garage garage V U4, 90
Garten garden I
Gast guest IV
Gate gate IV
Gebäude building II
geben to give I
Gebet prayer V U4, 98
Gebiet field III; area IV
geboren werden to be born IV
gebratener Reis mit Hühnerfleisch chicken fried rice II
gebraucht second-hand I
Geburtsdatum date of birth IV
Geburtstag birthday I
Gedicht poem III
Gefahr danger V U1, 20
gefährlich dangerous III
Gefallen finden an to enjoy IV
Gefallen finden an to enjoy + -ing V U2, 38
jmdn. **gefangen** halten to keep sb prisoner IV
Gefangene prisoner IV
Gefangener prisoner IV
Gefängnis prison V U2, 46
gegen against III
etwas gegen etw. haben to mind sth V U4, 90
Gegend area IV
gegenseitig each other III
Gegenstand item IV
gegenüber opposite II
Gehalt salary IV
gehen to go I; to walk; to leave IV
aus dem Weg gehen to avoid IV
campen gehen to go camping III
fischen gehen to go fishing IV
inlineskaten gehen to go skating II

ins Bett gehen to go to bed I
raften gehen to go rafting III
Schlittschuhlaufen gehen to go skating II
zelten gehen to go camping III
Gehör hearing II
Geist ghost IV
gelb yellow I
Geld money I
Geld aufbringen to raise money II
Geld sammeln to raise money II
Geldbeutel wallet V U3, 64
Geldbörse wallet V U3, 64
Gelegenheit chance III; opportunity IV
gelegentlich occasionally III
Gemälde painting V U1, 12
Gemeinde community V U4, 94
Gemüse vegetable (veg) IV
genauso the same II
genießen to enjoy IV
genießen to enjoy + -ing V U2, 38
genießen, ... zu tun to enjoy + -ing V U2, 38
genug enough III
genügend enough III
geöffnet open I
gerade (eben) just III
geradeaus straight on II
Gerät tool V U4, 90
Geräusch noise I
gerecht fair IV
Gern geschehen. You're welcome. V U1, 16
ich hätte **gern** ... I'd love (to) ... (= I would love to) IV
ich würde sehr **gern** ... I'd love (to) ... (= I would love to) IV
... **gerne** like + -ing I
gernhaben to like I
Geruch smell IV
Geruchssinn sense of smell IV
Geschäft shop I; store *(AE)* III; business V ZI, 9
Geschäftsführer manager IV
Geschäftsführerin manager IV
Geschäftswelt business V ZI, 9
geschehen to happen II
Geschenk present I
Geschichte story I
Geschick skill IV
geschlossen closed I
Geschöpf creature V U1, 10
Gesellschaft company II
Gesetz law V U1, 20
gegen das Gesetz verstoßen to break the law V U2, 46
Gesicht face I
Gespenst ghost IV
Gespräch dialogue II; interview IV
Gestalt figure II
gestalten to design IV
Gestaltung design II
gestern yesterday I
gesund healthy III
Getränk drink I
Getreide corn IV
Gewalt violence *(no pl)* IV
gewaltfrei non-violent V U2, 46
Gewerbe industry V U4, 88
Gewinn prize II
gewinnen to win I
Gewinner winner I
Gewinnerin winner I
Gewinnspiel raffle II
sich **gewöhnen** an (etw.) to get used to (sth) IV
gewöhnlich usually II
Gitarre guitar V U3, 72
glauben to think; to believe II
gleich the same II; right away V U3, 68
der **gleiche** the same II
gleichzeitig at the same time II
Glocke bell II
Glück bringend lucky II
Glück haben to be lucky II
Viel **Glück**! Good luck! IV
zum **Glück** fortunately V U3, 72
glücklich happy I; lucky II
Glückstag lucky day II
Glückwunsch! Congratulations! II
Gold gold III
Gold- gold III
golden gold III
grau grey I
Grenze border IV
Grill barbecue I
Grillfest barbecue I
Grippe flu V U1, 16
Grizzlybär grizzly bear IV
groß big I; large; high; tall II; great III
großartig great I; fantastic II; awesome III
Größe size II
Großeltern grandparents *(pl)* II
Großmutter grandmother V U4, 98
Großstadt city I
Großvater grandfather II
grün green I
gründen to found V U4, 98
Grundschule primary school IV
Gruppe team I; group IV
gruselig scary I
Viele **Grüße** Best wishes, I
Mit freundlichen **Grüßen** Yours sincerely, IV
günstig cheap II
gut fine; good I; well II
gut sein in to be good at I
Gut gemacht! Well done! II
gut sein bei to be good at I
Gute Besserung! Get well soon! V U1, 16
Guten Flug! Have a good flight! IV
Mir geht es gut. I'm fine. I
Alles **Gute!** Best wishes, I; All the best, II; Good luck! IV
Güter goods *(pl only)* V U2, 38

H

haben to have I; to have got II
Angst haben to be scared I
Glück haben to be lucky II
Hähnchen chicken I
Hai shark I
halb half III
halb (acht) half past (seven) II
eine halbe Million half a million III
(die) **Hälfte** half V ZI, 8
Hallen- indoor III
Hallo. Hello.; Hi. I
Hallo! G'day! (= Good day!) V U1, 10
Hals neck II
Halsband collar I
Halt stop II
halten to hold; to keep II; to give V ZI, 9
davon halten to think of V U1, 12
jmdn. gefangen halten to keep sb prisoner IV
Haltestelle stop II; station III

Hamburger burger I
Hammer hammer III
Hammerwerfen hammer throwing III
Hamster hamster I
Hand hand II
aus zweiter Hand second-hand I
Handschuh glove II
Handy phone I
hart hard II
hassen to hate I
häufig often II
häufiger more often IV
Häuptling chief V U4, 98
Hauptpostamt GPO V U1, 21
Hauptstadt capital (city) I
Haus house I
nach Hause home I
zu Hause at home I
Hausaufgabe(n) homework I
Hausaufgabe(n) machen to do homework I
Hausmeister caretaker I
Hausmeisterin caretaker I
Haustier pet I
Heft book I
heilig sacred V U2, 54
Heim home I
Heimat home country IV
Heimatland home country IV
Heimweh haben to be homesick IV
heiß hot I
Ich **heiße** ... My name is ... I
helfen to help I
Helfer assistant IV
Helferin assistant IV
Helikopter helicopter V U1, 12
Helm helmet I
Hemd shirt I
herausfallen to fall out III
herausfinden to find I; to find out IV; to learn V U1, 12
herauskommen to get out IV
Herberge hostel II
Herbst autumn II; fall *(AE)* III
Herr *(Anrede)* Mr I
herstellen to produce IV; to make V U2, 38
herüber over III
herumhängen to hang about I
herunter down III
herunterfallen to fall off II
Herzliche Grüße Love, I
heute today I
heute Morgen this morning II
Hi! G'day! (= Good day!) V U1, 10
hier here I
hierher here III
hierhin here III
hiesig local II
High School *(weiterführende Schule, Oberstufe)* high school V U3, 63
Hilfe help I; support V U4, 90
hilfreich useful III
Himmel sky IV
Hin- und Rückfahrkarte return ticket III
hinauf up II
hinaus out V U4, 98
hinausbringen to take out II
hinbringen to take II
Hindu Hindu V U2, 47
hinduistisch Hindu V U2, 47
in ... **hinein** into II
hinfallen to fall I
sich **hinsetzen** to sit (down) I
hinter behind I
Hintergrund background III
hinterlassen to leave III
hinunter down III
hinunterfallen to fall off II
Hinweis clue I
hinzufügen to add V U3, 64
hispanisch Hispanic IV
Hispanoamerikaner Hispanic IV
Hispanoamerikanerin Hispanic IV
HIV HIV V U3, 68
HIV- HIV V U3, 68
HI-Virus HIV V U3, 68
Hobby hobby II
hoch high; up; tall II
hochladen to upload II
Hochzeit wedding V U2, 37
arrangierte Hochzeit arranged marriage V U2, 37
Hockey hockey IV
hoffen (auf) to hope (for) II
Hoffnung hope V U3, 73
Höhe height II
Höhle cave IV
holen to get IV
Holz wood I
homosexuell lesbian V U3, 68; gay V U3, 68
hören to listen (to) I; to hear II
hören von to hear about IV
kurze **Hose** shorts *(pl)* II
Hostel hostel II
Hotdog hot dog II
Hotel hotel IV
hübsch pretty II; beautiful III
Hubschrauber helicopter V U1, 12
Hügel hill IV
Huhn chicken I
gebratener Reis mit **Hühnerfleisch** chicken fried rice II
Hund dog I
den Hund ausführen to take the dog for a walk I
hundert a/one hundred I
hungrig hungry I
hüpfen to bounce III
Hurrikan hurricane IV
Husky *(Schlittenhunderasse)* husky IV
Hut hat II
hüten to look after II

I

ich I; me I
ich hätte gern I'd (= I would) I
ich hätte gern ... I'd love (to) ... (= I would love to) IV
ich möchte ... I'd like (to) ... (= I would like to) I
ich würde I'd (= I would) I
ich würde gerne ... I'd like (to) ... (= I would like to) I
ich würde nicht gerne ... I wouldn't like (to) ... I
ich würde sehr gern ... I'd love (to) ... (= I would love to) IV
Idee idea I
ihm it; him II
ihn it; him II
Ihnen you I
ihnen them II
ihr you; her; their; its I
Ihr your I
Ihre yours III
ihre hers; theirs III
im in I
im Fernsehen on TV III

im Freien outside II
im Jahr a year IV
im Moment at the moment II
im Norden von in the north of III
im Wert von worth of V U4, 94
Imbissstube snack bar I
immer always I
für immer forever IV
immer noch still II
schon immer always III
Immigrant immigrant IV
Immigrantin immigrant IV
in to; in; at I; into II
in der Schule at school I
in der Woche a week V U3, 73
in ganz all over II
in Ordnung fine I
in Richtung towards V U4, 99
inbegriffen sein to be included V U4, 94
Inder Indian V U2, 36
Inderin Indian V U2, 36
Indianer Native American III
Indianerin Native American III
indianisch Native American III
indisch Indian V U2, 36
Industrie industry III
Industriezweig industry V U4, 88
Informatik IT (Information Technology) V U2, 38
aktuelle **Information** update IV
Information(en) information II
Ingenieur engineer II
Ingenieurin engineer II
inlineskaten to skate II
inlineskaten gehen to go skating II
Innen- indoor III
Insel island IV
Inspiration inspiration V U3, 68
inspirierend inspiring V U3, 68
interessant interesting I
Interesse interest IV
sich **interessieren** für to be interested in III
interessiert sein an to be interested in III
international international V ZI, 9
Internetseite website III
Internettagebuch blog I
Interview interview IV
Interviewer interviewer IV
Interviewerin interviewer IV
irgendeine any I
irgendeiner anyone IV
irgendetwas anything III
irgendjemand someone; anybody III; anyone IV
irgendwelche any I
Irisch Irish III
irisch Irish III
Italiener Italian IV
Italienerin Italian IV
Italienisch Italian IV
italienisch Italian IV

J

ja yes I
Jacke coat I
Jahr year I
im Jahr a year IV
Jahre alt year-old V U2, 42
pro Jahr a year IV
Jahreszeit season II
Jahrgangsstufe year I; grade *(AE)* II
Jahrhundert century IV
-jährig year-old V U2, 42
Jahrmarkt fair II
Januar January I
Japaner Japanese IV
Japanerin Japanese IV
Japanisch Japanese IV
japanisch Japanese IV
jede every I
jeder everyone II; anybody III
jedoch however V U1, 20
jemals ever III
jemand somebody I; someone; anybody III
jene that I; those II
jetzt now I
Job job I
Jugend- youth I; teen II
Jugendliche teen II; teenager V U2, 42
Jugendlicher teen II; teenager V U2, 42
Juli July I
jung young II
Junge boy I
Juni June I
Jurist lawyer V U2, 46
Juristin lawyer V U2, 46

K

Käfig cage II
Kajak kayak IV
Kajakfahren kayaking IV
Kalender planner II
kalt cold I
Kälte cold II
kämpfen to fight II; to struggle V U1, 11
Kanadier Canadian IV
Kanadierin Canadian IV
kanadisch Canadian IV
Kanal canal III
Känguru kangaroo V U1, 11
Kaninchen rabbit I
Kanone cannon III
Kanonenkugel cannon ball III
Kanu canoe IV
Kanufahren canoeing I
Kapitän captain II
Kapitänin captain II
kaputt machen to break V U1, 11
Karibe Caribbean IV
Karibin Caribbean IV
karibisch Caribbean IV
Karneval carnival I
Karriere career IV
Karte map II; card III
Kartoffel potato IV
Käse cheese I
Kasse checkout V U4, 94
Katze cat I
kaufen to buy I
kein no I; not … any III
keine no I; not … any III
Keks biscuit; cookie *(AE)* III
kennen to know I
kennenlernen to meet I
Kenntnis skill IV
Kette chain III
Kfz-Werkstatt garage V U4, 90
Kilo (kg, Kilogramm) kilo (kg, kilogram) I
Kilometer (km) kilometre (km) IV
Kilt kilt III
Kind kid I
Kinder children *(pl)* I
Kindergarten kindergarten V U3, 73
Kinderzimmer bedroom II
Kino cinema I
Kirche church II

Kiste box I
Kiwi *(Kosename für Neuseeländer)* Kiwi V U4, 106
klagen to lament V U4, 98
klar clear III
Klasse year; class I; grade *(AE)* II
Klassenarbeit test V U4, 90
Klassenfahrt school trip II
Klassenzimmer classroom I
Kleeblatt shamrock III
Kleid dress I
Kleider clothes *(pl only)* I
Kleiderschrank wardrobe II
Kleidung clothes *(pl only)* I
klein little; small I
Klettern rock climbing I
klettern to climb II
Klima climate IV
Klimawandel climate change V U1, 20
klingeln to ring I
klingen to sound III
Klub club I
Knall bang V U3, 64
Koala koala V U1, 11
Koch chef II
Koch- cooking II
Kochen cooking II
kochen to cook II
Koffer suitcase IV
Kohlenbergwerk coal mine III
Kohlengrube coal mine III
Kolonie colony IV
komisch funny I
kommen to come; to get I
zu spät kommen to be late II
Kommentar comment IV
kommentieren to comment (on) IV
Kommunikation communication V U4, 90
kommunizieren to communicate V ZI, 9
kompliziert difficult III
König king II
Königin queen II
können can I; may V U1, 20
(etw. tun) können to be able to (do sth) IV
nicht können can't I
konnte could III
könnte could V U3, 81; might V U4, 90
konstruieren to design IV
Kontakt contact I
in Kontakt bleiben to keep in touch II
Kontinent continent II
kontrollieren to check II; to control V U3, 72
Konzert concert I
Kopf head II
Kopfschmerzen headache II
Kopfweh headache II
Koralle coral V U1, 20
Korb basket III
Korbball netball I
Korn corn IV
Körper body IV
korrekt right I
korrigieren to correct II
kosten to cost III
kostenlos free III
köstlich delicious V U1, 12
Kostüm costume; fancy dress I
krachen to crash V U3, 64
Kraft energy V U1, 21
krank ill V U1, 16
Krankenakte medical record V U1, 16
Krankenhaus hospital II
Krankenpfleger nurse IV
Krankenschwester nurse IV
Krankenversicherung medical insurance V U3, 73
Krankheit disease V U3, 68
Kratzer scratch IV
Kreatur creature V U1, 10
Kricket cricket II
Kronjuwelen crown jewels *(pl)* II
Kruste crust IV
Küche kitchen II
Kuchen cake I
Küchenchef chef II
Kugel ball III
Kuh cow III
Kulissen scenery III
Kultur culture III
sich **kümmern** um to look after II
Kunde customer I
Kundenbetreuung customer service IV
Kundendienst customer service IV
Kundenservice customer service IV
Kundgebung march V U2, 47
Kundin customer I
Kunst Art I
Künstler artist III
Künstlerin artist III
Kunststück trick I
Kurier messenger IV
Kurierin messenger IV
Kurs class IV
kurz short II
kurze Hose shorts *(pl)* II
küssen to kiss V U4, 99
Küste coast III

L

lachen to laugh II
Laden shop I; store *(AE)* III
Lager camp III
Lampe lamp II
Land country I; nation III
landen to land IV
ländliche Gegend country I
Landschaft landscape V U4, 89
Landwirt farmer I
Landwirtin farmer I
Landwirtschaft farming V U2, 42
lang long III
länger longer I
langsam slow IV
Languste crayfish V U4, 99
langweilig boring I
Laptop laptop I
lassen to leave II
lass(t) uns let's (= let us) I
Laterne lantern II
Laufbahn career IV
laufen to run II; to walk IV
Schlittschuh laufen to skate II
laut loud I; noisy III
läuten to ring I
Leben life II; living V U2, 42
leben to live I
Lebensart lifestyle V U1, 12
Lebenslauf CV (curriculum vitae) IV
Lebensmittel food I
Lebensstil lifestyle V U1, 12
Lebensweise lifestyle V U1, 12; living V U2, 42
Lebewesen creature V U1, 10
lecker delicious V U1, 12
legen to put I
lehren to teach IV

Lehrer teacher I
Lehrerin teacher I
Leiche body IV
leicht easy I
Es tut mir **leid.** I'm sorry. II
Tut mir **leid.** Sorry. I
leider I'm afraid IV; unfortunately V U2, 47
leise quiet II
leisten to achieve V U3, 68
leistungsfähig efficient IV
leiten to lead V U2, 37; to be in charge (of) V U3, 72
Leiter ladder I; leader III
Leiterin leader III
(für) etw. **lernen** to study (for) sth V U4, 90
lernen to learn II
Lesbe lesbian V U3, 68
lesbisch lesbian V U3, 68
lesen to read II
letzte last I
Leute people I; persons *(pl)* II
Liebe(r) ..., *(Anrede in Briefen)*
Dear ..., I
Liebe Grüße Love, I
lieben to love I
Lieblings- favourite I; favorite *(AE)* III
am **liebsten** best II
Lied song I
Liedermacher songwriter V U3, 68
Liedermacherin songwriter V U3, 68
liefern to deliver IV
Lieferwagen van IV
Lineal ruler I
Linie line III
links on the left; left II
Liste list V U1, 16
Loch hole I
lokal local II
lösen to solve V U2, 38
Löwe lion V U3, 63
Luft air III
lügen to lie IV
lustig funny I; fun III

M

machen to do; to make I; to complete V U4, 90
eine Ausbildung machen to train IV
Fotos machen to take photos (of) II
Hausaufgabe(n) machen to do homework I
kaputt machen to break V U1, 11
Mach die Musik leiser. Turn the music down. I
Mach dir keine Sorgen. Don't worry. I
Mach dir nichts draus. Never mind. II
Macht nichts. Never mind. II
Mädchen girl I
Mahlzeit meal II
Mai May I
Mais corn IV
Mal time I; base III
das erste Mal the first time I
zum 200. Mal for the 200th time III
malen to paint II
Mama mum I; mom *(AE)* III
Manager manager IV
Managerin manager IV
manchmal sometimes I
Mann man I
Mannschaft team I
Mannschaftsführer captain II
Mannschaftsführerin captain II
Maori Maori V U4, 89
Maori- Maori V U4, 89
maorisch Maori V U4, 89
Markt market I
Marsch march V U2, 47
März March I
Maschine machine V U2, 38
Maske mask V U4, 99
Match match I
Mathe Maths I; Math *(AE)* III
Mathematik Math *(AE)* III
Matsch mud I
Mauer wall II
Maus mouse I
Mechaniker mechanic V U4, 90
Mechanikerin mechanic V U4, 90
Medaille medal II
soziale **Medien** social media III
Medikament medication; drug V U3, 68
Medikamente medicine V U1, 16
Medizin medicine V U1, 16
Meer sea I
am Meer at the seaside I
Meerschweinchen guinea pig II
mehr more II
nicht mehr not ... any more III
mehrere several V U2, 37
Mehrheit majority V ZI, 8
die Mehrheit most III
Mehrzahl majority V ZI, 8
meiden to avoid IV
Meile mile III
mein my I
meine mine III
meinen to mean IV
anderer **Meinung** sein to disagree IV
einer **Meinung** sein (mit) to agree (with) II
am **meisten** most III
die **meisten** most III
eine **Menge** a lot of I
Mensa cafeteria I
Mensch person *(sg)* II
Menschen people I; persons *(pl)* II
Menschenhändler slave trader IV
sich **merken** to remember III
merkwürdig funny I
Messe fair II
Metall- metal III
metallen metal III
Meter metre II; meter *(AE)* III
mich me I; myself III
mich selbst myself IV
mild mild II
Milliarde billion V ZI, 8
Million million I
eine halbe Million half a million III
Minute minute I
mir me I; myself IV
mit with I; on II; of III
mit (dem Zug) by (train) I
mit enthalten sein to be included V U4, 94
Mitarbeiter employee; assistant IV
Mitarbeiterin employee; assistant IV
mitbringen to bring II
Mitglied member V U4, 89
mitmachen (bei) to take part (in) II
mitnehmen to take I
mitspielen to act III
Mittagessen lunch; dinner I

Mittagspause lunchtime I
Mittagszeit lunchtime I
Mitte centre; middle; center *(AE)* III
Mittelschule secondary school IV
mitten in in the middle of II
mittlerer Schulabschluss secondary school leaving certificate IV
Mittwoch Wednesday I
Mode fashion IV
modern modern I
mögen to like; to want (to) I; to enjoy + -ing V U2, 38
gern mögen to love I
nicht mögen to hate I
ich möchte nicht … I wouldn't like (to) … I
ich möchte … I'd like (to) … (= I would like to) I
Möchtest du …? Would you like (to) …? I
Möglichkeit chance III; opportunity IV
im **Moment** at the moment II
momentan at the moment II
Monat month II
Montag Monday I
Morgen morning I
heute Morgen this morning II
morgen tomorrow II
motivieren to motivate III
müde tired I
Muffin muffin II
Mühe haben to struggle V U1, 11
Müll rubbish I
multikulturell multicultural IV
Mund mouth II
Museum museum II
Musik music I
Musikgruppe band II
Muslim Muslim I
Muslimin Muslim I
müssen to have to; must II; to need to III
mutig brave III
Mutter mother I
Mutti mum I
Mütze hat II

N

Na ja, … Well, … II
nach to; after I
nach *(bei Uhrzeitangaben)* past II
nach Hause home I
Nachbar neighbour I
Nachbarin neighbour I
nachdem after IV
nachdenken über to think about III
nachhaltig sustainable V U2, 42
Nachmittag afternoon I
nachmittags *(Uhrzeit)* p.m. III
Nachricht message II
Nachricht(en) news II
nachschauen to look I
nächste next I
als Nächstes next II
Nacht night I
nachts at night IV
Nacken neck II
nah near II
in der **Nähe** von near I
Name name I
Nase nose II
die Nase voll haben (von) to be fed up (with) III
nass wet I
Nation nation III
national national III
National- national III
Nationalität nationality IV
Nationalpark national park III
Natur nature V U3, 81
natürlich of course II
Naturwissenschaft science III
neben next to I; by III
nebenher at the same time II
nehmen to take I; to use III
nehmen (Bus/Zug) to catch (bus/train) III
Nehmen Sie Platz. Take a seat. IV
Nimm Platz. Take a seat. IV
nein no I
nennen to call III
nett nice I
neu new I
Neuigkeit(en) news II
neun nine I
neunzehn nineteen I
neunzig ninety I
nicht not I
auch nicht not … either III
nicht können can't I
nicht mögen to hate I
nicht einverstanden sein to disagree IV
nicht mehr not … any more III
nichts nothing II; not … anything III
nicken to nod V U4, 99
nie never II
niemals never II
niemand no one I; nobody II
noch still II
immer noch still II
noch ein another IV
noch einmal again I
noch nicht not … yet III
Nord- north III
Norden north III
im Norden von in the north of III
normalerweise usually II
Note grade *(AE)* II
Notfall emergency V U3, 80
November November I
null zero I
Null *(bei Uhrzeiten und Telefonnummern)* oh III
Nummer number I
nun now I
nur only I; just III
nutzen to use III
nützlich useful III

O

ob if IV
als ob like IV
oben up II; at the top V U1, 28
oberer Teil top II
oberes Ende top II
oberhalb above II
Obst fruit I
obwohl although V U4, 94
oder or I
offensichtlich certainly V U2, 46
öffentliche Verkehrsmittel public transport III
öffnen to open I
oft often II
öfter more often IV
ohne without II
Oje. Oh dear. V U1, 16
okay OK (okay) I
Oktober October I

Öl oil II
Ölpest oil spill V U1, 20
Ölteppich oil spill V U1, 20
Oma grandma I
Onkel uncle I
online online II
online stellen to post III
Online- online II
Orange orange I
orange orange I
in **Ordnung** fine I
in Ordnung bringen to tidy II
Organisation organization V U3, 72
organisieren to organize I
Orkan hurricane IV
Ort place I
örtlich local II
Ost- east III
Osten east III
das **Outback** *(australisches Hinterland)* the outback V U1, 11
oval oval III

P

ein **paar** some I; a few IV
packen to pack III
Paket package IV
Papa dad I
Papier paper III
Parade parade IV
Park park I
Parlament parliament V U3, 62
Partner partner I
Partnerin partner I
Partnerstadt twin town III
Party party I
eine Party feiern to have a party I
Pass passport IV
Passagier passenger IV
Passagierin passenger IV
passieren to happen II
Das ist passiert. That's what happened. II
Patient patient V U1, 16
Patientin patient V U1, 16
Pause break I
Pausenhof playground I
peng bang V U3, 64
Person person *(sg)* II
Pferd horse I
Pflanze plant III
Pflaume plum I
Pfund *(brit. Währungseinheit)* pound (£) I
Picknick picnic I
Pier pier II
pink pink I
Pistole gun IV
Pizza pizza I
Plan map II; plan IV
planen to plan IV
Planer planner II
platt flat V U1, 11
(Kontinental-)**Platte** plate IV
Platz place I
plaudern to chat II
plötzlich suddenly I
Podcast podcast V U3, 68
Polizei police IV
Polizeibeamter police officer I
Polizeibeamtin police officer I
Polizeirevier police station V U3, 64
Polizeiwache police station V U3, 64
Pommes frites chips *(pl)* I
Pop *(Musik)* pop II
positiv positive III
posten to post III
Poster poster II
Postkarte postcard I
Praktikant intern V U4, 94
Praktikantin intern V U4, 94
Praktikum internship IV
Präsentation presentation III
präsentieren to present V U4, 94
Präsident president III
Präsidentin president III
Preis price I; prize II
prellen to bounce III
Prinz prince V U2, 38
pro Jahr a year IV
pro Woche a week V U3, 73
probieren to try III
Problem problem I
Produkt product V U4, 94
Profil profile III
Programm programme III
(Software)**Programm** (software) program V ZI, 8
Programmierer computer programmer V U2, 38
Programmiererin computer programmer V U2, 38
Projekt project II
Prospekt brochure III
Protest protest V U2, 37
protestieren to protest V U1, 21
Prozent percent (%) III
Prozession parade IV
prüfen to test II
Prüfung exam V U4, 90
eine Prüfung schreiben to take an exam V U4, 90
Pullover pullover I
Puma mountain lion II
Punkt point III; dot V U1, 12
pünktlich in time V U2, 54
Pute turkey IV
putzen to clean II

Q

Quadrat- square V U3, 63
Qualifikation qualification IV
qualifiziert qualified V U4, 112
Quiz quiz IV

R

Rad wheel II
Radiergummi rubber I
Radio radio III
Raft raft III
raften gehen to go rafting III
Rafting rafting III
Rakete rocket III
rammen to hit V U3, 64
Ranger ranger *(AE)* IV
Rangerin ranger *(AE)* IV
Rap rap I
Rat advice III
raten to guess I
Ratespiel quiz IV
Ratschlag advice III
Rauch smoke IV
Raum room I
Raumfahrt space III
Realschulabschluss secondary school leaving certificate IV
Du hast **recht**. You're right. I
Recht right V U1, 11
rechte right II

rechts on the right; right II
Rechtschreibung spelling I
rechtzeitig in time V U2, 54
reden (mit) to talk (to) I
Redner speaker V ZI, 8
Rednerin speaker V ZI, 8
reduzieren to reduce V U4, 94
Referat presentation III
Referenz reference IV
Regal shelf II
Regalbrett shelf II
Regel rule V U3, 80
Regenbogen rainbow III
Reggae *(Musik)* reggae IV
Regierung government V U1, 20
Regisseur director V U3, 68
Regisseurin director V U3, 68
sich **registrieren** lassen to register V U1, 16
regnen to rain I
regnerisch rainy II
reich rich V U3, 63
Reihenhaus townhouse III
Reis rice II
gebratener Reis mit Hühnerfleisch chicken fried rice II
Reise trip I; tour; journey III
Reisebüro travel agent's IV
Reisebürokauffrau travel agent IV
Reisebürokaufmann travel agent IV
Reiseleiter tour guide V U2, 38
Reiseleiterin tour guide V U2, 38
reisen to travel II
Reisepass passport IV
Reiten horse riding I
reiten to ride I
Reiter rider V U4, 98
Reiterin rider V U4, 98
Religion religion V U2, 47
Rennen race II
rennen to run II
reparieren to repair IV
Reservat reservation III
reservieren to book III; to make reservations IV
Reservierung reservation III
respektieren to respect V U2, 47
Rest rest II
Restaurant restaurant II
retten to save II
Rezept *(für Arzneimittel)* prescription V U1, 16
Richterskala Richter scale *(no pl)* IV
richtig right I; true V U2, 38
richtigstellen to correct II
in **Richtung** towards V U4, 99
Riesen- giant V U1, 12
Riesenrad big wheel II
riesig great III; giant V U1, 12
Riff reef V U1, 20
Rinde crust IV
ringen to struggle V U1, 11
Ritt ride II
Rock skirt III
Rolle part II
Rollstuhl wheelchair I
rosa pink I
rot red I
Hin- und **Rückfahrkarte** return ticket III
rufen to shout I; to call III
Rugby rugby III
ruhig quiet II; calm V U4, 90
Russe Russian IV
Russin Russian IV
Russisch Russian IV
russisch Russian IV

S

Sache thing I
Sack bag I
Sackhüpfen sack race II
Safari safari V U3, 63
Saft juice I
sagen to say; to tell I
Saison season II
Salat salad I
Salz salt V U2, 47
Geld **sammeln** to raise money II
Sammlung collection III
Samstag Saturday I
samstags on Saturdays I
Sandwich sandwich I
Sänger singer I
Sängerin singer I
sanitäre Anlagen sanitation V U2, 42
sauber machen to clean II
Saxofon saxophone I
Schachtel box I
Schade! That's too bad. II
Schaden damage IV
schaden to damage V U2, 42
Schäden damage IV
Schaf sheep I
Schal scarf II
Schatzsuche treasure hunt II
schauen to look I
Schauspieler actor III
Schauspielerei drama III
Schauspielerin actor III
Schauspielworkshop acting workshop III
scheinen to seem V U4, 99
schenken to give I
schicken to send I
schieben to push I
schiefgehen to go wrong V U4, 90
schießen to kick III; to shoot IV
Schiff ship I; boat IV
Schild sign IV
Schimpanse chimpanzee II
schlafen to sleep II
Schlafzimmer bedroom II
schlagen to hit III
Schläger stick III
Schlagfrau batter III
Schlagmann batter III
Schlamm mud I
schlecht bad I; ill V U1, 16
schlechter worse II
schlechteste worst II
schleudern to skid V U3, 64
schließen to close I
Freundschaft(en) schließen to make friends II
schlimm bad II
schlimmer worse II
schlimmste worst II
Schlitten sled IV
schlittern to skid V U3, 64
Schlittschuh laufen to skate II
Schlittschuhlaufen gehen to go skating II
Schloss castle III
Schlumpf smurf I
Schluss end II
Schlüssel key III
Schminken face painting II
schmutzig dirty I
Schnee snow II
schneereich snowy II

schnell fast II; quick IV
Schnitzeljagd treasure hunt II
Schnitzerei carving V U4, 99
Schokolade chocolate I
schon already; yet III
schon einmal ever III
schon immer always III
Schon gut. Never mind. II
schön fine; nice I; beautiful III
High **School** *(weiterführende Schule, Oberstufe)* high school V U3, 63
Schottenrock kilt III
schottisch Scottish III
schrecklich awful I
Schreiben letter IV
eine Prüfung **schreiben** to take an exam V U4, 90
ein Examen schreiben to take an exam V U4, 90
Schreibtisch desk II
schreien to shout I
Schritt step II
Schuh shoe I
Schulabschluss qualification IV
mittlerer Schulabschluss secondary school leaving certificate IV
Schul-AG club I
Schulausflug school trip II
Schule school I
in der Schule at school I
weiterführende Schule secondary school IV
Schüler student I
Schülerin student I
Schulfach subject I
Schulhof playground I
Schulstunde lesson I
Schusswaffe gun IV
schütteln to shake IV
schützen to protect III
Schwanz tail I
schwarz black I
schwenken to swing III
schwer hard; serious II; heavy; difficult III
Schwert sword III
Schwester sister I
schwierig hard II; heavy; difficult III
Schwimmbad swimming pool I
schwimmen to swim I
schwimmen gehen to go swimming I
schwingen to swing III
schwul gay V U3, 68
Schwuler gay V U3, 68
Science-Fiction science fiction I
sechs six I
sechzehn sixteen I
sechzig sixty I
secondhand second-hand I
See lake IV
Seele soul V U2, 46
sehen to spy; to see; to look I
Wir sehen uns. See you. II
Sehenswürdigkeit sight II
sehr very I
Sehr geehrte(r) ..., Dear ..., IV
Seilbahn cable car IV
seilgezogene Straßenbahn cable car IV
Seilrutsche zip line III
sein his; to be; its I
einer Meinung sein (mit) to agree (with) II
weit weg sein to be a long way away II
seine his III
seit for; since IV
seitdem since IV
Seite side II
selbst myself; themselves; yourself III; himself; ourselves; yourselves; herself IV
selbstbewusst confident IV
selbstsicher confident IV
selbstverständlich of course II
Selfie selfie IV
selten rarely III
Seminar workshop III
senden to send I
Sendung programme III
September September I
Serie series *(no pl)* IV
Servus. Goodbye. I
Sesotho *(Sprache in Südafrika)* Sesotho V U3, 73
setzen to put I
sich setzen to sit (down) I
Setz dich. Take a seat. IV
Setzen Sie sich. Take a seat. IV
Shirt shirt I
Shorts shorts *(pl)* II
Show show I
sich each other; themselves III; himself; yourselves; herself; yourself IV
sich selbst himself; herself; themselves; yourself IV
sicher sure II; safe; confident IV; certainly V U2, 46
in **Sicherheit** safe IV
sie it; she I; her II
Sie you I
Sie sich yourselves IV
Sie sich selbst yourselves IV
sie *(Pl.)* they; them I
sie selbst themselves III
sieben seven I
siebzehn seventeen I
siebzig seventy I
Siedler settler V U1, 11
Siedlerin settler V U1, 11
siegen to win I
Sieger winner I
Siegerin winner I
singen to sing I
singe nicht don't sing I
singt nicht don't sing I
Sinn sense IV
Situation situation V U3, 80
Sitz seat III
sitzen to sit IV
Sitzplatz seat III
Skateboard skateboard I
Skater skater I
Skaterin skater I
Sklave slave IV
Sklavenhändler slave trader IV
Sklavin slave IV
Slum slum V U2, 36
SMS message II
Snowboard snowboard I
so so II
so ... wie as ... as III
sodass so that IV
soeben just III
sofern as long as V U3, 80
sofort right away V U3, 68
Software software IV
Sohn son IV
solange as long as V U3, 80
sollte should III

Sommer summer II
Songschreiber songwriter V U3, 68
Songschreiberin songwriter V U3, 68
Sonne sun II
sonnig sunny II
Sonntag Sunday I
sich **Sorgen** machen to worry I
Mach dir keine Sorgen. Don't worry. I
sorgfältig careful III
Sorte kind II
Souvenir souvenir II
sowohl ... als auch ... ... as well as ... II
soziale Medien social media III
Spanisch Spanish IV
spanisch Spanish IV
spannend exciting I
sparen to save II
Spaß fun I
Spaß haben to enjoy oneself IV
Spaß machen to be fun II
spaßig fun III
(zu) **spät** late II
zu spät kommen to be late II
später later I
Spaziergang walk I
Speck bacon I
spenden to donate V U4, 94
speziell special I
Spiel game; match I
spielen to play I; to act III
Spieler player II
Spielerin player II
Spielfeld field III
Spielplatz playground I
Spitze top II
Sport sport III
Sportarten sports *(pl only)* I
Sportfest sports day II
Sportgeschäft sports shop II
Sportplatz playing field II
Sportunterricht PE (Physical Education) I
Sportzentrum sports centre I
Sprache language IV
sprechen to say; to speak I
sprechen (mit) to talk (to) I
Sprecher speaker V ZI, 8
Sprecherin speaker V ZI, 8
springen to jump III
spülen to wash II
die **Spülmaschine** ausräumen to empty the dishwasher II
die **Spülmaschine** einräumen to load the dishwasher II
Spur clue I
Staat state; nation III
von allen Staaten of all the states IV
Staatsangehörige citizen IV
Staatsangehöriger citizen IV
Staatsangehörigkeit nationality IV
Staatsbürger citizen IV
Staatsbürgerin citizen IV
stabil strong IV
Stadion stadium I
Stadt city; town I
Stadtmitte city centre II
Stadtteil borough IV
Stadtzentrum city centre II
Stamm tribe V U1, 12
Stand stall I
Star star I
stark heavy; strong III
starten to start I
Station station III
Statue statue IV
staubsaugen to hoover II
Steckbrief profile III
stecken to put II
stecken bleiben to be stuck I
stehen to stand II
stehen für to stand for III
steigen to climb II
in etw. steigen to get on sth IV
Stein stone III; rock V U1, 12
Steinstoßen stone put III
Stell dir vor! Guess what? II
Stelle place I
stellen to put I
online stellen to post III
Stellt euch vor! Guess what? II
sterben to die III
Stift pen I
stiften to donate V U4, 94
Stiftung charity II
still quiet II
Stimmt etwas nicht? Is something wrong? II
Stock stick III
Stockwerk floor II
stolz (auf) proud (of) IV
stören to disturb V U3, 80
jmdn. von etw. **stoßen** to knock sb off sth IV
Strand beach I
Straße street; road I
Straßenbahn tram I
seilgezogene Straßenbahn cable car IV
Streich trick II
streichen to paint II
Streit argument II
(sich) **streiten** to fight II
Strom electricity V U3, 63
Stromschnelle rapid III
Strömung current III
ein **Stück** ... a piece of II
(auf einen Abschluss) **studieren** to study (for) sth V U4, 90
Stufe step II
Stuhl chair I
Stunde hour II
Stundenplan timetable I
Sturm storm I
von etw. **stürzen** to fall off II
suchen (nach) to look for IV
Suchplakat lost and found notice III
Süd- south III; southern IV
Südafrikaner South African V U3, 63
Südafrikanerin South African V U3, 63
südafrikanisch South African V U3, 63
Süden south III
südlich southern IV
Südstaaten- southern IV
super cool I
Supermarkt supermarket I
Surf- surfing IV
Surfen surfing IV
surfen gehen to go surfing III
Süßigkeit sweet I
Symbol symbol III
sympathisch friendly IV

T

Tablette tablet V U1, 16
Tafel blackboard I
Tag day I
ein ausgefüllter Tag a busy day II
eines Tages one day I
Tag! G'day! (= Good day!) V U1, 10

Tagebuch diary I
Tal valley III
Talent talent I
Talentwettbewerb talent show I
Tandem tandem II
Tandem fahren to go tandem bike riding II
Tankstelle garage V U4, 90
Tante aunt I
Tanz dancing; dance III
Tanzen dancing III
tanzen to dance I
Tänzer dancer I
Tänzerin dancer I
tapfer brave III
Tasche bag I
Taschenlampe torch I
Taschenrechner calculator I
eine **Tasse** ... a cup of II
Tätigkeit job III
Tatsache fact II
Tauglichkeit suitability V U4, 90
tausend a/one thousand II
Team team I
Technik DT (Design Technology) I; technology III
Techniker engineer II
Technikerin engineer II
Technologie technology III
Teddybär teddy I
Tee tea I
Teenager teen II; teenager V U2, 42
Teenagerin teen II
Teil part II
oberer Teil top II
teilen to share III
teilnehmen (an) to take part (in) II
Telefon phone I
Telefonanruf phone call I
telefonieren to phone II
Telefonzelle telephone box II
Teller plate IV
Temperatur temperature V U1, 20
Tennis tennis I
Teppich carpet II
Termin appointment V U1, 16
Test test V U4, 90
testen to test II
teuer expensive I
Theater theatre; theater *(AE)* III
Theater- drama III
Theaterstück play III
Thema topic IV
Ticket ticket II
tief deep V U4, 98
Tier animal I
Tierarzt vet IV
Tierärztin vet IV
Tierheim animal rescue shelter I
Tierpark zoo IV
Tisch table I; desk II
Tochter daughter I
Toilette toilet V U2, 42
toll great I; amazing II; awesome III
Tomate tomato I
Tombola raffle II
Topf pot III
Tor goal III; gate V U3, 80
Torpfosten goalpost III
Torstange goalpost III
tot dead IV
töten to kill V U1, 11
Tour tour III
Tourismus tourist industry; tourism IV
Tourist tourist II
Touristin tourist II
Touristeninformation tourist information centre V U4, 90
Township *(ehemalige Wohnsiedlungen für die schwarze Bevölkerung in Südafrika)* township V U3, 62
Tradition tradition III
tragen to wear I
trainieren to train IV
Training practice I; training IV
Transport transport II
Transporter van IV
transportieren to transport IV
Traum dream I
traurig sad I; unhappy II
Treff club I
treffen to meet I; to hit III
(sich) treffen to meet II
Treffer goal III
treiben to drive IV
trennen to separate V U3, 62
treten to kick III
Trick trick I
Trink- drinking V U2, 42
trinken to have I; to drink II
trocken dry II
Trompete trumpet II
Truthahn turkey IV
Tschüss. Bye. I; See you. II
T-Shirt T-shirt II
Tsunami *(durch Seebeben ausgelöste Flutwelle)* tsunami IV
Tuch scarf II
tun to do; to make I
Tut mir leid. Sorry. I
Tür door II
Türkisch Turkish IV
türkisch Turkish IV
Türklingel doorbell I
Turm tower II
Turnschuh trainer II
Tüte bag I
Tutorial tutorial IV

U

U-Bahn underground I
über about I; above; across II; over III
überall all over; everywhere II
überallhin everywhere II
sich **übergeben** to be sick I
überhaupt ever III
überlegen to guess I
sich überlegen to think about III
übernachten to stay I
überprüfen to check II
überrascht surprised II
Überraschung surprise III
übrig left III
Übung exercise; practice I
Übungsheft exercise book I
Uhr clock II
Uhr *(Zeitangabe bei vollen Stunden)* o'clock I
Uhrzeit time I
um at I; around III
um zu to II
um ... herum around II
(sich) **umdrehen** to turn over III
Umgebung environment II
umkippen to turn over III
umsteigen to change III
Umwelt environment II
Umwelt- environmental V U2, 37
umziehen to move II
Umzug procession II; parade IV
unabhängig independent V U2, 37

Unabhängigkeit independence IV
und and I
Und ...? What about ...? II
Unfall accident I
ungefähr about II
ungefährlich safe IV
unglaublich amazing II
unglücklich unhappy II
unglücklicherweise unfortunately V U2, 47
unheimlich scary I
Uniform uniform I
unmöglich impossible IV
Unordnung mess I
uns us II; ourselves IV
uns selbst ourselves IV
unser our I
unsere ours III
unten at the bottom V U1, 28
unter under I
Unternehmen company II
Unterricht lesson I; class IV
unterrichten to teach IV
Unterrichtsstunde class IV
unterschiedlich different I
Unterstützung support V U4, 90
unterwegs out and about III
unterwegs (in) around V U1, 10
unversehrt safe IV
Update update IV
Ur- great- V U4, 98
Ureinwohner Amerikas Native American III
Ureinwohnerin Amerikas Native American III
Urheberrecht copyright IV
Urkunde certificate V U4, 90
Urlaub holiday II; vacation *(AE)* III
Ururopa great-great-grandad I
US-amerikanisch US III

V

Vater father I
Vati dad I
Vegetarier vegetarian I
Vegetarierin vegetarian I
verändern to change II
Veranstaltung event II
die **Verantwortung** tragen (für) to be in charge (of) V U3, 72
verärgert angry II; annoyed IV
verbessern to correct II
sich verbessern to get better V U1, 16
in **Verbindung** bleiben staying connected III
verbringen *(Zeit)* to spend II
Verein club V U4, 89
verfügbar available IV
Vergangenheit past III
vergessen to forget II; to leave III
sich **verirren** to get lost IV
verkaufen to sell I
Verkäufer assistant I; shop assistant V U4, 94
Verkäuferin assistant I; shop assistant V U4, 94
Verkehr transport II; traffic III
öffentliche **Verkehrsmittel** public transport III
Verkleidung fancy dress I
verlassen to leave II
sich auf jmdn. verlassen to count on sb V U4, 90
sich verlassen (auf) to rely (on) IV
verlässlich reliable IV
verletzen to hurt II; to injure V U3, 64
verletzt hurt III
verlieren to lose II
verloren gehen to get lost IV
vermeiden to avoid IV
vermindern to reduce V U4, 94
vermissen to miss II
verpassen to miss II
verringern to reduce V U4, 94
verrückt crazy V U2, 54
verschieden different I
verschiedene several V U2, 37
verschmutzen to pollute V U2, 42
Verschmutzung pollution V U2, 37
verschneit snowy II
verspätet delayed IV
sich **verständigen** to communicate V ZI, 9
verstehen to understand II
Versuch experiment II
versuchen to try III
vertrauen (auf) to rely (on) IV
vertrauenswürdig reliable IV
verunreinigen to pollute V U2, 42
verursachen to cause IV
vervollständigen to finish I
verwenden to use III
Video video III
viel a lot of; lots of; much I
Viel Glück! Good luck! IV
viele a lot of; lots of; many I
Viele Grüße Best wishes, I
vielleicht maybe II
vier four I
Viertel vor/nach quarter to/past II
vierzehn fourteen I
vierzig forty I
virtuell virtual V U2, 38
Vogel bird IV
Volk nation III; people V U4, 89
Volksstamm tribe V U1, 12
vollbringen to achieve V U3, 68
völlig quite II; completely V U1, 20
von from; of I; by III
vor in front of I; before II; of III
vor ago II
vorbei (an) past I
Vorbild role model V U3, 68
Vordergrund foreground III
vorher before III
vorkommen to happen IV
vorlesen to read II
Vormittag morning I
vormittags *(Uhrzeit)* a.m. III
vorn in front II
Vorräte supplies *(pl)* IV
Vorschul- preschool V U3, 73
Vorschule preschool V U3, 73
vorsichtig careful III
jmdn. jmdm. **vorstellen** to introduce sb to sb III
Vortrag presentation III
Vulkan volcano V U4, 89

W

Wachs wax II
wachsen to grow V U2, 42
Waffe gun IV
wählen to choose III
während while; during IV
Wahrheit truth IV
wahrscheinlich probably IV
Wahrzeichen landmark IV
Wal whale IV

Walbeobachtungs- whale-watching IV
Wald wood IV
Walisisch Welsh III
walisisch Welsh III
Wand wall II
Wanderung walk I
Wandmalerei wall painting II
wann when I
Waren goods *(pl only)* V U2, 38
warm warm II
warten (auf) to wait (for) II
Warteschlange queue II
warum why I
was what I; which II
Was hast du? What's the matter? V U1, 16
Was ist los? What's the matter? V U1, 16
Was ist mit ...? What about ...? II
Was kann ich für euch/dich tun? How can I help you? I
Waschbär raccoon I
Wäsche wash II
(sich) **waschen** to wash II
Wasser water I
Website website III
Wechselgeld change I
wechseln to change II
Weg way I
aus dem Weg gehen to avoid IV
weg away II
weit weg sein to be a long way away II
wegen about IV; because of V U4, 98
wegfahren to drive off IV
weggehen to leave II
weglaufen to run away II
wehtun to hurt II
Weihnachten Christmas I
Frohe Weihnachten! Merry Christmas! I
weil because I
Art und **Weise** way III
weiß white I
weit far II; long V U1, 11
weit weg sein to be a long way away II
weitere more II
Weitsprung long jump II
welche what I; which II
Welle wave III
Wellenreiten surfing IV
Welt world I; earth III
in aller Welt all around the world II
Weltraum space III
ein (klein) **wenig** a little (bit) II
wenige a few IV
weniger less III
wenn when II; if IV
wer who I
Werbung ad(vert) (= advertisement) III
werden to get I; will II
etw. tun werden to be going to do sth III
nicht werden won't (= will not) II
(zu etw.) werden to become II
werfen to throw II
Werk factory III
Werkzeug tool V U4, 90
im **Wert** von worth of V U4, 94
wert worth V U4, 94
West- west III
Westen west III
Wettbewerb competition V ZI, 8
Wetter weather II
Wettlauf race II
Wettrennen race II
wichtig important III
wie how; like I; as II
so ... wie as ... as III
Wie alt bist du? How old are you? I
Wie geht es dir? How are you? I
Wie heißt du? What's your name? I
Wie ist das Wetter? What's the weather like? II
wie man ... how to ... IV
Wie spät ist es? What time is it? I
Wie viel (kostet/kosten) ...? How much (is/are) ...? I
Wie viel Uhr ist es? What time is it? I
wieder again I
wiederaufbauen to rebuild IV
wiederholen to repeat V U3, 81
Auf **Wiedersehen**. Goodbye. I
wild wild IV
Wildnis wilderness IV
willkommen (bei/in) welcome (to) I
Wind wind I
windig windy II
Winter winter I
wir we I; us II
Wirbelsturm hurricane IV
wirklich really I
Wirtschaft economy V U2, 42
wissen to know I
Ich weiß (es) nicht! I don't know. I
Wissenschaft science III
Witterung weather II
witzig sein to be fun II
wo where I
Woche week I
in der Woche a week V U3, 73
pro Woche a week V U3, 73
Wochenende weekend I
woher where I
Woher kommst du? Where are you from? I
wohin where I
wohltätige Zwecke charity II
Wohltätigkeits- charity II
Wohltätigkeitsorganisation charity II
Wohnen living V U2, 42
wohnen to live I
Wohnung flat I; apartment *(AE)* IV
Wohnzimmer living room II
Wolf wolf II
Wolke cloud II
wolkig cloudy II
Wolldecke blanket IV
Wolle wool I
wollen to want (to) I
Workshop workshop III
Wort word II
Wunder wonder V U4, 99
wunderschön beautiful III
wünschen to wish V U4, 98
ich würde I'd (= I would) I
ich würde gerne ... I'd like (to) ... (= I would like to) I
ich würde nicht gerne ... I wouldn't like (to) ... I
ich würde sehr gern ... I'd love (to) ... (= I would love to) IV
Würdest du gern ...? Would you like (to) ...? I
wütend angry II

Z

Zahl number I

Zahn tooth II
Zauberer wizard II
Zauberkünstler magician II
Zauberkünstlerin magician II
zaubern to do magic II
zehn ten I
Zeichen sign IV
zeigen to show II; to point V U4, 99
Zeit time I
Zeiten hours *(pl)* IV
Zeitpunkt date IV
Zeitschrift magazine IV
Zeitung newspaper III
Zeitungsstand newspaper kiosk II
Zelt tent II
zelten gehen to go camping III
Zeltplatz campsite III
Zentrum centre; center *(AE)* III
zerbrechen to break V U1, 11
zerstören to destroy IV
zerstört wrecked IV
Zerstörung destruction V U1, 21
Zertifikat certificate V U4, 90
zertrümmert wrecked IV
Zeuge witness IV
Zeugin witness IV
Zeugnis certificate V U4, 90
Ziege goat III
ziehen to pull I; to move IV; to grow V U2, 42
Ziel goal III
ziemlich quite II
Zimmer room I
zittern to shake IV
Zoo zoo IV
zornig angry II
zu to; at; too I
  auf … zu towards V U4, 99
  zu Fuß on foot I
züchten to grow V U2, 42
zuerst first II; at first V U3, 68
Zug train I
Zuhause home I
zuhören to listen (to) I
Zukunft future IV
zukünftig future V U4, 90
Zukunfts- future V U4, 90
Zulieferer supplier V U4, 94
zum 200. Mal for the 200th time III
zum Beispiel for example III
zum Glück fortunately V U3, 72
zumachen to close I
zunächst at first V U3, 68
zurück back II
zurückgehen to get back V U4, 98
zurückkommen to get back V U4, 98
zusammen together I; everyone II
zuschauen to watch II
zusehen to watch II
zuständig sein (für) to be in charge (of) V U3, 72
zustimmen to agree (with) II
zuverlässig reliable IV
zuvor before III
zwanzig twenty I
wohltätige **Zwecke** charity II
zwei two I
zweit- second IV
zweite second II
  aus zweiter Hand second-hand I
zwischen between III
zwölf twelve I

Instructions

Arbeitsanweisungen mit Operatoren

Act the dialogue with your partner.	**Spiele** den Dialog mit deinem Partner / deiner Partnerin.
Add more words.	**Füge** weitere Wörter **hinzu**.
Agree on the most important questions.	Einigt euch auf die wichtigsten Fragen.
Answer the questions.	**Beantworte** die Fragen.
Ask questions.	**Stelle** Fragen.
Ask your partner.	**Frage** deinen Partner / deine Partnerin.
Ask for feedback.	**Bitte um** Rückmeldung.
Change roles.	**Tauscht** die Rollen.
Change the dialogue.	**Ändere** den Dialog.
Check the sentences • your draft.	**Überprüfe** die Sätze • deinen Entwurf.
Choose one of the tasks • the right answers • the right words.	**Wähle** eine der Aufgaben • die richtigen Antworten • die richtigen Wörter aus.
Collect ideas • pictures.	**Sammle** Ideen • Bilder.
Compare the activities • the people • the things.	**Vergleiche** die Aktivitäten • die Leute • die Dinge.
Complete the dialogue • the sentences.	**Vervollständige** den Dialog • die Sätze.
Copy the table.	**Schreibe** die Tabelle **ab**.
Correct the wrong sentences • words.	**Verbessere** die falschen Sätze • Wörter.
Decide who can start.	**Entscheidet euch**, wer anfängt.
Describe the picture.	**Beschreibe** das Bild.
Discuss in groups.	**Besprecht** euch in Gruppen.
Draw a picture.	**Zeichne** ein Bild.
Explain.	**Erkläre**.
Find the answers • the names • the true statements • the words.	**Finde** die Antworten • die Namen • die richtigen Aussagen • die Wörter.
Find out about the country.	**Finde** etwas über das Land **heraus**.
Finish the sentences.	**Vervollständige** die Sätze.
Give a presentation.	**Halte** eine Präsentation.
Give feedback.	**Gib Rückmeldung.**
Guess.	**Überlege.**
Interview your partner.	**Interviewe** deinen Partner / deine Partnerin.
Listen, **read** and **say**.	**Höre zu**, **lies mit** und **sprich nach**.
Listen to the announcements • the dialogue • the interview.	**Höre** dir die Durchsagen • den Dialog • das Gespräch **an**.
Look at the photos • the pictures (again).	**Schaue** dir die Fotos • die Bilder (noch einmal) **an**.
Make questions • sentences.	**Bilde** Fragen • Sätze.
Make a chart • a dialogue • a list • a mind map • a poster • a table.	**Erstelle** ein Diagramm • einen Dialog • eine Liste • ein Wörternetz • ein Poster • eine Tabelle.
Make notes.	**Mache** dir Notizen.
Match the sentences • the words.	**Ordne** die Sätze • die Wörter **zu**.
Match the sentences with the pictures.	**Ordne** die Sätze den Bildern **zu**.

Organize your information.	**Ordnet** eure Informationen.
Pass on information.	**Gib** die Informationen **weiter**.
Plan your e-mail • your event.	**Plant** eure E-Mail • eure Veranstaltung.
Practise with a partner.	**Übe** mit einem Partner / einer Partnerin.
Prepare a presentation.	**Bereite** eine Präsentation **vor**.
Present your poster to your class.	**Stellt** euer Poster der Klasse **vor**.
Put in the right form • the right word • the right verbs.	**Setze** die richtige Form • das richtige Wort • die richtigen Verben **ein**.
Put the pictures • the sentences • the words **in the right order**.	**Bringe** die Bilder • die Sätze • die Wörter **in die richtige Reihenfolge**.
Put the words into groups.	**Sortiere** die Wörter in Gruppen.
Read, say and **listen**.	**Lies, sprich nach** und **höre zu**.
Read the dialogue • the story • the text.	**Lies** den Dialog • die Geschichte • den Text.
Read your sentences • your text to your class.	**Lies** deine Sätze • deinen Text der Klasse **vor**.
Report in class.	**Berichte** der Klasse.
Are the sentences **right or wrong**?	Sind die Sätze **richtig oder falsch**?
Say the names • the numbers.	**Nenne** die Namen • die Zahlen.
Show your brochure • your report to your group.	**Zeige** deiner Gruppe deine Broschüre • deinen Bericht.
Take notes.	**Mache dir Notizen.**
Talk about the film • the photos • your free time.	**Sprich über** den Film • die Fotos • deine Freizeit.
Talk to your partner.	**Sprich mit** deinem Partner / deiner Partnerin.
Tell the class.	**Erzähle** der Klasse davon.
Tell your partner **about** what you do at home.	**Erzähle** deinem Partner / deiner Partnerin, was du zu Hause machst.
Think about these questions.	**Denke über** diese Fragen **nach**.
Think of questions.	**Denke** dir Fragen **aus**.
Use your own ideas.	**Benutze** deine eigenen Ideen.
Watch the film.	**Schaue** den Film **an**.
What are the words?	**Wie** heißen die Wörter?
What (else) can you see in the photo?	**Was** kannst du **(noch)** auf dem Foto sehen?
Where are the things?	**Wo** sind die Dinge?
Which sentences are right?	**Welche** Sätze sind richtig?
Who is • says it?	**Wer** ist • sagt das?
Why (not)?	**Warum** (nicht)?
Work with the text.	**Arbeite** mit dem Text.
Write a diary entry • a draft • an e-mail • a text.	**Schreibe** einen Tagebucheintrag • einen Entwurf • eine E-Mail • einen Text.
Write sentences.	**Schreibe** Sätze.

Classroom phrases

Before or after the lesson

Good morning, Mr/Mrs/Miss	Guten Morgen, Herr/Frau ....
I'm sorry I'm late.	Tut mir leid, dass ich mich verspätet habe.
I'm sorry I don't have my exercise book/ my homework with me.	Tut mir leid, ich habe mein Heft/ meine Hausaufgaben nicht dabei.
What's for homework?	Was haben wir als Hausaufgabe auf?

Asking for help

What page are we on?	Auf welcher Seite sind wir?
Can you help me, please?	Können Sie / Kannst du mir bitte helfen?
What does ... mean?	Was heißt ...?
Can you say that again, please?	Können Sie / Kannst du das bitte wiederholen?
Can you write that on the board?	Können Sie das an die Tafel schreiben?
Can I go to the toilet, please?	Kann ich bitte auf die Toilette gehen?
Mr/Mrs/Miss ..., I don't feel well.	Herr/Frau ..., mir geht es nicht gut.

Asking for information

What page is it on, please?	Auf welcher Seite ist das?
What's the German/English word for ...?	Was ist das deutsche/englische Wort für ...?
How do you spell ...?	Wie schreibt man ...?
What's this in English, please?	Was heißt das bitte auf Englisch?
What does that mean?	Was heißt/bedeutet das?
Sorry, I don't understand.	Tut mir leid, ich verstehe das nicht.
Sorry, I don't know.	Tut mir leid, ich weiß es nicht.

Working together

Can we work in pairs/groups?	Können wir zu zweit / in Gruppen arbeiten?
Do you want to work with me/us?	Willst du / Wollt ihr mit mir/uns arbeiten?
Let's make/draw a	Lass(t) uns ein ... machen/zeichnen.
Whose turn is it?	Wer ist dran?
It's my/your turn.	Ich bin dran. / Du bist dran.
Who is going to do our presentation?	Wer macht unsere Präsentation?

Your teacher can say ...

Listen, please.	Hört bitte zu.
Listen to the dialogue.	Höre dir / Hört euch den Dialog an.
Open your books at page	Öffnet eure Bücher auf Seite ....
Turn to page	Schlagt Seite ... auf.
Read the text on page	Lest den Text auf Seite ....
Look at line	Schaue/Schaut in Zeile ....
Take out your pens.	Holt eure Stifte raus.

Show me your homework, please.	Zeigt mir bitte eure Hausaufgaben. / Zeige mir bitte deine Hausaufgaben.
Where's your homework?	Wo sind deine/eure Hausaufgaben?
Get into pairs/groups.	Bildet Paare/Gruppen.
Learn these words for homework.	Lernt diese Wörter als Hausaufgabe.
Look at the board.	Schaut an die Tafel.
Who can do number …?	Wer kann Nummer … machen?
Put your hands up, please.	Meldet euch, bitte.
Try again.	Versuche es noch einmal. / Versucht es noch einmal.
Sit down, please, and be quiet.	Setz dich bitte und sei ruhig. / Setzt euch bitte und seid ruhig.
Talk to your partner.	Sprecht mit eurem Partner / eurer Partnerin.
Talk about the pictures.	Redet über die Bilder.
Please speak up.	Bitte sprich lauter.
Well done.	Gut gemacht.

Abbildungsverzeichnis

I Dekelver, Christian, Weinstadt; **Cover.1** Avenue Images GmbH (Dave and Les Jacobs), Hamburg; **Cover.2** plainpicture GmbH & Co. KG (Angela Elbing), Hamburg; **8.1** .; graphitecture book & edition, Bernau am Chiemsee; **8.2** stock.adobe.com (mavoimages), Dublin; **8.3** Getty Images Plus (monkeybusinessimages), München; **9.1** ShutterStock.com RF (almonfoto), New York, NY; **9.2** Getty Images Plus (DGLimages), München; **10.1** Getty Images Plus (sarra22), München; **10.2** Alamy stock photo (Greg Balfour Evans), Abingdon; **11.1** Dekelver, Christian, Weinstadt; **11.2** Getty Images Plus (4FR), München; **11.3** Getty Images (Universal Images Group), München; **11.4** Getty Images (National Geographic), München; **12.1** Alamy stock photo (david a eastley), Abingdon; **12.2** F1online digitale Bildagentur (imagebroker.com), Frankfurt; **12.3** Thinkstock (esancai), München; **14.1** Alamy stock photo (Hideo Kurihara), Abingdon; **16.1** Getty Images Plus (Tim Kitchen), München; **18.1** ShutterStock.com RF (i viewfinder), New York, NY; **18.2** Alamy stock photo (martin berry), Abingdon; **18.3** Bláha, Marek, Offenbach am Main; **20.1** ShutterStock.com RF (Kristina Vackova), New York, NY; **20.2** Dekelver, Christian, Weinstadt; **22.1** Getty Images Plus (alvarez), München; **23.1** Thinkstock (esancai), München; **23.2** © BBC Motion Gallery — British Broadcasting Corporation — Media Centre, London; **23.3** © BBC Motion Gallery — British Broadcasting Corporation — Media Centre, London; **23.4** © BBC Motion Gallery — British Broadcasting Corporation — Media Centre, London; **23.5** © BBC Motion Gallery — British Broadcasting Corporation — Media Centre, London; **24.1** stock.adobe.com (Joe Gough), Dublin; **24.2** Bláha, Marek, Offenbach am Main; **25.1** Kramer, Peer (Peer Kramer), Düsseldorf; **25.2** Wolters, Dorothee, Köln; **25.3** Wolff, Steffen, Herzogenrath; **25.4** Schwarzstein, Jaroslaw, Hannover; **25.5** Ablang, Friederike, Berlin; **26.1** Alamy stock photo (David Wall), Abingdon; **26.2** ShutterStock.com RF (Alisia Luther), New York, NY; **26.3** Getty Images Plus (travellinglight), München; **26.4** ShutterStock.com RF (robert paul van beets), New York, NY; **26.5** Thinkstock (esancai), München; **27.1** Getty Images Plus (mollypix/iStock), München [Stanley Geebung (1956-): Kangaroo, Aboriginal Dot Painting, Ochre on Card, ca. 1995]; **27.2** ShutterStock.com RF (Peter Waters), New York, NY; **27.3** Getty Images Plus (tomograf), München; **27.4** imago images (UIG), Berlin; **28.1** ShutterStock.com RF (amophoto_au), New York, NY; **28.2** Alamy stock photo (JUPITERIMAGES/ STOCK IMAGE), Abingdon; **29.1** Bláha, Marek, Offenbach am Main; **30.1** Thinkstock (Wavebreakmedia Ltd), München; **30.2** Thinkstock (amazingmikael), München; **30.3** Thinkstock (ajr_images), München; **30.4** Thinkstock (123ducu), München; **32.1** Alamy stock photo (Rob Walls), Abingdon; **35.1** Bláha, Marek, Offenbach am Main; **36.1** Getty Images (Aleksandra Ladygin / EyeEm), München; **36.2** Getty Images (moodboard), München; **37.1** Dekelver, Christian, Weinstadt; **37.2** Getty Images (Jupiterimages), München; **37.3** Getty Images Plus (ra-photos), München; **37.4** Alamy stock photo (Aravind Teki), Abingdon; **38.1** Alamy stock photo (Stuart Forster India), Abingdon; **38.2** ShutterStock.com RF (CRS PHOTO), New York, NY; **38.3** Getty Images Plus (GCShutter), München; **38.4** Alamy stock photo (PhotosIndia.com LLC), Abingdon; **38.5** stock.adobe.com (Ray), Dublin; **39.1** Wolff, Steffen, Herzogenrath; **40.1** Alamy stock photo (Joerg Boethling), Abingdon; **42.1** stock.adobe.com (PRASANNAPIX), Dublin; **42.2** ShutterStock.com RF (David Davis), New York, NY; **44.1** ShutterStock.com RF (Indian Food Images), New York, NY; **44.2** stock.adobe.com (Phuong), Dublin; **44.3** stock.adobe.com (V.R.Murralinath), Dublin; **44.4** ShutterStock.com RF (Henk Bogaard), New York, NY; **44.5** Alamy stock photo (zah108 / Alamy Stock Foto), Abingdon; **44.6** Getty Images (Mint / Kontributor), München; **45.1** Getty Images Plus (SilviaJansen), München; **46.1** Alamy stock photo (Pictorial Press Ltd), Abingdon; **47.1** stock.adobe.com (Ray), Dublin; **47.2** Alamy stock photo (Science History Images), Abingdon; **48.1** Alamy stock photo (Jeffrey Isaac Greenberg 4), Abingdon; **48.2** stock.adobe.com (Ray), Dublin; **48.3** Thinkstock (Wavebreak Media), München; **48.4** stock.adobe.com (Ray), Dublin; **48.5** ShutterStock.com RF (Production Perig), New York, NY; **48.6** stock.adobe.com (Ray), Dublin; **49.1** © BBC Motion Gallery — British Broadcasting Corporation — Media Centre, London; **49.2** © BBC Motion Gallery — British Broadcasting Corporation — Media Centre, London; **49.3** © BBC Motion Gallery — British Broadcasting Corporation — Media Centre, London; **49.4** © BBC Motion Gallery — British Broadcasting Corporation — Media Centre, London; **49.5** stock.adobe.com (Ray), Dublin; **50.1** ShutterStock.com RF (nomads.team), New York, NY; **52.1** iStockphoto (DrRave), Calgary, Alberta; **53.1** Getty Images Plus (powerofforever), München; **53.2** ShutterStock.com RF (Matt Hahnewald), New York, NY; **53.3** ShutterStock.com RF (Paksongpob Kasempisaisin), New York, NY; **53.4** Getty Images Plus (hadynyah), München; **53.5** ShutterStock.com RF (Cavan-Images), New York, NY; **53.6** Alamy stock photo (Subhash Sharma/ ZUMAPRESS.com), Abingdon; **53.7** stock.adobe.com (Ray), Dublin; **54.1** Wolff, Steffen, Herzogenrath; **54.2** Wolff, Steffen, Herzogenrath; **54.3** Wolff, Steffen, Herzogenrath; **54.4** Wolff, Steffen, Herzogenrath; **57.1** ShutterStock.com RF (MD ZAKIR HOSSAIN SOHEL), New York, NY; **58.1** Alamy stock photo (Aditya "Dicky" Singh), Abingdon; **61.1** ShutterStock.com RF (Saurav022), New York, NY; **61.2** Bláha, Marek, Offenbach am Main; **62.1** ShutterStock.com RF (Robyn Gwilt), New York, NY; **62.2** Alamy stock photo (Adam Welz), Abingdon; **63.1** Dekelver, Christian, Weinstadt; **63.2** ShutterStock.com RF (Theodore Mattas), New York, NY; **63.3** Alamy stock photo (Roger Sedres), Abingdon; **63.4** Getty Images Plus (THEGIFT777), München; **64.1** stock.adobe.com (Ray), Dublin; **65.1** ShutterStock.com RF, New York, NY; **66.1** Wolff, Steffen, Herzogenrath; **66.2** Wolff, Steffen, Herzogenrath; **66.3** Wolff, Steffen, Herzogenrath; **66.4** Wolff, Steffen, Herzogenrath; **66.5** Wolff, Steffen, Herzogenrath; **66.6** Wolff, Steffen, Herzogenrath; **68.1** Alamy stock photo (RTNFreeberg / MediaPunch), Abingdon; **68.2** Picture-Alliance (REUTERS/Mike Hutchings), Frankfurt; **68.3** stock.adobe.com (Ray), Dublin; **69.1** Bláha, Marek, Offenbach am Main; **69.2** Bláha, Marek, Offenbach am Main; **69.3** Alamy stock photo (Africa Media Online), Abingdon; **70.1** stock.adobe.com (Ranta Images), Dublin; **70.2** stock.adobe.com (Daniel Ernst), Dublin; **71.1** ShutterStock.com RF (Africanstar), New York, NY; **72.1** ShutterStock.com RF (WAYHOME studio), New York, NY; **72.2** ShutterStock.com RF (Maridav), New York, NY; **73.1** stock.adobe.com (RichTphoto), Dublin; **73.2** stock.adobe.com (ajr_images), Dublin; **74.1** ShutterStock.com RF (JaneHYork), New York, NY; **75.1** © BBC Motion Gallery — British Broadcasting Corporation — Media Centre, London; **75.2** stock.adobe.com (Ray), Dublin; **76.1** Bláha, Marek, Offenbach am Main; **78.1** stock.adobe.com (WitR), Dublin; **78.2** Alamy stock photo (Bartek Wrzesniowski), Abingdon; **78.3** Alamy stock photo (Realy Easy Star/Giuseppe Masci), Abingdon; **79.1** Alamy stock photo (Africa Media Online), Abingdon; **79.2** Picture-Alliance (dpa), Frankfurt; **79.3** ShutterStock.com RF (Roger Sedres), New York, NY; **79.4** graphitecture book & edition, Bernau am Chiemsee; **79.5** stock.adobe.com (Ray), Dublin; **80.1** ShutterStock.com RF (Dirk M. de Boer), New York, NY; **84.1** Alamy stock photo (Gary Eastwood Photography), Abingdon; **85.1** Wolff, Steffen, Herzogenrath; **85.2** Wolff, Steffen, Herzogenrath; **85.3** Wolff, Steffen, Herzogenrath; **85.4** Wolff, Steffen, Herzogenrath; **86.1** ShutterStock.com RF (WitR), New York, NY; **86.2** ShutterStock.com RF (Moobatto), New York, NY; **86.3** ShutterStock.com RF (Elnur), New York, NY; **87.1** Bláha, Marek, Offenbach am Main; **88.1** Getty Images Plus (Robert CHG), München; **88.2** ShutterStock.com RF (sianc), New York, NY; **89.1** Dekelver, Christian, Weinstadt; **89.2** Getty Images Plus

(SolStock), München; **89.3** ShutterStock.com RF (atthle), New York, NY; **89.4** Alamy stock photo (Blaine Harrington III), Abingdon; **90.1** Wolff, Steffen, Herzogenrath; **92.1** ShutterStock.com RF (Gorodenkoff), New York, NY; **92.2** Bláha, Marek, Offenbach am Main; **94.1** Wolff, Steffen, Herzogenrath; **96.1** Wolff, Steffen, Herzogenrath; **96.2** Wolff, Steffen, Herzogenrath; **96.3** Wolff, Steffen, Herzogenrath; **96.4** Wolff, Steffen, Herzogenrath; **96.5** Wolff, Steffen, Herzogenrath; **96.6** Wolff, Steffen, Herzogenrath; **97.1** Getty Images Plus (fstop123), München; **99.1** Alamy stock photo (Moviestore collection Ltd/ Whale Rider, 2003), Abingdon; **99.2** Alamy stock photo (Entertainment Pictures/Whale Rider, 2003), Abingdon; **100.1** Getty Images Plus (FlairImages), München; **100.2** ShutterStock.com RF (StGrafix), New York, NY; **100.3** stock.adobe.com (ADESIGN), Dublin; **101.1** Alamy stock photo (eye35.pix), Abingdon; **101.2** ShutterStock.com RF (Peter Hermes Furian), New York, NY; **101.3** stock.adobe.com (ADESIGN), Dublin; **102.1** ShutterStock.com RF (Urban Napflin), New York, NY; **103.1** Getty Images Plus (Manchan), München; **104.1** ShutterStock.com RF (TDway), New York, NY; **104.2** stock.adobe.com (ADESIGN), Dublin; **105.1** stock.adobe.com (Dmitrii), Dublin; **105.2** Alamy stock photo (Wendy Johnson), Abingdon; **105.3** ShutterStock.com RF (Tim90), New York, NY; **105.4** ShutterStock.com RF (Paolo Bona), New York, NY; **108.1** Alamy stock photo (Gary Webber), Abingdon; **110.1** ShutterStock.com RF (vectorfusionart), New York, NY; **111.1** Bláha, Marek, Offenbach am Main; **113.1** Bláha, Marek, Offenbach am Main; **114.1** Alamy stock photo (Hideo Kurihara), Abingdon; **115.1** Alamy stock photo (martin berry), Abingdon; **116.1** Alamy stock photo (Joerg Boethling), Abingdon; **117.1** stock.adobe.com (PRASANNAPIX), Dublin; **117.2** ShutterStock.com RF (David Davis), New York, NY; **118.1** ShutterStock.com RF (Indian Food Images), New York, NY; **118.2** stock.adobe.com (Phuong), Dublin; **118.3** stock.adobe.com (V.R.Murralinath), Dublin; **118.4** ShutterStock.com RF (Henk Bogaard), New York, NY; **118.5** Alamy stock photo (zah108 / Alamy Stock Foto), Abingdon; **118.6** Getty Images (Mint / Kontributor), München; **121.1** Alamy stock photo (RTNFreeberg / MediaPunch), Abingdon; **121.2** Picture-Alliance (REUTERS/Mike Hutchings), Frankfurt; **122.1** Bláha, Marek, Offenbach am Main; **122.2** Bláha, Marek, Offenbach am Main; **122.3** stock.adobe.com (Ranta Images), Dublin; **122.4** stock.adobe.com (Daniel Ernst), Dublin; **123.1** Bláha, Marek, Offenbach am Main; **124.1** Wolff, Steffen, Herzogenrath; **125.1** Getty Images Plus (fstop123), München; **126.1** Klett-Archiv (Mo Büdinger), Stuttgart; **128.1** Klett-Archiv (Mo Büdinger), Stuttgart; **129.1** Bláha, Marek, Offenbach am Main; **130.1** Klett-Archiv (Mo Büdinger), Stuttgart; **131.1** Klett-Archiv (Mo Büdinger), Stuttgart; **133.1** Bláha, Marek, Offenbach am Main; **133.2** Klett-Archiv (Mo Büdinger), Stuttgart; **135.1** Klett-Archiv (Mo Büdinger), Stuttgart; **139.1** Bláha, Marek, Offenbach am Main; **146.1** Getty Images Plus (DigitalVision / Jacobs Stock Photography Ltd), München; **146.2** ShutterStock.com RF (Andriy Solovyov), New York, NY; **146.3** Getty Images RF (Photodisc), München; **146.4** Alamy stock photo (PhotoAbility), Abingdon; **146.5** BigStockPhoto.com (Jeni Foto), Davis, CA; **146.6** stock.adobe.com (Pavel Losevsky), Dublin; **146.7** ShutterStock.com RF (Alex Melnick), New York, NY; **146.8** iStockphoto (winhorse), Calgary, Alberta; **146.9** ShutterStock.com RF (Celso Diniz), New York, NY; **146.10** stock.adobe.com (Achim Thomae), Dublin; **148.1** Hesselbarth, Susann, Leipzig; **148.2** Jähde, Steffen, Sundhagen; **148.3** Reich, Bettina, Zwenkau/Leipzig; **148.4** Grafik wurde speziell für Redaktion F angefertigt und darf nur dort verwendet werden; **148.5** Fröhlich, Anke, Leipzig; **148.6** Wolff, Steffen (Steffen Wolff), Herzogenrath; **148.7** Wolff, Steffen, Herzogenrath; **148.8** Wolff, Steffen, Herzogenrath; **148.9** Wolf, Sylvia (Sylvia Wolf), Wiesbaden; **148.10** Wolf, Sylvia (Sylvia Wolf), Wiesbaden; **149.1** Rau, Katja, Berglen; **149.2** Wolff, Steffen (Steffen Wolff), Herzogenrath; **149.3** Ablang, Friederike, Berlin; **149.4** Wolff, Steffen, Herzogenrath; **149.5** Wolters, Dorothee, Köln; **149.6** Hochmann, Carmen, Gütersloh; **149.7** Wolff, Steffen, Herzogenrath; **149.8** Hoffmann, Martin, Stuttgart; **149.9** ShutterStock.com RF (Beny1), New York, NY; **149.10** Rockstroh, Myrtia, Berlin; **149.11** Wolff, Steffen, Herzogenrath; **149.12** Wolff, Steffen, Herzogenrath; **153.1** Kramer, Peer, Düsseldorf; **153.2** Wolters, Dorothee (Dorothee Wolters), Köln; **153.3** Wolf, Sylvia, Wiesbaden; **153.4** Wolf, Sylvia, Wiesbaden; **155.1** Hesselbarth, Susann, Leipzig; **155.2** Jähde, Steffen, Sundhagen; **156.1** Wolters, Dorothee, Köln; **156.2** Wolf, Sylvia (Sylvia Wolf), Wiesbaden; **161.1** Wolters, Dorothee, Köln; **162.1** Rau, Katja, Berglen; **163.1** Fröhlich, Anke, Leipzig; **163.2** Wilder, Marcus, Hamburg; **165.1** Schwarzstein, Jaroslaw, Hannover; **166.1** Burghart-Vollhardt, Martina, Kamenz; **167.1** Burghart-Vollhardt, Martina, Kamenz; **168.1** Nicolai, Axel, Sönnebüll; **169.1** Merkle, Helga, Albershausen; **170.1** Burghart-Vollhardt, Martina, Kamenz; **170.2** Kranenberg, Hendrik, Drolshagen; **170.3** Ablang, Friederike, Berlin; **232.1** Dekelver, Christian, Weinstadt; **233** Dekelver, Christian, Weinstadt; **234** Dekelver, Christian, Weinstadt

Textquellennachweis

98–99 From The Whale Rider, Witi Ihimaera, 2008

Cape York
Darwin
Kakadu National Park
Pacific Ocean
Indian Ocean
Great Barrier Reef
Cairns
Townsville
NORTHERN TERRITORY
AUSTRALIA
Ningaloo Reef
QUEENSLAND
Alice Springs
Uluru
Hervey Bay
Sunshine Coast
Brisbane
Monkey Mia
WESTERN AUSTRALIA
SOUTH AUSTRALIA
NEW SOUTH WALES
Sydney
Perth
Canberra
Adelaide
VICTORIA
Melbourne
Tasman Sea
NEW ZEALAND
TASMANIA
Hobart
0
500 km
1000 km
AUSTRALIA

CHINA
PAKISTAN
NEPAL
BHUTAN
BANGLA-
DESH
MYANMAR
SRI LANKA
INDIA
Srinagar
LADAKH
JAMMU &
KASHMIR
HIMACHAL PRADESH
PUNJAB
CHANDIGARH
UTTARAKHAND
HARYANA
Himalayas
ARUNACHAL PRADESH
New Delhi
RAJASTHAN
Agra
Taj Mahal
Jaipur
UTTAR
PRADESH
SIKKIM
NAGALAND
ASSAM
MEGHALAYA
MANIPUR
Imphal
BIHAR
Patna
Ganges
GUJARAT
Gandhinagar
Sanand
Ahmedabad
Porbandar
Dandi
Surat
MADHYA PRADESH
JHARKHAND
TRIPURA
MIZORAM
CHHATTIS-
GARH
Kolkata
Raipur
MAHARASHTRA
WEST BENGAL
Arabian Sea
Mumbai
ODISHA
TELANGANA
Hyderabad
Panaji
GOA
KARNATAKA
ANDHRA
PRADESH
Bay of Bengal
Bangalore
Chennai
PUDUCHERRY
TAMIL
NADU
KERALA
ANDAMAN AND
NICOBAR ISLANDS
LAKSHADWEEP
0
500 km
1000 km
INDIA

NAMIBIA
BOTSWANA
ZIMBABWE
MOZAMBIQUE
Kruger National Park
LIMPOPO
Polokwane
Kgalagadi Transfrontier Park
Nelspruit
MPUMALANGA
Mahikeng
Pretoria
GAUTENG
Johannesburg
NORTH WEST
Soweto
ESWA-TINI
Klerksdorp
Hluhluwe-Imfolozi Park
FREE STATE
Maloti-Drakensberg Park
KWAZULU-NATAL
Upington
Orange
Kimberley
Bloemfontein
LESOTHO
Drakensberg
Pietermaritzburg
Durban
NORTHERN CAPE
Orange
SOUTH AFRICA
South Atlantic Ocean
Cederberg Mountains
EASTERN CAPE
Indian Ocean
Bhisho
WESTERN CAPE
Table Mountain National Park
Cape Town
Makhanda
Port Elizabeth
Cape of Good Hope
0
500 km
REPUBLIC OF SOUTH AFRICA